CRE**A**TIVE
HOMEOWNER®

PLUMBING
BASIC, INTERMEDIATE & ADVANCED PROJECTS

MERLE HENKENIUS

CREATIVE HOMEOWNER®, Upper Saddle River, New Jersey

CREATIVE HOMEOWNER®

A Division of Federal Marketing Corp.
Upper Saddle River, NJ

EDITORIAL DIRECTOR: Timothy O. Bakke
PRODUCTION MANAGER: Kimberly H. Vivas

AUTHOR: Merle Henkenius
PROOFREADERS: Dan Houghtaling, Sharon Ranftle
PHOTO RESEARCHER: Sharon Ranftle
TECHNICAL CONSULTANTS: Richard Day, Master Plumber, Templeton, CA; Rex Caldwell, Master Plumber, Copper Hill, VA; Jim Weflen, Copper Development Association; Jeff Watson, LP Gas Association; Bob Williams, Genova Products, Inc.
INDEXER: Sandi Schroeder/Schroeder Indexing Services

SENIOR DESIGNER: David Geer
DESIGNER: Scott Molenaro
COVER DESIGN: Clarke Barre
ILLUSTRATIONS: Frank Rohrbach
PRINCIPAL PHOTOGRAPHER: Merle Henkenius

Manufactured in the United States of America

Current Printing (last digit)
10 9 8 7 6 5 4 3 2 1

Plumbing
Library of Congress Control Number: 2001090769
ISBN: 1-58011-085-1

CREATIVE HOMEOWNER®
A Division of Federal Marketing Corp.
24 Park Way, Upper Saddle River, NJ 07458
Web site: **www.creativehomeowner.com**

Photo Credits

All photography by Merle Henkenius except for the following.

Directionals: T-top, M-middle, B-bottom, R-right, L-left, C-center

Front cover: Freeze Frame Studio, Hackensack, NJ
p. 6: all Nancy Hill, Ridgefield, CT
p. 30BR: David Geer/CH
p. 33: all Gary David Gold/CH
p. 60: John Parsekian/CH
p. 65: Brian C. Nieves/CH
p. 72: Freeze Frame Studio/CH
p. 108: courtesy Kohler Plumbing, Kohler, WI
p. 139: all John Parsekian/CH
p. 174BL: courtesy Moen, North Olmstead, OH BC: courtesy Delta Faucet Company, Indianapolis, IN BR: courtesy American Standard, Piscataway, NJ
p. 175: Freeze Frame Studio/CH
p. 183T: Freeze Frame Studio/CH
p. 185T: Freeze Frame Studio/CH
p. 190: Freeze Frame Studio/CH
p. 226: all courtesy Jason International, North Little Rock, AR
p. 237: courtesy Marathon Water Heaters, Eagan, MN
p. 238B: courtesy State Industries, Ashland City, TN
p. 255: courtesy Culligan, Northbrook, IL

Illustration Credits

All illustrations by Frank Rohrbach except for the following.

p. 99: courtesy American Standard
p. 225B: Ian Warpole
p. 230B: Ian Warpole
p. 238T: Clarke Barre
p. 256T: courtesy Pure Water, Lincoln, NE
p. 262: George Retseck
p. 263T: George Retseck

Safety

Although the methods in this book have been reviewed for safety, it is not possible to overstate the importance of using the safest methods you can. What follows are reminders—some do's and don'ts of work safety—to use along with your common sense.

- ◪ Always use caution, care, and good judgment when following the procedures described in this book.

- ◪ Always obey *local* plumbing codes and laws, available from the building inspector. This book is based on the National Standard Plumbing Code, which despite its name, is one of several regional plumbing codes in force in the United States. As of the time of publication, there is no truly national plumbing code.

- ◪ Always use a flame shield to protect combustible materials when using a torch for soldering. And keep a fire extinguisher nearby whenever using a torch, just in case.

- ◪ Always be sure that the electrical setup is safe, that no circuit is overloaded, and that all power tools and outlets are properly grounded. Do not use power tools in wet locations. Use a battery powered flashlight when working near or with water.

- ◪ Always read labels on solvents and other products; provide ventilation; and observe all other warnings.

- ◪ Always read the manufacturer's instructions, especially the warnings, for using a tool or installing an appliance.

- ◪ Always remove the key from any drill chuck (portable or press) before starting the drill.

- ◪ Always use a drill with an auxiliary handle to control the torque when using large-size bits.

- ◪ Always pay deliberate attention to how a tool works so that you can avoid being injured.

- ◪ Always wear the appropriate rubber gloves or work gloves when handling chemicals, soldering, or doing heavy construction.

- ◪ Always wear a disposable face mask when you create dust by sawing or sanding. Use a special filtering respirator when working with toxic substances and solvents.

- ◪ Never try to light a gas appliance, like a water heater, if you smell gas. Do not touch any electrical switch or use any telephone in the same building. Go to a neighbor's house, and call the gas supplier. If you cannot reach your gas supplier, call the fire department.

- ◪ Always wear eye protection, especially when soldering, using a plunger or auger, using power tools, or striking metal on metal or concrete; a chip can fly off, for example, when chiseling concrete.

- ◪ Never work while wearing loose clothing, open cuffs, or jewelry; tie back long hair.

- ◪ Always be aware that there is seldom enough time for your body's reflexes to save you from injury from a power tool in a dangerous situation; everything happens too fast. Be alert!

- ◪ Always keep your hands away from the business ends of blades, cutters, and bits.

- ◪ Always hold a circular saw firmly, usually with both hands.

- ◪ Always check your local building codes when planning new construction. The codes are intended to protect public safety and should be observed to the letter.

- ◪ Never work with power tools when you are tired or when under the influence of alcohol or drugs.

- ◪ Never cut tiny pieces of pipe or wood using a power saw. When you need a small piece, saw it from a securely clamped longer piece.

- ◪ Never change a saw blade or a drill bit unless the power cord is unplugged. Do not depend on the switch being off. You might accidentally hit it.

- ◪ Always know the limitations of your tools. Do not try to force them to do what they were not designed to do.

- ◪ Never work in insufficient lighting.

- ◪ Never work with dull tools. Have them sharpened, or learn how to sharpen them yourself.

- ◪ Never use a power tool on a workpiece—large or small—that is not firmly supported.

- ◪ Never carry sharp or pointed tools, such as utility knives, awls, or chisels, in your pocket. If you want to carry any of these tools, use a special-purpose tool belt that has leather pockets and holders.

Contents

Introduction

These are good times for do-it-yourself plumbers. Plumbing materials are lighter and easier than ever to install, and the range of quality products sold to homeowners is unprecedented. Fifteen years ago, many of these products were sold only through wholesalers to plumbers.

And the materials are affordable. Many faucets and fixtures cost less at home centers than they do at wholesale houses. This may be bad news for plumbers, but it's good news for you. With these advantages, all you need is help with the installations. That is the purpose of this book.

Plumbing: Basic, Intermediate & Advanced Projects is, of course, loaded with detailed projects, but it also provides context. The first five chapters provide the background needed to accomplish almost any plumbing task, from the materials and tools needed to the importance of vents and traps in a properly functioning plumbing system, from soldering and solvent-welding techniques to the ins and outs of almost every imaginable type of valve.

The balance of the book takes you step by step through installation projects, improvements, repairs, and solutions

This handsome single-lever faucet has a pullout spout that doubles as a sprayer—practical for use in the kitchen.

An offset bath faucet makes an impressive design statement, but it's installed the same as any through-the-deck faucet.

to specific problems. Chapter 6 deals with toilet repairs and installations. Chapters 7 and 8 help you with sinks and faucets as well as waste-disposal units, dishwashers, and hot-water dispensers. Chapter 9 teaches you how to clear all kinds of drainpipes; then it's on to repairing and installing tubs and showers in Chapter 10. The final three chapters deal with so-called mechanicals: water heaters in Chapter 11; sump pumps, filters, and water softeners in Chapter 12; and septic systems and wells in Chapter 13. Every major (and some minor) system is covered to help you successfully complete just about any plumbing chore.

About Plumbing Codes

Many plumbing projects require permits, so *Plumbing: Basic, Intermediate & Advanced Projects* discusses industry standards and code compliance, project by project. All projects in the book are based on the National Standard Plumbing Code, which despite its name is one of several regional plumbing codes, along with countless local codes, in force in the United States. As a practical matter, the only codes that really matter are those adopted by your local municipality. You'll learn enough about the fundamentals to work intelligently with your codes office.

About the Projects

Every numbered step-by-step project is keyed to the level of difficulty (above, right) and the average time required by a reasonably skilled homeowner to complete the project. Each project also has a listing of tools and materials as well as a useful tip for getting the job done right.

In addition, you'll find a host of Smart Tips®, or insider information based on the author's many years of practical plumbing experience, and informative sidebars, which provide additional information on points of interest, products, and techniques relating to plumbing.

With the arsenal of information that is *Plumbing: Basic, Intermediate & Advanced Projects* at your side, you'll feel confident to tackle the very next plumbing challenge that comes along. Let the good times roll.

Smart Tips®

Insider information, shortcuts, new techniques, pitfalls to watch out for: this (and more) is the stuff of Smart Tips®.

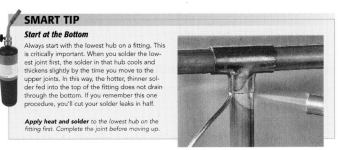

SMART TIP

Start at the Bottom
Always start with the lowest hub on a fitting. This is critically important. When you solder the low-est joint first, the solder in that hub cools and thickens slightly by the time you move to the upper joints. In this way, the hotter, thinner sol-der fed into the top of the fitting does not drain through the bottom. If you remember this one procedure, you'll cut your solder leaks in half.

Apply heat and solder to the lowest hub on the fitting first. Complete the joint before moving up.

Guide to Skill Level

Look for these estimates of job difficulty.

Easy, even for beginners.

Challenging. Can be done by beginners who have the patience and willingness to learn.

Difficult. Can be handled by most experienced do-it-yourselfers who have mastered basic plumbing skills. Consider consulting a specialist.

Introduction

Step-by-Step Photo Sequences

A listing of skill level, project time, tools, materials, and a helpful tip accompanies each step-by-step photo sequence.

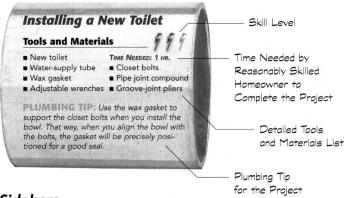

Installing a New Toilet

Tools and Materials
- New toilet
- Water-supply tube
- Wax gasket
- Adjustable wrenches

TIME NEEDED: 1 HR.
- Closet bolts
- Pipe joint compound
- Groove-joint pliers

PLUMBING TIP: *Use the wax gasket to support the closet bolts when you install the bowl. That way, when you align the bowl with the bolts, the gasket will be precisely posi-tioned for a good seal.*

— Skill Level

— Time Needed by Reasonably Skilled Homeowner to Complete the Project

— Detailed Tools and Materials List

— Plumbing Tip for the Project

Sidebars

The numerous sidebars focus on a product, technique, or situation, providing additional detail or insight.

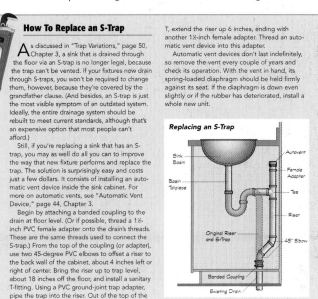

How To Replace an S-Trap

As discussed in "Trap Variations," page 50, Chapter 3, a sink that is drained through the floor via an S-trap is no longer legal, because the trap can't be vented. If your fixtures now drain through S-traps, you won't be required to change them, however, because they're covered by the grandfather clause. (And besides, an S-trap is just the most visible symptom of an outdated system. Ideally, the entire drainage system should be rebuilt to meet current standards, although that's an expensive option that most people can't afford.)

Still, if you're replacing a sink that has an S-trap, you may as well do all you can to improve the way that new fixture performs and replace the trap. The solution is surprisingly easy and costs just a few dollars. It consists of installing an auto-matic vent device inside the sink cabinet. For more on automatic vents, see "Automatic Vent Device," page 44, Chapter 3.

Begin by attaching a banded coupling to the drain at floor level. (Or if possible, thread a 1½-inch PVC female adapter onto the drain's threads. These are the same threads used to connect the S-trap.) From the top of the coupling (or adapter), use two 45-degree PVC elbows to offset a riser to the back wall of the cabinet, about 4 inches left or right of center. Bring the riser up to trap level, about 18 inches off the floor, and install a sanitary T-fitting. Using a PVC ground-joint trap adapter, pipe the trap into the riser. Out of the top of the

T, extend the riser up 6 inches, ending with another 1½-inch female adapter. Thread an auto-matic vent device into this adapter.

Automatic vent devices don't last indefinitely, so remove the vent every couple of years and check its operation. With the vent in hand, its spring-loaded diaphragm should be held firmly against its seat. If the diaphragm is down even slightly or if the rubber has deteriorated, install a whole new unit.

Replacing an S-Trap

Autovent
Sink Basin
Female Adapter
Basin Tailpiece
Tee
Riser
Original Riser and S-Trap
45° Elbow
Banded Coupling
Existing Drain

CHAPTER 1

Plumbing Basics

A home's plumbing system, with its tangle of pipes appearing here and disappearing there, can be daunting. If you think your plumbing system looks like a can of worms and it's completely unapproachable, take heart. It's really not as complicated as it appears. In fact, the entire system is comprehensible if you take a few minutes to organize the confusion into manageable segments, according to function.

Even if you go only so far as to separate the incoming water pipes from the outgoing drainage pipes, most of the battle is won. Separating these two systems is easy because the pipe sizes are different. Drainpipes are larger than water pipes, ranging between 1¼ and 4 inches in diameter. Water pipes are typically ½ and ¾ inch in diameter. These are inside diameters, so exterior measurements will be a little larger.

To get a sense of how plumbing systems work, it helps to follow the route that fresh water takes as it enters your home, passes through your fixtures and appliances, and drains to your septic system or public sewer.

Water Supply System

Each home has a water service pipe that travels underground from its supply source—either a private well and pump or public water main. Service lines are buried between 1 foot and 6 feet deep, depending on climate. The colder the climate, the deeper the lines are buried. City water services typically have three or four shutoff valves, offering several points at which to interrupt service. Only the last two valves are readily accessible to homeowners, however.

SMART TIP

Digging in Public Property

Although you're charged with maintaining the sidewalk in front of your house and the space, if any, between the sidewalk and street, this area is really public property. It's sometimes known as the public parking, and any qualified person needing to work on buried pipes can dig in this ground, even if it seems to be part of your lawn. You have a right to dig across the street to make installations and repairs, and your neighbor from across the street has the right to dig on your side. There is no need to tear up an area of more than about 4 by 8 feet. Whoever does the digging, whether by hand or machine, should also try to restore the grass.

Municipal Supply Lines

The first shutoff in the water line is actually part of the water-main tap mechanism, in which a motorized tapping machine has bored a self-tapping valve directly into an iron or plastic water main. The tap/valve, once in place, is called a *corporation stop*, or more commonly, a *corpcock*. You can reach it only by excavating the soil above it.

The second shutoff is also underground, usually in the public area between the street and sidewalk. The term for this in-line valve is a *curb stop*. It's only accessible with a long street key—which plumbers carry—and

has a pipelike sleeve that reaches to grade level. This vertical extension is called a *stopbox*. If you've been mowing around a protruding stopbox for years, you should know that it is adjustable, up or down. Call a plumber to adjust it.

A final pair of valves connects directly to the water meter, although in some houses there is only one valve. The valve on the street side of the meter is called a *meter valve* and the one on the house side, a *house valve*. These are the valves you'll use to shut down the system for emergencies and repairs, so it pays to know where your meter is located and how to reach both valves.

Where Are the Water and Sewer Mains Hidden?

Water and sewer mains are usually located near the street curb, with the sewer on one side of the street and the water on the other. Plumbers usually have to bore under the street with a mechanical boring machine to reach a main. Both mains need to be unearthed to make the service connections. Water mains are usually 3 to 6 feet deep, while sewers are between 3 and 15 feet deep,

with most in the 8- to 10-foot range.

In older neighborhoods, city mains may be located under the street. To gain access for installations or repairs, you must cut out a section of street. Street repair costs generally accrue to the homeowner. In the oldest neighborhoods, sewers are often located in alleyways. Your town's public works department should be able to tell you exactly where your sewer and water mains lie.

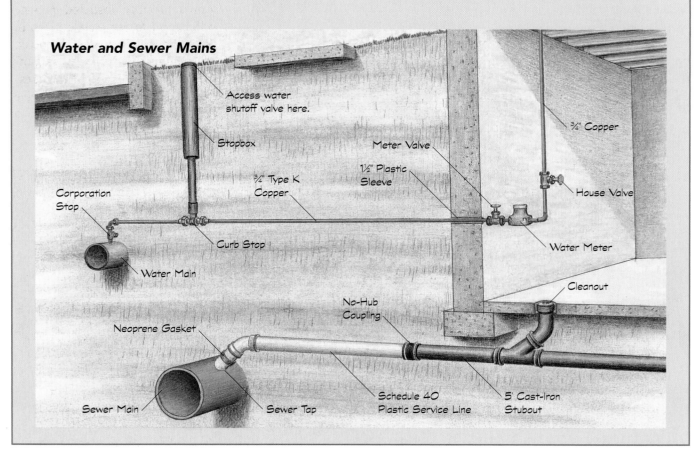

Water and Sewer Mains

Access water shutoff valve here.

Stopbox

Corporation Stop

Curb Stop

Water Main

Neoprene Gasket

Sewer Main

Sewer Tap

¾" Type K Copper

1½" Plastic Sleeve

Meter Valve

¾" Copper

House Valve

Water Meter

Cleanout

No-Hub Coupling

Schedule 40 Plastic Service Line

5' Cast-Iron Stubout

Water Meters

The water meter marks the end of the service line and the beginning of the in-house plumbing system. In some cases, the city owns the meters, while in others, users buy and maintain them at their own expense. Meters are usually inside the house, in a utility room, basement, or crawlspace, but some are outside, buried in *meter pits*. Meter pits are usually near the street, on either side of the sidewalk. If the meter is in a pit, the system rarely has a curb stop. In this case, the system has an additional valve just inside or outside the house, depending on the climate.

Types of Service Line

Service Lines in Older Homes. In homes built before World War II, the original service line is usually galvanized steel with a ¾-inch inside diameter. Pipes predating 1930 may terminate in a lead pipe loop. To identify

a lead loop, look for a blackish gray pipe that curves between the meter valve and the galvanized-steel service line. You should see a bulge at each end where the loop joins the pipe and meter valve. These hand-formed splices are called *wiped-lead joints* and are now a lost art. Plumbers made them with candle wax and molten lead, sweeping the lead repeatedly around the joint with the aid of a heat-resistant glove.

Plumbers also used lead underground at the water main because it was soft enough to accommodate seasonal ground movement. If you see a lead loop at the meter-end of your service line, expect one at the other end as well. While clearly obsolete, millions of lead loops are still in place, even though lead is now known to be extremely toxic. In most cases, mineral deposits sealed the water from the lead long ago. (See pages 72, 84, and 257, in Chapters 5 and 12).

Service Lines in Newer Homes. Homes built after 1950 have soft-copper service pipes. Again, the predominate size was ¾ inch, though larger diameters—up to 1¼ inch—were sometimes used to compensate for low pressure. Today 1-inch services are common, especially when plans include underground sprinkler systems. If your system draws water from a recently installed private well, expect to see plastic pipes in place, 1 to 1¼ inches in diameter. Most plumbers place a shutoff valve on the well side of the pressure tank. (Never shut off this valve without also shutting off power to the pump.)

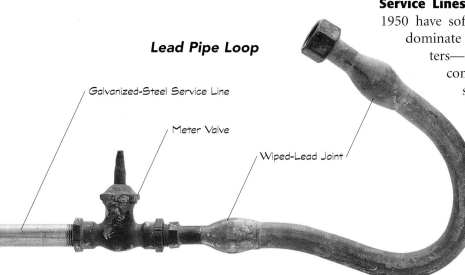

Lead Pipe Loop

Galvanized-Steel Service Line

Meter Valve

Wiped-Lead Joint

The Midcentury Benchmark

The 1950s were watershed years in home building, with methods and materials changing dramatically. A house built in the 1950s not only looks different from its 1940s predecessor, it is in fact built differently. In the 1950s, balloon framing was out; platform framing was in. Plaster was out; drywall was in. Knob-and-tube wiring was out; sheathed cable was in. Galvanized-steel piping was out; copper piping was in. And so on.

The end of World War II had a great deal to do with these changes. Thousands of returning

young soldiers sought affordable housing through the GI Bill as they settled down to start families. Builders began to use mass-production building methods to meet the demand for housing, and once-rationed materials of every description were readily available. Not surprisingly, some of the 1950s tract homes, furrowed in neat rows, bore a noticeable resemblance to military-base housing. In any case, this midcentury benchmark is useful when assessing the best approach for repairs and upgrades. Different methods and materials require different approaches.

Interior Water Supply Systems

A home's in-house water system starts with the water meter or, in the case of a private well, a pressure tank. If your home has an outdoor meter pit, consider the first full-size shutoff valve in the house as the starting point. From here, a single supply line—the *cold-water trunk line*—travels to a central location where a T-fitting splits it into two lines. One of these enters the top of a water heater while the other continues to feed cold water to the house. A third line exits the heater and becomes the system's *hot-water trunk line*. The hot-and-cold-water trunk lines usually run side by side along the center beam of the house, branching to serve isolated fixtures or fixture groups along the way.

In most cases, the trunk lines are ¾ inch in diameter and run under the floor joists, near the beam. The branch lines are usually tucked up between the joists so that most of the basement ceiling can be finished. While trunk lines are typically ¾ inch in diameter, branch lines are usually reduced to ½ inch in diameter at some point. Most codes allow only two fixtures on a ½-inch line, so plumbers will run ¾-inch branch lines until they reach the third-to-last fixture on the run. They also reduce to ½ inch in diameter the dedicated fixture risers that extend directly from the trunk lines.

No Basement?

Where are the water pipes if you live in a house without a basement? It depends on the type of home. If your ground floor spans a crawl space, the piping is likely to resemble that of a basement installation, except that the water heater may be located on the main floor in a utility closet.

If yours is a slab-on-grade home with a concrete floor, expect to find soft-copper water piping buried under the concrete slab. The water service in this case will usually enter a utility room through the floor. In most cases, the fixture supply piping will also be run under the slab, surfacing in the utility room, near the meter and water heater, on one end and near each fixture or group of fixtures on the other. In the extreme southern reaches of the country, where hard freezes are unlikely, copper or plastic water lines may be run in the attic, with branch lines dropping into plumbing walls.

Water Supply Lines

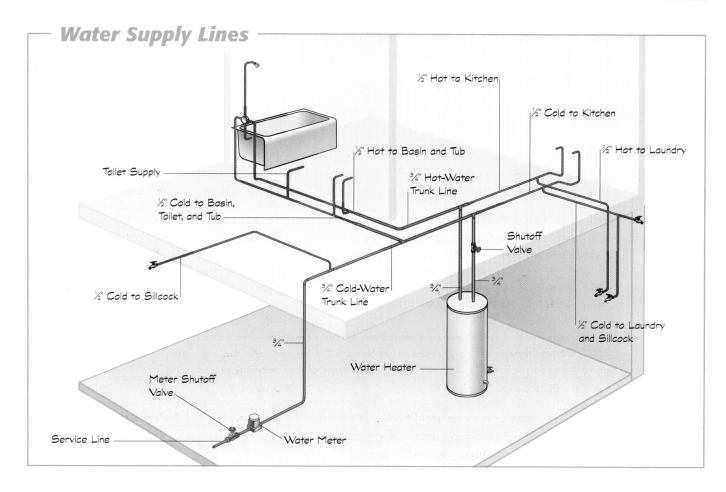

½" Hot to Kitchen
½" Cold to Kitchen
½" Hot to Basin and Tub
¾" Hot-Water Trunk Line
½" Hot to Laundry
Toilet Supply
½" Cold to Basin, Toilet, and Tub
Shutoff Valve
¾" Cold-Water Trunk Line
¾"   ¾"
½" Cold to Sillcock
½" Cold to Laundry and Sillcock
¾"
Water Heater
Meter Shutoff Valve
Service Line
Water Meter

Types of Pipe

Characteristics	Cutting Tools	Joining Method
PVC Pipe. Polyvinyl chloride plastic pipe is the preferred drain and vent piping for houses. It can't corrode, and it's easy to assemble.	Wheel cutter, hacksaw, scissor cutter	PVC solvent cement
ABS Pipe. Acrylonitrile butadiene styrene is a black plastic used in the same applications as PVC. It is not as rigid as PVC.	Wheel cutter, hacksaw	ABS or PVC solvent cement
Cast-Iron Pipe. Once used in drain and vent systems, this durable but brittle metal pipe has been largely replaced by PVC and ABS plastic.	Snap cutter, chisel	Banded neoprene couplings or rubber gaskets
Rigid Copper Pipe. The dominant water piping material today, copper pipe is usually joined with soldered (sweat) fittings.	Wheel cutter, hacksaw	Sweat or compression fittings
Soft Copper Pipe. Used primarily for natural gas and propane but also for water, this pipe is allowed under concrete.	Wheel cutter, hacksaw	Compression, solder, or flare fittings
Chromed Copper Tubing. This flexible piping is used as fixture water-supply tubes between fixtures and permanent piping.	Wheel cutter, hacksaw	Compression fittings
Flexible Braided-Steel Supply Line. This flexible piping, often used as fixture supply tubing, is easier to use than chromed copper tubing.	Fixed length	Factory-installed fittings
Chromed Ribbed Copper Pipe. Available only as fixture supply tubing, the ribbed section of this pipe makes it easy to bend.	Can't cut	Compression fittings
CPVC Pipe. Chlorinated polyvinyl chloride plastic water piping was created to replace rigid copper. Does not meet all local codes.	Wheel cutter, hacksaw, or scissor cutter	PVC cement or compression or crimp ring fittings
Pex Pipe. Cross-linked polyethylene plastic pipe is a flexible piping material gaining acceptance for in-house water systems. It requires few fittings.	Scissor tool, hacksaw	Several brands of proprietary fittings
Galvanized-Steel Pipe. Once used for in-house water systems, steel pipe is now used mostly in repair situations.	Wheel cutter and threading dies	Threaded fittings
Black Steel Pipe. Steel pipe was once used for in-house gas piping, though it's fast losing ground to soft copper and CSST.	Wheel cutter and threading dies	Threaded fittings
CSST. Corrugated stainless-steel tubing is a flexible, plastic-coated pipe made of stainless steel for in-house natural gas and propane.	Hacksaw or wheel cutter	Proprietary compression fittings

Drain, Waste, Vent

Water Supply

Gas

1 Plumbing Basics

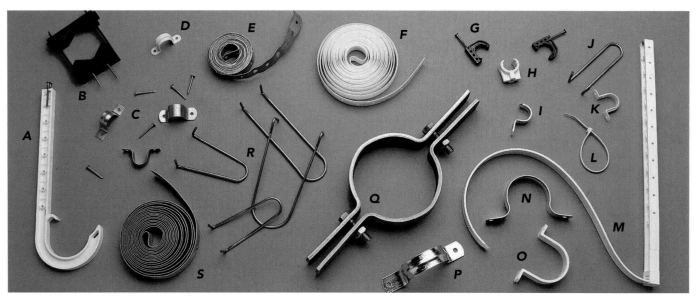

Hangers and Straps: A—plastic waste-pipe hanger, **B**—plastic water-pipe support, **C**—copper pipe straps, **D**—plastic pipe strap, **E**—copper hole strap, **F**—plastic hole strap, **G**—plastic pipe hook, **H**—plastic pipe clamp, **I**—conduit strap, **J**—copper pipe hook, **K**—plastic pipe strap, **L**—zip tie, **M**—plastic drainpipe support, **N**—galvanized drainpipe strap, **O**—plastic drainpipe strap, **P**—galvanized drainpipe strap, **Q**—stack clamp, **R**—wire pipe hooks, **S**—plastic hole strap

Copper or Plastic? While copper piping still dominates the market and likely will for a long time, plastic is gaining ground, especially in warmer climates. In some areas, including parts of the Desert Southwest, acids in the soil attack copper pipes, so plastic really is a better choice. And where codes allow plastic underground, you will usually find it approved for aboveground use as well. Do-it-yourselfers have long favored chlorinated polyvinyl chloride (CPVC) plastic water pipe because it requires little in the way of special skills or tools. Newer cross-linked polyethylene (PEX) plastic pipe is gaining in popularity with DIYers because of its ease of use. This white, red, or blue tubing is flexible and has little coil memory, so you can unwind it easily. You stretch it over rigid brass or plastic fittings to make a seal. Although it may require a special fitting tool and is usually connected to copper stubs at fixtures, PEX piping saves labor. It can also take a freeze better than copper or CPVC and is impervious to corrosive water or soil.

Connecting Fittings. Fittings for water piping are limited. They include male and female threaded adapters, 90-degree elbows, 45-degree elbows, T-fittings, couplings, and unions. Copper and brass fittings that are made to be soldered are called *sweat fittings*.

Elbows, as the name implies, create right-angle turns. Couplings join pipes end to end, and Ts split one pipe run into two separate lines. All of these fittings are available as copper or brass sweat types for copper tubing; threaded steel or brass types, which are threaded onto steel or copper pipes, respectively; and plastic types,

which are cemented to plastic pipes. Push-fit and barbed fittings may be used with some plastic pipe.

You'll use a special coupling called a *dielectric union* when you need to connect copper to iron. This fitting prevents electrolytic corrosion, which is caused by electrochemical reactions that take place when the dissimilar metals like iron and copper come in direct contact in the presence of water.

Dielectric unions have one side made of brass, and the other made of steel; a plastic bushing separates the two sides. The nonconducting bushing prevents the transfer of electrons that leads to electrolytic corrosion. Corrosion rates vary widely by locale, so some codes require dielectric unions and others don't. You'll have to check.

Fixture and Appliance Connections

Most fixture, faucet, and appliance connections are mechanical, meaning that they can be taken apart. (Two exceptions are those on water heaters and tub/shower faucets.) Sinks, waste-disposal units, laundry hookups, dishwashers, toilets, and bidets all have mechanical connections, which make them easy to service and replace.

The transition fittings that join permanent pipes to fixture-supply tubes take several forms. Prior to the 1950s, most of these connections were made with cone-shaped rubber washers, called *friction washers*. Plumbers simply slid a friction nut and cone washer onto a ¼- or ⅜-inch supply tube and inserted the tube into the larger ½-inch riser pipe. They then threaded the nut onto the pipe, forcing the tapered washer between the pipe and supply tube to make the seal. Because faucet and ball-

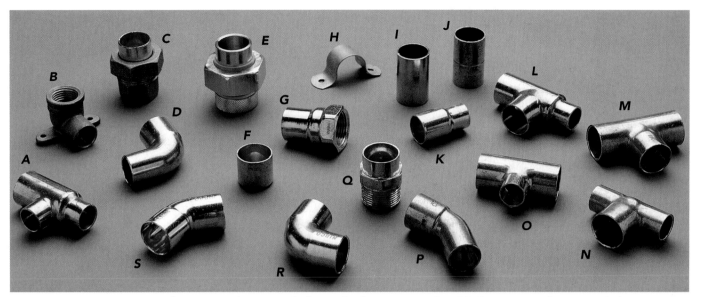

Fittings: **A**—¾ x ½ x ½-in. T-fitting, **B**—drop-eared elbow, **C**—brass union, **D**—90-deg. street elbow, **E**—dielectric union, **F**—copper sweat cap, **G**—sweat × female adapter, **H**—pipe strap, **I**—repair coupling, **J**—coupling, **K**—reducing coupling, **L**—¾ x ½ x ¾-in. T-fitting, **M**—¾-in. T-fitting, **N**—½ x ½ x ¾-in. T-fitting, **O**—¾ x ¾ x ½-in. T-fitting, **P**—45-deg. street elbow, **Q**—sweat × male adapter, **R**—90-deg. elbow, **S**—45-deg. elbow

cock shanks (toilet inlet valves) are similar in size to ½-inch threaded pipes, the top end connections of the supply tubes were formed exactly the same as cone washers. Though seldom installed today, plenty of these connections are in place. Both the nuts and washers remain common hardware store items.

Since the 1960s, compression fittings—both adapters and shutoff valves—have almost completely replaced cone washers. A compression fitting consists of a brass body with a tapered seat at top; a beveled compression ring, or *ferrule*; and a compression nut with a tapered inner rim. You slide the nut onto the supply tube, and follow it with the ferrule. When you insert the pipe and

tighten the nut, the pressure drives the ferrule into its tapered seats until it compresses around the supply tube and locks into place. You can loosen and reconnect the seal several times without ruining any parts.

Compression adapters and shutoffs—stops—are available to fit both copper pipe and threaded steel pipe risers. Those made for ½-inch steel pipe have female threads at their lower ends, while those for copper have a second, larger compression nut and ferrule that grips the copper. While adapters do a good job of connecting risers to supply tubes, many codes now require shutoffs. With shutoffs under every fixture, you won't have to shut down the entire system to make repairs.

Friction and Compression Fittings

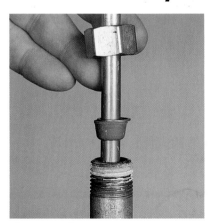

Cone washers *were common before compression fittings.*

Modern installations *use brass compression valves and fittings.*

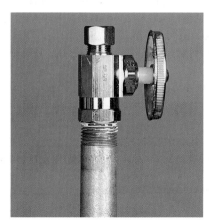

Compression valves *are also available with pipe threads.*

Supply Tubes. Supply tubes take several forms. The oldest and simplest is the copper ball-head tube, which is usually chrome plated. It's a simple ¼-inch flexible copper tube with a formed ball at the top. To make the connection, you place the ball against the tapered inner rim of the faucet shank and tighten a coupling nut over it. As the nut draws down, the formed-copper ball crushes against the shank's taper, making the seal. You trim the lower end to length, and join it to the supply riser with a compression adapter or shutoff valve. Plastic versions are also available but often don't meet requirements of local codes.

A new user-friendly version of the supply tube is the stainless-steel-enmeshed polymer tube (or flexible braided-steel tube), which is made for both sinks and toilets. Available in several lengths, it comes with compression and coupling nuts already installed. Homeowners much prefer this braided-steel tube because they don't have to trim it to fit, bend it into shape, or deal with separate fitting components. They just buy the lengths they need and tighten the coupling nuts in place. These tubes cost a few dollars more than their traditional counterparts, but they are usually worth it. Braided nylon and polybutylene versions are also available, but again, code compliance may be a problem depending on local codes.

And finally, a simple extension tube with a compression coupling is sometimes useful. Some modern faucets don't have threaded brass or plastic shanks. Instead, they have ¼-inch copper supply tubes brazed directly to the faucet body. These are usually long enough—about 18 inches—to reach wall-mounted stub-outs, but when the water pipes come through the floor, extension tubes are in order.

Drainage & Vent Systems

A plumbing drainage system has three basic segments, each with its own function: drainpipes, vent pipes, and fixture traps.

- *Drainpipes* direct wastewater away from the fixtures and house to the sewer, septic tank, or cesspool.

- *Vent pipes* allow air to enter the drainage system to equalize air pressure, allowing the wastewater to flow freely, and prevent suction.

- *Fixture traps* hold a small amount of water at fixtures to prevent the passage of sewer gas and vermin from the drainpipes into a living area.

Unlike potable-water systems, which flow under pressure, waste systems operate by gravity. Consequently, designers of these fittings emphasize gradual flow patterns and broad sweeps instead of abrupt turns. The abrupt geometry of water fittings is too severe for drain fittings. It's a difference you can see.

Sizes and Materials

As noted earlier, drainpipes are larger than water pipes, ranging in diameter from 1¼ to 4 inches. Any pipe 1½ inches in diameter or larger is likely to be a drainpipe or vent pipe; most 1¼-inch pipes are drainpipes only. Galvanized steel, copper, cast iron, and plastic are all common drainage and vent-pipe materials. Cast-iron stacks were standard for decades, usually with galvanized-steel or copper branch lines. Galvanized steel was used through the 1940s, and copper and brass emerged in the

---

Types of Supply Tubes

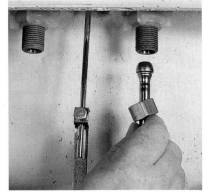

The ball head of this water supply tube crushes against the faucet shank.

Flexible braided-steel water supply tubes come equipped with factory-installed fittings.

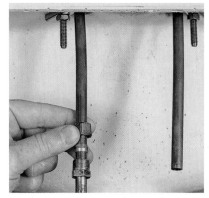

Compression coupling tubes are often used for faucets that have built-in supply tubes.

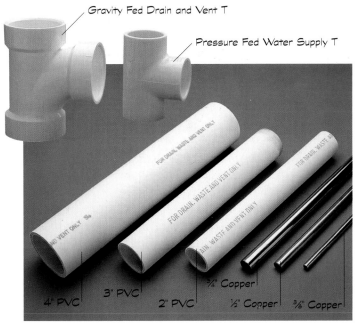

Gravity Fed Drain and Vent T

Pressure Fed Water Supply T

4" PVC 3" PVC 2" PVC ½" Copper ⅜" Copper

The plastic pipes carry wastewater; the copper pipes, fresh water. These are the most common sizes for modern homes. Note the gradual flow pattern in the drain tee.

1950s. The 1950s and 1960s also saw the installation of a good many copper and brass systems. After the mid-1970s, drain/vent systems usually tended to be plastic, either black acrylonitrile-butadiene-styrene (ABS) or white polyvinyl chloride (PVC).

The Drainpipe System

The in-house waste drainage system starts with a main pipe several feet outside an exterior wall, which passes under the house footing and into the basement or crawl-space. This below-floor drainpipe, usually 4 inches in diameter, is called the *main soil pipe*. (Any pipe carrying solid waste is technically a soil pipe.) The main soil pipe continues horizontally under the basement floor or slab (or along a wall), sometimes branching off—and reducing—to serve a laundry standpipe, maybe a floor drain or two, and possibly a basement bathroom and kitchen riser. Where the main soil pipe runs under the basement floor, it terminates in a 90-degree sweep bend through the floor and becomes the base for the primary vertical stack, or the main stack. Smaller drain stacks also come off of the main soil pipe and continue upward. These secondary drain and vent stacks may tie into the main stack above the highest fixture or pass through the roof independently.

Every home should have a full-size (3- or 4-inch-diameter) stack that travels from the soil pipe to roughly 12 inches above the point of exit through the roof. Think of this main stack as the trunk of a tree. At each floor, horizontal branch lines reach out to serve individual fixtures or fixture groups.

1 Plumbing Basics

Drain and Vent Lines

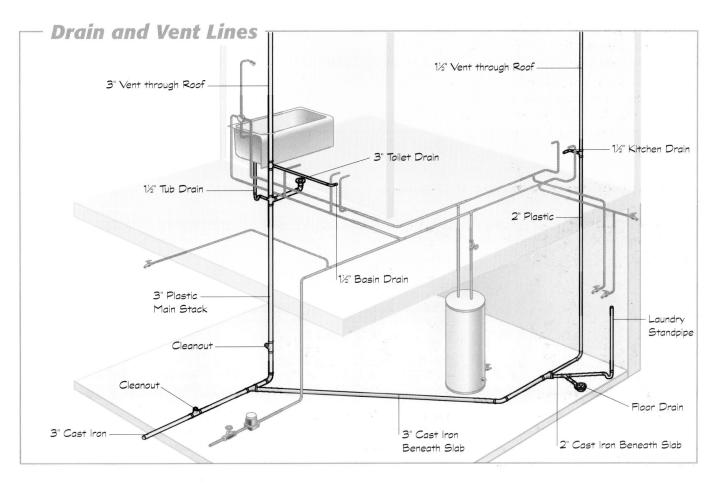

3" Vent through Roof

1½" Vent through Roof

3" Toilet Drain

1½" Kitchen Drain

1½" Tub Drain

2" Plastic

1½" Basin Drain

3" Plastic Main Stack

Cleanout

Laundry Standpipe

Cleanout

3" Cast Iron

Floor Drain

3" Cast Iron Beneath Slab

2" Cast Iron Beneath Slab

Types of Drain Traps

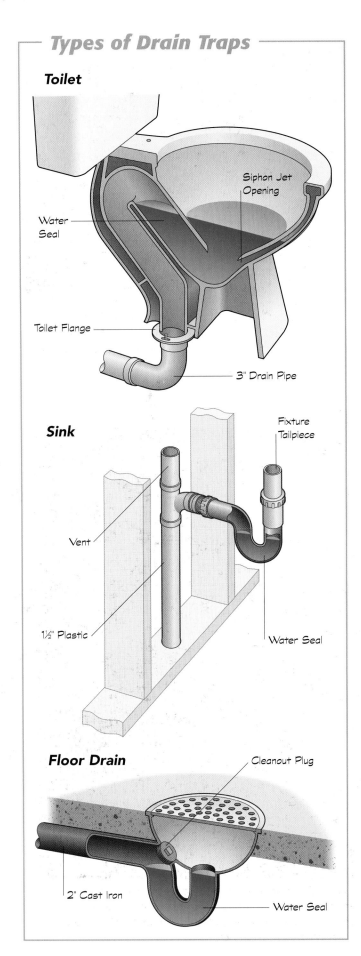

Toilet

Siphon Jet Opening

Water Seal

Toilet Flange

3" Drain Pipe

Sink

Fixture Tailpiece

Vent

1½" Plastic

Water Seal

Floor Drain

Cleanout Plug

2" Cast Iron

Water Seal

Drain Traps. Each fixture in the system is joined to its branch line via a water trap. These are critical components because they hold back the considerable volume of sewer gas present in every sewer system. While every fixture and drain must have a trap, not all traps are the same. Toilets, for example, have built-in, or *integral*, traps. The water you see standing in a toilet bowl is trapped there by an outlet passage that sweeps up before it sweeps down to its drainpipe connection. Floor drains also have integral traps, as do bidets and some urinals.

Sinks have sharply curved external chrome or plastic tube traps (P-traps), which can be disassembled for service work. Tub, shower, and laundry traps, in contrast, are usually fixed one-piece units.

Vent Pipes. Vents are important to a drainage system because they allow traps and drains to function properly. When water flows from a fixture through a pipe, it displaces an amount of air equal to its own volume, creating negative pressure behind the flow. This localized suction can be quite strong, especially at bends in the pipe. A toilet flushing near a sink, for example, can easily pull water from the sink's P-trap, allowing poisonous sewer gas into the living quarters. In fact, without adequate venting, a toilet won't flush properly.

Every home needs a stack vent through the roof, of course, but that's not always enough. All sorts of common situations can choke a vent, so it's necessary to have auxiliary vents, called *re-vents*. The shape, size, and location of these vents are critically important. (See Chapter 3, starting on page 40, for an in-depth discussion of venting.)

Fixtures. The point of all this piping begins and ends with the fixtures: sinks, toilets, tubs, and shower stalls. Fixtures are not as permanent as they appear. They are designed to be taken up and put back with relative ease and at moderate expense. Even bathtubs, which can look as though they've grown right out of the structural timbers of a home, are not that difficult to replace. If an old or defective fixture has you mumbling to yourself with every use, don't be intimidated: tear it out and put in a new one.

Appliances. The list of plumbing-related appliances has grown over the years to include water heaters, dishwashers, water softeners, water purifiers, clothes washers (which are not really plumbed in), waste-disposal units, hot-water dispensers, whirlpool tubs—and even refrigerators, with their ice makers. However, only the water heater is an essential and code-required part of every home's plumbing system.

Tools

It's easy to get carried away when buying tools, so focus on the basics first. A good rule is to hold off buying specialty tools until you need them. And if you can't imagine needing a large expensive tool more than once or twice, rent it if possible. You're likely to find many large tools, like chain wrenches and oversize pipe wrenches, in the local rental store. And finally, if you need to do special work on piping, many full-service hardware stores will cut, thread, or flare pipes for you in the store.

Of the specialty holding and turning tools shown here, the basin wrench and spud wrench are the real problem solvers. They will save you a lot of headaches, and they are not that expensive to buy.

Good tools can last a lifetime, so buy the best you can afford, especially when it comes to essentials you'll use often: pliers, screwdrivers, adjustable wrenches, and hammers.

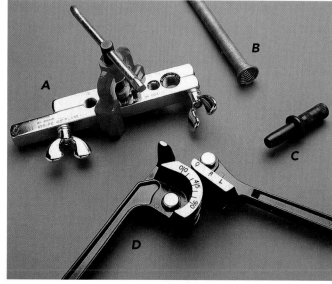

Forming Tools: **A**—*clamp-type flaring tool,* **B**—*spring-type tubing bender,* **C**—*hammer-type flaring tool,* **D**—*mechanical tubing bender*

1 Plumbing Basics

Holding and Turning Tools: **A**—*slip-joint pliers,* **B**—*nut drivers,* **C**—*strap wrench,* **D**—*adjustable wrenches,* **E**—*groove-joint pliers,* **F**—*offset screwdriver,* **G**—*spud wrench,* **H**—*Allen wrenches,* **I**—*chain wrench,* **J**—*sink-clip (Hootie) wrench,* **K**—*locking pliers,* **L**—*basin wrench,* **M**—*stop-box wrench,* **N**—*faucet-seat wrench,* **O**—*needle-nose pliers,* **P**—*deep-set faucet sockets,* **Q**—*combination wrench,* **R**—*pipe wrench*

Shopping for Tools

The right tools really do make the work easier and, in the end, better. While you can certainly cut water and gas piping with a hacksaw, a wheel cutter is faster and leaves a cleaner pipe edge. This may seem insignificant, but a crooked or ragged pipe end can affect fit and create turbulence as water passes through it. Excess turbulence can erode the pipe wall, greatly shortening its service life. The inexpensive little pipe reamer shown in the photograph below serves a similar purpose with plastic water pipe.

Similarly, a high-quality saber saw with an auto scroll feature cuts more accurately and is less damaging to countertop laminates than bargain saws, and a good heavy-duty reciprocating saw makes difficult jobs much easier. And finally, no one who remembers life before cordless drills will ever take them for granted. If you doubt their contribution to quality, count the number of screws used in older homes.

Drill Bits

All drill bits cut holes, but they do it differently, with differing results. The two self-feed bits shown here are for rough-in work, for chewing quick, crude holes through framing lumber. They work best on a right-angle drill, especially in wall and joist spaces. The hole-saw, in contrast, cuts a neat, precise hole, so it's better suited to drilling countertops, plastic sinks, and tub-shower surrounds, where chipping may be a problem. Speed bits are good starter bits. For only a few dollars, they bore a quick, moderately clean hole. Spiral bits work best when you need to drill a lot of holes; the spiral literally pulls the bit through. The high-speed bit is good for small holes in metal.

Cutting Tools: A—*scissor-type tubing cutter,* ***B***—*wheel cutter,* ***C***—*plastic-pipe saw,* ***D***—*reciprocating saw,* ***E***—*rat-tail and slim tapered files,* ***F***—*bastard-cut (flat) file,* ***G***—*multi-tool,* ***H***—*utility saw,* ***I***—*hacksaw,* ***J***—*utility knife,* ***K***—*cold chisel,* ***L***—*plastic-pipe reamer,* ***M***—*faucet valve seat grinder,* ***N***—*saber saw,* ***O***—*miniature tubing cutter*

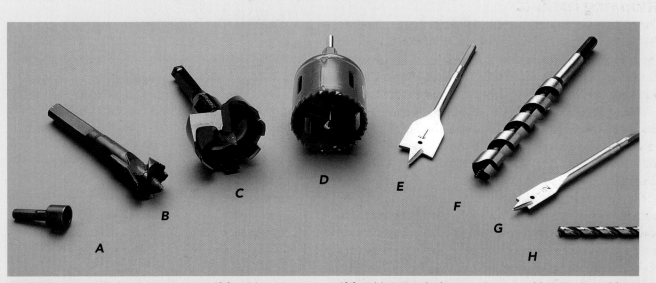

Drill Bits: A—nut driver, **B**—1-in. self-feed bit, **C**—2-in. self-feed bit, **D**—hole saw, **E**—speed bit, **F**—spiral bit, **G**—speed bit, **H**—high-speed bit

Common General Tools: A—claw hammer, **B**—multitester, **C**—stud finder, **D**—flashlight, **E**—chalk-line box, **F**—caulking gun, **G**—aviation snips, **H**—cordless drill/driver, **I**—measuring tape, **J**—2-ft. level, **K**—small sledgehammer, **L**—flat-blade screwdriver, **M**—Phillips screwdriver, **N**—putty knife, **O**—torpedo level, **P**—drywall taping knife

Plumbing Tools

Most plumbing tools are very specialized, so they have to earn their keep on plumbing projects alone. Basic tools, like plungers, pipe wrenches, and drain augers, should be part of every homeowner's tool kit. You'll use these items many times over the years.

The snap-cutter for cast-iron pipe and threading die for galvanized or black steel piping probably occupy the far end of the spectrum. With such limited application, snap-cutters and dies are almost always rental tools. The rest of these tools are more house specific. If you plan to add a bathroom or do other major additions or rerouting to copper water piping, then you need a soldering torch. If you have small children, you may find yourself needing a closet auger to retrieve small toys or other objects flushed down the toilet. If you live in an older home that has chronic drain problems, a few hundred dollars for a medium-size electric power auger may be a small price to pay.

Plumbing Supplies

The products shown at right cover a variety of projects. Silicone and latex tub-and-tile caulk are essential for preventing leaks around sinks, tubs, and showers. Silicone is more durable and generally lasts longer before you must replace it, but it requires more skill. You'll need PVC primer and solvent cement when working with PVC drainpipes and CPVC water pipes. Both PVC cement and ABS cement work on ABS plastic pipe. You'll need leak-detection soap when working with gas pipe and pipe joint compound or pipe-thread tape for sealing threaded connections. And finally, for soldering copper pipe you'll need flux, solder, and abrasives to clean the pipe surface.

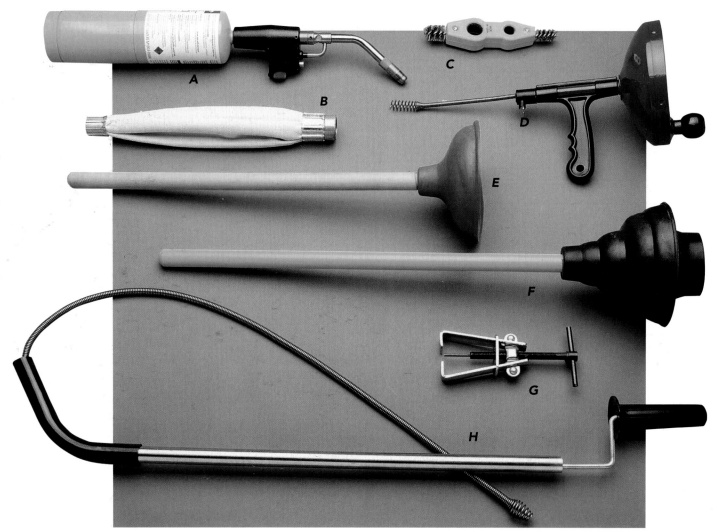

***Common Plumbing Tools: A**—soldering torch, **B**—blow bag, **C**—pipe-cleaning tool, **D**—hand auger, **E**—standard plunger, **F**—combination plunger, **G**—handle puller, **H**—closet auger*

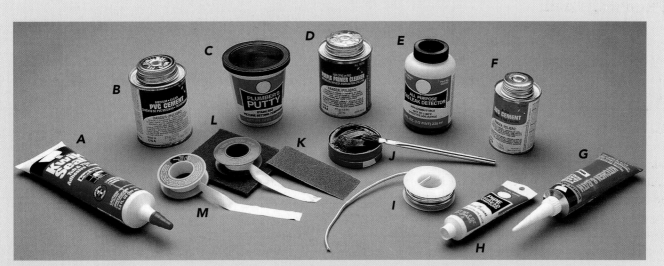

Plumbing Supplies: A—*latex tub-and-tile caulk,* **B**—*PVC solvent cement,* **C**—*plumber's putty,* **D**—*PVC primer,* **E**—*leak-detection fluid,* **F**—*ABS solvent cement,* **G**—*silicone caulk,* **H**—*pipe joint compound,* **I**—*solder,* **J**—*flux,* **K**—*grit cloth,* **L**—*abrasive pad,* **M**—*pipe-thread sealing tape (yellow spool: gas, blue spool: water)*

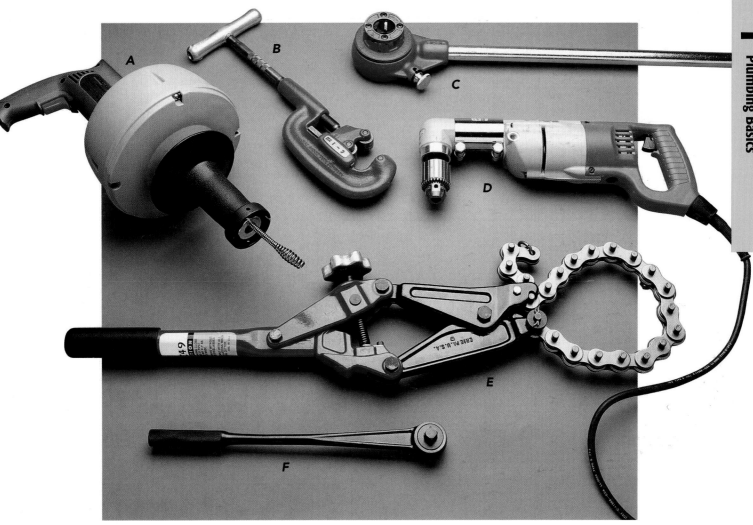

Rental Tools: A—*power drain auger,* **B**—*steel-pipe cutter,* **C**—*steel-pipe threading die,* **D**—*right-angle drill,* **E**—*snap-cutter for cast-iron pipe,* **F**—*snap-cutter drive wrench*

1

Plumbing Basics

CHAPTER 2

Planning Plumbing Changes & Additions

 f you are planning to make improvements that require installation of plumbing fixtures or appliances where there are no water or drainage facilities, draw up a detailed plan to scale before proceeding. Once you have prepared the plan (along with a list of materials), have someone with experience doing similar projects check to see whether you have overlooked anything. The local plumbing-supply store may have trained consultants on staff who can provide this service. The two main tasks ahead of you will be 1) to make sure your plans comply with code and 2) to make accurate rough-in measurements.

Building Codes

A building code is a collection of legal statutes that specify which building materials may be used and how these materials are to be assembled in the construction of residential and commercial buildings. A code office has legal authority within its jurisdiction, be it state, county, or municipality. A typical building code covers everything from framing to concrete installations to ventilation and insulation. To comply with code, you must secure a building permit from the local building department and allow the building inspector or inspectors access to the work for inspection and approval at various stages of completion.

Lack of Uniformity. Unlike electrical codes, which are written at the national level (the National Electrical Code, or NEC) and enforced (and sometimes modified) at the state, county, and city level, plumbing codes are often written and enforced only at the city or county level. So while electricians normally carry both state and county licenses, plumbers are usually licensed only at the city/county level. Plumbers who work in more than one county or city must often have more than one license.

Many small towns and rural areas remain entirely without plumbing codes. More and more codes are going on the books in these areas, but the conversion is far from complete and may never be. The most far-reaching enforcement bodies are state and county health departments, which have little to do with home construction but claim jurisdiction over private wells and septic systems. You should check with the local building department to see what plumbing codes, if any, are enforced.

Properties financed with the aid of government guarantees, such as those of the U.S. Department of Housing and Urban Development's Federal Housing Administration (FHA) and the U.S. Department of Veterans Affairs (VA), must meet the guidelines established by these agencies in addition to meeting any applicable state, county, and municipal codes. These federal guidelines are not considered codes, however, and have more to do with home financing than home building.

Permits and Inspections

If you're planning to install a permanent appliance like a water heater or to make a plumbing upgrade that will require piping changes or additions, visit the local building department and apply for a permit. You may be asked several questions about how you plan to accomplish this work, but don't be intimidated. Explain exactly what plumbing is in place and how you plan to expand or change it. If your plan is not likely to meet applicable codes, the code official will most likely be ready with suggestions to make it code-worthy.

Once you have worked out the details of your plan, you'll need to fill out a permit application. The form will probably have a list of fixtures and project descriptions. In most cases, you'll simply check the boxes next to each appropriate fixture or work category. If you plan to remodel a bathroom, for example, check the boxes next to Sink, Toilet, and Tub/Shower. The cost of the permit is usually determined by the number of boxes you check, but don't let this intimidate you. Permit fees are seldom expensive, especially for simple upgrades.

Inspections. You'll need to call for an inspection, usually a minimum of a day ahead of time, at the completion of each stage of work. Try to set up a time when you can meet the inspector on the job. At the very least, arrange for a friend or family member to open the door for him or her.

Just how many plumbing inspections will you need? It depends. If your remodeling involves in-wall piping and fixture installations, you'll need two inspections—a rough-in inspection and a finish inspection. But if you're simply replacing a water heater, where all of your work will be visible at a glance, then only a final inspection will be necessary. (New-home construction usually requires four plumbing inspections: one for the under-

ground sewer and water service lines and taps, one after the installation of any under-slab or basement floor piping, another after the installation of above-floor rough-in piping, and a final inspection when the work is complete.)

Remember that an inspector must approve all in-wall and underground work before you cover it up. A building inspector has the authority to make you remove drywall, soil, or even concrete if he or she suspects substandard work. Covering your work prior to inspection automatically makes it suspicious.

Layout & Feasibility

Before making any plumbing improvements, you'll need to assess feasibility. To do that, you'll need to know how much space each new fixture will require, both practically and as a matter of local codes. You'll also need to know the rough-in specifications for each new fixture. Most are standard, meaning that they'll work with any common brand of fixture. If you choose a specialty fixture with nonstandard dimensions, make certain that you get the rough-in measurements from the manufacturer's product literature or from the retailer before you start.

Standard Rough-In Measurements

Roughing-in piping for fixtures and appliances in exactly the right places is critical because finished walls and cabinets usually cover the piping by the time you install the fixtures. Going back to reposition connector fittings at the finishing stage is costly and time-consuming. The following sections give standard fixture and appliance rough-in measurements. Note: All measurements are taken from the center of the pipe or fitting.

SMART TIP

Grandfather Clause to the Rescue

If you're like many homeowners, what keeps you from applying for permits and calling for inspections is the fear that once an inspector darkens your door, he or she will storm through the house condemning everything in sight. Is this possible? Perhaps, but it's not likely. Unless inspectors see something that is clearly a health hazard, there isn't much they can do.

If you have water running properly to the basic fixtures, reasonably few appliances plugged into

working electrical outlets, no missing steps, and walls and a roof that appear as if they'll stay put, you are pretty much covered by the grandfather clause. The clause basically applies common sense by stating that new standards cannot be applied to old work unless that work now poses a genuine health risk to inhabitants or passersby. If older installations met the standards of their day, they will do until you decide to improve them. When you make those improvements, however, current standards will apply.

SMART TIP

Do You Need a Permit?

In areas with enforced plumbing codes, only those plumbing projects with pipe changes and permanent appliance installations generally require permits and inspections. If, for example, you plan to take up your old toilet and replace it with a new one, you usually don't need a permit or inspection. But if you plan to move the toilet from one wall to another, which would require changing the permanent piping, you'll need to apply for a permit and have your work inspected and approved. The reasoning here is simple: replacing a fixture does nothing to compromise the plumbing system, but piping changes can alter the balance between drain and vent segments; therefore, they deserve closer scrutiny.

Water heaters are another case in point. The issue, as always, is safety. Code officials need to know whether you've vented your gas water heater adequately or wired your electric heater properly. They'll also check the temperature-and-pressure-relief valve. If the relief-valve installation is wrong, the heater can explode when its thermostat fails. Too often, homeowners plug relief-valve openings with iron plugs or transfer the old water heater's nearly spent temperature-and-pressure-relief valve to the new heater. In other cases, homeowners install relief valves that have pressure ratings higher than those of the heaters they are meant to protect. Code officials, therefore, have several good reasons to check your water-heater installation.

Water-Heater Relief Valves: Permit Required

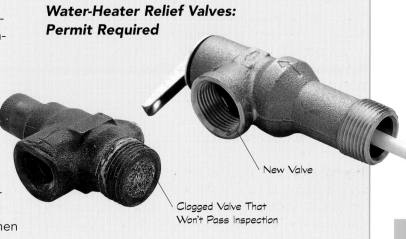

New Valve

Clogged Valve That Won't Pass Inspection

Toilets. Most toilets fit into a space that is 22 inches wide, but codes require a 30-inch opening. The toilet flange fitting should be centered in this opening, with at least 15 inches between the center of the toilet flange and the nearest side wall or cabinet. Spot the center of the flange 12½ inches out from the stud wall in the back, or 12 inches out from a finished wall. All standard toilets are set up for this 12-inch rough-in, but toilets with 10-inch and 14-inch rough-ins are available for special situations. These work fine, but they're always more expensive. You'd use one if you mismeasured or if a structural framing member kept you from roughing-in the flange at 12 inches. Some plumbers might accommodate the difference of an inch or so by using an offset flange. Offset flanges are not as sturdy as standard flanges, however, so avoid them if possible. A 12-inch rough-in is the best way to go, even if it means cutting floor joists and installing structural headers on each side of the cut.

When it comes to a toilet's water-supply rough-in, you'll have two choices. You can bring the supply riser through the floor or through the back wall. Both work, but a wall installation makes floor cleaning easier. If you use a floor riser, center it 6 inches to the left of the drain outlet and 3 inches from the back wall. For a wall installation, spot the stub-out 6 inches to the left of the outlet and 6 inches off the floor. If a stud or floor joist forces you to fudge by an inch or two, don't worry, the toilet supply tube will handle the offset.

Kitchen Sinks. The water piping for a kitchen sink should be centered on the eventual placement of the sink. Again, these pipes can enter from the wall or floor. Wall installations make it easier to set the cabinet, however. The standard height for water pipes exiting a wall is 18 inches. Kitchen sinks have 8-inch center spreads, so place each pipe (hot and cold water) 4 inches off center.

The drain piping should exit the wall at least 16 inches above the kitchen floor (not the cabinet floor). With a 36-inch cabinet base (and double-basin sink), position the drain 12 inches in from one or the other side of the cabinet wall. The side from which you'll measure depends on whether you plan to install a waste-disposal unit. If so, position the unit for convenience, and install the drain on the remaining side, measuring from that side of the cabinet. With a single-basin sink, locate the drain 2 inches off center in either direction.

2 Planning Plumbing Changes & Additions

Standard Rough-In Measurements

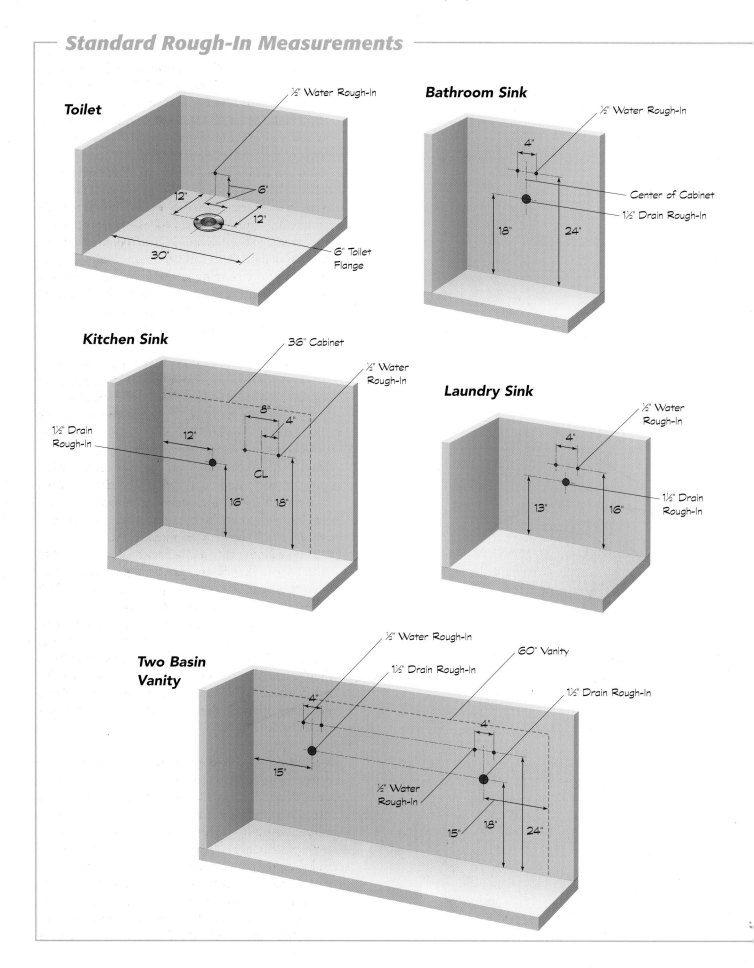

Toilet

½" Water Rough-In

12"

6"

12"

30"

6" Toilet Flange

Bathroom Sink

½" Water Rough-In

4"

Center of Cabinet

1½" Drain Rough-In

18"

24"

Kitchen Sink

36" Cabinet

½" Water Rough-In

1½" Drain Rough-In

8"

4"

12"

CL

16"

18"

Laundry Sink

½" Water Rough-In

4"

1½" Drain Rough-In

13"

16"

Two Basin Vanity

½" Water Rough-In

1½" Drain Rough-In

60" Vanity

1½" Drain Rough-In

4"

4"

15"

½" Water Rough-In

15"

18"

24"

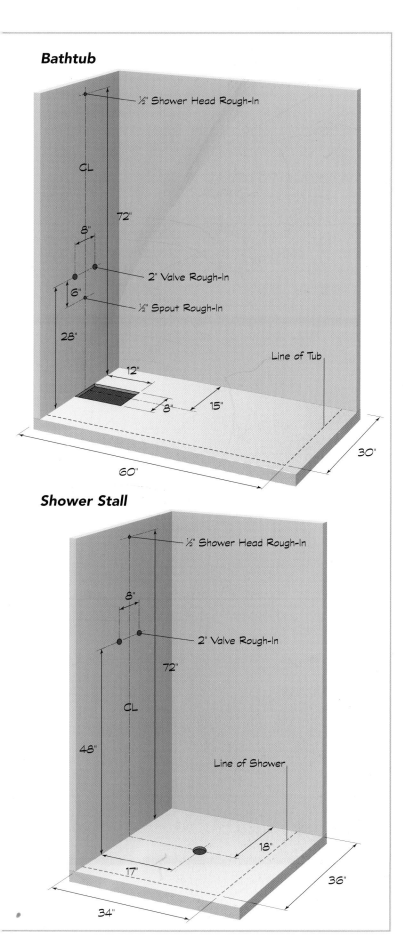

Bathtub

½" Shower Head Rough-In

CL

72"

8"

2" Valve Rough-In

6"

½" Spout Rough-In

28"

Line of Tub

12"

8"   15"

30"

60"

Shower Stall

½" Shower Head Rough-In

8"

2" Valve Rough-In

72"

CL

48"

Line of Shower

18"

17"

36"

34"

Bathroom Sink. If you are using a single bathroom sink (sometimes called a lavatory basin), position the water piping a distance of 2 inches from each side of the centerline. For two sinks in the same cabinet, install two sets of stub-outs and two drains. A workable height for in-wall water stub-outs is 24 inches above the bathroom floor.

You can center drains inside the vanity cabinet, 18 inches off the bathroom floor. When installing two basins in a larger cabinet, divide the width of the cabinet into four equal parts and center the two drains on the second and third dividing lines. Pedestal lavatories are always a tight fit, so check the manufacturer's specifications before running any pipe. When installing a wall-hung lavatory, locate the rim of the fixture 32 inches off the floor. The rough-in placements are the same as those for a single-basin vanity.

Bathtubs. Because bathtubs have bulky waste-and-overflow drain assemblies, you must cut a relatively large hole in the bathroom floor, under the drain, to accommodate them. Make the cut before setting the tub. Standard tubs are 30 inches wide, while some fiberglass models and most whirlpool tubs are 32 inches wide. In any case, measure 15 or 16 inches from the back wall to establish the drain center. Then cut an 8 × 12-inch opening in the floor. This will allow you to set the tub, install the waste assembly, and attach the P-trap, in that order.

Standard height for a tub-faucet valve is 28 inches off the floor. That places the spout pipe at 6 inches below the center of the valve and the shower head 72 inches above the floor. While these placements work well, there's nothing particularly special about them. If local codes specify other placements, use those. And if you'd like to raise the faucet and shower head slightly, feel free to do so. Many people prefer a 76-inch position for the shower head because it places the connection well above the tops of manufactured tub surrounds.

Shower Stalls. Standard shower-valve height is 48 inches above the bathroom floor, with the shower head 72 inches above the floor. Again, many people prefer a 76-inch shower head height. Always install a shower head in a sidewall, never in a back wall.

Proper drain placement can vary, so be sure to read the product specifications. In most cases, the drain is centered in the pan. For example, for a 34 × 36-inch pan, measure 18 inches in from the side walls and 17 inches in from the back wall. As with a bathtub, you'll cut the floor opening—which

2 Planning Plumbing Changes & Additions

should be at least 6 inches in diameter—and install the pan or one-piece stall before connecting the P-trap. The only case when a trap needs to be piped first is when you are setting a shower on concrete.

Laundry Sinks. Laundry sinks have rough-in placements different from those of other sinks. Plan for a drain outlet no more than 13 inches above the floor and water stub-outs 16 inches above the floor. The drain can be centered or up to 2 inches off center. Laundry sinks, made of fiberglass and ABS plastic, are available in stand-alone, wall-hung, and floor-supported models and in drop-in models for cabinet installations.

Laundry Standpipes. A laundry standpipe (the riser drainpipe) should reach 36 inches above the floor. For in-wall installations, a recessed laundry box is a good idea. In this case, the water lines and standpipe terminate inside the box.

A laundry standpipe must be 2 inches in diameter and have a fixed, 2-inch trap. In basements and slab-on-grade homes, the trap can be below the floor and may not need to be vented. In basements, mount the shutoff valves about 42 inches above the floor. Secure all pipes to the wall to counter the back-shock, or water hammer, caused by a washer's electric solenoid valve.

Designing Efficient Plumbing Installations

The best plumbing configuration for a larger home is the back-to-back bathroom grouping shown on the opposite page. In this two-bathroom arrangement, both tubs, both sinks, and both toilets are stack-vented. Only the first floor kitchen line travels any distance, and so only that line is vented separately. A back-to-back layout also holds water piping to an absolute minimum. Less water piping means less heat loss through pipe walls and, therefore, less wasted energy. Having to drain the cooled water from a long hot-water piping run in order to get the hot water behind it is enormously wasteful and perpetually annoying. In a small home, another way to save piping is to back the kitchen up to the bathroom. If you don't intend to install a dishwasher, you

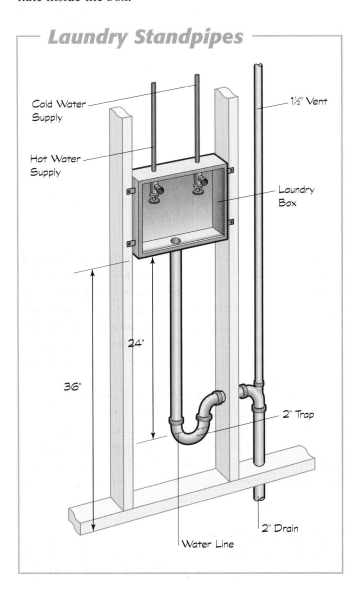

Laundry Standpipes

Cold Water Supply

Hot Water Supply

1½" Vent

Laundry Box

24"

36"

2" Trap

2" Drain

Water Line

SMART TIP

Freeing Up Floor Space

If you have to accommodate the cramped space of an extremely small bathroom where a conventional toilet will get in the way, you can use a corner toilet. This kind of toilet has a wedge-shaped tank to fit an inside corner and free up some floor space. The rough-in for this toilet is centered 12½ inches from the rough framing of each of the walls that form the corner.

This corner toilet is shaped to save floor space, but you plumb it as you would any other toilet.

Back-to-Back Bathroom Layout

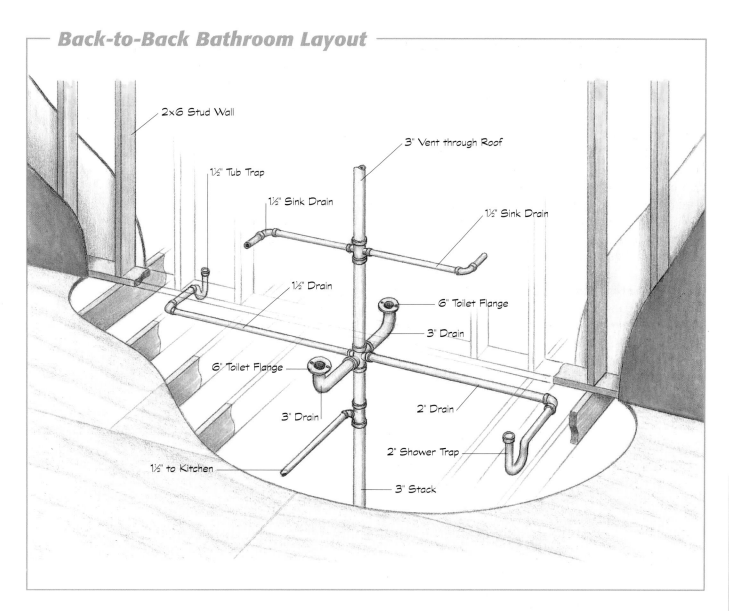

2×6 Stud Wall

3" Vent through Roof

1½" Tub Trap

1½" Sink Drain

1½" Sink Drain

1½" Drain

6" Toilet Flange

3" Drain

6" Toilet Flange

2" Drain

3" Drain

2" Shower Trap

1½" to Kitchen

3" Stack

can plan on stack-venting all of the first-floor fixtures.

When it comes to fixture layout within a bathroom, the most economical and easy-to-vent approach is to place the toilet between the sink and tub/shower. This is a perfect small-bathroom configuration: it saves water pipe, drainpipe, and fittings. Older homes, in which the sink and tub share a common floor-mounted drum trap, have an older layout. In these cases, the sink occupies the space between the toilet and tub. Whenever possible, remove a troublesome drum trap, and trap each fixture independently.

Planning for Access

In a few instances, you can install new plumbing without opening walls and ceilings, but these situations are limited. In many cases, you'll need to open at least one side of a wall so that you can install and secure the new piping. This is especially true when working in multistory houses.

Don't let the notion of tearing into walls and ceilings scare you. Cutting out drywall or plaster is easy, and if you don't feel up to repairing these openings yourself, you shouldn't have a problem finding a drywall or plaster contractor to do it for you. In any case, don't let a few dollars' worth of drywall or plaster repair keep you from having the bath, kitchen, bar, laundry, or whirlpool you've always wanted.

If you're simply remodeling a bathroom or kitchen, most of the piping from the old bath or kitchen will do. Although you may need to replace or move some of it, there will always be existing plumbing with which to work. But if you hope to bring plumbing to a new area of the house, then planning the pipe route is an important first step.

Planning New Vents. If you have a crawl space or unfinished basement, chances are you'll be able to run water and drainage piping easily to any area of the

2 Planning Plumbing Changes & Additions

SMART TIP

Cluster for Efficiency

As a general rule, it's less expensive and less complicated to cluster plumbing groups near one another and close to the main stack. The farther one bath is from another or the farther any fixture is from the main stack and water heater, the more piping is required. While this may seem obvious, there's more to it than mere distance. Fixtures near the main stack can often be stack-vented. When they are spread out, these same fixtures will need secondary vents, or re-vents, which can more than double the amount of piping needed for the job. (See Chapter 3, beginning on page 34, for more on venting.)

house from existing lines. The trickiest part will be venting your new fixtures. The new vent will need to extend into the attic, where it must either join an existing vent stack or exit the roof directly. If you are working in a two-story home and the plumbing to be installed is in the basement or on the first floor, you may need to open a wall or build an enclosed chimneylike pipe chase to cover the pipes. Some codes may allow an exterior vent as long as it terminates above the roof, away from attic windows or dormers.

If your upgrade involves a single, low-volume fixture—a bar sink, for example—you might consider an

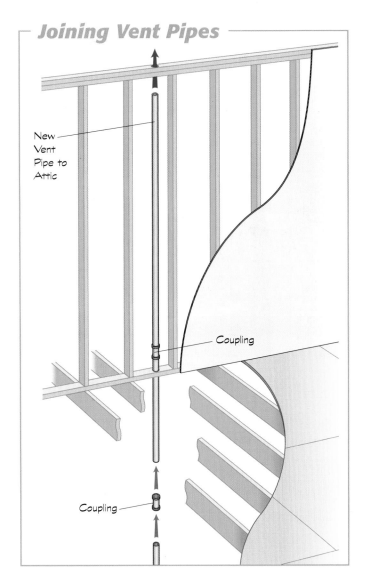

Joining Vent Pipes

New Vent Pipe to Attic

Coupling

Coupling

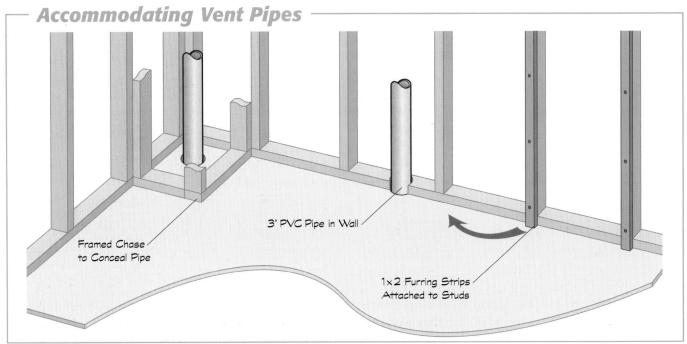

Accommodating Vent Pipes

Framed Chase to Conceal Pipe

3" PVC Pipe in Wall

1x2 Furring Strips Attached to Studs

automatic vent device or a loop vent. Neither requires open-air access. Both vents are discussed in Chapter 3, pages 42 and 44.

If you live in a single-story home, venting basement plumbing is relatively easy. You can usually drill the top and bottom plates of an interior wall and then slide pipe from the basement into the attic. It takes careful measuring, but it's not difficult. If that's not workable, consider running the vent pipe through a first-floor closet. You can then enclose the pipe with studs and drywall or caulk it where it passes through the closet floor and ceiling.

The size of the vent is another consideration. An isolated sink, laundry, or shower will only need a 1½-inch vent. A bath group, consisting of a tub/shower, sink, and toilet, can all be vented with a 2-inch vent as long as your house already has a 3- or 4-inch stack extending through the roof.

If you have a two-story home, you'll likely need to cut access openings in finished walls and ceilings. If you need to extend a 3-inch stack from the basement to the attic—to add an upstairs bath, for example—a conventional wall will be too narrow. You'll need to build a pipe chase or widen the entire plumbing wall about an inch. To widen the wall, nail 1×2 furring strips to the existing studs, and then screw and glue new drywall to these strips.

Before

After

Often you can leave the fixtures in place when you remodel a bathroom or kitchen. That way you don't have to worry about rerouting plumbing.

2 Planning Plumbing Changes & Additions

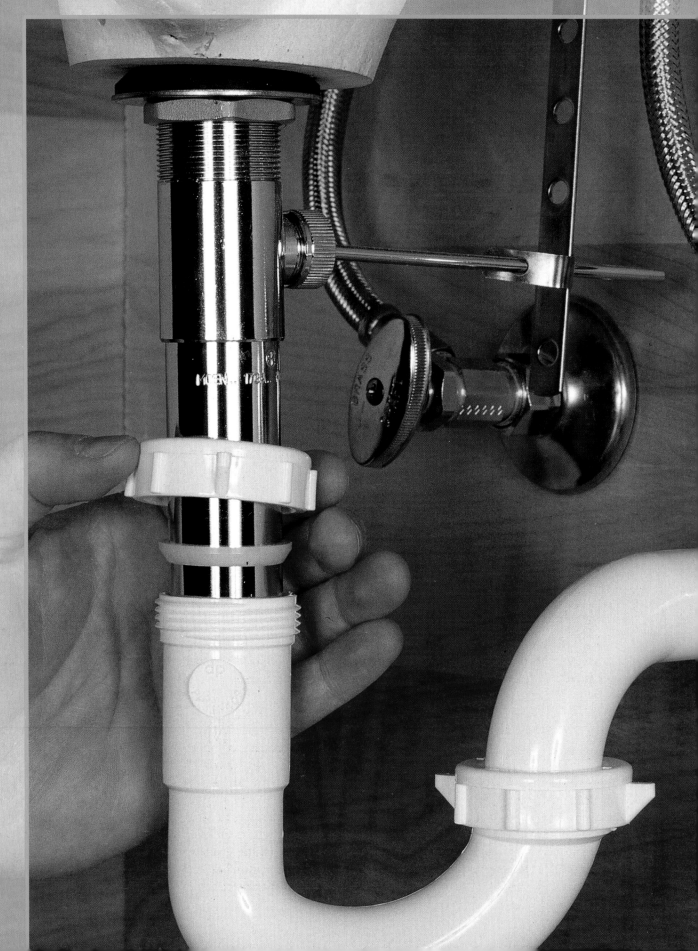

CHAPTER 3

Drains, Vents & Traps

**D**rainpipes have the important job of carrying all the wastewater a household generates away from the house and into a sewer or septic system.

The sewer or septic system creates a poisonously gaseous environment, however, and all that stands between you and that environment is the water in your fixture traps. If you lose the water in one of these traps (by evaporation, suction, or some other means), noxious sewer gases will rise into your living quarters, possibly causing headaches and even respiratory illnesses in those exposed to the gases. This is why traps are so important in your drainage system.

A properly designed venting system is the only way to ensure that you maintain adequate water flow in drainpipes and water levels in fixture traps, so vents are also vitally important.

Drains

The drawing on the following page shows a typical plumbing system. Imagine that this is a one-story ranch-style home, with one bath on the main floor and another in the basement. The water piping is included to give a greater sense of perspective and detail. While not every house will be plumbed just like this one and codes may vary slightly, this is a good example of a code-worthy piping schematic.

Basic Drainage Considerations

Establishing an easy, gradual flow of wastewater is the prime consideration with drains. (Similarly, airflow is the critical, overriding objective of venting, which is essential to proper drainage.) Therefore, every drainpipe, whether buried under soil or threaded through walls, must be sloped just right. When installing drainpipes, shoot for a slope of $\frac{1}{4}$ inch per foot. If structural barriers force a compromise, try to maintain at least $\frac{1}{16}$ inch per foot.

Too Much Slope. As you've seen, a drain must slope downward if water is to flow by gravity, but you may not know that it's possible to have too much slope. When water moves through a horizontal pipe too quickly and that water is carrying solids, the water can outrun the solids. This is especially true of longer drain lines, such as the sewer service pipe between the house and sewer main. New low-flush toilets only compound the problem because they use less water. Even gray water—water that doesn't carry solids—leaves grease, soap, hair, and food particles behind when it moves through the system too quickly. Eventually these accumulations can cause the line to clog.

To prevent accumulation problems, limit the fall of any drain line to no more than $\frac{1}{4}$ inch per foot. If structural barriers force a slope greater than $\frac{1}{4}$ inch per foot or if the line will slope a distance greater than its own diameter along its length, use fittings to step up the line. Hold the line before and after the step at $\frac{1}{8}$ to $\frac{1}{4}$ inch per

Typical Drainage System

Working backward—that is, starting with where the wastewater exits the house—the drainage system begins with the 4-inch soil pipe, which enters the house under an exterior footing or slab. (In some cases the soil pipe may enter the house through the basement or crawlspace wall, especially in a septic-system arrangement.) Just after the cleanout, a 4 x 2-inch Y-fitting splits off to drain the laundry in the basement and the kitchen on the main floor. Codes often require that this takeoff be downstream of the larger toilet-branch line.

The next in-line fitting is a 4-inch Y-fitting that serves the basement bath group—toilet, tub, and sink. The toilet line is re-vented because it is a lower floor installation; it does double duty as a wet vent for the shower and sink.

Before the soil pipe sweeps up to become the primary 3-inch vertical stack, an unvented 2-inch Y-fitting serves a trapped floor drain. On the stack, a 3-inch T-fitting with a 1½-inch side inlet serves the toilet and shower. The fitting allows both fixtures to enter the stack at the same level and, therefore, allows both to be stack-vented.

Approximately 16 inches above the floor, a second T-fitting drains the sink basin, which is also stack-vented. From the top of this T, the stack continues through the roof.

Whole-House Drain and Vent System

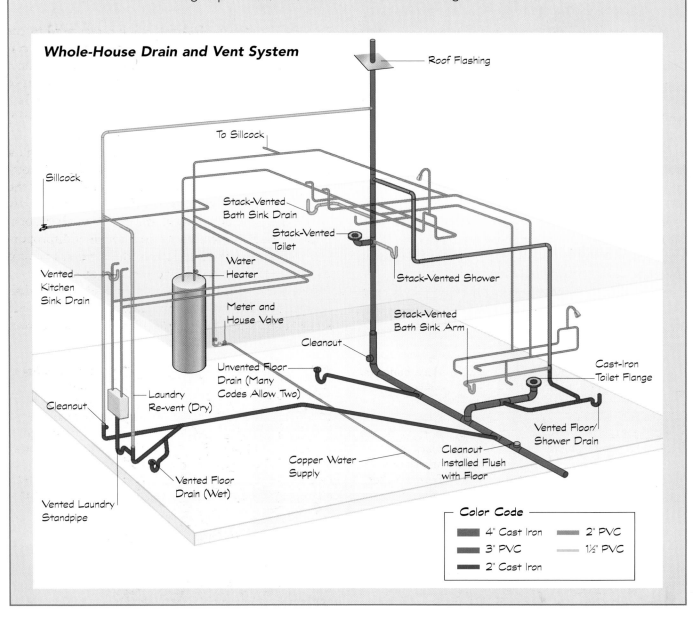

Roof Flashing
To Sillcock
Sillcock
Stack-Vented Bath Sink Drain
Stack-Vented Toilet
Water Heater
Vented Kitchen Sink Drain
Stack-Vented Shower
Meter and House Valve
Stack-Vented Bath Sink Arm
Cleanout
Unvented Floor Drain (Many Codes Allow Two)
Cast-Iron Toilet Flange
Cleanout
Laundry Re-vent (Dry)
Vented Floor/ Shower Drain
Vented Floor Drain (Wet)
Copper Water Supply
Cleanout Installed Flush with Floor
Vented Laundry Standpipe

Color Code

■ 4" Cast Iron	■ 2" PVC
■ 3" PVC	■ 1½" PVC
■ 2" Cast Iron	

foot. You must re-vent any line that slopes, from start to finish, more than its own diameter.

Fitting and pipe selection is also important. In a waste system, use only code-approved sanitary fittings. Do not use T-fittings in drainpipes except to drain and stack-vent the top fixture or the top bath group on a stack. A Y-connector, used in combination with a 45-degree elbow, offers a much more gradual flow, which is less likely to clog. This is true whether the stack is vertical or horizontal.

When you install a 90-degree elbow at the base of a vertical stack, use a long-sweep L configuration, or install two 45-degree elbows. Standard short-sweep elbows will do fine elsewhere in the system, but water falling vertically from a height of 8 to 24 feet needs a buffer as it changes direction. A more gradual turn will keep water from filling the elbow completely and prevent a momentary loss of vent.

When you install plastic drain and vent pipe—above or below the basement floor—make sure that it has a Schedule 40 rating. While codes once allowed thinner-walled pipe in underground sewer service lines, most codes today require Schedule 40 throughout, from sewer to roof.

Supporting Pipe. When you run pipe through stud walls or through floor and ceiling joists, always drill the pipe holes slightly larger than the outside diameter of the pipe. Plastic pipe expands when warm water passes through it, and if the pipe fits too tightly, you'll hear a steady ticking sound when warm water is used. This annoying sound is the pipe rubbing against the wood as the plastic expands and contracts.

When you hang plastic drainpipes and vent pipes under floor joists, support the pipe with hole strapping or the appropriate pipe hangers. (See "Hangers and

PVC Drainpipe

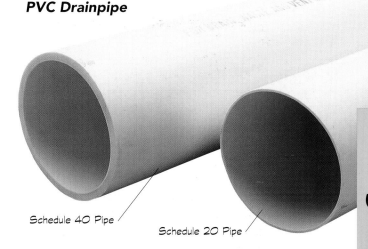

Schedule 40 Pipe

Schedule 20 Pipe

Straps" photograph, page 14.) Support plastic waste piping at least every 4 feet.

Cutting Structural Timbers. You'll rarely need to cut into load-bearing timbers to install drainpipes. You can usually hang a horizontal fixture line (extending from a vertical stack) under the joists near the center beam of the house and box the area in later. When a drain line needs to travel with the joists toward an outside wall, you can usually tuck it up between the joists.

You may occasionally need to run pipes through a few joists to maintain an adequate ceiling height, however. This is usually not a problem, but drill only the center one-third of each joist, and where possible, stay within a few feet of a support wall. Never notch the bottom of a joist, because the bottom carries a disproportionate share of the load. Break these rules, and you could threaten the floor's load-bearing capacity.

The best approach is to use a right-angle drill equipped with a self-feed bit. Lacking these, drill four small holes to form a square (or circle), and cut between

Wire hangers, which you just hammer into joists to support pipes, are quick and affordable. Several other types of hangers are available.

Use a right-angle drill and a large self-feed bit to bore pipe holes in studs. Make the holes at least ⅛ in. oversize.

3 Drains, Vents & Traps

Installing Pipe through Joists

Drill four holes if you don't have a large bit or hole saw.

Use a saber saw to cut out the lumber between the holes.

Fit short pieces of pipe between joists, and couple them together.

them using a reciprocating saw. Remember that each succeeding hole must be slightly higher (or lower) than the last to maintain an adequate slope. With 1½-inch pipe, you can often bend it enough to start it through the first two holes. After that, drive it through with a hammer, using a block of wood to protect the pipe. With larger pipes, you'll have to splice short lengths together using couplings, one coupling per joist space. This looks piecemeal, but it works well, and it's legal.

When installing 1½-inch plastic pipe through stud walls, you can usually bend it between the first two studs and drive it the rest of the way. With an open wall, it's sometimes easier to remove one stud to get it started, and then toenail the stud back in place. You may need to splice 2-inch pipe because it is less forgiving.

Installing In-Ground Piping

Every plumbing system has some portion of its drainage piping underground, even if it's only the sewer service line. Many houses with basements and all slab-on-grade homes will have soil pipes trenched in place before the concrete goes down. If you build an addition that requires below-grade piping or if you break out some portion of your existing concrete to add piping, you'll need to know the basics.

In-ground piping must be able to support the substantial weight of the soil and concrete above it. This means that the trench you dig for the pipe must be uniform, with adequate slope, and without extreme high spots or voids. High spots can squeeze a pipe out of round, hindering flow. Voids beneath the pipe can cause sags and breaks.

When you install in-ground piping, take all the time you need to perfect the trench bed. **1.** Use a level on each length of pipe to ensure adequate slope. **2.** As always, shoot for ¼ inch of slope per foot. Dig as deep as you must to meet an existing pipe or sewer service line. In the case of a new home, this may mean digging under an exterior footing. In a remodel, dig to the same level as the pipe into which you need to splice. Always try to square the sides of the trench. A 12- to 16-inch width is ideal, but try not to overexcavate. If you happen to dig too deeply, don't try to undo your mistake by packing soil back into the trench. Disturbed soil will continue to settle for years. Bring a low spot back to grade with compactible sand or gravel. Sand is really the best way to ensure a uniform trench. Many plumbers lay a bed of sand in the entire trench.

When installing cast-iron pipe—or even plastic pipe—be sure to dig shallow depressions for the hubs. If you don't, the weight bearing down on the pipe can break it. With plastic pipe, the weight can cause the pipe to drape from hub to hub, creating flow problems.

Protect the Piping. If careless concrete workers are likely to bump into floor drains, laundry stands, and stack risers and leave them permanently out of position, stake these fittings in place with ½-inch iron rebar topped with a pipe holder. **3.** This will keep the pipes stable and help them resist any inadvertent manhandling. Also, be sure to cover the top of each riser and floor-drain screen with duct tape when you're finished installing the pipe. **4.** This will keep concrete and other debris from falling into them. Many a homeowner has had to jackhammer the floor of a spanking-new home to retrieve a chunk of construction debris from the soil pipe. If you're installing a toilet in the addition, cover the top of the toilet drain with a plastic cap before the concrete goes down. **5.**

Installing In-Ground Drainpipes

Tools and Materials

- Cast-iron pipe
- Hubs, connectors
- Duct tape
- Hammer, stakes

TIME NEEDED: WEEKEND
- Shovel
- 4' spirit level
- Plastic cap

PLUMBING TIP: *If the cast iron won't slide into the gasket, sink a tile spade in the dirt in front of the pipe and lever the pipe with the shovel.*

1 Dig the soil-pipe trench at a slight downward slope, and tunnel a minimum of 20 in. under the basement footing.

2 Install the first length of cast-iron pipe under the footing, and use a spirit level to check that its slope is adequate.

3 Drive a stake clamp next to the toilet riser and stack fittings to hold them in place until the concrete is poured.

4 Cover the tops of all floor drains and stacks using tape to keep construction debris from falling into the piping system.

5 Instead of sealing it with tape, install a plastic closet cap over the toilet riser. The concrete floor will be poured around this cap.

Providing Cleanout Access. Codes stipulate that each drain stack must have a permanently accessible cleanout fitting at its base. (Dry-vent stacks don't need cleanouts.) Where you have reduced a 4-inch soil pipe to a 3-inch stack, make the cleanout T-fitting the size of the larger pipe. If the stack is more than 10 feet from the wall, codes require an additional cleanout fitting. You can place this cleanout just inside the wall, in the basement floor, or just outside the house, brought to grade. If you'll be finishing that area of the basement, an exterior cleanout fitting is practical. And, finally, most codes require additional cleanout fittings in above-grade kitchen lines. Install one after a change of direction.

Vents

As mentioned in Chapter 1 (pages 16 to 18), vents play a vital part in a home's drainage system. A faulty venting system will not only cause aggravation when the drainage system malfunctions, it could also make you and your family ill if it compromises the seal the traps are supposed to maintain against sewer gases. It is important to understand the various venting options possible, as well as size and installation basics, if you plan to alter or add to your current system.

Vent Types and Terms

The most common vent installations are illustrated and discussed in the following pages. If your planned system varies from those described here, draw a picture of it and ask the local building (or plumbing) inspector to check it before you do the work.

• **Vent Terminal.** A *vent terminal* is roughly equivalent to the distance between floors, but because of layout considerations, it often starts a foot below one floor and ends a foot below the next.

• **Broken Vent.** The term *broken vent* refers to an improperly installed vent that, consequently, is ineffective. A broken vent is little better than no vent at all. Often the problem stems from the location and elevation of the vent's takeoff fitting. The illustrations in "4 Common Broken Vents," opposite, show the situations you're most likely to face.

• **Stack Vent.** Vertical drainage stacks are also considered vents because, in addition to carrying water, they pull relief air from above the roof. Short horizontal branch lines extending from a vertical stack do not require additional venting and, therefore, are said to be stack-vented.

• **Vent Stack.** A *vent stack* is a vertical stack installed for the sole purpose of providing relief air. It does not carry water. A vent stack can be tied into the stack vent above the highest fixture or exit the roof independently.

You may have seen plumbing diagrams in the past with vent stacks starting below the lowest fixture on the stack and continuing into the attic. All fixtures are shown connected to this stack vent. However, dedicated system-wide vent stacks are rarely found in residential installations. They work best in tall commercial buildings.

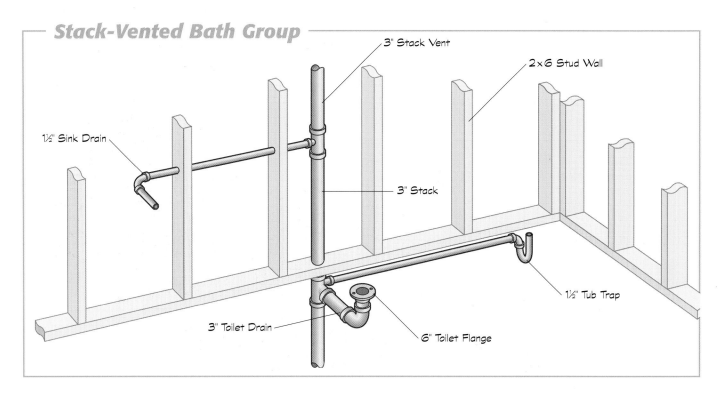

Stack-Vented Bath Group

3" Stack Vent

2×6 Stud Wall

1½" Sink Drain

3" Stack

1½" Tub Trap

3" Toilet Drain

6" Toilet Flange

4 Common Broken Vents

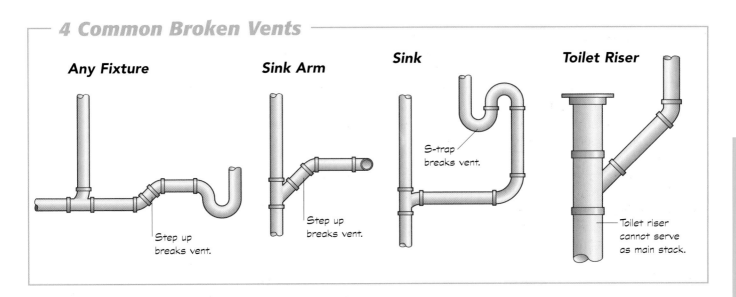

Any Fixture

Step up breaks vent.

Sink Arm

Step up breaks vent.

Sink

S-trap breaks vent.

Toilet Riser

Toilet riser cannot serve as main stack.

Vent Stack

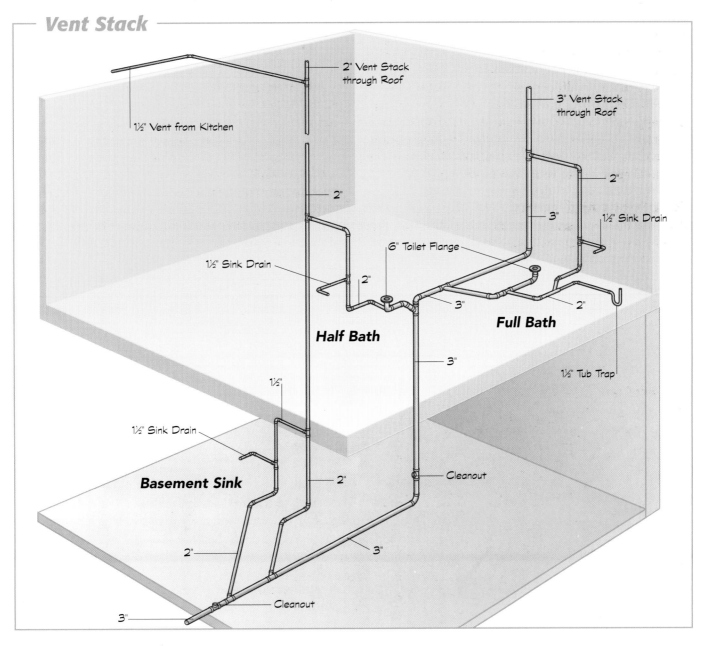

2" Vent Stack through Roof

1½" Vent from Kitchen

3" Vent Stack through Roof

2"

2"

3"

1½" Sink Drain

6" Toilet Flange

1½" Sink Drain

2"

3"

2"

Half Bath

Full Bath

1½" Tub Trap

3"

1½"

1½" Sink Drain

Basement Sink

Cleanout

2"

Cleanout

2"

3"

3"

• **Stack-Vented Branch Arm.** In a properly designed system, fixture drain lines are sized so that they can never run more than one-half full. (See "Sizing Fixture Drains and Vents," page 45.) If a horizontal branch pipe is not too long, the unused top half of the pipe can serve as a vent. It feeds air from the stack to the back of the flow, preserving the trap seal. But such a *stack-vented branch arm* is limited.

• The stack fitting must be a T-fitting and not a Y-fitting.

• The branch must serve the highest fixture or fixture combination on the stack. This "highest fixture" rule applies to each individual stack, even when the highest fixture on a second stack is a floor or two above or below that of the primary stack, providing that all stacks extend to the open air above the roof. However, there are always exceptions: this rule does not apply to a basement bath group, because most of that piping is horizontal.

• The length of the branch should not exceed the limits established by code. The larger the pipe diameter, the longer the allowed length. For example, most codes specify that a 1½-inch-diameter branch arm can extend 5 feet from the stack to the trap, although many further limit that to 3½ feet. Most codes allow 8 feet for a 2-inch line and 10 feet for a 3-inch line. You must re-vent anything longer. (See "Maximum Stack-Vented Branch Arm Lengths," below.)

Maximum Stack-Vented Branch Arm Lengths

Fixture	Pipe Size (inches)	Max. Length of Branch Arm (feet)
Toilet	3"	10'
Toilet	4"	12'
Sink	1½"	5'
Lavatory	1½"	5'
2 Lavatories	2"	8'
Tub	1½"	5'
Shower	2"	8'
Laundry	2"	8'

All horizontal branch arms longer than noted must be re-vented.

Stack-Vent Exception

There is one exception to the "highest fixture" rule regarding stack-vented branch arms, and it's an important one. When the uppermost fixture is part of a bathroom group, you can also join the toilet piping to the stack with a T-fitting, even though it's technically the second-highest branch on the stack. Making the most of the rule that says two fixtures can be stack-vented if their pipes enter the stack at the same level, manufacturers now sell 3-inch T-fittings with 1½- or 2-inch side inlet fittings. A T-fitting with a side inlet allows a nearby tub or shower to enter the stack at the same level as the toilet. What this means, of course, is that you can stack-vent the entire bath group. You can handle the toilet and tub/shower with a 3-inch side inlet T, and the lav with a standard T-fitting. (See "Side Inlet Ports," page 47.)

• **Re-vent.** A *re-vent* is a vent added to a fixture drain when the primary vent is broken in some way. When a branch arm is too long, for example, or when it must step up to accommodate structural barriers, you must install a re-vent.

• **Wet and Dry Vents.** A *wet vent* carries water as well as air through some part of its piping. A basement bathroom provides a good example, because the vent for the toilet line also carries water from the tub and lavatory. While wet vents are handy and efficient, they have their limits. Because air must share space with water, wet vents are low-volume vents. They cannot vent many fixtures. A *dry vent* does not carry water, so it has greater fixture capacity. (See "Vent/Drain Sizes per Fixture/Appliance" and "Assigned Fixture Units per Fixture," page 45.)

• **Common Vent.** A *common vent* is a single vent pipe that provides relief air to two or more fixtures on a single branch line. When you are venting two fixtures, you must place a common vent between the drain outlets. When you are venting more than two fixtures, install the vent between the last and second-to-last fixture outlets.

• **Loop Vent.** When you want to install a sink in a kitchen island, a conventional vent will not work. In this situation, a *loop vent* is appropriate. Loop vents easily handle the low-volume fixtures (such as kitchen sinks) that are installed in island cabinets.

Re-vented Branch Arm

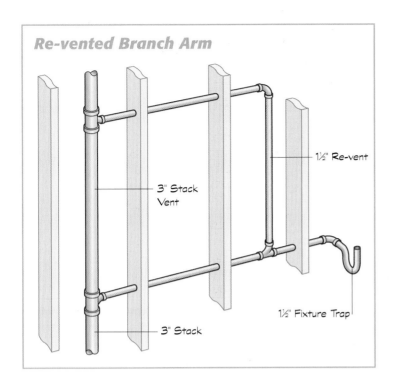

1½" Re-vent

3" Stack Vent

1½" Fixture Trap

3" Stack

Common Vent

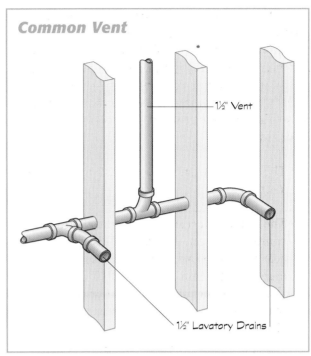

1½" Vent

1½" Lavatory Drains

Toilet, Tub, and Sink Served by a Wet Vent

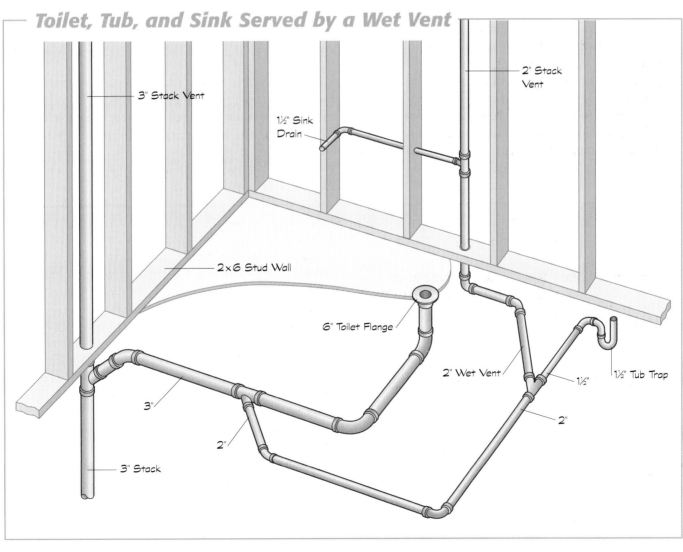

3" Stack Vent

2" Stack Vent

1½" Sink Drain

2×6 Stud Wall

6" Toilet Flange

2" Wet Vent

1½"

1½" Tub Trap

3"

2"

2"

3" Stack

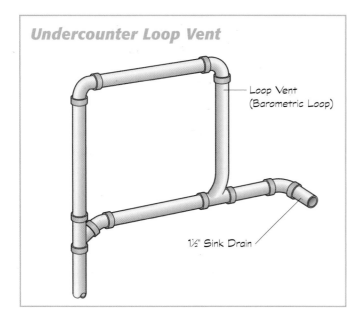

Undercounter Loop Vent

Loop Vent
(Barometric Loop)

1½" Sink Drain

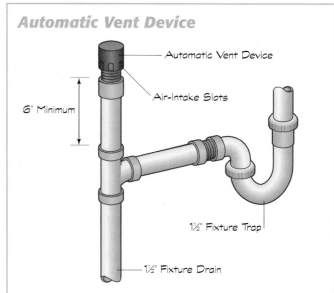

Automatic Vent Device

Automatic Vent Device

Air-Intake Slots

6" Minimum

1½" Fixture Trap

1½" Fixture Drain

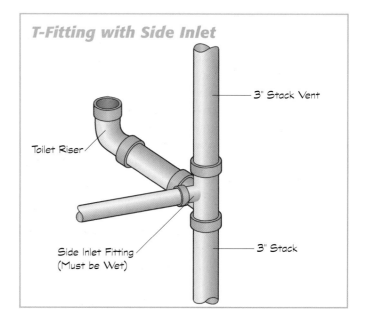

T-Fitting with Side Inlet

3" Stack Vent

Toilet Riser

Side Inlet Fitting
(Must be Wet)

3" Stack

Loop vents do not extend to open air or tie into stacks or vent stacks. They have no direct, fresh-air connections. Instead, the volume of air in the piping loop provides the needed pressure relief. For this reason, loop vents are also known as *barometric vents*.

• *Automatic Vent Device.* An *automatic vent device* can take the place of a loop vent. It consists of an inverted cup with a spring-loaded diaphragm. The spring allows the piping system to pull air from the cabinet space but keeps gas from escaping. It's basically a kind of check valve, allowing air to flow in only one direction.

While automatic vent devices can be system savers, do not use them where it's possible to install conventional vents. Because automatic vents have limited capacity, don't use them to vent high-volume drains or to vent more than one fixture. Install them so that they always remain accessible because they can wear out and may need replacing.

Basic Drain and Vent Considerations

Codes stipulate that you can stack-vent only branch lines that stem from a vertically positioned T-fitting and that Ts can only be used in drainpipes when the fixture to be drained is the highest fixture on a vertical stack. When two uppermost fixtures are stack-vented, their drain lines must enter the stack at the same level. Therefore, to connect two lines to the stack you will need a *Side-inlet fitting* or a *cross-fitting* (a cross fitting is basically a double T-fitting). (See the photo on page 48.)

Re-venting. Some codes state that any time a horizontal branch line falls more than its own diameter along its length, it too must be re-vented. Y-fittings, by their very shape, constitute what's called in the industry a step-up and cause the line to fall by more than its diameter, so all branch lines connected to a stack via a Y-fitting should also be re-vented. (Some codes waive this rule for 1½ inch lines, so you may want to check with your local building department.)

Whenever you install a vertical stack that jogs horizontally, you must re-vent all fixture lines attached to the horizontal section and all fixtures below the horizontal section. And finally, you must re-vent even an uppermost branch arm if it's too long, as defined by local codes.

Some codes allow one or two unvented traps below the basement floor, but check with your local building department to learn whether this is true in your area. If these exceptions are granted, plan on re-venting every other branch line in the system—except stack-vented branches. Place these vents near the fixtures, and always install the takeoff fitting on the highest horizontal plane of a branch line. If the drain line steps up, install the vent between the step and the fixture trap.

Secondary Stacks. Some codes require that homes have at least one full-size stack, but if you need additional stacks to serve bath groups elsewhere in the house, you can reduce the vent portions of the other stacks to 2 inches in diameter. Bring these vents through the roof, or tie them into the primary stack. Tie all of the secondary vents into a stack at least 6 inches above the flood plane of the highest fixture on that stack. For a 36-inch-high kitchen sink, for example, you would connect the re-vent to the stack no lower than 42 inches above the floor.

Sizing Fixture Drains and Vents

Code officials use a formula known as the fixture-unit measurement to determine the minimum allowable pipe size for each fixture or group of fixtures. This is a fairly complicated formula. You won't need to know it in detail, but the results—as organized in the tables at right—are important. Use the tables to customize your plans and solve specific problems.

In brief, engineers on standard-setting boards have assigned each household fixture and appliance a numerical value based on the maximum flow rate that each is likely to produce. (See "Assigned Fixture Units per Fixture," at right.) The goal is to size each drainpipe so that it will never run more than one-half full, leaving the remaining half of the pipe open to carry vent air. When a single line serves multiple fixtures, the total number of fixture units it will carry dictates the line size. Because drains and vents work together, fixture units are used to size both drain and vent lines. (See "Vent/Drain Sizes per Fixture/Appliance," top right.)

Installing Vents and Vent Fittings

Vent fittings don't normally carry water, so they don't need the gradual sweeps and curves that drainage fittings use. Their turns are abrupt and short, like water fittings. Special vent fittings are seldom used at the residential level, however. This makes them difficult to find in retail outlets.

Most plumbers, and nearly all weekend plumbers, use drainage, or sanitary, fittings in both the drain and vent segments of the system. Because you must use drainage fittings for wet vents, this is a reasonable approach. Moreover, because drainage fittings are read-

Vent/Drain Sizes per Fixture/Appliance

Fixture	Drain Size	Vent Size
Sink	1½"	1½"
Lavatory	1½"	1½"
Tub	1½"	1½"
Shower	2"	1½"
Laundry	2"	1½"
Floor Drain	2"	1½"
Toilet	3–4"	2"

Vents for below-grade traps may be waived.

Assigned Fixture Units per Fixture

Fixture/Appliance	FU
Clothes washer (2" trap)	3
Bath group (toilet, lav & tub)	6
Bathtub, w/wo shower (1½" trap)	3
Dishwasher	2
Floor drain (2" trap)	3
Kitchen sink (1½" trap)	2
Kitchen sink w/disposer & dishwasher	3
Kitchen w/dishwasher	3
Lavatory (1¼" trap)	1
Laundry sink (1½" trap)	2
Shower stall (2" trap)	2
Toilet (3.5 gal./1.6 gal.)	4/3

ily available, sold everywhere in quantity, they cost less.

While you must connect most drainage lines with Y-fittings, you can often use T-fittings in vent connections. When a re-vent takes off vertically from a horizontal branch line (which is wet), you can use a T-fitting on its back—that is, with its in-line openings positioned horizontally and its branch inlet facing up. You can also use a T-fitting with its branch inlet facing down or to either side when a horizontal vent is dry. These positions are common when tying several vents together in an attic.

When you use a T-fitting to stack-vent a horizontal

Designing a Code-Approved Drain and Vent

Here's how to use the fixture-unit and pipe-size tables on pages 42, 45, and 47 to ensure a code-worthy installation. Let's say that you would like to stack-vent a horizontal branch arm that serves a bathtub and a freestanding shower. Assume that the tub will be 6 feet from the stack and the shower 9 feet from the stack in the same direction. According to the table "Maximum Stack-Vented Branch Arm Lengths," page 42, a shower requires a 2-inch trap and pipe diameter, and the maximum length of its branch arm is 8 feet. In this case, you can't stack-vent the shower because it is too far away (9 feet), so there's little point in stack-venting the tub. You should still drain the tub and shower through a common line, however, because that's the most economical way and you may have limited room to fit the piping. But where should you place the re-vent, and what size must it be to pass inspection?

As described under "Common Vent" (page 42), if one vent serves two fixtures, you must place it between them. In this case, you can vent the shower through the Y-branch serving the tub. This will make a short length of the tub branch a wet vent, in that it will both drain and vent the tub while also venting the shower.

What size will this branch need to be? If you check the table "Assigned Fixture Units Per Fixture," page 45, you will see that a tub and shower have a combined value of four fixture units. Refer to the table "Maximum Fixture Units Per Vent Size," page 47, and you will see that a 1½-inch wet vent accommodates only two fixture units, but a 2-inch wet vent will carry four fixture units. This means that from a 2-inch drain line, you will need to branch off with a 2-inch Y-fitting to serve the tub, and you'll need to continue this size until the pipes branch again. You can reduce to 1½ inches out of the front in-line opening of this second Y-fitting because a tub requires only a 1½-inch trap and drain, and this section serves only the tub drain. The vent from this point on will be dry and will extend upward from the branch of the Y-fitting.

To determine the size of the dry vent you will need to continue to the open air above the roof, see "Vent/Drain Sizes per Fixture/Appliance," page 45. The table shows 1½ inches for a shower and 1½ inches for a tub. But according to the table "Maximum Fixture Units Per Vent Size," a 1½-inch dry vent can handle only three fixture units, which is not enough. You have four, which means that you must maintain a 2-inch re-vent.

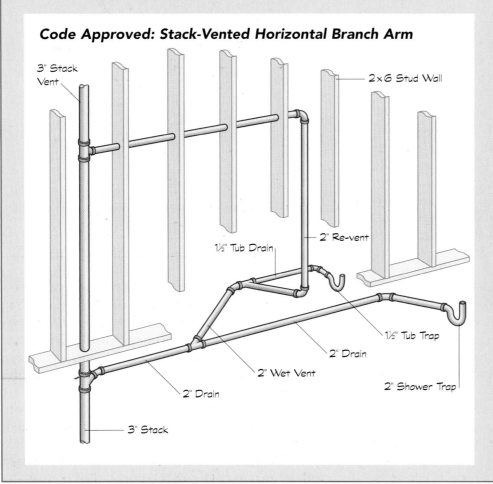

Code Approved: Stack-Vented Horizontal Branch Arm

- 3" Stack Vent
- 2×6 Stud Wall
- 1½" Tub Drain
- 2" Re-vent
- 1½" Tub Trap
- 2" Drain
- 2" Wet Vent
- 2" Shower Trap
- 2" Drain
- 3" Stack

Maximum Fixture Units per Vent Size

Vent Size	FU/Wet	FU/Dry	Total for 2–3 Floors (Dry)*
1½" hor.	2	3	—
1½" vert.	2	3	4
2"	4	6	10
3"	—	20	48
4"	—	160	240

*A dry vent at its fixture unit limit on a lower floor is allowed additional capacity as it reaches second and third vent terminals.

fixture drain, position the branch inlet so that the flow pattern sweeps downward, facilitating the flow of water. But do the opposite when connecting a horizontal dry vent to a vertical vent stack. In this case, you should install the T-fitting upside down, so the flow pattern of the branch sweeps upward, in keeping with the direction of airflow. Follow the same patterns when sloping piping that is connected to vent fittings. Just as you always position drainpipes to slope downward, you must always position horizontal vents to slope upward. A rise of ⅟₁₆ to ¼ inch per foot is adequate.

When a wet re-vent takes off from a horizontal drain line, you must use a Y-fitting, of course, because a wet vent carries water through its lower section, and drainage rules take precedence. In this case, you must rotate the Y-fitting, used on its side, slightly upward. Canting the Y's inlet ⅛ inch above level is enough to ensure adequate flow and air intake. Because you often use Y-fittings in conjunction with 45-degree elbows, slightly cant the elbows, too.

• **Cross-Fittings.** Codes stipulate that you can stack-vent two or more fixtures on the same level only when their drains enter the stack at the same level, so you'll need connectors with more than one inlet port to accomplish this. Cross-fittings, which are essentially double T-fittings, are examples of such connectors, as are Ts and crosses with side-inlet ports. All of these fittings expand the practical limits of stack-venting. Crosses work well when you splice them into vertical stacks, but do not work in horizontal piping runs. Additionally, some code authorities don't allow crosses on small drains because drain-auger cables tend to pass through them horizontally instead of dropping into the stack.

Installing Fittings

When you install drainpipe, make sure the flow pattern of T-fittings runs downward.

Invert the T-fittings for vent pipes, with the flow pattern running upward.

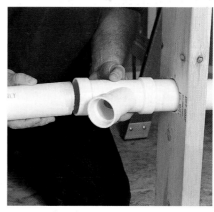

When you install a horizontal Y-fitting, rotate the branch upward slightly.

When two sinks are in the same wall, you can use a cross-fitting, with one sink on each side of the stack. You can also use cross-fittings to drain and stack-vent two toilets, again, with one toilet on each side of the stack, as is the case with back-to-back bathrooms. As always, codes allow Ts and crosses only on uppermost fixtures or fixture groups and on dry vents.

• **Side-Inlet Ports.** T-fittings and cross-fittings with side-inlet ports are doubly useful in top-floor bathroom plumbing. You can drain and stack-vent a toilet with a 3-inch T-fitting, but you can also drain and vent a bathtub with a T that has a 1½ inch side inlet. In like manner, you

Types of Drain and Vent Fittings

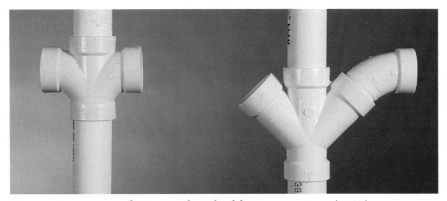

Comparing a cross-fitting with a double Y-connector, *the Y has a more gentle sweep and requires two 45-deg. elbows but takes up more space.*

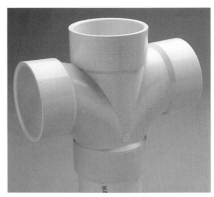

A 3- or 4-in. cross-fitting *serves two toilets in back-to-back baths.*

can use a 3-inch cross-fitting to drain and vent two toilets, but a cross with two inlets also allows you to drain and vent a shower on one side and a bathtub on the other. When you use a 3 × 1½-inch cross-fitting above the toilet cross, it can drain and vent the two bath sinks if the bathrooms share a common wall. With stack-venting, you can plumb back-to-back bathrooms efficiently. Without these multiport fittings, you would have to re-vent all but one sink, using three to four times the piping and fittings.

• ***Heel-Outlet 90-degree Elbows.*** Heel-outlet elbow fittings can also save piping. The savings here are not in length but in diameter. The typical use for a heel-outlet 90-degree elbow is to vent a single toilet that is on a secondary stack. You bring a 3-inch vertical stack up to the basement ceiling and use the heel-outlet elbow (with the 2-inch outlet facing upward) to change from vertical to horizontal. A standard 90-degree elbow returns vertically into the toilet flange. In this case, the heel-outlet not only facilitates a smaller vent but allows the vent to be placed in a wall with standard 2×4s. You would have to fur out the wall at least an inch if you used a 3-inch vent. You can also cut lesser, nearby fixtures into the stack below the heel-outlet elbow, using a Y-fitting, and tie the vent serving these fixtures into the toilet vent 42 inches above the floor. Again, you can do all this within a standard wall.

Heel-outlet elbows work well in these situations, but code does not allow the small port to carry water. While you can use a side inlet port wet—washed by at least one fixture—you must always keep a heel-outlet port dry. If you need to drain and vent a toilet-and-sink combination, use a 3-inch elbow with a 2-inch side-inlet to drain the bathroom sink and create a vent. Install the elbow right below the toilet, and drain the sink through the inlet. Continue the inlet piping into the attic as a vent.

Roof Vent Considerations

Plumbing-stack flashing comes in three forms: lead and the more conventional neoprene rubber and sheet metal with neoprene inserts. You can also get a special sheet-metal flashing designed to prevent frost problems in northern climates.

Lead Flashing. Lead flashing was the standard for many years, but sheet metal and neoprene are better for today's modern asphalt shingles. Roofers still use lead when installing a wood-shake shingle roof, however, because lead flashing has a larger apron, so it offers greater leak protection with shake shingles.

Conventional Flashing. Neoprene flashing and sheet-metal flashing with neoprene inserts are easy to install. In new construction, simply press the flashing over the vent stack. When installing a new vent through an existing roof, you'll need to work harder for a watertight fit. Start by considering whether a new roof hole is even necessary. It's often easier and cheaper to tie the new vent into an existing stack in the attic, avoiding the roof entirely. If this isn't possible, proceed from the attic. Bring the new stack through the attic floor, and suspend a plumb line above the vent to determine the exact location of the roof cut. If the vent falls too near an existing structure (roof window, roof vent, or the like), offset it a couple of feet with 22-, 45-, or 90-degree elbows. When you've determined the best location, mark a circular opening on the roof sheathing about 6 inches in diameter. Drill ¼-inch holes in at least four equidistant spots along the cut line. Then go on top of the roof, and use a reciprocating saw or saber saw to cut through the sheathing and shingles by connecting the drill holes. You can also cut the shingles first using a utility knife.

Installations vary, but it is often easier to splice the

Side inlets *allow a cross-fitting to serve toilets, plus shower and tub.*

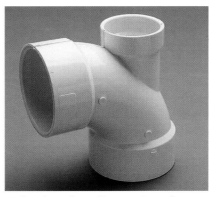

A heel-outlet elbow's *2-in. fitting, used vertically, can vent a toilet.*

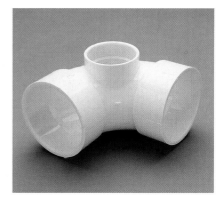

A side-inlet elbow's *2-in. inlet can vent a toilet and drain a sink.*

new flashing into the existing shingles before bringing the vent through the roof. Slide the top half of the flashing under the shingles above the opening, and allow the bottom half to lie on top of the shingles below the opening. This will require removing a few nails from the shingles above the opening. Slide a hacksaw blade under the appropriate shingles, and cut through the nails. Then slide the flashing under these shingles so that the opening in the flashing is directly over the vent opening. You may also need to trim the top shingle flaps a bit to accommodate the raised insert.

With the flashing in place, go into the attic to install the last section of pipe, feeding it through the flashing opening from below. Return to the roof, and apply roofing compound—fiber-reinforced tar in a caulk tube—under the exposed outside edges of the flashing. Lastly, nail through the bottom corners of the flashing and apply a dab of compound to each nailhead.

This method works well, but you can also install the vent pipe before installing the flashing. In this case, press the flashing over the vent, turn it sideways, and rotate it under the upper shingles. Again, you may need to remove a nail or two.

Frost-Proof Flashing. In northern climates, frost can be a problem: the warm, damp air flowing up from a stack can freeze when it reaches the cold roof area, forming frost that looks a bit like a snow cone sitting atop the vent pipe and blocking it. When this happens, fixtures respond as if they are unvented; the toilets flush slowly, and you can hear the drains choke and gurgle. Small vents freeze over more easily, so many codes stipulate that roof vents must be at least 3 inches in diameter. Smaller vents must be increased in size 12 inches below the roof and extend above the roof 12 inches.

Some manufacturers offer a mechanical solution: frost-inhibiting roof-vent flashing. This flashing has double sheet-metal walls with an air space between them. The air space serves as an insulator between the warm stack and the cold surrounding roof surface.

Types of Vent-Pipe Flashing

Lead vent-pipe flashing *can be made watertight by folding its excess length into the stack.*

Sheet-metal flashing *with a neoprene insert can sometimes be rotated under existing shingles.*

Traps

Traps vary in size and shape, according to the volume of water they handle. Traps that serve high-volume appliances, such as washing machines, are usually 2 inches in diameter. Toilet traps are even larger. A bathroom sink trap, in contrast, usually has a 1¼-inch trap.

Volume and trap size are not the only considerations, however. Modern traps have a precise geometry that permits them to allow wastewater to pass yet retain a reservoir of water as a seal, even under slight negative pressure. Because of this precision in design, you should always use manufactured traps; do not make your own from conventional fittings.

Trap Variations

Older houses can have a variety of fixture and drain traps, some good and some not so good. Two traps that were popular earlier in this century, the S-trap and drum trap, for example, are no longer permitted by codes, although hundreds of thousands of them may still be in use. Even though these traps are protected by the grandfather clause (page 26), it's best to upgrade them when making piping changes.

• **Drum Trap.** Used almost exclusively in bathrooms, the drum trap was installed in the floor, usually near the toilet. This trap has a juglike shape, with two inlets and one outlet. The top, usually capped with a brass cleanout plug, is usually visible in a bare floor. The inlet pipes enter the drum at a point lower than the outlet, which creates the water seal. (See the illustration at right.) The two inlet pipes typically drain the bathtub and sink, while the outlet empties into cast-iron toilet piping. Drum traps are often plumbed with lead pipes.

You can determine whether an older home has a drum trap in any of several ways. The easiest is to look for the cleanout fitting in the bathroom floor, although a floor covering may now conceal it. If your home was built before the 1940s and the bath has not been substantially remodeled, you'll likely find a drum trap. Layout can be another indicator. In drum trap installations, the sink is usually between the tub and toilet, while in modern installations the toilet is often between the sink and the tub. Slow drains also yield good information. A sink that backs up into the tub may signal a drum trap. For more on replacing a drum trap, see "Replacing an Old Drum-Trap System," page 128.

• **S-Trap.** The S-trap has its drain connection in the floor. Because these traps are impossible to vent, do not install them unless you are directly replacing a leaking or broken one. Building codes do not allow using them for new construction or remodels.

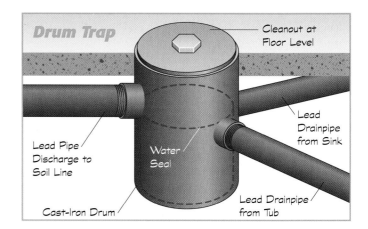

Drum Trap

Cleanout at Floor Level

Lead Drainpipe from Sink

Water Seal

Lead Pipe Discharge to Soil Line

Lead Drainpipe from Tub

Cast-Iron Drum

Connecting Traps

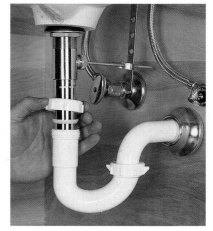

Join chrome traps using flat rubber friction washers.

S-traps connect to drainpipes at floor level. Try to avoid them.

Join plastic P-traps using nylon compression washers.

• **P-Trap.** The only code-worthy external trap is the P-trap. You can easily take these traps apart. They consist of a U-shaped bend and trap arm, plus several nuts and washers. P-traps come in plastic and chrome-plated brass. Plastic lasts longer, but chrome looks better. Many people install chrome P-traps only where they will be visible, such as under wall-hung and pedestal sinks.

Chrome trap connections have hex nuts and flat rubber friction washers. Plastic traps have beveled joints and tapered nylon compression washers with nuts that you can tighten by hand. In contrast, you tighten chrome traps using a pipe wrench. Use pipe joint compound on chrome traps but not on plastic traps.

You will find the second type of P-trap on built-in fixtures, such as bathtubs and showers, and on laundry stands. These traps may come in two pieces, but once assembled, they are not meant to be taken apart. Older-type cast-iron and -brass P-traps are made in one piece.

• **Running Traps.** A running trap is a variation on the P-trap. Plumbers use this specialty fitting only when a permanent P-trap is not workable—such as in situations where structural framing members are in the way or where a P-trap could freeze. A drain at the bottom of an external stairwell gives a good example: you install the drain basin outdoors but move the trap indoors where the water stays warm. Codes require that the trap be within 2 feet of the fixture outlet or floor drain that it serves. Greater distances can cause the trap to siphon. (For more on this, see "Siphoning Action," page 52.)

• **Built-in Traps.** Some fixtures, such as toilets and bidets, have built-in traps. (See the cross-sectional drawing of a toilet on page 98.) These fixtures do not need, and cannot have, additional traps. In fact, double trapping of any fixture is prohibited by code. House traps, as described below, are the only exception. Two traps in close proximity to each other can be a problem; the second trap can siphon the first—and be depleted itself—by momentum.

• **House Traps.** Some local codes require the use of a house trap in a dwelling. This trap is in the soil pipe beneath the basement floor and is the same size as the soil pipe, usually 4 inches in diameter. If a house trap is not required in your area, don't use one. When a house trap is required, note that you generally need a vent on each side of it: one on the house side and one on the service side. (See the illustration at right.)

• **Area Drains.** Garage floors often have built-in drains called area drains, although they are not required by code. Builders frequently stand a square clay-tile flue liner on end to make the drain reservoir. Factory-made plastic drains are also now available. The top is usually fitted with a drain screen measuring 12 × 12 inches.

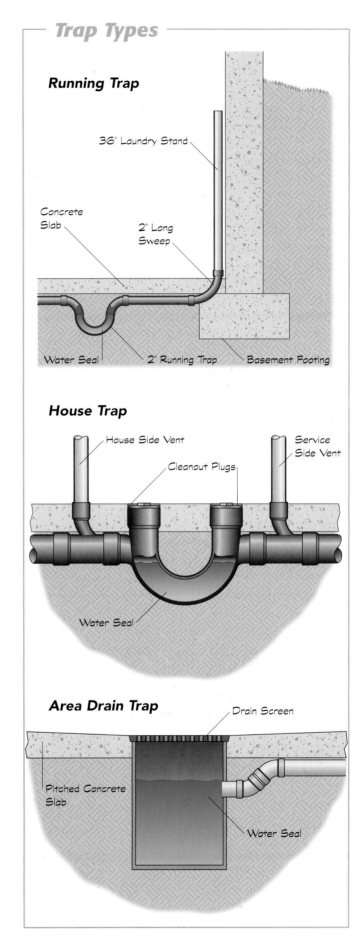

Trap Types

Running Trap

36" Laundry Stand

Concrete Slab

2" Long Sweep

Water Seal   2" Running Trap   Basement Footing

House Trap

House Side Vent   Service Side Vent

Cleanout Plugs

Water Seal

Area Drain Trap

Drain Screen

Pitched Concrete Slab

Water Seal

Broken Trap Seals

A broken trap seal occurs when the water level in the trap recedes enough to allow sewer gas to escape. Broken seals may be caused by aspiration, capillary attraction, evaporation, momentum, or siphoning action.

Aspiration. Aspiration occurs when a large volume of water flows near the trap and creates negative pressure, which pulls standing water from the trap.

There are two major symptoms of aspiration. One is the possible odor of sewer gases, although most of the poisonous gases are odorless. The other is the familiar choke and gurgle of unvented low-volume drains. If you have a fixture drain in your house that goes "glug-glug-glug" when a nearby fixture or appliance is used, that's the unmistakable sound of aspiration resulting from improper venting. You should call in a plumber.

Every fixture with an S-trap is subject to aspiration because you can't vent S-traps. Short of replacement or installing an automatic vent device (page 155), you can do little about S-trap problems.

Momentum. The momentum of water passing through traps can also empty them. This occurs when the vertical distance between the fixture outlet and the trap is too great; limit it to around 12 inches. Most codes prohibit a vertical distance greater than 24 inches, except for laundry standpipes.

Capillary Attraction. Capillary attraction lifts water the way a wick lifts lamp oil. All it takes is a few strands of fabric caught by a rough edge in the trap. The threads absorb water from the bottom of the trap and lift it into the drainpipe. This process takes a few days, so it's most noticeable in drains that are used only once or twice a week. Laundry drains are particularly prone to broken seals caused by capillary attraction. Trim the streamers from frayed towels and blue jeans before they go into the wash, and keep dental floss out of the drains.

Evaporation. If you've ever returned from a long vacation to find that your house has a foul smell, chances are that evaporation opened a trap to sewer gas. Floor drains are especially prone to evaporation because they are so seldom used. Your basement floor drain should have a float ball, a lightweight plastic ball that drops to seal the drain if the water evaporates. When water flows into the drain, the ball floats, allowing the water to escape through the drain. If your drain does not have a float ball, either pour a pint of water into it every week or so to maintain the seal or install a retrofit float ball.

Siphoning Action. Siphoning, which can deplete the water in an S-trap, occurs as follows: When a rapid flow of water runs through an S-trap, the water fills the entire trap. The resulting water pressure is not relieved by vent-supplied air at the top of the trap bend, as it is in a P-trap, and a siphon occurs, in which the pressure created at the front of the flow pulls too much of the back of the flow through the trap, leaving too-little water behind. A fixture that chokes and gurgles when you use it is a sure sign of siphoning.

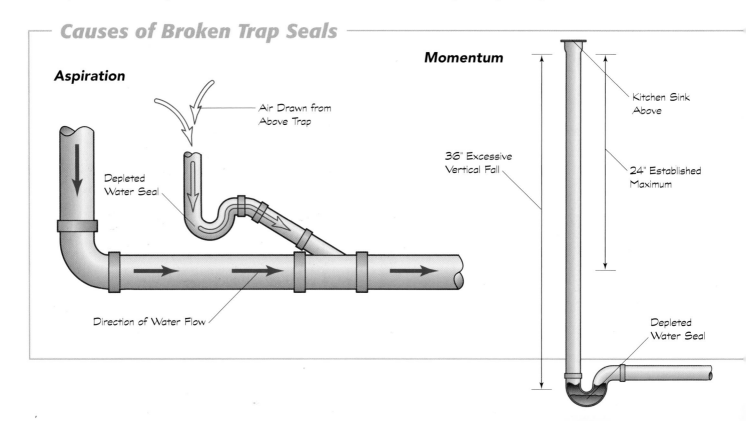

Causes of Broken Trap Seals

Aspiration

Air Drawn from Above Trap

Depleted Water Seal

Direction of Water Flow

Momentum

Kitchen Sink Above

36" Excessive Vertical Fall

24" Established Maximum

Depleted Water Seal

SMART TIP

How to Avoid Aspiration

When water flushes through a drainpipe, it displaces a quantity of air equal to its own volume. The water pulls air in behind it to fill the void as it moves through the pipe. If air does not move into the pipe, a partial air lock occurs, slowing the water flow.

While flow through a drainage system never completely stops, local airflow problems are common. Unless a plumbing system—with its many bends, turns, vertical drops, and horizontal runs—is well designed with careful attention to venting, it may be subject to areas of isolated pressure when water moves through it in volume. Water from a high-volume fixture rushing past a smaller branch line that serves a bathroom sink or tub is more likely to pull air from that branch than it is to pull from the open air above the roof stack, which can be 20 to 30 feet away. When air is pulled from an improperly vented branch line, it pulls water from the trap at the end of that line.

However, if you drilled a hole in the top of that branch line, a short distance from the trap, the rushing water moving past the branch would pull its air through that hole, leaving the water in the trap undisturbed and the seal intact. This hole would be a trap-preserving vent. Of course, holes in plumbing pipes won't do, so plumbers splice a

T-fitting into the line instead of drilling a hole. They run piping up from the T until they can tie the pipe back into the main stack above the highest fixture or run it through the roof independently, creating a vent. (See "Vents," page 40.)

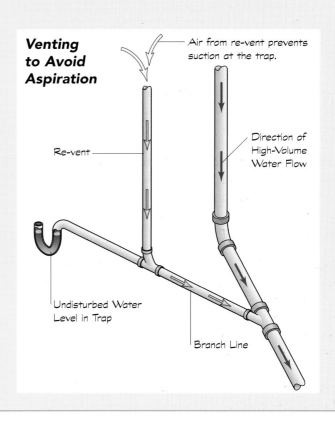

Venting to Avoid Aspiration

Air from re-vent prevents suction at the trap.

Re-vent

Direction of High-Volume Water Flow

Undisturbed Water Level in Trap

Branch Line

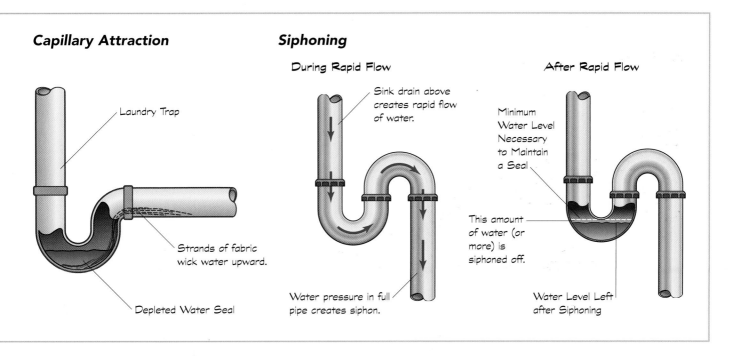

Capillary Attraction

Laundry Trap

Strands of fabric wick water upward.

Depleted Water Seal

Siphoning

During Rapid Flow

Sink drain above creates rapid flow of water.

Water pressure in full pipe creates siphon.

After Rapid Flow

Minimum Water Level Necessary to Maintain a Seal

This amount of water (or more) is siphoned off.

Water Level Left after Siphoning

CHAPTER 4

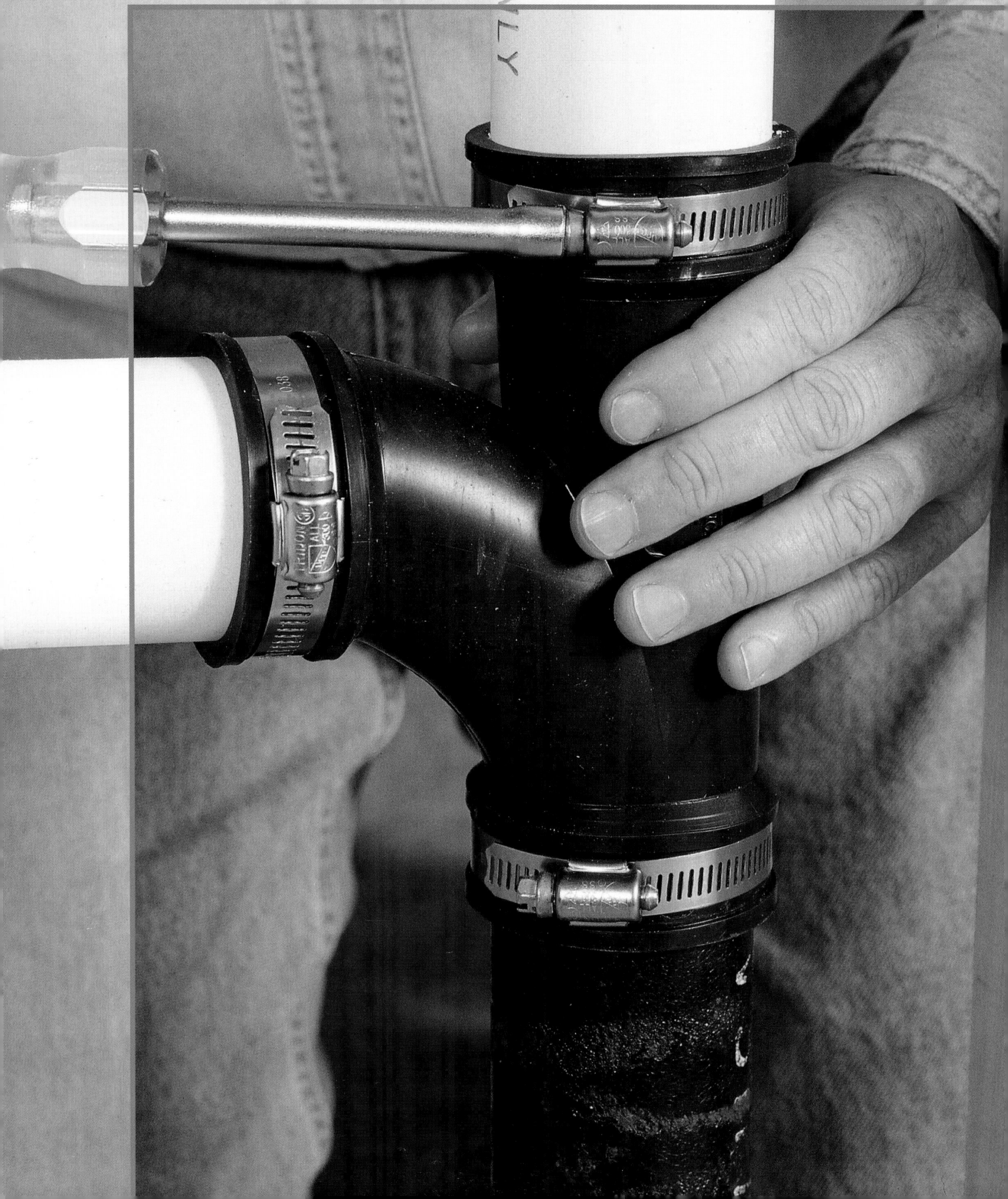

Working with Waste & Vent Pipes

By learning to work with drain, waste, and vent (DWV) pipe and fittings, you'll be able to extend or replace some of the piping in your home rather than just make simple faucet and toilet repairs and improvements. Although having basic knowledge such as how to work with fixtures and faucets is useful and can save you money, making real upgrades involving new pipe and fittings will give you great satisfaction and can potentially save even more money.

Until about the 1960s and '70s, the traditional materials for waste and vent piping were cast-iron and copper. Modern plastic piping makes it easier to upgrade your plumbing, but most retrofits require splicing into those older materials, which in some cases requires fairly specialized skills. Only if you're plumbing a new home will you have the luxury of using new materials from start to finish.

As is so often the case, the things that seem the simplest need the most careful attention. Choosing drainage fittings that encourage gradual flow patterns, installing drain lines at just the right pitch, installing enough vents, and sizing pipes for the best efficiency—these are the things that matter most when working with the DWV system. In comparison, it's easy to learn to solder a T-fitting, solvent-weld plastic pipes, and cut cast iron. (For specific information on fitting selection, venting applications, and drainage installations, review Chapter 3, "Drains, Vents & Traps," pages 34 to 53.)

Cast-Iron Drainage Piping

Cast-iron pipe was once the universal material for underfloor, or basement, soil piping. It was also common in vertical stacks in houses built prior to the early 1960s. The above-floor branch lines serving these stacks may have been made of galvanized iron or copper, but cast iron was the backbone of every DWV system.

Some codes today still require cast iron below the basement floor, but the trend is clearly toward plastic drain and vent piping, from street to roof. Still, cast iron is present in most homes built prior to the 1980s, and builders in some areas continue to install it. If you hope to make any changes or additions to a cast-iron plumbing system, you'll need to know how to cut it. You'll also need to know how to fit it with either cast-iron or plastic fittings.

Cast-iron pipe comes in 3-, 5-, and 10-foot lengths, in no-hub, single-hub, or double-hub configurations. Two hubs make for less waste when you need custom-cut lengths, but you can't use them as they are because one of the hubs would always be backward. A double-hub pipe has to be cut in two.

Cast-iron pipes without hubs are available for use with no-hub fittings. Standard cast-iron pipe diameters for residential use are 2, 3, and 4 inches. Most existing homes have 4-inch soil and sewer-service pipes. However, with today's EPA mandated low-volume 1.6-gallon toilets, it is becoming less common to install 4-inch pipes in new construction because, with so little liquid volume, toilet water outruns the solids in larger pipes.

Cast-Iron Fittings

Cast-iron fittings come in a variety of configurations, as shown in the illustration below. Several of the fittings also have side-inlet or heel-outlet openings. (For more on side inlets and heel outlets, see "Side-Inlet Ports" and "Heel-Outlet 90-Degree Elbows," pages 47 to 48.)

Traditional cast-iron pipes and fittings are formed with bells and spigots. A spigot, or male end, fits into a bell, or female hub. This is a loose fit, however, so you need a neoprene gasket or packing material to make the joint watertight. Prior to the 1970s, all cast-iron joints were packed with lead and an oily ropelike material called oakum, which expands when wet.

Today, however, plumbers join bell-and-spigot cast-iron fittings with neoprene rubber gaskets. You press the gasket into the cast-iron bell and lubricate it with a soapy gel before pushing the spigot end of the drainpipe through the gasket.

As mentioned earlier, you join no-hub pipes and fittings with banded (no-hub) couplings, which are remarkably easy to use. There are several banded coupling styles, but all work similarly. Each consists of a neoprene rubber sleeve banded by stainless-steel clamps,

Making Lead-and-Oakum Joints

Use a packing tool *to tamp the joint two-thirds full of oakum.*

Cap the oakum with lead wool, *and tamp it into solid packing.*

Cast-Iron Fittings

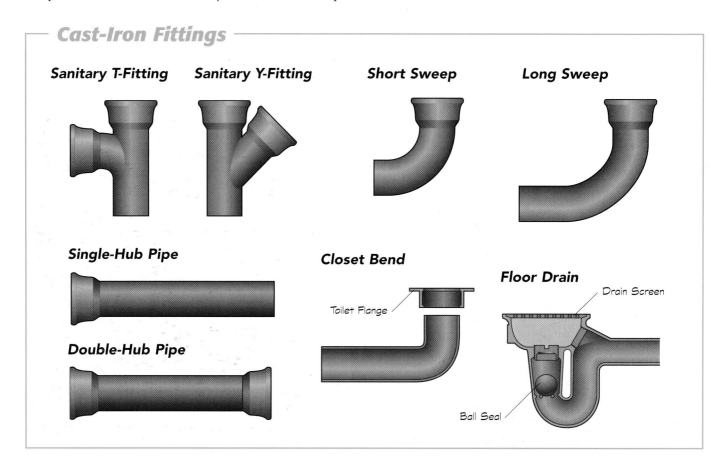

Sanitary T-Fitting

Sanitary Y-Fitting

Short Sweep

Long Sweep

Single-Hub Pipe

Double-Hub Pipe

Closet Bend

Toilet Flange

Floor Drain

Drain Screen

Ball Seal

Connections with Neoprene Fittings

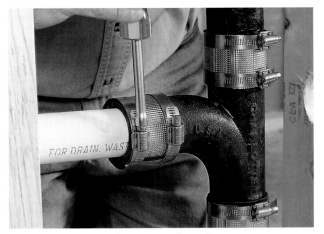

Use banded couplings to splice plastic piping into a cast-iron drainage line.

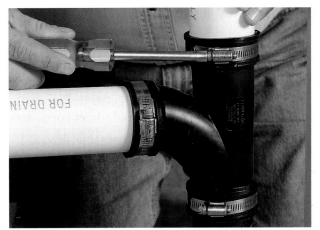

Install a no-hub flexible fitting for greater ease in retrofitting drainpipes.

one at each end. Some brands use a thick but pliable neoprene sleeve and two stainless-steel clamps, while others use a thin neoprene sleeve backed by a wide stainless-steel band and two clamps. Both types are available as straight couplings; reducers, which allow you to join pipes of different diameters; and connectors such as sanitary T-fittings.

Because these couplings can also join dissimilar materials, such as cast iron and plastic or copper and plastic, they are perfect remodeling fittings, making permanent, corrosion-free joints. The thick-walled, heavy-duty all-neoprene type can be used underground, while the stainless-steel-collar type cannot.

How to Cut Cast Iron

You have a choice of methods when cutting cast-iron pipe. While a hacksaw will work, it's a tedious process and sometimes requires several blades per cut. When professionals cut cast iron, they use a snap-cutter. As its name implies, this tool doesn't saw through, but snaps—breaks—a pipe in two. A snap-cutter consists of a roller chain that has hardened steel wheels built into it, spaced an inch apart. The chain is connected to a ratchet or scissor head. As you lever the head, the chain tightens, and the cutter wheels bite into the pipe with equal pressure. When you apply enough pressure, the pipe snaps in two. Snap-cutters are common rental items.

Lead and Oakum Seals a Toilet Flange

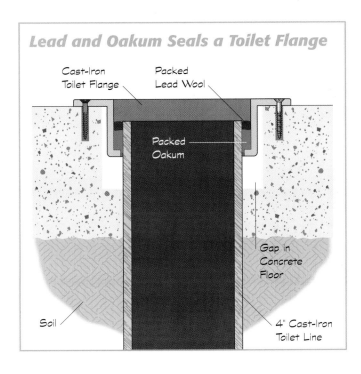

Cast-Iron Toilet Flange

Packed Lead Wool

Packed Oakum

Gap in Concrete Floor

Soil

4" Cast-Iron Toilet Line

A rented snap-cutter makes cutting cast-iron drainpipes quick and easy.

Another cutting method is to repeatedly score the pipe with a ball-peen hammer and cold chisel. This method is slow and requires access to the entire circumference of the pipe, but it works surprisingly well. To cut cast-iron pipe with a cold chisel, draw a line completely around the pipe at the appropriate spot using chalk or a grease pencil. Then strike the chisel along this line until you've made it completely around the pipe. **1.** Repeat the rotation until the pipe breaks apart. As you tap—usually five to seven rotations—the chisel weakens the cast along the line and eventually breaks it more or less evenly.

If the pipe breaks unevenly, you can break off any high spots using an old adjustable wrench. **2.** Just grip about ¼ inch of pipe with the jaws of the wrench, and strike the handle. With several strikes, you'll chip away enough material to even the edge.

Choosing a Method. Which method is best? It all depends on the location of the pipe and the amount of room in which you have to work. When installing new piping or cutting into an existing line underneath the basement floor, a snap-cutter is quick and easy. But if the pipe rests against a wall, a cutter chain may not fit between the wall and pipe. This pipe position would also prohibit the cold-chisel approach. In this case, a hacksaw is your best choice.

Installing New Cast Iron

These days, you join cast-iron pipes with easy-to-use neoprene gaskets or no-hub couplings, depending on your choice of bell-and-spigot or hubless pipe. With bell-and-spigot piping, lay the work out as you go, push-

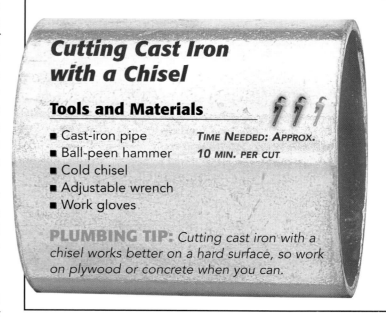

Cutting Cast Iron with a Chisel

Tools and Materials

- Cast-iron pipe
- Ball-peen hammer
- Cold chisel
- Adjustable wrench
- Work gloves

TIME NEEDED: APPROX. 10 MIN. PER CUT

PLUMBING TIP: Cutting cast iron with a chisel works better on a hard surface, so work on plywood or concrete when you can.

ing the male end of each pipe or fitting into the previous hub. Just remember that water should flow into, and not out of, the open end of a hub.

The easiest way to install a gasket is to roll it into the hub. With the gasket flange facing you, reach through the gasket and fold half of the gasket up, toward yourself. Press the untwisted half into the hub, and release the twisted half. **1.** This will usually seat the gasket nicely. Because all methods of cutting cast iron leave a sharp edge, you'll need to dull this edge before using gaskets. A file works well, but it's faster to grind the pipe edge along a concrete footing.

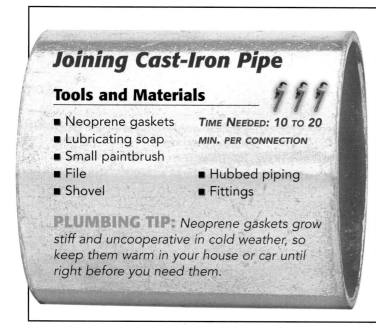

Joining Cast-Iron Pipe

Tools and Materials

- Neoprene gaskets
- Lubricating soap
- Small paintbrush
- File
- Shovel
- Hubbed piping
- Fittings

TIME NEEDED: 10 TO 20 MIN. PER CONNECTION

PLUMBING TIP: Neoprene gaskets grow stiff and uncooperative in cold weather, so keep them warm in your house or car until right before you need them.

1 To install a gasket, reach through and roll half of it up. Press the other half into the hub and release.

1 Draw a line around the pipe, and score along this line until the pipe breaks in two.

2 If the cut leaves any unevenness, break off the high spots using an old adjustable wrench.

With the gasket in the hub, lubricate it and the male end of the pipe or fitting. **2** (inset). If you don't have access to gasket lubricant, liquid dish soap will work. Don't use petroleum products such as grease or pipe joint compound, however, because they can destroy the gasket. Push the new pipe section through the gasket until it bottoms out in the hub. When working in soil, use a shovel to pry against the pipe, driving it through the gasket. **2.** You should hear a metal-to-metal "clunk" as the male end bottoms out, so don't stop until you do. If you don't hear that reassuring "clunk" (or you're installing a Y-fitting), rotate the pipe in the hub. **3.** You should hear and feel the pipe grinding against the hub. If you can't tell whether the male end has bottomed out, pull the joint apart and try again from a slightly different angle. You'll get the most consistent results with a straight-on approach, giving the pipe a slight twist if it binds.

When joining no-hub pipe with banded couplings, the procedure is even easier. All you do is slide the coupling onto one pipe or fitting, and slide the next pipe or fitting into the other end of the coupling. With the joint assembled, tighten the bands with a nut driver or a small wrench. In a few cases, you might even choose to use flexible banded neoprene elbows and T- and Y-fit-

2 Lubricate the gasket with soap, and use a shovel to force the pipe through it. You should hear the pipe bottom out.

3 Install a Y-fitting in a fashion similar to that for the hub connections, and then rotate it into position for the branch line.

4 Working with Waste & Vent Pipes

Yoke Fitting: Bad Idea

A yoke fitting clamps onto a cast-iron stack or branch after you have cut a hole in the pipe. While this sounds reasonable, it's really not a good idea, and most code authorities don't allow yokes, even though you can buy them. The reasons are two-fold. First, it's tough to establish a good flow pattern. Second, cutting a hole in a cast-iron pipe with a cutting torch is messy business that burns off the protective coating around the hole. Without this coating, the stack deteriorates near the yoke. You also risk dropping the cut piece into the stack. You can find plastic yokes for plastic pipes, but again, they're usually not code compliant.

tings. While these specialty fittings are a bit expensive, they can simplify your work.

Working with Existing Cast Iron

Retrofit work differs from new installations in two ways. First, you don't usually have as much room to work. Second, in addition to extending the new, you'll need to adapt to the old. In the case of cast iron, that means finding the best place to splice into the line. In some

Install a stack clamp *to secure the upper section of a cast-iron stack when cutting out a lower section.*

cases, it means making the whole project fit current code requirements. Once you cut into grandpa's work, you lose the benefit of the grandfather clause. (See "Grandfather Clause to the Rescue," page 26.)

Where you choose to cut into an older cast-iron piping system will depend on what you hope to add or improve. If you've built a home addition that includes plumbing, you'll likely need to cut into the stack in the basement. If you're adding a bath in a basement, in an area without rough-in piping for a bath, you'll need to break the basement floor and cut into the underslab soil pipe. If you are simply remodeling an upstairs bath, you may not need to cut into the stack at all. You may be able to simply cut into the existing horizontal toilet piping, just beyond the stack fitting. You can then extend all the fixtures from this full-size line. You may need to cut the stack in the attic to tie in a new vent, but that's usually easier than breaking the stack in a wall.

Hazards of Cutting Vertical Stacks. If you need to cut out a section of cast-iron stack on a lower floor, it's important that you make sure the stack above the cut can't come crashing down. Most stacks won't fall when cut, because upper-story vents or branch lines hold them in place. Still, it pays to check, especially when you consider the weight of a 20-to-30-foot cast-iron pipe. The most surefire precautionary measure is to install a stack clamp that grips the stack and is supported by nearby wall studs. (See the photo at left.)

If you can't locate a stack clamp or the local wholesaler won't sell one to you, you'll have to improvise. If necessary, you can make a clamp with strap iron and bolts. In most cases, you only need to support the stack until you can splice in the new fitting. Dimensional lumber works well as blocking. If you're working in the basement, for example, and you plan to cut out a section of stack just below the toilet fitting, jam a 2×4 stud between the toilet T-fitting and the basement floor. If you've opened a wall to make your improvements, a short 2×4 jammed between the floor's soleplate and the sink's branch arm will work. You could also go into the attic and prop lumber under a re-vent just as it enters the stack. In this case, you'd use the lumber to bridge two ceiling joists or to block up from the plumbing wall's top plate. A final option is to suspend the pipe with hole strap or lightweight chain. This is the best way to support horizontal piping.

Splicing T- and Y-fittings

All the new drainage piping you install can be made of Schedule 40 PVC pipe unless code requires cast-iron under the basement slab. This means that once you get

Splicing No-Hub Cast-Iron Fittings

Tools and Materials

TIME NEEDED: 1 HR.

- Grease pencil
- Snap-cutter or hacksaw
- Cast-iron no-hub T- or Y-fitting
- Banded couplings
- Nut driver

PLUMBING TIP: No-hub couplings are easy to use, and they also allow future access and make good cleanout fittings.

1 Hold the new fitting against the pipe, and mark the area to be removed. Add ½-in. clearance to the cutout for fitting room.

2 Cut out the pipe (inset), roll the neoprene sleeve down, slide the T-fitting in place, and roll the sleeve back up over the pipe.

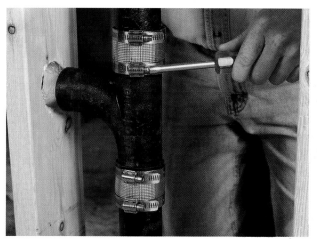

3 Tighten all clamps on the banded couplings using a nut driver. Extend Schedule 40 PVC from the T-fitting's branch.

4 Working with Waste & Vent Pipes

past that one cast-iron T- or Y-fitting, it's smooth sailing. In most cases, that fitting will be easy to install as well. (In fact, a T- or Y-fitting spliced into a cast-iron line does not need to be made of cast iron. Schedule 40 PVC pipe has about the same wall thickness, so it's a good match.)

After deciding where to cut into the existing line and making sure the line will not drop when cut, start by holding the new fitting against the old trunk or branch line. Mark one end of the fitting on the old line with a grease pencil or chalk. Then add ½ inch to the length of the fitting, and chalk a second mark. **1.** Cut on these marks. **2** (inset). The extra ½ inch will provide valuable working space when banding the new fitting in place.

If you have chosen the banded couplings without stainless-steel sleeves or center stops, just slide one coupling onto each end of the existing line. Set the new fit-

ting—either a no-hub cast-iron fitting or plastic fitting with glued stubs—into the gap, and slide the banded couplings halfway onto the new fitting at each end. Then draw the bands tight using a nut driver, screwdriver, or open-end wrench.

If you have purchased banded couplings with a center stop, or ridge, in the middle of their neoprene sleeves, the job becomes only slightly more complicated. Start by sliding only the stainless-steel bands onto the pipe. Then slide the neoprene sleeves onto the pipes until the pipe ends come to rest against the center stops. With the sleeves in place, fold each one back over itself. This will give you the clearance you'll need to set the fitting in place. Then roll the folded halves of the sleeves onto the fitting. **2.** Slide the stainless-steel band over each neoprene sleeve, and tighten the clamps. **3.** This variety of banded coupling is not approved by code for use underground.

Other Methods of Tapping into Cast Iron. Not all cast-iron fittings have bell-and-spigot inlets. Some older types accept threaded pipes or threaded adapters. You'll find these fittings in homes that have cast-iron stacks with copper or galvanized-steel branch lines. These threaded fittings offer yet another method of adapting plastic to cast iron, though not always as easily as with banded couplings. They also have the advantages of being extremely inexpensive and making neat, professional-looking retrofit connections.

In the case of copper or brass threaded adapters, just cut the old copper line near the cast-iron fitting, and back the adapter out with a large pipe wrench. Because brass and copper are relatively soft, their threads break loose easily.

Galvanized-steel threads, in contrast, fuse with the cast iron over time. To break these threads free, you often need to heat the cast iron with a torch. Heat causes the female half of the fitting to expand slightly, loosening its grip. In any case, when you've removed the old threaded piece, clean the rust from the cast-iron threads using a wire brush. Then wrap plumber's pipe thread-sealing tape—only two full rounds—onto the threads of the new plastic adapter, and screw the adapter into the cast-iron fitting.

New Piping into Old Hubs

In some situations, the best approach is to start your new piping inside an old hub. One example is when a stack hub rests at basement floor level and you'd like to extend a branch line horizontally just above the floor. There are times when using an old hub can also save you from having to cut into a stack. Removing an old iron pipe from a lead and oakum joint is well within a homeowner's abilities. The job requires digging both the lead and oakum from the old joint so that you can lift out the pipe.

Special tools for this job are available, but an old flat-blade screwdriver will work. Begin by driving the blade of the screwdriver diagonally through the ring of lead, prying it up. Grip the pried-out piece of lead with pliers, and peel the rest of it out. You can dig out the

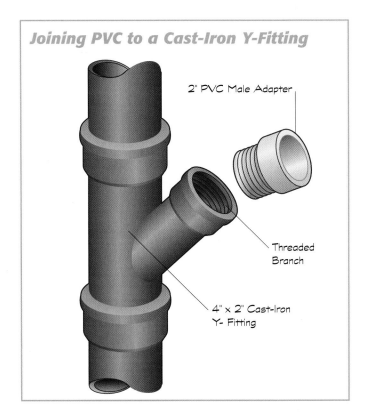

Joining PVC to a Cast-Iron Y-Fitting

2" PVC Male Adapter

Threaded Branch

4" x 2" Cast-Iron Y- Fitting

Removing Galvanized-Steel Waste Pipes

Plumbers no longer install galvanized-steel waste piping at the residential level, so you will only be replacing or repairing this material. In either case, you must always cut galvanized steel into two pieces to work on it. This is because galvanized-steel piping sections were always installed sequentially, with threaded fittings: when you try to loosen a length of pipe at one end, you're tightening it at the other. The only solution is to cut the pipe so that you can back each end from its threads.

This is always easier said than done because steel threads rust almost from the moment they're installed. Coming along 40 years later, you're going to have to work to break this oxidation seal. It can be done, but you'll need to heat the female half of the joint and then use a large pipe wrench and all the leverage you can muster to break free the threads. When you've removed both ends of the pipe, thread plastic male adapters into the fittings and install PVC plastic piping between the adapters. An easier approach is to just cut out the steel and splice it with banded couplings.

Joining PVC to a Cast-Iron Hub

Tools and Materials

- Hacksaw
- File
- Gasket, lubricant, and brush
- Hammer
- PVC piping

TIME NEEDED: 10–20 MIN. PER FITTING

PLUMBING TIP: *Schedule 40 PVC piping has a similar outside diameter as cast iron, so it can be used to make direct connections in hub fittings.*

1 Press a 2-in. neoprene gasket directly into the cast-iron fitting hub until it seats. These gaskets can't be rolled.

2 To make the PVC plastic pipe fit the gasket, file the pipe edge to smooth it out, and lubricate the gasket (inset).

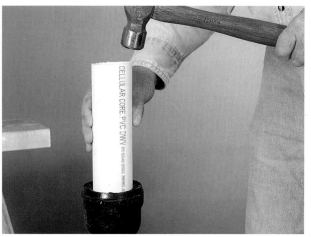

3 Align the plastic pipe with the cast-iron fitting, and drive the pipe into the hub until you feel it bottom out.

oakum in a similar fashion, but you'll have to remove it bit by bit. Needle-nose pliers work well. When you have cleaned out the joint and removed the old pipe, begin the new piping by installing a neoprene gasket made for cast iron in the hub. **1.** These gaskets accept Schedule 40 PVC pipe as well as cast iron. Reducing gaskets are also available. Lubricate the gasket as you would if you were working with cast-iron pipe. **2** (inset). Cut the PVC pipe to the size you need, and file the sharp, ragged edge left by the saw. **2.** Then force the PVC pipe into the gasketed hub until it bottoms out. You may need to tap the pipe in place using a ball-peen hammer. **3.**

If you are using a thick reducing gasket, slide the gasket onto the plastic pipe first. Then insert the pipe into the cast-iron hub. Lubricate the outside of the gasket, and drive it into the hub using a hammer.

Tearing Out a Cast-Iron System

Sometimes you simply have to replace an outdated drainage system. Those with drum traps, rusted cast iron, leaky joints, grossly inadequate venting, and permanently slow drains all fit into this category. In fact, when you are doing a substantial remodel and gutting extensive areas of a house, there's no point in saving the old system. Retrofits are almost always compromises, and with full access, there's no advantage in compromise.

To dismantle an antiquated galvanized-steel or copper plumbing system, you can cut it apart with a hacksaw or reciprocating saw. You can also cut out cast iron, but an easier method is to shatter the hubs with hammers. This may seem extreme, but it works well and gets the job done quickly. It also works when galvanized steel is joined using cast-iron elbows and T- and Y-fittings.

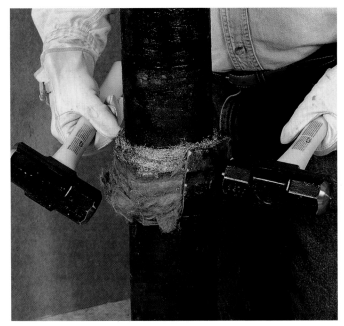

The quickest way to dismantle an old cast-iron system is to smash the hubs with two hammers.

You'll need to wear face and eye protection, of course, but the method is simple. Starting near the top of the stack, strike the first hub with two hammers of equal weight. (See the photo above.) Three-pound sledgehammers work well. The hammers should strike opposite sides of the cast-iron hub, hitting at roughly the same time. That's about all there is to it. With two or three hammer blows, one side of the hub will break away, allowing you to lift the pipe from its lead-and-oakum seat. Work carefully at first until you get the hang of it.

When you reach the lowest section of piping on the stack, stop. From the basement ceiling on down, use a snap-cutter or a ball-peen hammer and cold chisel to make clean cuts. At this point, either dig the lead and oakum from the lowest hub or use a snap-cutter to cut the stack a foot or so above the floor. Using a neoprene gasket or banded coupling, you can then extend the new piping upward.

Plastic Drainage Piping

The plastic piping materials allowed by codes for use in drain and vent systems are Schedule 40 PVC, and to a lesser extent, Schedule 40 ABS. PVC is white; ABS plastic is black.

PVC has gained almost universal acceptance, so this discussion focuses on it; however, little difference exists between the two plastics in terms of installation. If you have ABS-plastic piping in place, you can make repairs and additions using ABS or PVC fittings, but use the more aggressive PVC joint cement or a universal solvent cement. ABS cement does not bond well enough to PVC.

Converting a Lead Toilet Riser to Plastic

Years ago, plumbers used lead drain lines to join cast-iron and galvanized-steel pipes to traps and fixtures. The two most common places to find lead are on outdated drum traps and old toilet risers. No matter where you find these fittings, replace them. Lead is easy to recognize, as it shows a dull gray with age and is shiny bright when scratched. It is also soft. You can cut through lead easily using a hacksaw or even a sharp utility knife.

To replace a lead riser, cut through the lead with a utility knife. Remove the riser and flange, and cut the lead again, this time just above the hub. Install a banded coupling on the insert, and finish with a PVC pipe and flange.

Replacing an Old Cast-Iron Toilet Flange

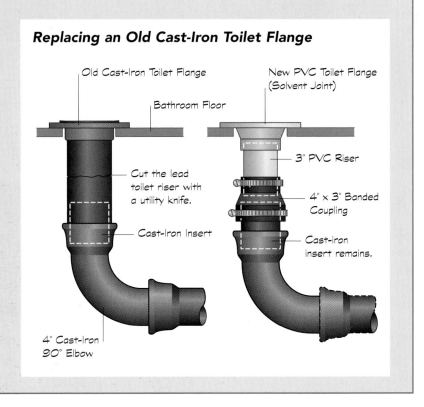

Old Cast-Iron Toilet Flange

New PVC Toilet Flange (Solvent Joint)

Bathroom Floor

Cut the lead toilet riser with a utility knife.

3" PVC Riser

Cast-Iron Insert

4" x 3" Banded Coupling

Cast-iron insert remains.

4" Cast-Iron 90° Elbow

Advantages and Disadvantages. Over the years, plastic has had to overcome an image problem as nothing more than a cheap substitute for metal. Actually, it's hard to imagine a better material for residential waste and vent systems. Almost every conceivable fitting is available in PVC or ABS. Plastic is remarkably easy to install with the simplest of household tools. Once installed, it's easy to alter. It fits in tight spaces and is universally available at reasonable prices. Plastic never rots or corrodes, and it stands up well to caustic drain-cleaning chemicals.

What are its disadvantages? It's noisy. You can hear water run through it, which some homeowners find annoying. It expands and contracts more than cast iron or copper with changes in water temperature, and if it's wedged against structural timbers, it makes a persistent ticking sound with the expansion and contraction. It also tends to have more abrupt flow patterns, which can lead to clogs. But for all of that, the advantages outweigh the disadvantages for most people.

Licensed plumbers often cut PVC pipe with a power miter saw (or cutoff saw), but a hacksaw or tubing cutter works about as well. If you use a hacksaw, be sure to clear the resulting ridges or burrs from the pipe edge before installing it. Deburring tools are available, but a pocket-knife or a file works just as well. In a pinch, you can even rub off the burrs with your thumb.

Before cementing PVC joints, be sure to deglaze, or prime, both the pipe end and the fitting to roughen the surfaces and make it easier for the solvent to achieve a good bond. You can do this most easily using a primer-solvent, but sanding *lightly* or scuffing with an abrasive pad will also work. Many primers have a bright color additive, called an indicator. This additive has nothing to do with how the primer works. Rather, it reveals whether or not a primer has been used and is primarily for the benefit of the plumbing inspector.

Because primers are thin and tend to run all over the pipe and fitting, indicator colors tend to make a job (as well as hands, clothes, shoes, walls, floors, tools, and the like) look messy. Understandably, many people prefer primers without indicator colors. When color indicators are required by code, however, ugly wins.

4 Working with Waste & Vent Pipes

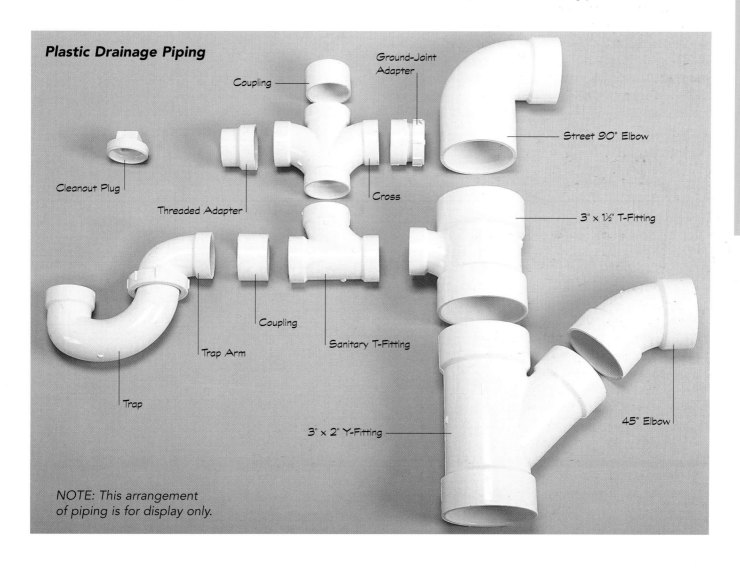

Plastic Drainage Piping

Coupling

Ground-Joint Adapter

Street 90° Elbow

Cleanout Plug

Threaded Adapter

Cross

3" x 1½" T-Fitting

Coupling

Trap Arm

Sanitary T-Fitting

Trap

3" x 2" Y-Fitting

45° Elbow

NOTE: This arrangement of piping is for display only.

Working with Plastic Drainpipe

PVC (and ABS) pipes and fittings, once cemented together, stay that way. Unlike wood glues, which bind each piece of wood to itself, plastic pipe solvents actually melt one surface into the other, creating a chemical weld. With a 1½-inch pipe and fitting, you'll have about 30 seconds to change your mind about the joint. After that, it's permanent. So test-fit and mark each group of fittings with a pencil or felt-tip marker before gluing them in place.

When measuring for a pipe cut, be sure to include the depth of the fitting hubs in your total. **1.** You can make this calculation in your head, but holding an actual fitting in place helps to eliminate errors. When you've determined the exact pipe length needed, mark the pipe and cut it. You can use a hacksaw, handsaw (with miter box), PVC saw, wheel cutter, or power miter saw (cutoff saw). **2.** Be careful to keep the cut square, because an angled pipe won't fit as well into the fitting. And when cutting, make long, easy strokes. Moving the saw too fast can cause the saw blade to overheat, gumming it up and leaving hard-to-remove burrs in the pipe.

Smooth the inside of the pipe end using a knife, sandpaper, or a deburring tool before cementing the joint together. **3.** Any rough edges will attract hair and strands of fabric sent though the system, causing clogs, and in some cases, depleting a trap seal through capillary attraction. (See "Capillary Attraction," pages 52 and 53.)

With the end of the pipe cleared of burrs and rough spots, apply primer-solvent to the outer edge of the pipe and to the hub of the fitting. **4.** Both primer-solvent and joint-cement containers come with applicators. When the primer evaporates, test-fit the joints, making sure that the pipe bottoms out in the fittings. When you're sure the joint is right, mark the pipe to show where the fitting should land on it in final assembly. **5.** Next, coat the first 1 inch of the pipe and the entire inside of the fitting hub with cement. **6.** Immediately insert the pipe and fitting. As soon as the pipe bottoms out in the hub, rotate the fitting about one-quarter turn. **7.** This fills any voids in the joint by breaking up the insertion lines. Of course, if you've test-fitted your joints first, you'll need to push the pipe into the fitting with the alignment marks about one-quarter turn out of sync, then rotate the fitting until the marks line up. Hold the parts together for about 10 seconds. Wipe any excess cement from the outside of the pipe or fitting. Complete the assembly with any additional pipes or fittings. **8.**

Working with Plastic Drainpipe

Tools and Materials

- Measuring tape
- PVC pipe
- Hacksaw
- Deburring tool
- Pencil
- Primer and cement

TIME NEEDED: VARIES

PLUMBING TIP: *To take a cemented joint apart, cut the pipe flush with the hub, and slice into the stub several times with a hacksaw blade. Pry out the pieces with a screwdriver.*

3 *Use an inexpensive deburring tool or the rounded side of a file to smooth the ragged edge left by the saw.*

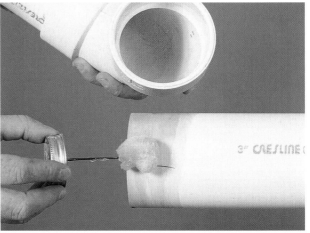

6 *Apply PVC solvent cement with the applicator contained in the can. Cover both the pipe ends and the inside of each hub.*

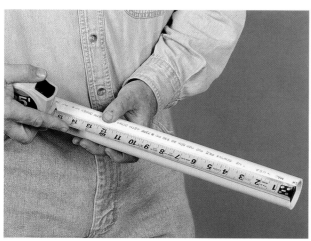

1 *Measure the pipe with a measuring tape. Don't forget to allow extra length to extend into the fitting's hub.*

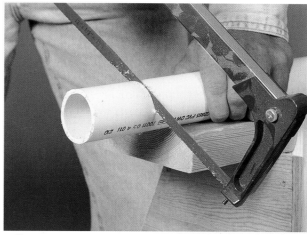

2 *Cut the pipe (here, with a hacksaw). You can also use a handsaw, special PVC saw, wheel cutter, or power miter saw. Be sure the cut is straight.*

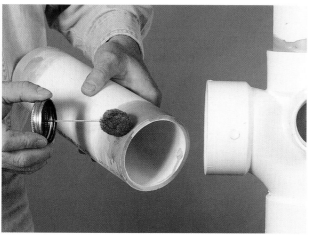

4 *Apply primer to the end of the pipe to cut the glaze. Many primers have an added colorant. Primer is often code required.*

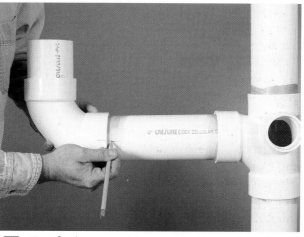

5 *Test-fit the assembly, and mark each joint for alignment with a pencil. You could also number the pieces.*

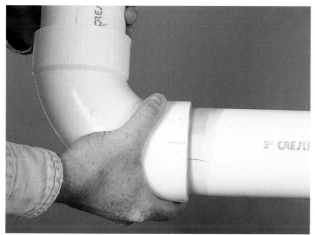

7 *Start the fitting slightly out of alignment, and rotate it one-quarter turn to line up the marks. This breaks up the insertion lines of the glue.*

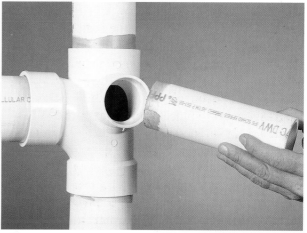

8 *Install the stack fittings first, then the branch lines. A side-inlet T-fitting (shown) can drain both toilet and shower.*

4 Working with Waste & Vent Pipes

CHAPTER 5

Working with Water Piping

Water piping is easier to install than waste and vent piping in many respects, and it's certainly easier to design. With no gravity or venting issues to worry about, size and efficiency become the focus.

Size is relatively easy to determine. A ½-inch line can serve only two fixtures, so in almost all cases you'll run water supply trunk lines in ¾-inch pipe until you reach the last two fixtures, and then reduce to ½-inch piping. (Sizes always indicate the inside diameter of the pipe.) The same sizing rule applies to branch lines extending from the main trunk lines. (See Chapter 2, "Planning Changes," starting on page 24, for more specific information on system design and code requirements.)

If you do the job neatly, using no more pipe than necessary, you'll have an efficient system. If you anchor all in-wall stub-outs and valves, support the pipe every few feet, and protect it from freezing, you can expect decades of trouble-free service. And if you insulate the hot-water lines, you'll save on water-heating costs.

One drawback might be the water-pipe joining method. Water pipes are usually made of copper, which must be soldered. Well soldered joints require some skill, but with practice and the information in this chapter, good soldering technique is not beyond your reach.

Of course, you might worry about leaks, but leaks are fairly easy to repair. Just drain the system, and redo the offending fitting. It may be inconvenient and time-consuming, but it's not difficult.

Cutting Water Pipes

The methods and equipment you need to cut water pipes depend on the piping material itself. Many people cut copper and galvanized steel with a hacksaw, but a tubing cutter leaves a more uniform edge. You can also cut plastic pipe with a tubing cutter, but most do-it-yourselfers reach for a hacksaw instead. The reason has less to do with the quality of the cut than with the availability of the tool. Tubing shears are probably the best cutting tool for plastic.

You can do an adequate job with a hacksaw if you're careful. The goal is always a straight cut. When you cut pipe at an angle, it won't fit fully into the fitting. Cemented plastic-pipe joints need all the surface contact they can get, so a fitting that doesn't bottom out is a problem. In the case of galvanized steel, it's difficult to get threading dies started over an angled pipe end.

A clean cut is also important. A tubing cutter can leave a compression ridge inside the pipe, while hacksaws leave coarse burrs. Ragged burrs protruding from a pipe's edge will eventually break off and make their way into control valves, appliances, and faucets. Severe edges also create friction in the water flow, called line friction, which can reduce pressure. And finally, raised edges generate turbulence, which can eventually erode the pipe wall. To prevent these problems, ream any severe edges left by a cutting tool before you install the pipe.

To ream a copper or plastic pipe, lift the triangular

reaming attachment from the top of the cutter, insert it into the end of the pipe, and give it several sharp twists. When dealing with steel pipe, you'll need a more aggressive reaming tool—one with hardened-steel cutting blades. If you rent other tools to work with steel pipe (such as a threader), rent a reamer as well. If you are making only a few cuts, use a rat-tail file.

Using a Tubing Cutter

Use all tubing cutters in a similar fashion. First, mark the pipe to length. **1.** Then clamp the cutter onto the pipe, centering the cutting wheel on your mark. Rotate the tool's handle clockwise until the cutting wheel bites into the pipe just a little. **2.** Don't overdo it. If it's difficult to rotate the cutter around the pipe, unscrew the handle, but just slightly. Rotate the tool around the pipe several times. You'll feel slight resistance on the first one or two turns, but after that, the cutter will roll easily around the pipe. This is your cue to tighten the wheel against the pipe again. Rotate the cutter, and repeat this procedure until you cut all the way through the pipe.

You use the same method for cutting plastic, steel, or copper. The only difference is that tubing cutters made for steel pipe are much heavier than those for copper and plastic. Because of this, there's a substantial cost difference. Buying a tubing cutter for plastic and copper makes sense—one will work for both—but cutters made for steel pipe are strictly rental items. In fact, if you have only one or two cuts to make, you should probably have your local hardware store or plumbing supply center cut and thread the pipes for you.

Thumb Cutter. You'll find a variety of tubing cutters on the market, most having an overall length of 5 to 6

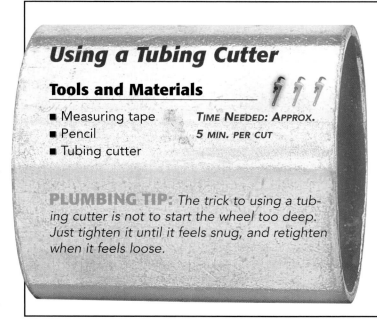

Using a Tubing Cutter

Tools and Materials

- Measuring tape
- Pencil
- Tubing cutter

TIME NEEDED: APPROX.
5 MIN. PER CUT

PLUMBING TIP: *The trick to using a tubing cutter is not to start the wheel too deep. Just tighten it until it feels snug, and retighten when it feels loose.*

inches. These do well in the open, but when working in walls and between joists, a close-quarters tubing cutter—sometimes called a *thumb cutter*—is often a better choice. Instead of a long handle, a thumb cutter has a knurled knob. The tool works surprisingly well, and some models handle pipes up to 1 inch in diameter. If you can afford only one tubing cutter for copper pipe, a thumb cutter is a good choice. It'll slow you down a little, but you'll be able to use it in more places.

Cutting with a Hacksaw

When you are using a hacksaw to cut pipe, don't rush it. Use as much of the blade as possible in long, easy strokes. If you work too fast, the blade will heat up and start binding. A hot blade also leaves a ragged pipe edge. The best approach is to steady the pipe on a solid surface and cut just to the left or right of the support. Some people like to use a miter box to ensure straight cuts.

Close-Quarters Hacksaws. Full-size hacksaws have the same limitations as full-size tubing cutters: in many situations, they're just too big. When you need a smaller saw, you'll find that there are a variety of miniature hacksaws on the market. While it's not sensible to try plumbing an entire job with a tiny saw, they work wonders in cramped spaces. In fact, close-quarters hacksaws often work in situations too cramped for thumb cutters. The design shown in the photo on the opposite page is usually preferable, but other designs can work well enough. In a pinch, some people remove the blade from a full-size hacksaw and use it alone. But hacksaw blades are fairly brittle, so remember to wear gloves.

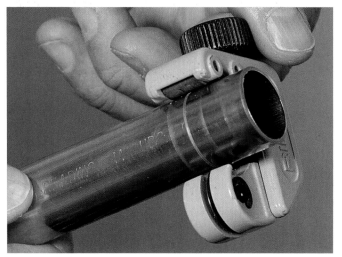

Use a thumb cutter *when you need to cut copper tubing and you're confined by a tight working space.*

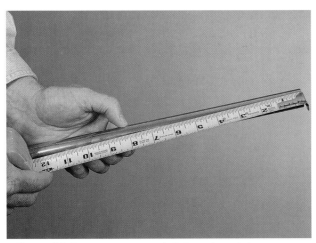

1 Hold the pipe in your left hand and the measuring tape in your right. Hold the location with your thumb; then mark it using a pencil.

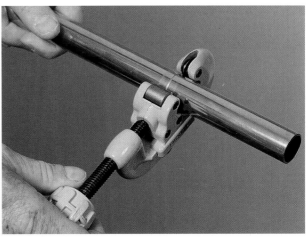

2 Tighten the wheel cutter to clamp it onto the pipe at the mark, and rotate the cutter with the wheel following the rollers.

Using Hacksaws

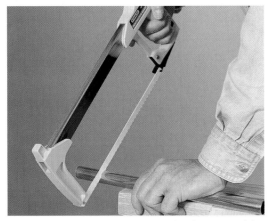

Use a fine-tooth blade in a hacksaw. Hold the pipe steady, cutting near the support.

You can use a miniature hacksaw as you would a full-size one, but it fits tight spaces.

Copper Water Piping

Copper pipe is available in two forms—*rigid*, or hard, and *drawn*, or soft. Rigid copper comes in 10- or 20-foot lengths, while soft copper comes in 60-, 100-, and 120-foot coils. You typically use rigid copper for in-house, above-concrete water-piping installations, and soft copper for belowground applications and for connecting stub-outs with faucets. Along with black steel pipe, some codes allow soft copper for both natural gas and propane piping installations.

Rigid copper is available in Type M and Type L wall thicknesses. Type M, thinner than Type L, is used predominantly in residential systems. Type L is more common in commercial installations. Soft copper comes in Type L and Type K wall thicknesses—Type K is heavier. You use Type L most often aboveground, as both water and gas piping, while you use Type K almost exclusively for underground water piping. Type K soft copper is also used to run water service lines between public mains and private homes.

You can join rigid copper with soldered—or sweat—fittings, compression fittings, and push-fit fittings. You can join soft copper with compression and flare fittings. Threaded adapters are available for joining copper to any other threaded material, including threaded steel and CPVC plastic. Only soldered and threaded fittings can be hidden in walls, however.

Solder

Solder is metallic filler that bonds two metallic surfaces to itself. Flux helps this bonding to occur. Flux works by

5 Working with Water Piping

ridding the copper surfaces of oxidation and other contaminants. It pulls molten solder into the joint, even when the fitting is upside down. Where the flux goes, solder will follow. Without flux, molten solder will just bead up and fall away.

Until the late 1980s, most of the solder used in residential plumbing was a 50-50 amalgamation of tin and lead. Other combinations included 60-40 and 95-5 tin and lead. Lead was almost always an ingredient. The industry used lead solder because it was a familiar product in sheet-metal work when copper pipe became popular after World War II. Lead melts at relatively low temperatures and bridges gaps well, so it's easier to use than other kinds of solders, which are harder. Lead also makes brass more easily machined, so most quality faucets contained lead until very recently.

The plumbing industry didn't realize that water, under fairly common conditions, could leach lead from soldered fittings. Even small amounts of lead ingested by a human being can cause brain damage. Today, the U.S. Environmental Protection Agency (EPA) bans the use of lead-based plumbing solder.

Existing Lead Hazards. What if your home already has lead-based solder joints? Short of installing an expensive distiller or an equally expensive reverse-osmosis water filter, both of which can eliminate even microscopic amounts of lead from drinking water, there's little you can do. However, you can take precautions, as discussed below.

Almost all soldered copper piping installed before 1988 had lead soldered joints. Does this mean that your home's plumbing puts you at risk today? It's hard to say with certainty, but probably not. There's a limit to the amount of lead available in a soldered fitting, and most of the exposed lead leaches out in the first 90 days. Water conditions also make a difference. Soft water is inherently more aggressive, so it dissolves some soft metals at a faster rate, depleting them sooner. With even slightly hard water, the joints scale over in a few years, sealing off the problem. The greatest likely hazard occurred when these systems were new, and even then, certain use habits may have diminished the risk.

Water must remain in contact with soldered joints six to eight hours before it can absorb much lead, so the greatest lead concentrations are present when the system hasn't been used for a while, such as overnight or while you're at work. If you flush a toilet, take a shower or let a little water run through the faucet before taking a drink, you pretty much avoid the lead risk. If you're concerned, let a faucet run for 15 to 20 seconds before drinking. It's somewhat wasteful but effective. And lastly, certain contaminants, including nitrates and heavy metals, become concentrated in heated environments, so avoid cooking with water from the water heater. Always use cold water.

Soldering Copper

The three most common mistakes in soldering are using dirty fittings and using too much or too little heat. If fitting and pipe aren't clean down to shiny copper, the solder may not adhere well to the metal. With too much heat, you'll cook the flux from the fitting hubs, resulting in a weak bond, and with too little heat, the solder may not flow properly, also resulting in a weak joint. Other trouble sources are water left in fittings, which prevents the metal from heating up as the water absorbs the heat; heating the top end of a fitting first, resulting in uneven heat distribution; and not allowing for the greater mass and density of brass valves and fittings when applying

SMART TIP

Start at the Bottom

Always start with the lowest hub on a fitting. This is critically important. When you solder the lowest joint first, the solder in that hub cools and thickens slightly by the time you move to the upper joints. In this way, the hotter, thinner solder fed into the top of the fitting does not drain through the bottom. If you remember this one procedure, you'll cut your solder leaks in half.

Apply heat and solder to the lowest hub on the fitting first. Complete the joint before moving up.

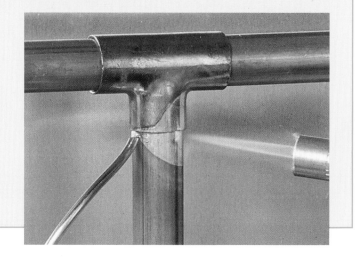

heat, which may result in the fitting not getting hot enough to melt the solder. You can avoid each of these problems. All it takes is an awareness of the potential pitfalls and the correct approach.

Cleaning. To begin, clean both the pipe ends and the fitting ports. The best approach is to sand them with grit cloth, fine sandpaper, an abrasive scouring pad, or a wire brush. Wire brushes for cleaning fittings are available at plumbing outlets. **1.** Many people get good results from using a wire brush for fittings and an abrasive pad for pipes. Sand each pipe at least 1 inch up from its end, even if the pipe is shiny and new. **2.** New pipes and fittings still need sanding because they may have a coating of oil or other substance.

After you have sanded the pipe and fitting and wiped them clean, use a small brush to apply a thin coating of flux to the pipe end as well as to the inner surface of the fitting. **3.** Insert each pipe into its fitting hub fully, and wipe away the excess flux. (If you're soldering an assembly that spans more than one joist or stud, secure the pipe to the structural framing using pipe clamps or hangers, as necessary, as you assemble the fittings. To save time, it pays to assemble a group of fittings, and then to solder them all in sequence, from the bottom up.) Once you start soldering a fitting, solder all the hubs on that fitting before moving on. Try to solder all the assembled fittings within 30 minutes, because some brands of flux will degrade the copper if they're left on the pipe or fitting surface longer.

Soldering Copper Tubing

Tools and Materials

- Cleaning tool or pad
- Flux & brush
- Solder
- Soldering torch

TIME NEEDED: 20–30 MIN.
- Tubing & fittings
- Gloves & goggles
- Rag

PLUMBING TIP: *If you don't have a wire brush, you can clean both pipe and fittings with a soap-free household abrasive scrubbing pad. Force the pad into the fitting hubs with your little finger.*

1 *Use a combination tool, wire brush, or abrasive pad to clean each hub on the fitting. Combination tools have two different brush sizes.*

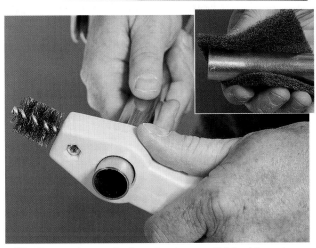

2 *Scour the end of each pipe until it's shiny at least 1 in. back where the fitting will be attached. Wipe the pipe and fitting with a rag.*

3 *Apply flux to the pipe end and the inside of the fitting with a small brush. Insert the pipe, and wipe away the excess flux.*

5 Working with Water Piping

Sequence continues on next page

Continued from previous page

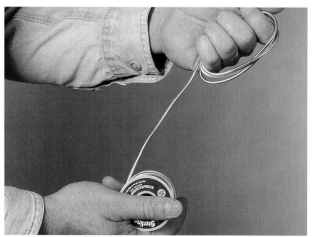

4 *Pull approximately about 24 in. of solder from the spool, and wrap it around your hand for a more comfortable grip.*

5 *To keep from scorching the rubber and plastic parts in a shutoff valve, remove the stem before soldering the valve.*

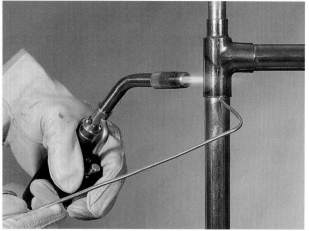

6 *Heat both sides of the lowest hub on the fitting. Touch the solder to the fitting. Continue to heat the fitting until the solder starts to melt.*

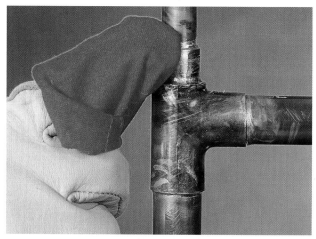

7 *When you've finished soldering the fitting and before the solder hardens, wipe the excess solder from each joint. Wipe away from yourself.*

When you have a group of pipes and fittings assembled, wrap a couple of feet of solder wire around your hand to form an oval-shaped spool. **4.** Remove the spool from your hand, and pull one end out roughly 10 inches. Then bend down the final 2 inches of this length into a 90-degree angle. This makes a convenient roll of wire that you can spool out as needed. The 90-degree bend allows you to comfortably approach the fitting from nearly any direction.

When you are going to heat a brass valve, it's a good idea to remove the cartridge or stem. **5.** This simple precaution helps to avoid warping the nylon and neoprene components. If you decide not to take the valve apart, at least turn the valve to its fully open position. Then angle the torch tip away from the valve body, and heat only the valve's hubs. In any case, try to keep the

flame from hitting the copper pipes directly. Copper heats faster than brass, and if you heat the copper first, it will cook the flux from the fitting before the brass is ready for solder.

Bringing the Heat. Use a mapp (methylacetyline propane) gas torch, available at hardware stores for soldering. No-lead solders require more heat than lead solders, and mapp gas makes a hotter flame than propane. When you heat a joint for solder, always heat the fitting, not the pipe. Keep the torch moving, side to side, to avoid hot spots that can cook the flux. Heat just one fitting hub at a time, not the entire fitting.

Before lighting the torch, gather everything you'll need, including the torch, solder, wiping rag, job light (if needed), ladder, and flux. Keep the flux nearby in case you inadvertently scorch a fitting. With everything ready, light the torch and turn the valve wide open. If you're right-handed, place the torch in your left hand and the solder and rag in your right. Heat the most accessible side of the lowest hub on the first fitting, moving the flame in an arc across the front half of the hub. **6.** Try to keep the torch tip about ¾ inch away from the fitting, and always keep it moving. As soon as the flux in the near side of the fitting begins to crackle and spit, move the flame to the far side of the fitting and heat it, again moving the torch in a side-to-side arc. At this point, the fitting will be almost ready, so repeatedly touch the solder wire to the near—preheated—side of the fitting hub. As soon as the fitting begins to melt the solder, pull the heat away and push more solder into the joint. Remember, the fitting, not the torch, should melt the solder.

How much solder should you give each joint? As a rule a ½-inch fitting should get ½ inch of solder wire per hub, a ¾-inch fitting, ¾ inch of solder, and so on. When the fitting is uniformly hot, the flux will draw the solder completely around the joint quickly. When the joint cools a bit, look for the solder to draw into the rim slightly. When this happens, you'll know that the joint was a good "take." If the solder seems to just lie on the rim, add a little more heat until it gets drawn in. If that doesn't do it, brush new flux around the rim and add a little more heat and solder.

As soon as the lower hub of the fitting takes, heat the next-highest hub and repeat the procedure. Keep in mind that the fitting is already quite hot, so it takes only a few seconds of heat on the remaining hubs. To avoid overheating, keep touching the solder to the joint. When you've finished soldering all hubs on the fitting and before the solder hardens, use your rag to wipe away the excess, always in a direction that's away from your face. **7.** In any case, don't leave sloppy globs of solder dripping from the fitting. Appearance counts.

Soldering Problems and Solutions. Not all soldering jobs are simple. Common problem situations include tight workspaces, fittings installed too closely to structural timbers, and pipes that trap water. The best way to avoid problems, of course, is to avoid problem situations. You can often pre-solder fittings that must rest against structural timbers or be installed deep inside cantilevers or walls. You solder the fitting or group of fittings out in the open and then install the soldered assembly. **A.**

When you can't avoid soldering against studs or joists, you can keep from scorching the wood by sliding a double thickness of sheet metal between the fitting

and the structural member. **B.** It's handy to keep a 6-inch fold of sheet metal in your toolbox for this purpose. In a pinch, even a smashed tin can will do the job. The important thing to remember is that the sheet metal must have two layers. Plumbing outlets also sell squares of woven fireproof protective fabric, which also work well. **C.**

Solder deep-set fittings, *like this freeze-proof sillcock, to their pipes before installing them.*

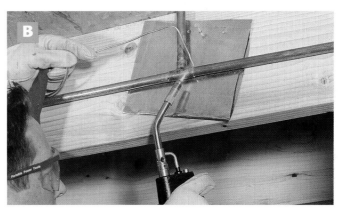

Use a double thickness of sheet metal *to keep from scorching the wood.*

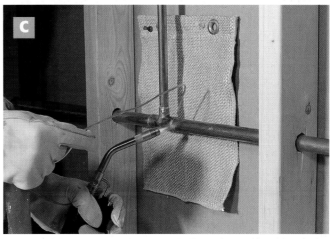

You can also use a flame shield *of fireproof woven fabric to protect larger areas.*

To stop a trickle of water, *insert a special liquid-filled capsule before soldering.*

A union installed at a low point *makes a good drain-down fitting.*

Safety Caution: *If you scorch lumber, brush the char mark clean using a wire brush to remove all carbon, and wet the area thoroughly. Burnt framing lumber has been the source of a good many house fires, and a fire can spring to life hours after the work was done if not taken care of.*

When old shutoff valves leak, the downstream pipes will continue to carry a trickle of water. It's difficult to make pipes and fittings that have even a small amount of water in them hot enough to accept solder. And even when you can make them hot enough, the escaping steam forces pinholes through the solder. You can usually avoid the problem by opening all other valves and faucets, thereby draining the water through another part of the system. Or you can loosen the water-meter union nuts and empty the pipe water into a bucket or nearby floor drain.

If that fails, you might try an old plumber's trick. Push several wads of white bread into the pipe with a pencil to hold back any water. Squeeze the bread into tight balls before pushing it in. If you work quickly, you can solder the fitting before the bread starts to disintegrate. When you have finished the job, detach the aerator from the nearest faucet and flush the sodden bread from the line. Plumbing outlets also sell liquid-filled plastic capsules for this purpose, which you later dissolve with heat. **D.**

If all else fails and you simply can't keep water from trickling through the fitting to be soldered, cut the line at its lowest point so that it drains, and install a union or freeze-repair fitting when you have finished the work. **E.** (For freeze repair, see the top photo on page 81.)

Other Methods of Joining Copper

While its best to assemble large piping projects with inexpensive soldered fittings, you can find other fittings for copper. These fittings fall into three categories, all of which are mechanical joints: compression fittings, flare fittings, and push-fit fittings.

Compression Fittings

A compression-type water fitting consists of a brass body—either an adapter body or valve body—with two or more pipe hubs. The fitting hubs have external threads and beveled rims. The nuts are open at the top so that you can insert pipes through them. A third component, a brass compression ring called a ferrule, makes the seal. The ferrule is also beveled, top and bottom.

You make the connection by sliding the nut and ferrule onto the end of a pipe and inserting the pipe into the fitting hub. As you tighten the nut, the beveled surfaces force the ring inward, cinching it around the pipe. Because the ring actually crushes the pipe a little, it locks the ring in place and makes the water seal.

The problem comes in not knowing how much to tighten the compression nut. If you overtighten it, you can reduce the ring too much, and water will seep past the nut. When you see a leak, your first impulse is to tighten the nut even more. But in this case, tightening just widens the gap and makes the leak worse. At this point, there's no chance of saving the connection. Your only option is to start over, using a new supply tube and ring.

You most frequently use compression fittings as conversion fittings under fixtures. Used in this way, they join rigid copper supply lines to flexible copper supply

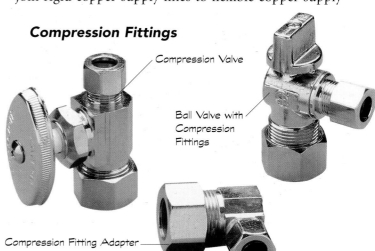

Compression Fittings

Compression Valve

Ball Valve with Compression Fittings

Compression Fitting Adapter

tubes. Compression-type connectors normally come with shutoff valves, but they're also available as couplings and 90-degree L-fittings, in sizes ranging from ⅛ to 1 inch in diameter. You can also find valves and adapters with one threaded hub and one compression hub. Use these to join threaded brass water fittings to copper supply tubes.

Installing Compression Fittings. If the alignment between faucet and riser requires an offset, begin by bending the supply tube to meet the fittings head-on. Use a tubing bender so that you don't crimp the soft copper tubing as you shape it. Then hold or temporarily fasten the supply tube in place, and mark it for length. **1.** Trim the tube, making sure that any bends are well away from its end. Bending a pipe forces it out of round, preventing the nut and ring from sliding on.

Once the supply tube is ready, slide the nut and ferrule onto it an inch or two, and lubricate both the ring and fitting threads with a thin coating of pipe joint compound. **2.** Insert the pipe into the fitting port; slide the compression ring down to meet the fitting; and thread the nut onto the fitting *finger-tight.* If the tube enters at a slight angle, the nut may bind against it, so wiggle the tube a bit to make sure the nut is tight. When the connection feels snug, use a 6-inch adjustable wrench to tighten the nut 1½ turns. **3.** Don't tighten any more unless you see a leak after the water is turned on. If you do find a leak, tighten the nut only until the leak stops, usually less than one-half a turn.

Installing Compression Fittings

Tools and Materials

- Stop valve & fittings   TIME NEEDED: 20 MIN.
- Supply tubing
- Pencil   ■ Tubing bender
- Adjustable wrenches ■ Tubing cutter

PLUMBING TIP: *To make sure a compression nut is really finger-tight, wiggle the supply tube while tightening.*

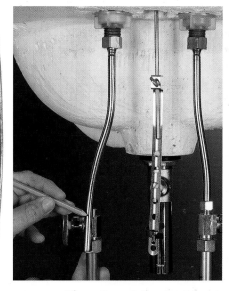

1 Bend the supply tube into shape using a tubing bender, test-fit it, and mark the length with a pencil. Then cut the tube with a tubing cutter, and slide the compression nut and ferrule onto its end.

2 Coat the ferrule and threads with pipe joint compound, insert the tube into the compression fitting, and slide the ferrule and nut down. Tighten the nut finger-tight.

3 Back-hold the valve with one 6-in. adjustable wrench, and tighten the top compression nut with another. Turn the nut only about 1½ turns.

5 Working with Water Piping

Flare Fittings

Compression fittings work on both rigid and soft copper tubing, but flare fittings work only on soft copper. Soft copper is not often used for in-house water piping, except as supply tubes. (Some people use it in rural areas because it's easy to bend and less likely to split when it freezes.) These days, it is more common to use soft copper for underslab water piping and in-house and underground gas piping. You'll find flare fittings with both short and deep-shoulder flare nuts. Deep-shoulder nuts provide greater support; most codes require them. Installation is the same with both types.

The goal with flared fittings is to expand—flare out—the end of the soft copper pipe to match the male end of the fitting. You'll find two tools for flaring soft copper tubing. The most common is a *clamp-type flaring tool*. It consists of a base clamp, which bites onto the pipe, and a flaring vise with a threaded stem and cone-shaped flare head, which slides over the clamp. As you screw the stem downward, you force the head into the end of the pipe, stretching it uniformly. The second tool, a *hammer-type flaring tool*, does the job more quickly but is less popular with homeowners. This tool is a one-

Flare Fittings

Deep-Shoulder Nut

Short-Shoulder Nut

Making Flare-Fitting Connections

Tools and Materials

- Tubing & fittings
- Tubing cutter
- Tubing bender
- Clamp flaring tool

TIME NEEDED: 30 MIN.
- Pipe joint compound
- Groove-joint pliers
- Adjustable wrenches

PLUMBING TIP: *Getting the correct flare is important for a good seal. To get it right, experiment a time or two. You can always cut the nut from the tube and start over.*

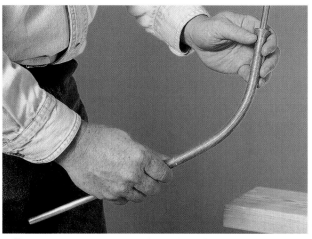

1 Use a spring-type tubing bender to avoid kinking soft copper tubes. These work on both copper and chrome-plated supply tubes.

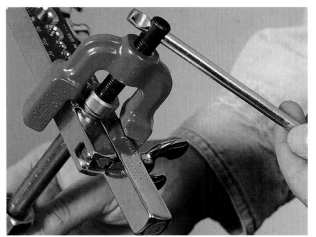

4 Continue threading the tool into the pipe until the rim becomes flared out about 1/16 in. Getting the right flare might take some trial and error.

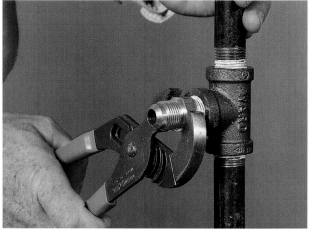

5 Apply a light coating of pipe joint compound to the male end of the flare fitting, and screw it into place.

piece, flared stud. You drive it into the pipe with a hammer. Each pipe size requires a different tool.

Making Flare-Fitting Connections. Cut the copper tubing using a tubing cutter, and bend it into shape. **1.** Slide the flare nut several inches onto the tube, and fasten the base clamp. **2.** To provide enough surface area for the flare, allow the tube to protrude above the clamp roughly ⅛ inch. (The holes in the base are chamfered, or beveled.) Unscrew the stem on the flaring vise enough so that it clears the end of the tubing, and slide the vise over the base clamp. Screw the stem downward until the flaring head enters the tube. **3.** Continue to drive the head into the end of the tube until the tube flares in the tapered jaws of the base clamp. **4.**

The goal is to flare the end of the tube enough for the flare nut to grip it and to provide an adequate surface area for the brass-to-copper mechanical seal. If the flare is too wide, it won't fit inside the nut; if it's too narrow, it won't seal. When you are satisfied with the flare in the tube, turn the male end of the flare fitting into the fitting you want to connect. **5.** Use plumber's joint compound on the flare fitting's threads before connecting it (to a black steel pipe fitting, for example). Now lubricate the other end of the fitting with pipe joint compound. **6.** Tighten the nut over the fitting until it is finger-tight. **7.** Using two wrenches of roughly equal size, one on the nut and one on the fitting, complete tightening the nut. Unlike compression fittings, the tighter you make this joint, the better.

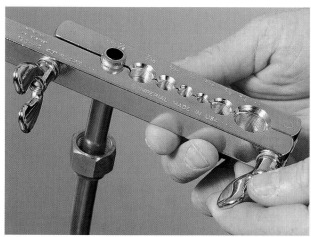

2 With a clamp-type flaring tool, clamp the base onto the pipe with about ⅛ in. of pipe showing above the top surface of the base.

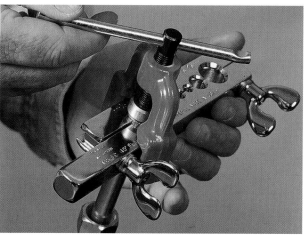

3 Make sure the stem will clear the pipe, and slide the flaring vise on from one end. Thread the head down into the pipe opening.

6 Coat the free end of the flare fitting with pipe joint compound, but avoid getting the material inside the fitting.

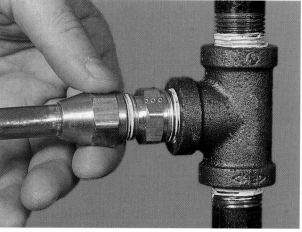

7 Thread the nut onto the fitting until it is finger-tight. Finish tightening using two adjustable wrenches, one to tighten and one to backhold.

5 Working with Water Piping

Using a Hammer-Type Flaring Tool

Begin by sliding the nut onto the pipe. Because these tools can force the pipe slightly out of round below the flare, hold the nut less than an inch below the end of the pipe. If you do this, you won't have to worry that a slightly mis-shapen pipe will hold up the nut. Drive the tool into the end of the pipe with sharp, steady hammer blows. If you notice that one side of the pipe is being flared more than the other, even things out by striking the tool at a slight angle. Stop flaring when you see the outside diameter of the flare approaching the inside diameter of the fitting nut.

Push-Fit Fittings

Push-fit fittings, also known as crimp-ring fittings, are relatively new. They've gained wide acceptance because they are remarkably easy to use and almost never leak. They work on a variety of piping materials and can join dissimilar materials. They are available in a variety of configurations, the most ingenious of which is a braided stainless-steel freeze-repair coupling. To make an in-line repair, such as fixing a freeze rupture, you simply cut out the damaged section and splice in the repair piece, pushing each end fitting over its pipe. (See the photo on the opposite page.) Some codes don't allow push-fit fittings, however, and others allow them only when they remain exposed.

Another advantage to push-fit fittings is that you can rotate them on the pipe after you have installed them. This feature is handy when you are making retrofit installations.

Similar braided stainless-steel tubing is now offered in many forms, including toilet, sink, and clothes-washer supply tubes. You can fit these tubes with compression fittings, friction fittings, and crimp-ring fittings. While all codes allow stainless-steel-encased tubes, many do not allow nylon-reinforced versions.

Natural- and Propane-Gas Piping

Professional plumbers are usually the only ones to install in-house gas piping because, while there's little procedural difference between running water pipe and gas pipe, there certainly is a liability difference. A water leak can be costly, but a gas leak can be fatal.

With that in mind, there are aspects of the job that you should know about, if only to check the plumber's work. The piping between the gas meter and your appliances will be under either high pressure or low pressure. High-pressure systems allow smaller pipes, while low-pressure systems require larger pipes. High-pressure systems also require a pressure reduction regulator at each appliance, while low-pressure systems have a single regulator mounted on the meter.

Three piping materials are allowed for in-house gas piping: black steel, flexible stainless steel, or soft copper in Type L or Type K thickness. Low-pressure systems can use ¾-inch black steel or ¾-inch soft copper, in either thickness. As the ¾-inch feed line reaches each appliance, the branch line serving that appliance will probably be reduced to ½ inch. When only one appliance remains, the feed line may also be reduced to ½ inch. With high-pressure systems, the entire run may be in ⅜- or ½-inch soft copper, with each branch line terminating in a regulator near the appliance. All flare fittings must have deep-shoulder nuts. Codes do not allow rigid copper. Some codes now disallow black steel, so make it a point to ask before any work is done on your system. It is being replaced by a new gas-only piping system made of flexible stainless steel, which is covered by a yellow plastic coating. Manufacturers use flare-type fittings, but each has its own design, and brands are not interchangeable. **Note:** *This new piping, called corrugated stainless-steel tubing (CSST), is not a DIY material.*

Codes require an approved gas shutoff valve within 36 inches of each appliance and a condensation-catching drip leg near each fixed appliance, including the furnace (or boiler) and water heater. All gas-pipe joints must be made with gas-compatible pipe joint compound, or in the case of black steel, gas-compatible pipe-thread sealing

A good use of a push-fit fitting is this freeze-repair kit. Cut out the bad section of pipe, and bridge the gap.

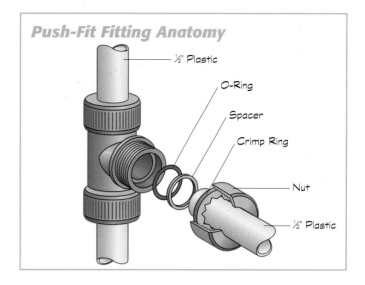

Push-Fit Fitting Anatomy

½" Plastic
O-Ring
Spacer
Crimp Ring
Nut
½" Plastic

How Push-Fit Fittings Work. Push-fit fittings come in two forms. You can remove the nuts from some of them, but others consist of one piece, so you cannot take them apart. If you take apart those with fastening nuts, you'll need to break off the crimping ring and install a new one. Push-fits are not always allowed inside walls.

Some push-fit fittings are brass, while others are plastic. The mechanism for all the fittings is similar. A push-fit consists of a fitting body, neoprene O-ring, and metal crimping ring. To install these fittings, you'll need to round the edge of both pipes with a file or grit cloth, lubricate the end of the pipes with plumber's grease—food-grade or heat-proof—and push the fitting onto the pipes. When the pipe bottoms out in the fitting hub, the O-ring makes the seal and the crimping ring grips the pipe, locking the fitting in place.

tape. And finally, most codes now require braided stainless-steel connectors on movable appliances such as dryers and ranges. Some are available with built-in safety valves. Should the connector ever break, the valve would close immediately.

Testing Gas Lines. After charging the system and bleeding the air from the line, through a union or drip-leg cap, the plumber will test all the joints using an electronic gas detector. You can also test joints if you ever suspect a leak. Use premixed testing soap (available at plumbing supply stores) or a mixture of dish detergent and warm water. Create a thick, soapy mixture by squirting about a tablespoon of liquid soap into a cup and mixing it with warm water. Then, using an inexpensive brush, coat each fitting connection with the mixture. A leaky fitting will produce bubbles. Have a plumber remake any joint where bubbles appear, and then retest it.

Plastic-coated CSST (corrugated stainless-steel tubing) for use with gas comes with a variety of proprietary fittings. This piping is not a do-it-yourself material.

Periodically test all gas fittings using liquid test soap or a mixture of household dish detergent and water. If you find a leak, turn off the gas and call in a plumber.

5 Working with Water Piping

Steel Piping

Galvanized and black steel are the two types of steel pipe used in residential plumbing. You can install galvanized steel as water or gas pipe. However, use black steel, where allowed, only as gas pipe. Don't be tempted to use black steel in your plumbing system. The use of black steel for water is prohibited by many codes because water causes black steel to rust quickly.

Aside from their separate uses, there's little difference in how the two are cut and fitted. You can cut both types of steel with a heavy wheel cutter or a hacksaw and use threaded fittings on both. You can purchase short, threaded nipples at any hardware store, but you'll need to rent threading dies to cut threads on custom lengths. (See the "Rental Tools" photograph, page 23.) While few people use either type today, there is plenty of it in place, and you may need to know something about it to make repairs and additions.

Cutting, Threading, and Fitting Steel Piping

You can use a bench vise to work with steel piping, but a tripod-mounted pipe vise is much better because it gives you greater mobility. You are likely to rent a cutter and threading dies anyway, so you may as well rent a pipe vise too.

To cut a steel pipe, simply measure for length, mark the desired length on the pipe, and grip the pipe in that spot with a steel-pipe wheel cutter. With the cutting wheel centered on your mark, tighten the cutter until the wheel begins to bite into the pipe. Rotate the cutter around the pipe, with the rollers preceding the cutting wheel. **1.** When you no longer feel steady resistance, tighten the handle a full turn or less and rotate again. Repeat this procedure until the wheel slices through the pipe wall all the way around. Once you have cut the pipe, clean any ridges or burrs left on the inside perimeter of the pipe end using a heavy-duty reamer. **2.** You can rent this tool when you get the threader.

To cut new threads to accept fittings on the pipe, keep the pipe in the vise, and coat the end with cutting oil. **3** (inset). Select the appropriately sized threading die, and attach it to the rachet head. You'll notice that one side of the die head has cutting blades, while the other has an open bore. Slide the die onto the end of the pipe, bore-first. **3.** Standing in front of the die, use one hand to press the die onto the pipe while cranking the ratchet handle in a clockwise direction. You should feel the cutting blades grip the pipe—but continue to press against

the die head until the blades cut into the pipe walls. This begins happening after approximately one rotation. Apply cutting oil.

When the cutting blades have begun tracing their way up the pipe, move to a more comfortable position and rotate the die two more turns. At this point, stop and oil the pipe and cutting die thoroughly. Then continue threading in a clockwise direction, re-oiling periodically, until the first threads appear through the front of the cutting blades. At this point, reverse the handle and back the die head off the pipe. **Caution:** be sure to oil the die blades and the pipe threads every few rounds. Without constant lubrication, the pipe may heat up and swell, which can break the cutting blades on the die and ruin the pipe threads.

Cutting, Threading, and Fitting Steel Pipe

Tools and Materials

- Steel pipe & fitting
- Pipe vise
- Pipe cutter & reamer
- Cutting oil

TIME NEEDED: 15 MIN.
- Threading die
- Pipe joint compound
- Pipe wrenches

PLUMBING TIP: If you have trouble starting a threaded fitting, place the pipe against it and slowly rotate the pipe backward. When you feel the threads mesh, begin tightening.

3 Apply oil to the pipe end, and slide the threading die onto the pipe. While applying pressure, slowly crank the tool in a clockwise rotation.

Using Steel Fittings. When threading steel pipe into steel fittings, use plenty of pipe joint compound on the male threads. **4.** In addition to providing lubrication, the compound fills any voids in the threads. When you first attach the fitting, use a pipe wrench to start threading it. **5.** It's a good idea to add a nipple to the other end of the fitting so that you don't damage the threads in the attachment process. As you tighten the pipe into the fitting, always use two pipe wrenches, one to tighten the new pipe, and the other to backhold the fitting. Backholding is especially important when working with older piping that has been in place for many years. (See the photograph at right.) When you are working on the fitting in front of you, it's easy to break the seal on a joint farther down the line. Backholding prevents this.

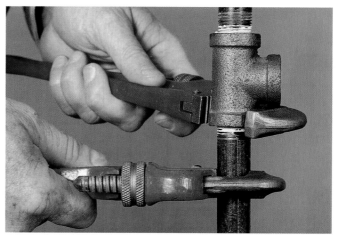

Whenever you work with threaded fittings, make sure you backhold the pipe with a second wrench.

1 Clamp the pipe in the vise, and clamp the wheel cutter onto the pipe. Tighten and rotate the cutter to make the cut.

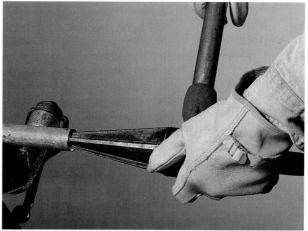

2 Cut any inside burr from the pipe using a heavy-duty reaming tool. Stop when you can no longer feel the burr.

4 Spread pipe joint compound over the newly cut male threads, using the applicator brush that comes with the container.

5 Use a pipe wrench to tighten the fitting onto the pipe. Tighten until it feels snug. Use a nipple in the fitting (right) to preserve the threads.

5 Working with Water Piping

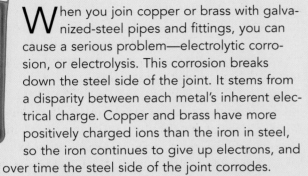

Electrolysis

When you join copper or brass with galvanized-steel pipes and fittings, you can cause a serious problem—electrolytic corrosion, or electrolysis. This corrosion breaks down the steel side of the joint. It stems from a disparity between each metal's inherent electrical charge. Copper and brass have more positively charged ions than the iron in steel, so the iron continues to give up electrons, and over time the steel side of the joint corrodes.

Electrolysis occurs when dissimilar metals come in contact, but the rate of corrosion varies locally. The damage may not reveal itself for decades, or it may take only a year or two. For example, hard water and high humidity accelerate corrosion because they increase conductivity, speeding the ion exchange and increasing the oxidation rate.

When joining dissimilar metals in plumbing, *dielectric unions* are normally required. A dielec-

A dielectric union allows you to join copper and iron without electrolytic corrosion.

tric union differs from a conventional union in that a plastic spacer separates the two halves of the fitting. The threaded adapters are also different. In most cases, one is brass and the other is steel. The plastic spacer prevents direct contact, which prevents corrosion. You install these unions just as you install other unions. To find out whether your home requires dielectric unions, check with the local building department.

Alternative Methods of Joining Steel Pipe. If the thought of all this threading and wrenching wears you down, take heart. You'll often be able to repair or extend steel lines with newer, more friendly materials. In the case of black-steel gas piping, you might be able to cut the line and splice-in soft copper tubing, using couplings that have a flared fitting on one end and male or female threads on the other.

If local codes allow plastic water piping, you might also splice in a length of CPVC plastic pipe, using easy-to-install threaded adapters. In this case, you'd remove the old pipe, thread male adapters in the female steel-pipe threads, and cement a length of plastic pipe into these fittings. But be sure you don't interrupt your home's electrical grounding system. (See "Electrical Grounding and Plastic," page 87.)

Lead Water Piping

In the early 1900s, plumbers used lead water piping. They considered lead a real problem solver because it is malleable and can accommodate moderate seasonal soil movement without creating pipe failure. Plumbers generally installed it in underground water service lines between public mains and private homes. They did not use it for the entire system. Even today, millions of homes still have lead loops in their water service lines.

In such cases, the first loop joins the public water main to the water service pipe, while the second joins the house end of the service pipe with the water meter.

To determine whether your older home—built prior to 1945—has lead service loops, check the service pipe as it enters the house. If you see galvanized-steel joints with visible threads, lead is not present. But if you see a dull gray loop of pipe that joins galvanized piping with bulging, seamless joints, that's lead. These joints are seamless because the plumber repeatedly wiped molten lead over the lead-steel transition. To confirm your suspicions, scrape the pipe surface with a knife. If the scraped area is soft and shiny, it's lead.

As noted in Chapter 1, page 11, the presence of calcified mineral deposits inside the pipes reduces the lead hazard in older systems. Because lead loops are part of the underground service pipe, replacement is costly. And because there's no way of knowing how a buried-service-line repair will go, few plumbers will give you a binding estimate. It will almost always be a cost-plus repair, and it's not something you can do on your own.

It is generally a good idea to replace ancient water service lines, even when lead is not part of the system. These lines are on their last legs and will break sooner or later, usually during the coldest time of the year in the north, when repairs are the most expensive. In addition, many of these old service lines are undersized, constricted by mineral deposits, or both.

Plastic Water Piping

Plastic water pipe, made of chlorinated polyvinyl chloride (CPVC), has been around for years, and when properly installed, has been proved to be durable. Its appeal, of course, is its ease of installation. CPVC piping can be installed with the most common of household tools and by people with almost no previous experience. The problem is that some plumbing codes have not come up to speed on CPVC as a potable water carrier.

Cutting and Fitting CPVC Pipe

CPVC piping comes in a variety of diameters: ⅜, ½, ¾, and 1 inch. The fitting assortment made for other kinds of piping is also available in CPVC. The best way to cut it is using special shears. **1.** These cutters slice the plastic cleanly, leaving almost no ridges or ragged edges. Like the PVC made for drainpipes, CPVC comes with a surface glaze that you must remove before you cement it. If you leave this glaze in place, you increase the chances of a leak. The best remover is a solvent-primer, which comes in containers with lid-mounted applicators. Dab primer on the pipe area to be cemented. **2.** Do the same to the inner surfaces of the fitting hubs. Allow the primer to evaporate before making the joint. You can also cut the glaze by scuffing the final 1 inch of the pipe and the inner surfaces of each fitting hub.

After you remove the surface glaze, test-fit the joints you want to make. Make alignment marks on the fitting and the pipe using a pencil or marker. **3.** You'll use

Cutting and Fitting CPVC Pipe

Tools and Materials

- Pipe-cutting shears
- CPVC pipe & fittings
- CPVC solvent primer ■ Pencil
- CPVC solvent cement ■ Measuring tape

TIME NEEDED: 20–30 MIN.

PLUMBING TIP: Make register marks on the tubing and fittings when you test-fit the assembly so you can tell how much to rotate the parts when you cement them together.

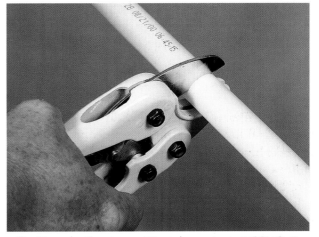

1 Use plastic-pipe-cutting shears to cut CPVC. Be sure to allow for the depth of the fitting hub. This tool makes the cleanest possible cut.

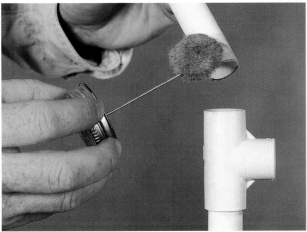

2 Apply primer to the pipe ends and fitting hubs. Primer removes the surface glaze and reduces leaks. Use sandpaper if you don't have primer.

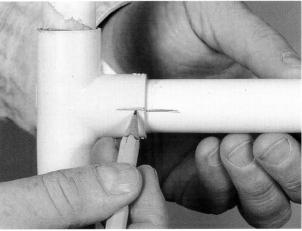

3 Test-fit the pipe and fittings. Before you disassemble the pipe and cement it, mark the final alignment with a pencil.

5 Working with Water Piping

Sequence continues on next page

Continued from previous page

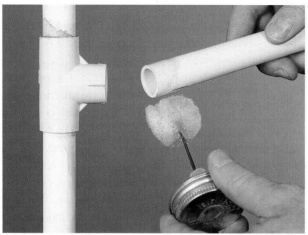

4 Apply CPVC solvent cement to the pipe and fitting hub, and insert the pipe about one-quarter turn out of alignment.

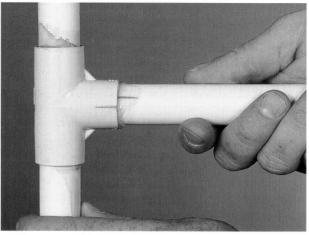

5 Rotate the pipe one-quarter turn after inserting it to line up the pencil marks. This spreads the cement and accelerates curing.

these marks later to line up the pipes and fittings in exactly the same positions when you rotate the parts as you put them together. Apply a thin but even coating of joint solvent cement inside the hub of the fitting and to the outside of the pipe, using the container's applicator. **4.** Insert the pipe into the fitting, and rotate it one-quarter turn, using the alignment marks you made previously as a guide. **5.** Rotating the pipe or fitting helps fill any voids in the cement and creates friction, which serves to accelerate the chemical bonding slightly. As with PVC drainpipe, once you have cemented the joint you'll have very little time to change your mind. If you find that you've made a mistake, pull the joint apart immediately. Then you can apply new solvent cement and remake the joint.

CPVC versus Copper

Is CPVC plastic as good as copper for common residential plumbing applications? In most cases, yes. But this is true only if it is not used underground or under concrete, if it has no chance to freeze, and when the installation is made according to manufacturer's specifications and is code-worthy. In some cases—for example, in cabins and second homes where water can stand long enough to corrode copper—plastic may actually be the best choice.

Other Plastic Pipe

Polybutylene pipe was used a good deal in the 1970s and '80s, but it is no longer on the market. There is plenty of it still in place, however. If you come across this flexible gray plastic pipe in a residential water system, you can make repairs using copper or CPVC and transition fittings.

Another plastic piping material, cross-linked polyethylene (PEX), is made in several colors, including red, blue, brownish-red, and white. It is used extensively in mobile and modular homes and in some site-built homes, though most local codes don't yet allow it for potable water. It is a high-quality material that is used extensively in the Southwest, where acidic water and soil eat through copper pipes. It is also used almost exclusively in radiant-floor applications, in which hot water is run through concrete floor slabs to warm the floor and heat the home. You'll most often find it in wholesale plumbing supply stores.

You can join PEX pipes using crimp-ring fittings, but codes allow these fittings only in exposed installations. For code-worthy in-wall installations, you'll need barbed fittings made especially for PEX tubing. Unfortunately, these fittings are proprietary and require special tools not readily available to homeowners.

Electrical Grounding and Plastic. Few homeowners understand the relationship between a home's plumbing and electrical systems. In many jurisdictions, the electrical panel is grounded through metallic water piping. Because the metallic piping inside the house connects to a metallic water service pipe that is buried underground, most codes require that the electrical system use this piping for all or part of its path to ground.

If you cut out a section of cold-water trunk line and splice a length of plastic piping in its place, there's a good chance that you'll interrupt this path to ground. That's a dangerous situation. If you decide to splice plastic into a cold-water trunk line, install a heavy grounding conductor across the span. This jumper wire should be the same size as the service panel's existing grounding wire, usually 6 gauge. Attach the wire to the metallic pipes using code-approved grounding clamps, one on each side of the splice. You won't need a jumper where the grounding wire connects directly to the water service pipe on the street side of the meter.

Insulating Water Pipes

You can do little that improves a water-piping job as much as pipe insulation. Inexpensive and easy to install, pipe insulation dampens much of the noise of running water and limits freezing. It also eliminates condensation in summer and reduces energy costs year-round in two ways. First, it reduces the amount of heat lost through the pipe walls. Second, because hot or cold water temperatures are maintained longer in their respective lines, you'll spend less time—and water—running the tap, waiting for it to warm up or cool down.

Pipe insulation comes in several forms. The easiest one to install is made of foam rubber. It comes in a variety of lengths and diameters, and is partially split along one side. When you install it on new piping, you slide it directly onto each new length, leaving the split intact. On existing installations, open the seam, slip the insulation over the pipe, and seal the joint with duct tape or plastic sealing tape. (See the photograph below.)

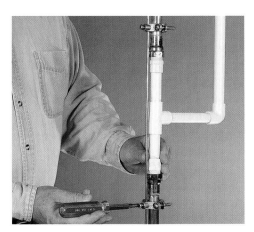

When splicing plastic into copper piping, you may need to install a copper jumper wire to maintain an unbroken ground for the home's wiring system.

To insulate existing pipes using foam insulation, open the seam and tape the insulation in place.

PEX pipe uses threaded barbed adapters to connect to valves. Install the fitting, and slide the pipe onto the barb.

To lock the PEX pipe onto a barbed fitting, plumbers use a proprietary crimp-ring tool.

5 Working with Water Piping

In-Line Water-Control Valves

Shutoff valves, or stops, for water piping have a variety of control mechanisms. Each mechanism type has its advantages and disadvantages, and understanding those pluses and minuses will help you decide where to use each one. For example, some valve mechanisms restrict flow by as much as 50 percent. This is a real concern in certain situations. The main house valve, for instance, should not restrict flow, because a reduction there could affect the performance of the entire system. In contrast, the small-bore compression valves under sinks have little effect because the faucets they serve are flow-restricting in the first place.

Gate Valves

Gate valves, along with some ball valves, allow an unrestricted flow of water. As the name implies, the control mechanism is an internal gate. Turn the handle to the left, and the gate rises out of its seat. Turn it to the right, and the gate moves downward, slicing off the flow. The sliding gate, which operates vertically, makes gate valves larger than other valves.

Like most full-bore water valves, gate valves are not meant to be used frequently. They can't survive the wear and tear that a faucet endures on a daily basis. If the gate valve has a serious nemesis, it's hard water. Calcified minerals can encrust the mechanism, rendering it inoperable. Forcing the valve can break the stem from the gate. Gate valves can be serviced but not always effectively. In most cases, replacement is the best option.

Because of their full-flow designs, gate valves are used close to the beginning of the water piping system, usually near the meter or pressure tank or in the cold-water inlet line of the water heater.

Ball Valves

Ball valves are available in flow-reducing and larger full-flow versions. The mechanism in these valves is a hollow nylon or metal ball that pivots in the valve body. Opposing sides of the ball are open. When these openings are oriented with the flow, water passes through the ball. When you rotate the valve against the flow, the closed sides of the ball stop the water. Ball valves are easy to use because it takes only one-quarter turn of the handle to open or close them. In addition, they are generally more durable than gate valves. They're certainly less vulnerable to calcification. Ball valves can be used anywhere a gate valve might be used, but they're also appropriate in frequent-use situations.

Globe Valves

Globe valves have been the standard in the industry for years and are used most often in full-size, in-line piping, although they can restrict flow by nearly 50 percent. Some newer designs—with slightly larger bodies—are less restrictive.

Globe valves are popular for several reasons. To begin with, they are the least expensive types of valve. They are small and compact, and because they use a compression mechanism, you can service them easily and inexpensively. All it takes is a 5¢ washer. Unlike ball valves, however, globe valves do not withstand frequent operation. While the valve seat and mechanism hold up well enough, the graphite stem packing in many models leaks after each use. A half-turn of the packing nut stops the leak, but it's a nuisance. Some models now have O-ring packing and nylon bonnet-nut seals, which correct the problem.

Globe valves, in ½- and ¾-inch diameters, are common in residential plumbing. They do not work well as the first valves in the system, but they work in branch

In-Line Valves

A gate valve has an internal wedge that controls water flow.

A ball valve uses a hollow ball at its core to control water flow.

A compression valve uses a threaded stem and rubber washer.

lines. Although not the best idea because they restrict flow, many people install them above water heaters in the cold-water inlet line. Check local codes, however.

Stop-and-Waste Valves

Stop-and-waste valves are usually globe valves that have a drain screw on the downstream side of the shutoff mechanism. This screw allows you to drain water from the downstream piping after you have shut off the valve. Stop-and-waste valves are useful for pipes that you need to shut down during winter, such as dedicated lines serving outdoor faucets, sprinklers, outbuildings, and the like. If you are draining an entire system, such as a summer home or cabin, however, a hose bibcock drain is the best choice. (See "Hose Bibcocks," page 90.)

Fixture Stops

Fixture stops, or shutoffs, come in two types: compression and ball-valve. Compression stops are small brass valves, usually chrome plated, that join permanent water piping to supply tubes. These stops have a compression-type shutoff mechanism, but they are called compression stops because compression fittings join them to piping. Valves that join copper pipes to copper supply tubes have two compression fittings, one large and one small. Those joining threaded iron pipe to supply tubes have ½-inch female threads at the lower end. The supply-tube connection has a compression fitting.

Ball-valve stops use a nylon ball mechanism instead of a compression-type one to control water. These stops cost a little more, but they're more durable.

The most common compression and ball-valve stops reduce in size from ⅝ inch outside diameter (O.D.) to ⅜ inch O.D., although other sizes are available. The valves come in straight (in-line) and angled (90-degree L-shape) configurations. You'll find straight stops when the water piping enters the room or cabinet through the floor and angle stops when it enters through the wall.

All codes require stops under toilets, and many now require them under sinks as well. Required or not, fixture stops are a good idea.

Dual Stops. Dual stops are merely compression stops with two outlet ports. You'd use a dual stop to join a kitchen's hot-water supply line to the kitchen faucet and a dishwasher, for example. Dual stops are available with one or two control mechanisms. A two-stop valve, which costs more, allows you to work on the dishwasher without shutting off the faucet and vise versa.

Confusing Terminology

The term "compression" has two meanings in plumbing. Any fitting that uses a tapered brass or nylon ring to make its seal is a *compression fitting*. These include water fittings and valves, as well as plastic tube traps and under-sink waste kits. Confusion arises when you talk about shutoff valves, however. People often call valves that have similar compression-style connectors *compression valves*. But the term compression also describes a shutoff mechanism in which a stem-fitted washer makes the seal when it is compressed against a raised seat. By this definition, globe valves, hose bibcocks, and many traditional sink faucets are compression valves, although they may or may not be joined to piping by compression fittings.

5 Working with Water Piping

A stop-and-waste valve is drained by unscrewing a threaded cap.

A ball-valve fixture stop is the most reliable form of shutoff valve.

A dual stop valve splits one water line (usually hot) into two.

Utility Faucet Valves

Some valves are intended to control water for utility purposes (to a yard hose, for example) or for occasionally draining appliances like water heaters.

Hose Bibcocks

A hose bibcock is a drain valve with external hose threads on its spout. While it may be connected to its piping via male or female threads or through a compression fitting, a hose bibcock's identifying feature is its hose threads, which are larger and coarser than iron-pipe threads. You can use hose bibcocks to join permanent water piping to clothes-washer hoses and garden hoses. Because you must occasionally drain water heaters and boilers, you'll also find hose bibcocks used as drain fittings for these appliances. For this reason, these valves are sometimes called boiler drains.

Most hose bibcocks are brass and use a compression mechanism for controlling water. A hose bibcock used as an outdoor sillcock (a wall-mounted outdoor faucet) usually has female threads and a brass flange that is predrilled to accept screws. In this case, a threaded water pipe extends through the exterior wall about ½ inch, and the valve is threaded onto the pipe. The flange is then screwed to the exterior wall.

Freeze-Proof Sillcocks

In areas with cold winter weather, sillcocks need some form of freeze protection. Traditionally, this has meant a two-valve assembly. You installed a hose bibcock valve outside, on the exterior wall, and an in-line valve just inside the house, in the joist space. When it began to get

---

Hose Bibcocks

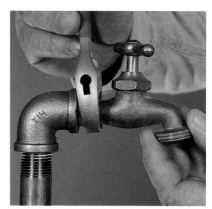

Male threads on some hose bibcocks allow you to attach the faucets to elbows and other appropriate fittings.

Female threads on other hose bibcocks allow you to thread the units onto supply pipes.

> ### SMART TIP
>
> #### Preventing Laundry-Room Water Hammer
>
> Hose bibcocks that have male threads are usually connected to female fittings mounted on a laundry room wall. When the system piping is copper, the female fittings should be 90-degree drop-eared elbows that have predrilled side tabs (ears), which allow the fitting to be anchored with screws. Because solenoid valves in washing machines shut off abruptly, causing the back-shock known as water hammer, it's imperative to have anchored fittings here. (See "Water Hammer Arrestors," page 240.)

---

cold, the homeowner dutifully shut off the inside valve and drained the outside valve.

While this setup works well enough, it has two disadvantages. First, the faucet can't be used during the winter months. Second, homeowners are generally not good at routine maintenance like this. They either don't know that the second valve exists, don't know what it's for, or don't get around to draining the line before the first hard freeze occurs.

First Freeze-Proofing Attempts. The freeze-proof sillcock, introduced more than 30 years ago, was an attempt to correct the freezing problem, with generally good results. The trick was to move the stop mechanism well inside the house, where it could stay warm, while maintaining the handle and spout outside, where you could use them year-round. Those first freeze-proof sillcocks had a long stem that extended through an oversize tube, or drain chamber. Because the washer and seat operated in a warm environment and any water left in the chamber drained out when you shut off the faucet, it was a truly all-weather faucet.

These faucets would have been perfect but for one flaw: they only drained when the hose was removed. An attached hose created an air lock, which held water in

Freeze-Proof Sillcocks

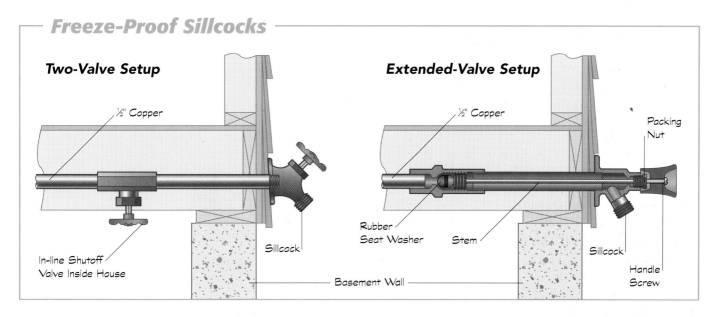

Two-Valve Setup

½" Copper

In-line Shutoff Valve Inside House

Sillcock

Basement Wall

Extended-Valve Setup

½" Copper

Packing Nut

Rubber Seat Washer

Stem

Sillcock

Handle Screw

the chamber. This water then froze and ruptured the sillcock. Because the freeze occurred in the chamber, on the downstream side of the stop mechanism, the leak only appeared when the sillcock was used again, usually the following spring. By then, of course, the hose had been stored away for months and the homeowner had forgotten last fall's early cold snap. Because an attached hose was about the only way to rupture a freeze-proof sillcock—and an attached hose voids the warranty—these sillcocks have been the source of a good many disputes between homeowner and plumber.

Modern Solution. Most new freeze-proof sillcocks have a vacuum breaker threaded onto the spout to solve the hose-related freeze problem and prevent back siphonage. The vacuum breaker releases the air lock created by the attached hose and drains the chamber. Some new so-called freeze-proof sillcocks include a top-mounted back-flow preventer instead of a vacuum breaker. These prevent contaminating backflows, but they're not always freeze-proof with a hose attached. Nevertheless, codes now require sillcocks with either backflow preventers or vacuum breakers. When installing a freeze-proof sillcock, always prop up the rear of the chamber so that water can drain through the spout.

Freeze-proof sillcocks come in lengths ranging from 6 to 36 inches. Choose a length that places the stop a foot or so inside the house. If you are installing a sillcock in a cantilevered floor or wall, it will need to be longer, of course, as will those you install through brick or stone facades. While you usually install sillcocks through the band joist of a home, you can also use them on houses that are built on concrete slabs. In these cases, an interior wall houses the drain chamber, keeping it reasonably warm.

Freeze-Proof Solutions

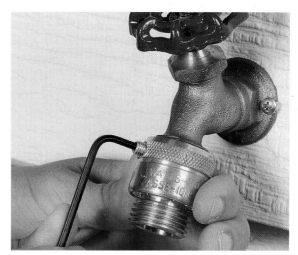

Aftermarket vacuum breakers can be installed on existing sillcocks.

Press plumber's putty around the freeze-proof sillcock mounting flange to seal the opening.

5

Working with Water Piping

Repairing a Freeze-Proof Sillcock

Tools and Materials

- Replacement washer *TIME NEEDED: 20 MIN.*
- Screwdriver
- Adjustable wrench

PLUMBING TIP: *To keep from damaging a sillcock's rubber washer, don't overtighten when shutting it off.*

1 Remove the handle, and loosen the bonnet nut to release the long faucet stem. Look for an arrow that shows turning direction.

2 Remove the stem, and replace the neoprene rubber washer. Be sure to coat the new washer with heat-proof grease before installing it.

3 Thread the stem back into the sillcock with the handle in place but not screwed on. Remove the handle, and tighten the bonnet nut.

Repairing Freeze-Proof Sillcocks. There's little difference between repairing sillcocks and repairing traditional stem-and-seat faucets. You simply remove the stem and replace the washer or rubber stopper. **1–3.** The only variant is that the bonnet nuts on some sillcocks have left-hand threads, which means that you'll need to turn the nut clockwise to remove it. Look for a rotation arrow stamped into the handle or bonnet nut.

Freeze-Proof Yard Hydrants

Freeze-proof yard hydrants are the rural equivalents of freeze-proof sillcocks. Instead of being mounted through a house wall, they are buried underground, with only a short length of riser and the handle and spout showing aboveground. People typically use hydrants for water gardens, remote buildings, and livestock tanks.

Like freeze-proof sillcocks, these hydrants have a long stem and a drain chamber. But instead of draining unneeded water through the spout, hydrants drain downward, into a drainage pit at the base of the hydrant near the shutoff mechanism. When you raise the on-off lever, it lifts the long stem and the rubber stopper attached to it. This allows water to fill the riser and flow from the spout. When you lower the lever, the stem forces the stopper back into its seat, blocking the flow. The water left in the riser then drains through a small opening just above the stop mechanism; this keeps the riser from freezing. A gravel pit at the bottom of the trench stores the water until the surrounding soil can absorb it. Because you bury the stop mechanism and drain fitting below frost level—typically 3 to 6 feet deep, you can use the hydrant year-round.

Freeze-Proof Yard Hydrant

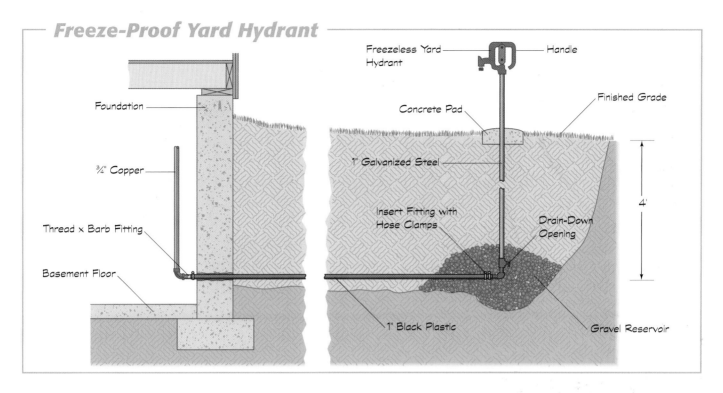

Foundation

¾" Copper

Thread x Barb Fitting

Basement Floor

Freezeless Yard Hydrant — Handle

Concrete Pad

Finished Grade

1" Galvanized Steel

Insert Fitting with Hose Clamps

Drain-Down Opening

4'

1" Black Plastic

Gravel Reservoir

Repairing a Hydrant. To repair a freeze-proof yard hydrant, shut off the water supply, thread the handle-and-spout assembly counterclockwise, and lift the assembly and stem from the riser. Remove the worn stopper from the stem, and install a new one. When you thread the handle-and-spout assembly off or on, be sure to backhold the riser with a second wrench. Backholding keeps you from damaging the piping connection at the bottom of the trench.

Regulators & Safety Valves

Sometimes you need to control the direction of water flow in a drainage or water-supply system so that contaminated water doesn't back up into the house or mix with potable water. That's where regulators like vacuum breakers and check valves come in.

Safety valves are important in controlling high-pressure systems like water heaters. If you didn't have a safety relief valve in such situations, dangerous explosions could easily occur.

Vacuum Breakers

As the name implies, vacuum breakers prevent air locks and back-siphoning of water in a piping system. As noted previously, modern sillcocks have a vacuum breaker that releases water held in the drain chamber. Vacuum breakers have an internal, spring-loaded diaphragm that is able to sense back-pressure. When

back-pressure occurs, the diaphragm opens, venting the airlock through a series of perimeter openings.

While sillcocks and toilets have vacuum breakers or built-in backflow preventers, you can also get add-on devices. (See the photographs on page 91 and below.) Some models fit the hose threads on outdoor faucets and laundry sinks, and others fit faucet aerator threads. When buying a toilet fill-valve or ballcock, make sure that it has built-in backflow protection. And if your current sillcock or hydrant doesn't have a vacuum breaker, buy an add-on breaker and install it. It's worthwhile protection for just a few dollars.

Laundry sink faucets *also have hose threads. If you use a hose, install a vacuum breaker.*

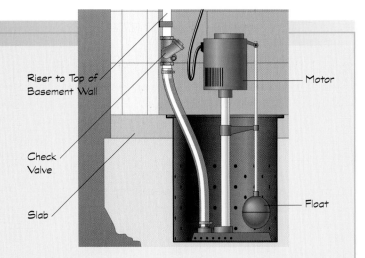

SMART TIP

Checking a Sump Pump

The most frequent use of check valves in drainage systems is in sump-pump installations. Without a check valve, the last bit of water pumped up the riser would fall back into the pit when the pump shuts off. This fallback water could be enough to activate the pump's float. Without a check valve to hold this quantity of water in the riser pipe, the pump would cycle on and off continuously, ruining the motor. Listen to the pump through a complete cycle. The easiest valves to replace are those with hose clamp connections, like those on a no-hub fitting. Simply loosen the clamps and pull the old valve out. Install a new valve in similar fashion.

If you find a check valve with threaded connections, you may need to cut the pipe. With plastic pipe, saw through it and thread a new valve in place. Then rejoin the pipe with a no-hub coupling. This coupling will provide easy access next time. If you hear the pump kick on soon after it has stopped running, suspect a leaky check valve.

Check Valves

Check valves keep water from flowing backward through a line. They are available for both water and drainage piping. A check valve has a weighted flapper that allows water to flow in only one direction. Should the flow ever reverse, the flapper would fall against its seat and check the flow.

In drainage piping installations, full-size check valves can keep the city sewer main from backing into your home through your sewer service line.

In water-supply installations, check valves keep hot and cold water from cross-migrating through faucets. If you have a faucet that runs hot when you first turn the cold water on, cross-migration is the likely problem, and a check valve the probable solution.

Pressure-Reduction Valves

City water mains do not all have the same pressure. Those nearest water towers or pumping stations have greater pressure than those miles away, at the end of the line. It's not unusual for homes near a pumping station to have static pressures averaging 120 pounds per

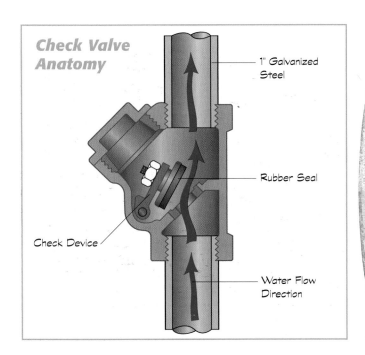

Check Valve Anatomy

- 1" Galvanized Steel
- Rubber Seal
- Check Device
- Water Flow Direction

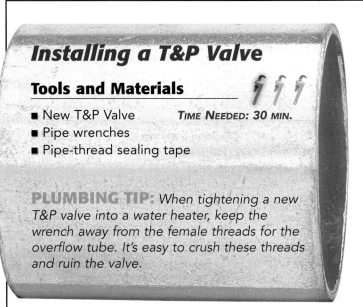

Installing a T&P Valve

Tools and Materials

- New T&P Valve   TIME NEEDED: 30 MIN.
- Pipe wrenches
- Pipe-thread sealing tape

PLUMBING TIP: When tightening a new T&P valve into a water heater, keep the wrench away from the female threads for the overflow tube. It's easy to crush these threads and ruin the valve.

SMART TIP

Reducing High Pressure Saves Water

Although the most important consideration in installing a pressure-reduction valve is to reduce excessively high, damaging water pressure, a hidden benefit in installing one is water savings. A faucet that runs for ten minutes at 100 psi delivers 45 gallons of water. At 50 psi, that volume is cut to 30 gallons. You'll still have plenty of water for your needs—without wasting it—at reasonably strong pressure.

Pressure-reduction valves are adjustable. Thread the adjustment screw up or down, then tighten the locknut.

square inch (psi). This is more pressure than fixtures and appliances can manage. Too much pressure causes water-heater relief valves to leak, toilets to keep running, and faucets to pulse and pound when turned on and off.

The only solution to high pressure is a mechanical pressure-reduction valve. These devices come in two forms. Some have a set pressure, while others can be adjusted through a modest range of settings. Pressure-reduction valves have threaded female ports and are usually installed in-line, just before the water meter. If you suspect unreasonably high pressure, ask a local plumber or the utility company to run a pressure test. Forty to 60 psi is ideal. Anything above 70 to 80 psi probably deserves to be cut back.

Temperature-and-Pressure-Relief Valves

Temperature-and-pressure-relief (often called T&P) valves release water from a water heater or boiler when the temperature and pressure in the heater become dangerously high. Temperature and pressure build when a thermostat sticks and won't shut off. This is a fairly common occurrence with potentially tragic consequences. People die from water-heater explosions every year, and defective or missing relief valves are almost always a factor.

When you replace a water heater, always install a new T&P valve. **1–2.** And make sure that the preset release pressure of the valve is less than the pressure rating of the heater. Whatever you do, don't be tempted to fill the relief hole with an iron plug, even temporarily.

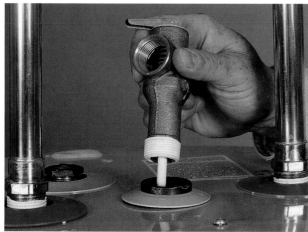

1 Wrap pipe-thread sealing tape around the threads of the new T&P valve, and tighten the valve into the heater.

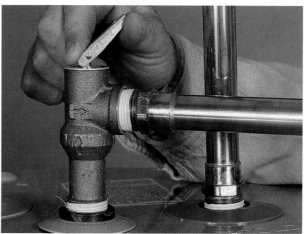

2 To test the T&P valve after installation, lift the release lever until water shoots through the overflow tube.

CHAPTER 6

Toilet Repairs & Installations

**W**ater-flush toilets are miracles of simplicity. In fact, few devices accomplish as much with so few parts. They're so simply built that you can completely overhaul one in about an hour, for about $20 in parts. The latest generation of water-savers may be a little more complicated, but repairing them is work you can still do.

Toilet Fundamentals

Water-powered toilets come in two forms, gravity-flow and pressure-assisted models. Gravity-flow toilets, as the name implies, use only the force of gravity to flush wastewater. Pressure-assisted models use the extra power of compressed air to push water more forcefully. The basic waste-removal system is similar in both types. Water flows into the tank via the fill valve. When you flush the toilet, the water flows through the flush valve, into and through the bowl, and through the trap, taking waste with it. Knowing this sequence will later help you match symptoms with solutions.

How Gravity-Flow Toilets Work

When you press down on the flush handle, its lever lifts a chain or lift wire attached to a flapper or tank ball. (Flappers have chains; tank balls have lift wires.) The chain or wire lifts the flapper or ball from its flush-valve seat, which allows water to escape through the valve.

Both flappers and tank balls are hollow. Some are open at the bottom, and some are closed, but both drain water and trap air, making them temporarily buoyant when you push down on the handle. Without this buoyancy, the flapper or ball would sink immediately, so you'd need to hold the flush lever down until the tank was empty.

As the flushing water recedes, the flapper or ball floats downward until it rests in the flush-valve seat and stops up the opening. Once seated, it is flooded with water and held down by the weight of the water rising above it.

After passing through the flush valve, the water from the tank travels in two directions. Much of it shoots through the siphon jet, the small opening across from the trap outlet. The rest flows to the hollow rim around the top of the bowl, where it spills through slanted holes in the underside of the rim.

The water rushing in through the siphon jet overflows the trap, priming it. Once primed, the trap siphons all the water it can over its weir, or crown, stopping only when there's not enough water in the bowl to sustain the siphon. At this point, all water on the house side of the trap slides back into the bowl.

Because the rim holes are slanted, the water entering the bowl through the rim travels diagonally around the bowl. This diagonal pattern scours the sides of the bowl, but it also sends the water over the trap in a spiraling motion, which improves the efficiency of the flush.

As the bowl empties, new water enters the tank through the ballcock or fill valve. (All ballcocks are fill valves, but not all fill valves are ballcocks. The term "ballcock" applies only to traditional fill valves, which have ball floats on the end of a pivoting arm. Newer fill valves use a vertically mounted float cup.) This flow begins the moment you flush the toilet. Most of the water entering the tank does so through a tube that terminates near the bottom of the tank. Delivering the water to the bottom of the tank provides a measure of noise control. The sound is muffled as soon as the water in the tank rises above the end of the tube. At the same time, a small stream of water is diverted into the flush valve overflow tube—via a ⅛-inch-diameter fill tube—and falls directly into the bowl's rim. This stream restores the water in the bowl to its maximum level. As soon as the tank fills, the float shuts off the fill valve, and the toilet is ready for another flush.

Water-Saving Toilets

Responding to legislation enacted several years ago, manufacturers reduced the volume of water needed to flush a toilet efficiently. Ironically, the very first toilets had small flush tanks, holding only about 3 gallons. These toilets worked because the tanks were mounted on the wall, high above the bowl. Elevating water in a column increases its downward force—an effect known as head pressure. The more pressure generated for the flush, the less water you need. The reverse is also true, so when tanks were moved down the wall and mounted on or just above the bowl, manufacturers increased the size of the tanks to as much as 8 gallons. This was clearly more volume than was needed, and the industry eventually settled on 5 gallons.

During the late 1960s and into the '70s, fresh water came to be recognized as a limited resource, and tank size was reduced again, to 3.5 gallons.

Water-Savers Are the Law. In the late 1970s, a number of Scandinavian countries began using—and mandating—super-low-flow toilets, which flushed with an amazingly skimpy 1.6 gallons of water. Before long, these toilets appeared at trade shows here in the United States, and manufacturers began experimenting with low-flow toilets, trying to improve performance. Eventually, the U.S. enacted a national standard that limits to 1.6 gallons per flush (gpf) the water used by residential toilets made in this country after January 1, 1994.

Do low-flow toilets work as well as 3.5-gpf ones? The early models certainly didn't. From the start, manufacturers offered two distinctly different low-flow toilets; a gravity-flow model and a pressure-assisted model. The gravity-flow models were like traditional toilets but with minor changes all around, including new fill valves and flush valves. Engi-

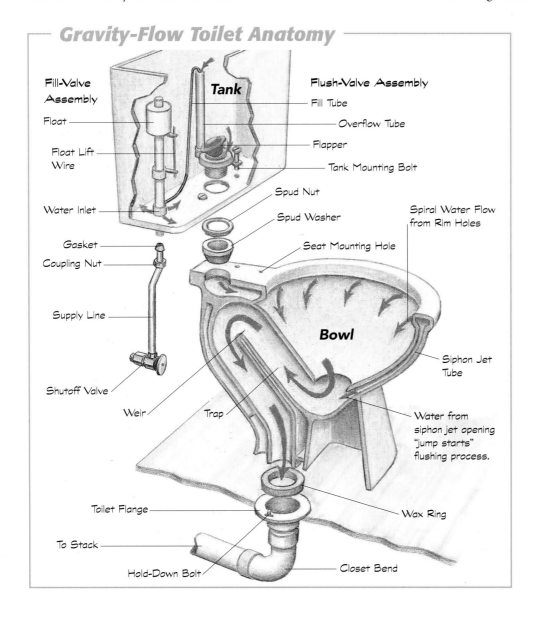

Gravity-Flow Toilet Anatomy

Fill-Valve Assembly
- Float
- Float Lift Wire
- Water Inlet
- Gasket
- Coupling Nut
- Supply Line
- Shutoff Valve
- Weir
- Trap
- Toilet Flange
- To Stack
- Hold-Down Bolt

Tank

Flush-Valve Assembly
- Fill Tube
- Overflow Tube
- Flapper
- Tank Mounting Bolt
- Spud Nut
- Spud Washer
- Seat Mounting Hole
- Spiral Water Flow from Rim Holes
- Siphon Jet Tube
- Water from siphon jet opening "jump starts" flushing process.
- Wax Ring
- Closet Bend

Bowl

Water Savers

1.6-Gallon Gravity-Flow Toilet

Pressure-Assisted Toilet

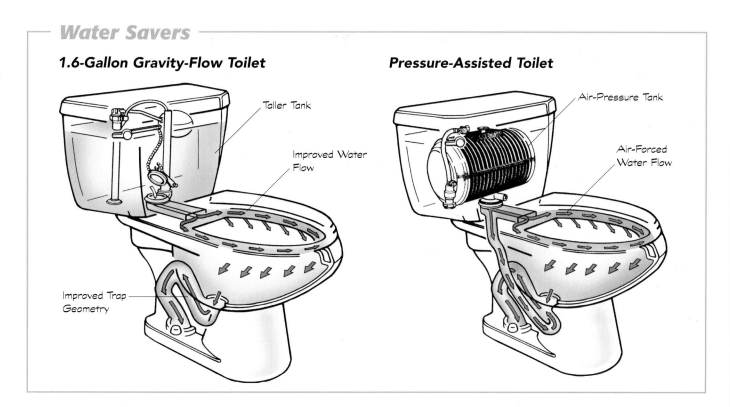

Taller Tank

Improved Water Flow

Improved Trap Geometry

Air-Pressure Tank

Air-Forced Water Flow

neers reduced trap geometry, along with water spots—the surface area of the bowl water—and outlet diameters to cut down the flow of water. These early water misers were so sluggish that they often needed additional flushes to clear and clean the bowl, and clogs were common. With steady engineering refinements, however, gravity-flow toilets now work reasonably well and are a good choice for most households.

Pressure-Assisted Toilets. In general, pressure-assisted toilets work better than gravity models. These toilets use incoming water to compress air in a chamber inside the tank. (A water pressure of at least 20 pounds per square inch is required.) Flushing releases this compressed air in a burst, forcing water to prime the trap almost instantly. Air assist allows the tank to operate with less water, making more water available for the bowl. More water in the bowl means a larger water spot and a cleaner bowl. And finally, the tank-within-a-tank construction completely eliminates tank sweat caused by condensation during hot, humid weather.

With these advantages, you'd think everyone would want a pressure-assisted toilet, but that hasn't been the case. The most common complaints are that they're too noisy and too complicated. Starting each flush with a burst of compressed air does make them noisy, and they're certainly less familiar. Most people would recognize the tank components in a traditional toilet, but lift the lid on a pressure-assisted unit, and all you'll see is a sealed plastic drum, a water-inlet mechanism, a hose,

and a flush cartridge. Most manufacturers use almost identical tank components, all made by a single supplier. It's easy to repair and replace these parts, but not all hardware stores carry them. Plumbing wholesalers do, but they don't often sell to non-plumbers. Plumbers may sell the parts, but they'd rather that you pay for installation as well.

SMART TIP

Which Toilet to Buy?

If you need a new toilet, which toilet should you buy: a pressure-assisted model or a gravity-flow unit? Price is one consideration. Pressure-assisted toilets are more expensive than conventional models, upwards of $150. Past experience and the condition of your existing plumbing is another consideration. If your old toilet clogged frequently or you have a system that is more than 50 years old, a pressure-assisted unit is probably your best bet. If you've had few clogs with your old toilet, you'll likely get along fine with a 1.6-gpf gravity-flow toilet, but buy a good, moderately priced one and not a bargain-basement model. For the best performance, look for a trap diameter on the large side: they range from 1⅝ to 2 inches.

Trouble-Shooting Gravity-Flow Toilets

Now that you know how traditional gravity-flow toilets are supposed to work, it's time to learn how and why they may not work and what to do when they don't. Keep in mind that poorly maintained toilets may display more than one symptom.

Problem 1: Slow Toilet

Your toilet seems sluggish. It once flushed vigorously, but now the water seems to move slowly through its cycle, often rising high in the bowl before passing through the trap. You also notice large bubbles rising out of the trap during the flush. Sometimes the bowl even seems to double flush.

These are classic symptoms of a partially blocked trap. An obstruction, such as a toy, comb, cotton swab, and the like, has made its way to the top of the trap and lodged in the opening. Paper then begins to accumulate on the obstruction, further closing the opening. In many cases, enough of the trap remains open to keep the toilet working, but in time, partial clogs become complete clogs.

To clear a partial blockage, start with a toilet plunger, forcing the cup forward and pulling it back with equal pressure. If a plunger doesn't clear the clog, try a closet auger. If the closet auger doesn't do it, bail out the bowl with a paper cup or other small container, and place a pocket mirror in the outlet. Shine a flashlight onto the mirror, bouncing light to the top of the trap. The mirror should allow you to see the obstruction. When you know exactly what and where it is, you should be able to

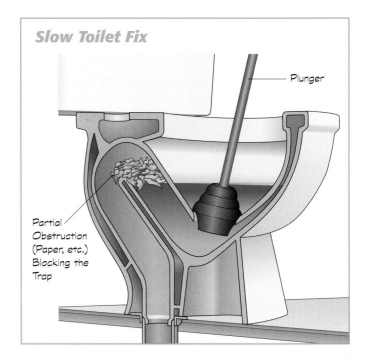

Slow Toilet Fix

Plunger

Partial Obstruction (Paper, etc.) Blocking the Trap

pull the obstruction into the bowl by using a piece of wire. In rare cases, you may need to remove the toilet and work from the other side. (For more on clearing clogs, see Chapter 9, "Clearing Drainpipes," starting on page 206.)

Problem 2: Dirty Toilet

The toilet does not appear clogged, because water doesn't rise unusually high in the bowl, but it flushes sluggishly, and the bowl doesn't stay clean for long.

These symptoms suggest that the toilet bowl's rim holes—and possibly the siphon jet hole—are clogged

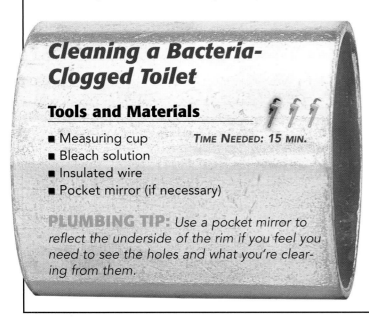

Cleaning a Bacteria-Clogged Toilet

Tools and Materials

TIME NEEDED: 15 MIN.

- Measuring cup
- Bleach solution
- Insulated wire
- Pocket mirror (if necessary)

PLUMBING TIP: *Use a pocket mirror to reflect the underside of the rim if you feel you need to see the holes and what you're clearing from them.*

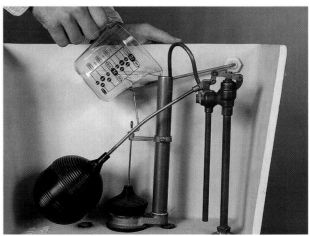

1 To kill bacteria buildup in and under the toilet bowl's rim, pour a bleach solution directly into the overflow tube.

with calcified minerals from hard water or with bacteria. To make sure, watch the water as it passes through the bowl. Open rim holes should send lots of water coursing diagonally across the sides of the bowl. If the water slides straight down, that may be a sign that the rim holes are partially clogged, either by bacteria or calcification. Dark, vertical stains beneath some of the holes suggest bacteria. Clogged siphon jets are almost always caused by bacteria.

How will you know whether blockages are made of mineral deposits or bacteria? Bacteria accumulations are soft and dark, ranging from orange to black. Mineral deposits are hard, scaly, and usually light in color.

Bacteria. To remove bacteria, first kill as much of it as possible, not just in the bowl but in the bowl's rim and rim holes. Pour a mixture of 1 part household bleach and 10 parts water directly into the tank's overflow tube. Just lift the tank lid, and direct a cup or more of the bleach solution into the overflow. **1.** Allow the bleach to work for a few minutes; then flush the toilet, and carefully ream the rim holes with a pen knife or a piece of wire. **2.** You can't see the rim holes from above, so use a pocket mirror to check your progress. Scour any bacteria stains from the underside of the rim, using bowl cleaner and an abrasive pad. Add a final dose of bleach through the overflow; wait a few minutes; and flush the toilet. To clear a clogged siphon jet, ream it thoroughly with a stiff wire. **3.** You'll probably have to do this all-out ream-and-scour cleaning only once or twice a year if you add one or two tablespoons of bleach to the overflow tube periodically.

Mineral Deposits. To remove calcified minerals left by hard water, you'll need slightly different tools. Instead of bleach, pour vinegar into the overflow tube, and let it stand for at least 30 minutes. Vinegar dissolves and loosens mineral deposits, allowing you to break and scrape thick accumulations that may have built up around the rim holes. Vinegar seems to work better when it's heated. Don't boil it, just heat it to shower temperature, about 104 degrees F.

After letting the vinegar stand, ream each hole thoroughly. On heavily clogged holes, use Allen wrenches as reaming tools. Start with a small wrench, and use larger ones as you gradually unclog the hole. Remember that porcelain chips easily, so work carefully and use a pocket mirror to check your work. (See the photo below.) This problem is a good indication that you might need to install a water softener. (See "Installing a Water Softener," page 258.)

Use a pocket mirror and Allen wrench to ream mineral-clogged holes around the underside of the rim.

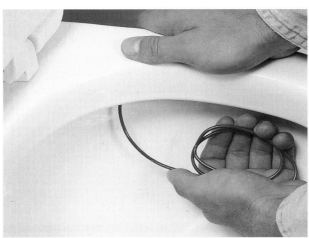

2 Clear bacteria from the rim holes using a short length of insulated electrical wire. Try approaching the hole from several angles.

3 Clear bacteria from the siphon jet (opposite the trap), again using a piece of wire. A dark opening may indicate the presence of bacteria.

Problem 3: Slow-Filling Toilet

The toilet flushes well enough, but the tank takes 10 to 15 minutes to fill. You also hear a slight hissing sound when the house is quiet.

This symptom indicates the presence of sediment in the fill-valve diaphragm. (Significant sediment problems may occur after the installation of a new toilet, after work is done on a nearby water main, or after a well is put into service.)

The solution is to remove the diaphragm cover and pick the grit from the valve. This is usually a quick and easy fix. If your toilet has a conventional brass or plastic ballcock (a fill valve with a float ball), shut off the water, and remove the two or three screws that secure the cover. **1.** Lift the cover and float rod from the riser. **2.**

You should be able to see sand or rust flakes scattered around the rim of the valve seat. Remove this grit using tweezers, and replace the cover. **3.**

Not all sediment in a line will work its way through at the same time, so you may need to clean the fill valve several times in the next few days or weeks. If sediment routinely plagues your water system, the best approach is to install a sediment filter in the cold-water trunk line. (See "Installing an In-Line Filter," page 256.)

Problem 4: Running Toilet

The toilet often keeps running until you wiggle the flush handle.

This symptom signals an adjustment problem, either in the flapper chain or tank-ball linkage. (It may also

Removing Grit from the Diaphragm

Tools and Materials

- Screwdriver
- Tweezers

TIME NEEDED: 30 MIN.

PLUMBING TIP: *Even tiny pieces of grit from a well or a plumbing repair can interfere with the operation of a fill valve. This easy repair can save thousands of gallons of water over time.*

1 To remove the ballcock's diaphragm cover, remove the three or four brass screws holding it down and lift the float mechanism.

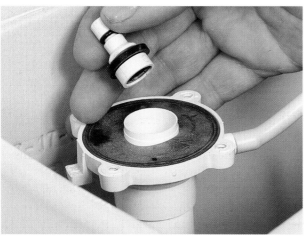

2 With the cover removed, lift the valve's plunger and diaphragm gasket to look for sand grit or other sediment.

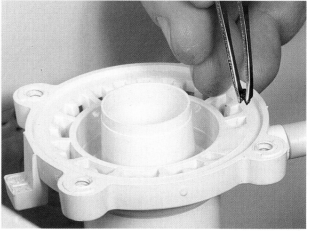

3 Use tweezers to lift out any sediment particles or rust flakes. You may need to repeat this sequence a time or two over the next month.

indicate a corroded flush lever, but in this case symptoms usually include the lever sticking in the up position.) If your toilet has a flapper, the lift chain may be too long. To correct the problem, remove the tank lid and lift the chain from the wire hook that secures it to the flush lever. Reconnect it so that it has less slack. With the chain hooked, top and bottom, press it to one side. You should see roughly 1 inch of sideways deflection. (See the photo at right, top.)

If your toilet has a tank ball, expect the lift-wire guide to be out of alignment. You'll find this guide clamped around the flush valve's overflow tube, secured by a setscrew. (See the photo at right, middle.) Begin by removing the tank lid; then flush the toilet several times. Keep flushing until you see the tank ball fall off-center, showing you which way to move the guide. If the ball falls to the left, for example, move the guide to the right.

Shut off the water, and loosen the setscrew about two full turns. Rotate the guide about $\frac{1}{16}$ inch, and then reset the screw. Turn the water back on, and watch the tank ball fall through several more flushes. If you've under- or over-corrected, you should be able to see it in the way the ball hits the flush-valve seat. It should hit dead center when it lands.

When making these adjustments, try not to apply too much pressure to the brass overflow tube. Brass gets brittle with age, and an old overflow tube might break off. If this should happen, simply pry the remaining bit of tube from its valve threads and screw a new brass tube in place. (See the photo at right, bottom.)

Problem 5: Rippling Water

The toilet comes on by itself, runs for a few seconds, and then shuts off. You may also hear a steady trickle and see tiny ripples in the bowl water.

This is most likely a sign that your toilet's flapper or tank ball is worn out. It may also signal a bad flush valve, but check the flapper/ball first. In any case, a small stream of water is leaking through the valve. As the tank level drops, the float activates the fill valve, which

Use a chlorine-resistant flapper for a longer useful service life. This flapper is clear.

Fixing Running Toilets

Adjust the flapper chain so that it has about 1 in. of slack.

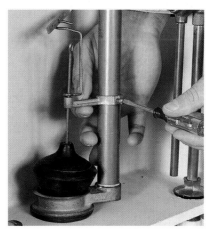

Adjust the lift-wire support if the tank ball falls off center.

When you replace an overflow tube that breaks off, coat the threads with pipe joint compound.

6 Toilet Repairs & Installations

---

replenishes the lost water and then shuts off. This cycle repeats itself every 20 to 30 minutes.

When a flapper or tank ball fails, it's usually because the rubber has broken down. In the worst cases, the flapper will literally fall apart in your hands. An early warning sign of deterioration is a stubborn black slime that covers the surface of the rubber.

Replacing the parts is cheap and easy to do. Flappers and tank balls are universal, so just about any brand will

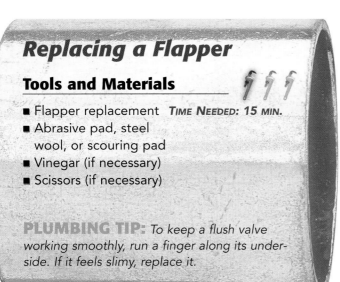

Replacing a Flapper

Tools and Materials

- Flapper replacement *TIME NEEDED: 15 MIN.*
- Abrasive pad, steel wool, or scouring pad
- Vinegar (if necessary)
- Scissors (if necessary)

PLUMBING TIP: *To keep a flush valve working smoothly, run a finger along its underside. If it feels slimy, replace it.*

1 *Clean the flush-valve seat by wiping it with an abrasive material like steel wool or a scouring pad. Feel for imperfections in the seat's surface.*

work. Chlorine degrades rubber quickly, so if you use chlorine toilet-tank treatments, it's a good idea to install a flapper or tank ball made to resist chlorine. (See the photo on page 103.) Even the small amount of chlorine in municipal water can do damage to rubber.

Flapper Replacement. With a flapper, shut off the water; unhook the chain; and lift the flapper from its pegs at the base of the flush valve or from around the overflow tube if the flapper has a collar. Before installing the new flapper, clear the valve seat of any old rubber (slime) or mineral deposits. Wipe the seat rim with a paper towel; then sand it lightly with fine sandpaper or steel wool. An abrasive pad from the kitchen will also work. **1.** You may need to use a little vinegar to dissolve mineral deposits.

The new flapper will likely have two types of flush-valve attachments for a universal fit: side tabs that hook over the valve's side pegs and a rubber collar for use on valves without side pegs. In the latter case, you'd slide the collar over the overflow tube. **2A.** If side pegs are present at the base of the flush valve, cut the rubber collar from the flapper and throw it away. **2B** (inset). Then hook the flapper tabs over the pegs. **2B.** Once you've attached the flapper, reconnect the chain.

Tank-Ball Replacement. To replace a tank ball, first shut off the water and grip the top of the lift wire with pliers. With your remaining hand, thread the ball from the lift wire. **1.** If the ball crumbles, leaving only the brass insert attached to the wire, use a second pair of pliers to grip this fitting. Brass is soft, so you won't have

any trouble backing the ball fitting from the lift wire with a good grip. In a few cases, the lift wire may break, but replacements are common hardware store items.

Again, dress the flush-valve seat with an abrasive and a paper towel; then insert the wire through its guide and into the new tank ball. **2.** Finally, make any needed adjustments in the lift-wire guide. (See "Fixing Running Toilets," on page 103.)

If the flapper (or tank ball) seems to be in good shape and creates a good seal, the problem lies with the flush valve, and you'll have to replace it. (See "Replacing a Flush Valve," page 109.)

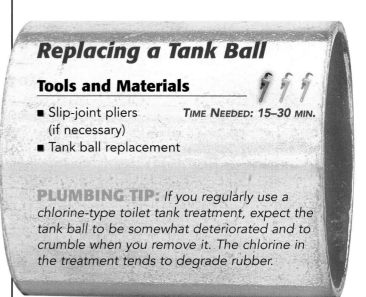

Replacing a Tank Ball

Tools and Materials

- Slip-joint pliers (if necessary) *TIME NEEDED: 15–30 MIN.*
- Tank ball replacement

PLUMBING TIP: *If you regularly use a chlorine-type toilet tank treatment, expect the tank ball to be somewhat deteriorated and to crumble when you remove it. The chlorine in the treatment tends to degrade rubber.*

2 Universal flush-valve flappers are made to fit either of two situations you'll encounter. If the flush valve has no side pegs at the bottom of the overflow tube, slide the collar over the tube (photo A). If it has side pegs, cut off the collar (inset), and hook the eyelets over the pegs (photo B).

Problem 6: Hissing Toilet

The toilet doesn't shut off completely. You hear a hissing noise and see ripples in the bowl. This behavior starts intermittently but over time becomes constant.

These symptoms suggest a problem with the fill valve or ballcock. (Remember that all ballcocks are fill valves, but not all fill valves are ballcocks. The term "ballcock" applies only to traditional fill valves, which have ball floats on the end of a pivoting arm.) It may be that you need to remove sediment from the fill-valve diaphragm. (See "Removing Grit from a Diaphragm," page 102.) Or you may be able to solve the problem by making a sim-

ple float adjustment. In most cases, however, the valve needs to be repaired or replaced. Don't put it off. A toilet that won't shut off completely wastes lots of water.

Do the simple things first. If the water level is so high that it spills into the overflow tube before the float ball or cup can shut off the fill valve, adjust the water level. Aim for a level about 1 inch below the top of the overflow. With a ballcock assembly, tighten the adjustment screw on top of the fill-valve riser. If that doesn't work, bend the float-ball rod down slightly. (See the photos on page 106.) Use both hands, and work carefully. Newer fill valves have other float adjustments. For example, a

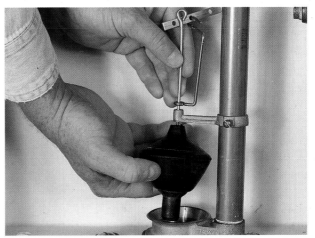

1 After you've drained the tank water, remove the tank ball from the lift wire. The tank ball may crumble if it is more than a few years old.

2 Thread the lift wire into the new tank ball, and check its operation through several flushes. This replacement type has a weighted bottom.

SMART TIP

Easy-Fix Flush Valve

Here's a flush-valve assembly unlike any other. It consists of an inverted cone that rides up and down on a plastic tower. A simple rubber gasket seals the valve. The design holds up well, but when it fails, all you'll need to do is replace the gasket. Thread the cap from the tower, lift the cone, and press a new gasket in place. (Mansfield Company, 150 First St., Perrysville, OH 44864; toll-free phone number: 1-877-850-3060.)

1 *Thread the plastic cap from the flush-valve tower.*

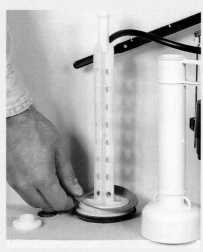
2 *Lift the tower to expose the sealing gasket.*

3 *Replace the gasket, and reinstall the tower.*

common type has a stainless-steel clip that you use to adjust the height of a float cup. (See "Replacing a Fill Valve," on page 112.) If adjustment doesn't solve the problem, a tiny amount of sediment may be in the diaphragm. See "Removing Grit from the Diaphragm," page 102, for how to clean the assembly.

Assuming that the float setting is fine and there is no sediment in the diaphragm, your next option is to replace the diaphragm and float-plunger seals. Begin by shutting off the water and removing the two or three screws that secure the combination diaphragm cover and float-arm assembly to the top of the riser. Lift the cover-and-float-arm assembly from the valve, and pull out the rubber seals. Expect a large rubber disk or stopper. (See the photo at bottom right.) Take these parts with you to a well-stocked plumbing outlet. If you can find replacement seals, install them in reverse order of removal, and test your work. You may be better off replacing the entire fill valve, especially if it's old. (See "When to Replace a Ballcock," opposite top.)

Fixing Fill Valves to Cure Hissing

Adjust the float rod *by bending it downward carefully.*

Fine-tune the float *by turning its adjustment screw.*

Replace the rubber seals *on the plunger of a brass ballcock.*

SMART TIP

When to Replace a Ballcock

While replacing only the seals of a ballcock is easier than replacing the entire unit, it's not always possible. Over the years, dozens of ballcocks have been made. It's not always easy to find replacement parts, and some were never meant to be serviced. Also, ballcock seats, like faucet seats, eventually wear out. In these cases you'll have to replace the ballcock, preferably with a modern fill valve. (See "Replacing a Fill Valve," page 112.)

Problem 7: Sticking Flush Handle

When you press down on the flush lever handle, it sticks— and you have to pull it back up.

Stiff flush levers are usually heavily corroded, while loose ones are probably broken. You may be able to free a sticking lever using a few drops of penetrating oil, but replacement is a good idea, especially considering how little a new one costs. Old lever handles also begin shedding their chrome or brass plating and look ugly.

There's nothing difficult about this repair, but in this case knowledge works better than leverage: you should know that the hex nut holding a flush lever assembly to the tank uses left-hand threads. (That's right, the threads are backward.) To loosen this nut, turn it clockwise rather than the usual counterclockwise. If the nut is too corroded to break free, cut the assembly apart with a hacksaw.

Your new lever and handle will likely come in one piece, with the fastening nut the only other component. The lever may be metal or plastic, while the handle will probably be chrome- or brass-plated metal. Snake the

lever through the tank hole; then slide the nut over the lever, and screw it onto its threads. (See the photos below.) Finally, connect the flapper chain or lift wire.

Problem 8: Stuck Seat

The toilet's seat is broken or worn. You've bought a new seat but can't get the old one off.

This is a common problem when an old toilet seat has brass bolts molded into the seat hinge. When you attempt to loosen the corroded fastening nuts, they stick tight, causing the bolt heads to break loose within their molded sockets. No matter what you do, the bolts just spin. The only way to deal with this situation is to saw through the bolts, just under the seat. To keep from marring the toilet's china surface, place a double thickness of duct tape on the bowl, all around the bolts. Remove the blade from a hacksaw, lay it flat against the bottom of the seat, and cut straight through the bolts.

With the old seat removed, position the new one, and insert the bolts through the seat and deck holes. Tighten the nuts. If cutting the old toilet-seat bolts is the bad news, the good news is that you'll only have to do it once. The plastic bolts on new seats will never corrode.

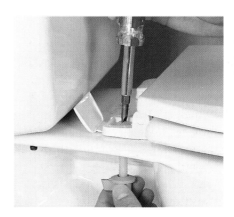

Tighten the new seat bolt using a screwdriver, and snap the hinged cover in place.

Replacing a Flush Handle

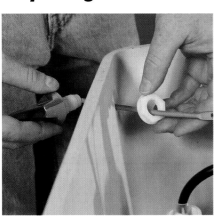

Remove the nut from the old lever, and pull the lever through the tank hole.

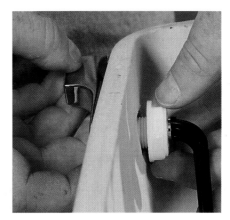

Slide the new lever in place, and tighten the nut. The nut has left-hand threads.

Problem 9: Leaking Base

Lately you've noticed water near the base of the toilet.

This is usually a sign that the bowl wax gasket on the toilet flange has failed. But that's not always the case, and because fixing a broken gasket requires taking up the toilet, it pays to investigate the quick fixes. Often water that appears on the floor is not bowl but tank water. If the tank has been bumped, it's not uncommon for water to leak past the tank bolts, dripping to the floor. Reach under the tank, and feel for moisture clinging to the tank bolts. If the bolts are wet, dry them using a paper towel. (Although a disturbed tank bolt may leak persistently, sometimes one bump makes one drip, and that's it. With that in mind, wipe the water from the floor, and go away for a while.)

After an hour or so, check the bolts again. If they're wet, you have a tank leak. Carefully tighten the nuts on the tank bolts a half-turn to a full turn to stop the leak. If the leak persists, then tighten the nuts one or two turns. If the leak still persists, remove the tank bolts and install new bolt washers. In this case, you usually will not need to disturb the tank-to-bowl seal or the water connection. Just turn off the water; flush the toilet; and sponge all the remaining water from the tank. Then remove the bolts; replace the washers; coat them liberally with pipe joint compound; and reinstall the bolts.

If the tank is not leaking, the problem is with the wax

◆ SMART TIP

Water Tank Condensation

If you see water on the floor near the toilet, it may be nothing more than moisture dripping from the sides of the water tank. Condensation on the sides of a tank occurs when air in the room is warm and the humidity is high. The warm air condenses when it meets the cool sides of the tank. Don't take this dripping moisture lightly. If you don't wipe up the puddles (or stop the dripping), water can seep beneath the flooring and cause the subfloor to rot. To prevent condensation problems, buy a toilet-tank insulation kit, which consists of polystyrene (usually) tank liners, from a home center. Shut off the water to the toilet, and drain the tank by flushing. Cut the insulating liners to size; apply the supplied adhesive; and install the liners to the inside of the tank. The polystyrene should prevent the tank sides from becoming so cool that they cause condensation.

gasket in the toilet flange. You'll have to take up the toilet and replace the seal. (See "Taking Up and Resetting a Toilet," page 121.)

One-Piece Silent-Flush Toilets

One-piece silent-flush toilets were the first alternatives to conventional two-piece toilets, hitting the market around the time Cadillacs grew fins and aimed at the same market. They were expensive, stylish, and discreetly quiet.

There are two basic types: One is a gravity-flow toilet with a conventional fill valve and flush valve. This type is easy to repair if you can find factory replacement parts. The other has a more complicated system of valves, which need to be calibrated to match a home's static water line pressure. One look at a repair kit, which resembles an automotive carburetor repair kit, and you'll get the picture: working on it is not easy. You should hire a good service plumber for this job. Ask up front whether the plumber is familiar with your particular make and model.

A silent-flush toilet *is made in one piece. They are usually very quiet but may be difficult to work on.*

Repairing Toilets

Replacing a Flush Valve

A flush valve fails when its valve seat can no longer form a seal to hold water. As water leaks past a defective flapper or tank ball, it can cut channels through the valve seat. When these voids appear, you have two repair options: install a retrofit flush-valve seat right over the damaged seat, or separate the tank from the bowl and replace the flush valve. Retrofit kits are easier, but a new flush valve makes a longer-lasting repair. (See "Retrofit Kits to the Rescue," page 111, for information on how to install a retrofit flush-valve seat.)

To replace a flush valve, start by shutting off the water, either at the main valve or at the shutoff valve beneath the toilet. Lift the lid from the tank, and flush the toilet to drain as much water as possible. Sponge out any remaining water.

Remove the Tank. With the tank empty, loosen the coupling nut that secures the water-supply tube to the fill-valve shank, and remove the tube. Reach under the tank, and using a socket wrench, remove the nuts from the two tank bolts. If the bolts spin, backhold them with a large screwdriver. **1.** In most cases, the nuts will turn free, but if your toilet is old and the nuts haven't been disturbed in many years, it's reasonable to expect them to resist. If the nuts seem really stuck, forgo the wrench and reach for a hacksaw blade. **2.** Brass bolts are relatively soft, and you should be able to cut through them

6 Toilet Repairs & Installations

Replacing a Flush Valve

Tools and Materials

- Socket wrench
- Flat-blade screwdriver
- Hacksaw blade
- Adjustable wrench

TIME NEEDED: 1–1½ HRS.
- Groove-joint pliers
- New flush valve
- Pipe joint compound

PLUMBING TIP: *Retrofit valve-seat kits for flush valves are readily available and are easier to install, but replacing a leaking flush valve is the most reliable repair.*

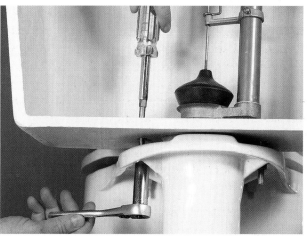

1 Loosen the tank bolts with a socket wrench while backholding the slotted bolt head within the tank using a flat-blade screwdriver.

2 If the tank bolt won't break free, you'll have to use a hacksaw blade to saw through it. Wrap one end of the blade to protect your hand.

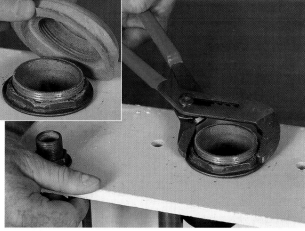

3 Remove the old flush valve's spud-nut washer (inset), and loosen the spud nut using groove-joint pliers. The nut should break free easily.

Sequence continues on next page

Continued from previous page

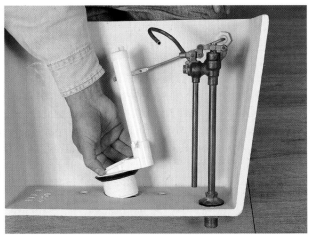

4. Install the new flush valve through the tank hole, and position the overflow tube to fit the fill tube on the fill valve.

5. Thread the large spud nut onto the flush valve at the bottom of the tank, and tighten the nut with pliers until it squeaks.

6. Fit the large rubber spud washer over the spud nut, and coat the washer with a generous layer of pipe joint compound.

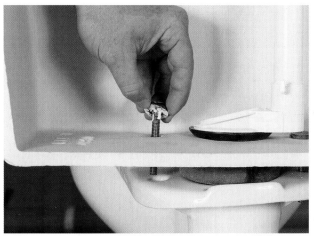

7. Install washers on the tank bolts, and coat them with pipe joint compound. Insert the bolts through the tank and bowl.

quickly and easily. Use the blade from a standard hacksaw, and wrap one end with duct tape to serve as a makeshift handle. You'll use only the blade because you can't fit a hacksaw between the tank and the bowl.

With the tank free, lift it from the bowl, and lay it on its back. (The photos show a cutaway tank upside down for clarity.) If you're working on a finished floor or other surface that you don't want to mar, spread newspapers or a folded drop cloth. Pull the rubber spud washer from the shank to expose the spud nut. **3** (inset, page 109). Back the spud nut from the shank with groove-joint adjustable pliers or a pipe wrench. **3** (page 109). You might have to grip the flush valve with one hand inside the tank or get a helper to lend a hand. Pull the old flush valve out, and scrape away any old putty from around the tank hole.

Install the New Flush Valve. Slide the rubber spud gasket over the new flush-valve unit's shank threads, tapered edge down. **4.** Insert the shank of the new valve body through the tank hole, and thread the spud nut onto the shank, finger-tight. **5.** Before tightening the nut further, rotate the flush valve so that the overflow tube is nearest the ballcock or fill valve and the seat and flapper face away from it. Then, while holding the valve in place, draw the spud nut down with pliers or a wrench until it feels snug. Slide the new spud washer over the spud nut, and coat its tapered edge with pipe joint compound. **6.**

Next, set the tank on the bowl. Slide washers onto the tank bolts; coat them with pipe joint compound; and install the bolts. **7.** Place a washer and nut on each bolt, and draw the nuts tight alternately, a little at a time. Keep in mind that the tank is not meant to rest directly on the bowl but should remain suspended on the flush-valve's spud washer. If you attempt to draw the tank down to meet the bowl, chances are you'll break one or the other. When the nuts begin to feel snug, stop and check the level and plumb alignment of the tank. The goal is a level tank that sits parallel with the back wall. Don't be concerned if the tank wobbles a bit on the spud washer. It will firm up when you fill the tank with water.

Connect the flapper. (See "Replacing a Flapper," page 104, for how to do this.) Then reinstall the water supply tube, and turn the water back on. Watch the flapper operate through several flushes, and make adjustments as needed. Check the bottom of the tank bolts for leaks, and continue to check them several times over the next few days. If no leaks appear in the first week or so, none should appear thereafter. If you feel dampness or see water at the ends of the tank bolts, tighten them just a little more and dry them. If they leak again, tighten them more, but only one-quarter to one-half turn or so at a time. Don't overdo it. The greater hazard is in over-tightening the bolts.

SMART TIP

Retrofit Kits to the Rescue

If you're not up to separating the tank from the bowl to repair a damaged flush valve or if the toilet has it's flush valve and overflow cast into the china, then a retrofit valve-seat replacement kit is a good choice. (Eljer and Crane are two manufacturers that may have toilets with these parts cast into the body of the tank.) The kit is an assembly that consists of a stainless-steel or plastic valve seat, an epoxy-putty ring, and a flapper. The super-tough epoxy putty ring adheres the entire unit onto the old seat. The kit can be used over brass, china, or plastic flush valves.

To install a retrofit valve-seat kit, start by shutting off the water and flushing the toilet to drain the tank. Sponge the remaining water from the tank. Remove the old flapper. If your toilet has a tank ball, remove the ball, the lift wire, and the lift-wire guide. Then sand the old seat to remove mineral deposits and to abrade the surface for better adhesion. (You may want to use vinegar if the mineral deposits are stubborn.) Wipe the seat clean, and allow the seat rim to dry.

With the old seat ready, peel one waxed-paper protector from the epoxy ring, and stick the ring to the bottom side of the retrofit seat. Peel the remaining waxed paper from the epoxy (photo at left), and press the assembly firmly onto the old valve seat (photo in middle). Finally, connect the flapper chain (photo at right), and turn the water back on.

Epoxy kits are not your only valve-seat repair option. A simpler kit consists of a tube of silicone adhesive, which cures under water, and a plastic replacement valve seat. Sand the seat, and then apply a bead of silicone to the seat rim. Press the new seat in place; install a new flapper; and turn the water back on.

1 Peel the protective paper from the epoxy ring.

2 Press the replacement seat over the old seat.

3 Connect the chain with about ½ in. of slack.

Replacing a Fill Valve

If you're having trouble with a toilet's fill valve, it's usually best to replace the entire unit. You'll see several types on the market. The most familiar is probably the traditional ballcock, in brass or plastic, but you'll also see some that have floats that slide up and down on a vertical riser and some low-profile valves that are activated by head-water pressure.

Codes require fill valves to have built-in backflow protection. Backflow preventers keep tank water from back-siphoning into the water system. Although all codes require them, some manufacturers make both protected and nonprotected fill valves. Check the product labeling, and choose a valve that lists built-in backflow prevention as one of its features.

Remove the Old Ballcock. To remove the old fill valve (ballcock), start by shutting off the water and flushing the toilet. Sponge any remaining water from the bottom of the tank. Loosen the coupling nut that binds the supply tube to the ballcock shank. **1.** Then loosen the compression nut that binds the bottom of the supply tube to the shutoff valve. Finally, remove the jamb nut from the ballcock shank, and lift the old assembly from the tank. **2.**

Install the New Valve. Scrape away any old putty or pipe joint compound from the area around the tank opening. Slide the sealing washer onto the new fill valve's threaded shank, and coat the bottom of the washer with pipe joint compound. Insert the shank through the tank hole, and thread the jamb nut onto the shank threads. **3.**

Replacing a Fill Valve

Tools and Materials

- New fill valve
- Pipe joint compound
- New supply tube (if necessary)
- Groove-joint pliers
- Adjustable wrench

TIME NEEDED: 1 HR.

PLUMBING TIP: When tightening any tank part from below, always hold it steady from above. It's easy to spin one component against another.

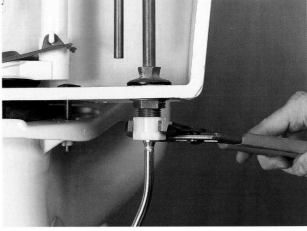

1 Using a pair of large groove-joint pliers, loosen the coupling nut that connects the supply riser to the ballcock shank.

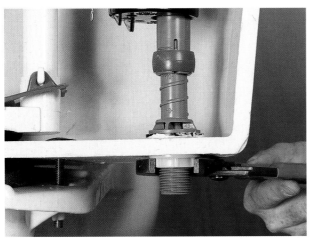

4 While holding the unit steady, carefully tighten the fill valve's jamb nut with pliers until the nut feels snug and begins to squeak.

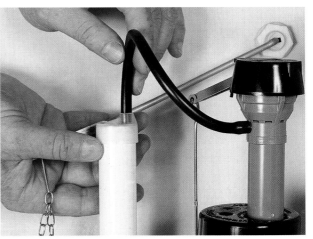

5 Measure, cut, and install the fill tube. Don't allow it to kink. Connect one end to the fill valve and the other to the overflow tube.

Before tightening the jamb nut, make sure the fill valve is aligned properly in the tank. If you're installing a traditional-style ballcock with a float ball, make sure the ball doesn't contact the tank wall or the overflow tube. Ideally, the ball should ride at least ½ inch away from the back of the tank. Grip the fill valve to keep it from rotating against the fill tube, and then tighten the jamb nut until the sealing washer flattens out and the nut feels snug. **4.**

Next, install the fill tube between the nipple on the fill valve and the flush valve's overflow tube. Use the provided fitting to hold the fill tube on the overflow. **5.** You can adjust the float (a ball float if you're installing a ballcock) now by approximating where you want the water level. With a vertical fill valve, pinch the stainless-steel adjustment clip on the float rod, and move the float cup up or down. **6.** To adjust a ballcock float, see "Problem 6: Hissing Toilet," page 105.

Hook Up the Supply Line. The last step is to reconnect the water supply. If the new fill valve's shank extends the same amount from the bottom of the tank as the old one's, you can just reconnect the old water supply tube. If the new shank is more than ⅛ inch longer or shorter than the old one, however, you probably need a new supply tube. The easiest to install is a prefitted tube made of polymer plastic encased in stainless-steel mesh. You just attach the couplings at each end of the tube, and you're done. **7.** To avoid damaging the tube, tighten the lower end first.

6 Toilet Repairs & Installations

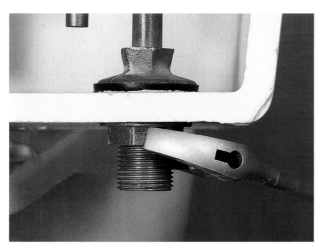

2 Loosen the ballcock jamb nut with an adjustable wrench while gripping the ballcock unit from above.

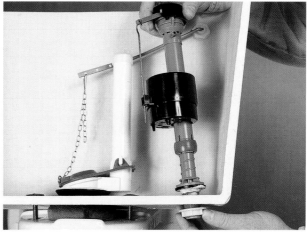

3 Insert the new fill valve through the tank hole, and tighten the jamb nut. Apply pipe joint compound to the washer.

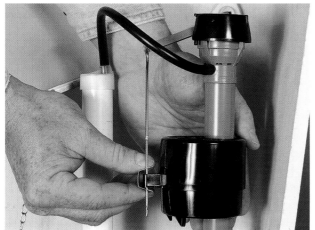

6 Adjust the fill valve's float by compressing and sliding the clip up or down the lift wire. This will control the water level in the tank.

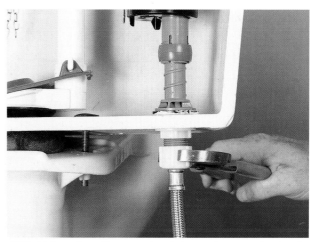

7 Using the pliers again, tighten the supply riser's coupling nut on to the fill valve's exposed shank threads.

Traditional Toilet Supply Line

Traditional supply risers use compression fittings to make the seal at the shutoff valve.

The traditional (but not necessarily the best) supply tube is made of chromium-plated copper, with a rubber cone washer or a plastic flat washer, fitted to meet the fill valve's shank. You cut the other end to length and join it to the shut-off valve with a compression fitting. These tubes are supple, and if the offset is not too severe, you can bend them without a tubing bender. Make the bend as high or low on the tube as possible.

Hold the tube between the fill valve's shank and the shutoff valve. This should give you a rough idea as to the degree of offset and the length you'll need. Make the offsets so that each end of the tube will enter its fitting dead straight. Trim the tube, and then slide on the coupling nut, followed by a compression nut and ferrule. Lubricate both ends with pipe joint compound.

To gain enough vertical clearance to fit the tube between the fittings, press down on the shutoff valve. If the valve won't budge, bend the supply tube just enough to clear the fittings, and then straighten it again. Make the compression connection at the shutoff valve first. To keep from over-tightening the compression nut, turn it finger-tight while wiggling the tube a little to keep it from binding. Then tighten it one full turn using a wrench. Finally, tighten the coupling nut at the tank, and turn on the water to test for leaks.

In addition to chromed-copper tubes and the stainless-steel mesh tubing mentioned earlier, you'll also see ribbed-copper tubes, which are easier to bend, polybutylene tubes, and polymer tubes reinforced with nylon webbing. Only the chromed copper, ribbed copper, and stainless-steel mesh tubes have wide code approval.

Trouble-Shooting Pressure-Assisted Toilets

Pressure-assisted toilets function differently from gravity-flow toilets. They are based on a different operating principle: use of air pressure. The toilets offer limited repair options, but you can attempt a few remedies.

Problem 1: Running Toilet

The toilet keeps running between flushes or produces a loud buzzing noise after each flush.

This behavior suggests that something is keeping the flush-valve cartridge—the central, top mounted fitting in the tank—from closing. Although an occasional trickle of water into the bowl between flushes is not unusual for these toilets, if the water actually seems to run while the toilet is idle, you'll need to investigate.

If the toilet has a flush button mounted in the tank lid, the button's trim collar may be riding on the activator. Remove the tank lid, and flush the toilet. If the toilet now flushes properly, the collar was the problem. Replace the tank lid, and remove the flush button. While sighting through the lid opening, move the collar until it is centered over the activator. When you replace the button, make sure it travels downward at least ⅛ inch before contacting the activator. If it doesn't, loosen the locking screw, adjust the activator, and reset the screw. **1.** If the flush button doesn't seem to be the problem or your toilet has a flush lever, shut off the water, drain the tank completely, and then turn the water back on. Hereafter, avoid pressing the flush button or lever before the tank fills completely. As with a flush button, the flush lever needs ⅛ inch of clearance. **2.**

If adjusting the activator doesn't help, suspect the pressure-regulating valve. (A faulty valve may also cause the toilet to take longer than normal to fill.) The regulating valve is sandwiched between the check valve and the relief valve in the water supply group. To replace it, you'll have to remove the entire supply group. Shut off the water, loosen the coupling nut beneath the tank, and remove the water supply tube. Then remove the jamb nut that holds the supply group in the tank. **3.** Lift the supply group out of the tank, and take it apart to expose the pressure-regulating valve. **4.** Remove the old regulating valve, and insert a new one. **5.** Reconnect the assembly, and tighten all connections with a wrench, backholding with a second wrench. Turn the water back on. If replacing the regulating valve doesn't correct the problem, suspect a faulty flush-valve cartridge. (See "Replacing a Flush-Valve Cartridge," page 116.)

Fixing a Running Pressure-Assisted Toilet

Tools and Materials

- Screwdriver
- Groove-joint pliers
- Adjustable wrench
- New pressure-regulating valve

TIME NEEDED: 1–1½ HR.

PLUMBING TIP: *Backholding threaded assemblies is as important in a repair like this as it is in larger plumbing applications, such as galvanized-steel water piping.*

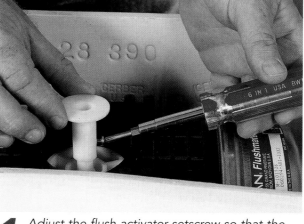

1 Adjust the flush activator setscrew so that the flush button (if you have one) has at least ⅛ in. of clearance before it contacts the activator.

2 If there's no button, adjust the flush lever or activator (or both) as needed so that there is ⅛ in. of clearance between lever and activator.

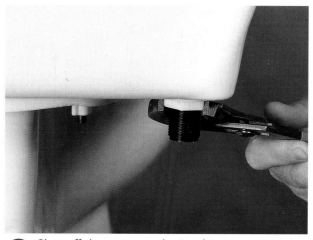

3 Shut off the water, and using large groove-joint pliers, loosen the jamb nut that holds the water supply group in the tank hole.

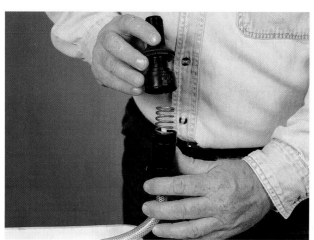

4 Twist the supply-group assembly apart to expose the pressure-regulating valve. Install a new valve.

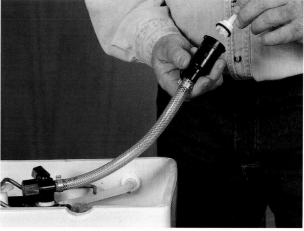

5 Assemble the supply group, and tighten all connections using an adjustable wrench. Back-hold nuts using pliers or another wrench.

Problem 2: Inefficient Flushes

The toilet flushes sluggishly and doesn't clear the bowl.

This symptom may simply mean a clogged trap, so use a plunger or closet auger on the bowl before tearing into the tank. If the trap is clear, suspect a faulty flush-valve cartridge. Lift the tank lid, and check for water on top of the cartridge. If you see any water at all, replace the cartridge. If you don't, you'll need to conduct a little flush-valve test.

Turn off the water, and flush the toilet. Hold the flush lever down a full 60 seconds to drain the tank completely. Then pour a little water into the hollow around the activator stem. (See the photo below.) Turn the water back on, and allow the tank to fill completely. Then check for air bubbles around the activator. If no bubbles appear, assume that you have a fouled air inducer. Remove the inducer and clean it. If you do see bubbles around the activator, you'll need to replace the entire cartridge.

Cleaning a Fouled Air Inducer. To clean a fouled air inducer, shut off the water and drain the tank by holding the flush lever down for a minute or so. Using pliers or an adjustable wrench, remove the inducer's plastic nut. **1.** Place a hand under the inducer to catch the internal components. Expect to find a small plastic or brass poppit fitted with a spring. **2.** Hold the poppit under running water, and roll it between a finger and thumb to remove any calcification. If the poppit is really crusty, soak it in vinegar for about 30 minutes, and then rub off the scale. Carefully reassemble the components, and test your work. If the cleaning doesn't solve the

problem, replace the pressure-regulating valve. (See "Fixing a Running Pressure-Assisted Toilet," page 115.)

Replacing a Flush-Valve Cartridge. To begin, shut off the water and drain the tank completely by holding down the flush lever for about a minute. Insert the ends of a large pair of needle-nose pliers into the fins of the cartridge's top nut. **1.** Carefully rotate the cartridge from the tank. If necessary, slide a large screwdriver between the pliers' handles for extra leverage. Discard the old cartridge, and buy an identical new one. Coat the top threads and the O-ring of the new cartridge with

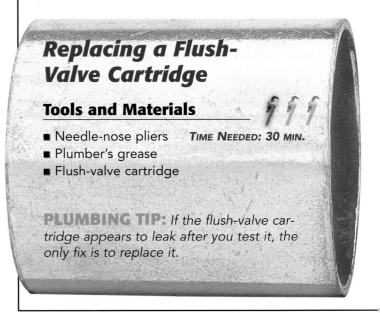

Cleaning a Fouled Air Inducer

Tools and Materials

- Groove-joint pliers or adjustable wrench
- Vinegar (if necessary)

TIME NEEDED: 30 MIN.

PLUMBING TIP: *You may not have to replace the pressure-regulating valve if you can clean the air inducer to make it more effective.*

To test for a leaky flush-valve cartridge, *remove the water-tank top, pour water around the activator stem, and flush. The appearance of bubbles indicates a leak.*

Replacing a Flush-Valve Cartridge

Tools and Materials

- Needle-nose pliers
- Plumber's grease
- Flush-valve cartridge

TIME NEEDED: 30 MIN.

PLUMBING TIP: *If the flush-valve cartridge appears to leak after you test it, the only fix is to replace it.*

1 With the tank drained, remove the inducer's plastic nut. Place a hand under the inducer to catch the parts.

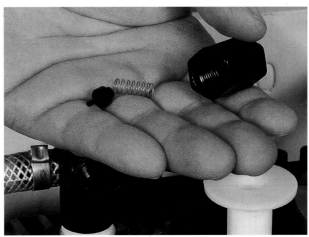

2 Hold the tiny brass or plastic poppit fitting under running water, and roll it between your fingers to clean it.

plumber's grease or petroleum jelly, and thread the cartridge into place. **2.** Tighten until it squeaks, then just a touch more. Turn the water back on, and test your work.

Toilet Flanges

A toilet flange, or closet flange, is a slotted ring, usually connected to a vertical collar. The collar fits through the floor, while the slotted ring, or flange, rests on top of the floor. Toilets are bolted directly to this fitting. In the case of a cast-iron flange, the collar slides over a riser pipe, which extends to floor level. The gap between the pipe and collar is packed with lead and oakum. If the pipe is cast iron and the collar is plastic, the gap is bridged by a rubber gasket. With plastic or copper piping, the flange is cemented or soldered to the riser. In all cases, the flange is anchored to the floor with screws.

When a flange will be installed on concrete, the plumber usually installs a plastic or styrofoam spacer around the waste-pipe riser. The concrete installer then finishes around the spacer, and when the time comes, the plumber removes the spacer and installs the flange. The spacer, in this case, provides fitting room for the

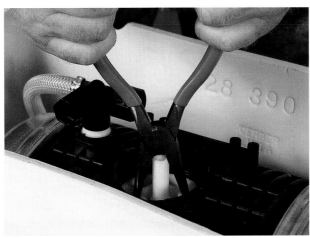

1 Insert the pointed ends of a large pair of needle-nose pliers into the fins of the cartridge's top nut.

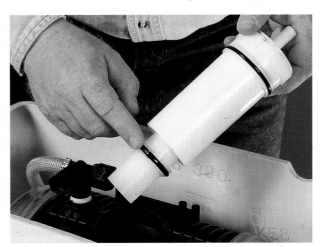

2 Coat the top threads and adjacent O-ring of the cartridge with plumber's grease, and tighten the cartridge in place.

Installing Toilet Flanges on a Wood Floor

This plastic insert flange fits neatly inside a cast-iron riser.

Apply PVC cement to the flange and riser, and press in place.

Attach the flange to the floor using panhead screws.

flange collar. While this is the most common approach, some jurisdictions allow a simpler method. In these cases, the plumber installs a plastic waste pipe at grade level and tapes it off. The concrete installer then finishes right up to the pipe. When it's time to set the toilet, the plumber cuts out the tape, drills holes in the concrete, and installs anchors for flange mounting screws. The plumber then screws a simple flange ring to the concrete floor. There is no direct connection between the flange and the waste pipe. A concrete-installation wax ring with a seep-proof insert keeps the joint from leaking.

Types of Flange Gaskets

Fifty years ago, the gasket material used to set toilets was plumber's putty. The plumber simply rolled out a quantity of putty and pressed it onto the flange. Putty, however, hardens with age, which can lead to leaks. The reason putty worked at all is because toilet bowls back then had four closet bolts instead of the two used today. Two were inverted, through the flange, as they are on modern toilets, but two more bolts located near the front of the flange anchored the bowl to the floor. Four bolts allowed very little flexing.

Wax. Beeswax rings, called bowl wax gaskets, eventually replaced putty as the preferred gasket material for toilets. (You'll also see the rings referred to as wax seals.) These wax rings were able to accommodate the slight flexing that occurs between a toilet and floor, so for generations bowl wax gaskets have been and

still are the standard. You can buy gaskets in 3- or 4-inch-diameter sizes by about 1 inch thick. They are inexpensive and durable—a hard combination to beat.

Still, improvements are always in the works. One improvement was to incorporate a plastic, funnel-like insert in the traditional wax gasket. The insert was designed to deliver the water well past the flange surface, thereby eliminating leaks between floor flange and the wax. These special seep-proof gaskets are often used when a toilet is installed on a concrete slab.

Rubber. Next in the progression came flexible-rubber gaskets, which when compressed, block the lateral migration of water. Rubber gaskets can also reseal themselves once disturbed, and they're reusable. They are sold in several thicknesses to accommodate a variety of flange heights relative to floor height, and you need to buy *precisely* the right thickness (unlike wax gaskets, which are more forgiving of small height differences). If a rubber gasket is even a little too thick, the toilet won't rest on the floor. If it's too thin, it won't seal.

The benefits of rubber and wax have recently been incorporated into a hybrid gasket, a neoprene rubber ring with a wax coating. (These gaskets are also available

Rubber Flange Gaskets

Neoprene Gasket with Wax Coating

Foam-Rubber Gasket

Wax Gasket with Seep-Proof Insert

Standard Wax Gasket

Installing Toilet Flanges on Concrete

Drill anchor holes and tap plastic anchors in place. Apply caulk to the bottom of the flange.

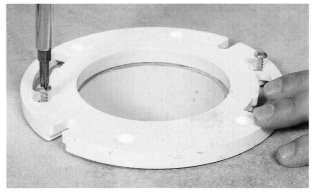

Attach the flange directly to the concrete using screws installed in the plastic anchors.

with seep-proof inserts.) The advantage is that the rubber will bounce back to reseal itself, while the layer of wax is more forgiving of sizing errors.

Measuring for Rubber. Wax gaskets come in standard thicknesses, and easily conform to slight job-site differences (flooring thickness and the like). In most cases, just knowing the horn length is good enough. To get the right thickness for a rubber flange gasket, you need to lay a straightedge across the base of the toilet and measure the length of the horn. Subtract the thickness of the toilet flange (minus any finish flooring such as tile), and add ⅛ to ¼ inch. The result is the ideal gasket thickness. Buy one as close to that thickness as possible. Measuring is not difficult, but it is bothersome. For that reason, you should use rubber gaskets only when the toilet is likely to be bumped frequently, as it might be when used by a physically handicapped person. A rubber gasket is better able to reseal itself after being disturbed.

Leaky Flange Gaskets

If you see water on the floor around the toilet, first try to determine whether it is from leaking tank bolts or condensation. (See "Problem 9: Leaking Base" and "Water Tank Condensation," page 108.) If you can't find the source or if more water appears with each use, the water is probably coming from the floor flange. Correct the situation as soon as possible. Water can delaminate plywood, blister underlayment, and rot the subfloor.

Quick Fix. If the toilet was installed within the past few months, then merely tightening the closet bolts on the base of the toilet may reseal the bowl's wax gasket. New wax gaskets almost always compress a little after installation, which can leave the bolts loose. Continued use can then cause the toilet to rock in place, breaking the

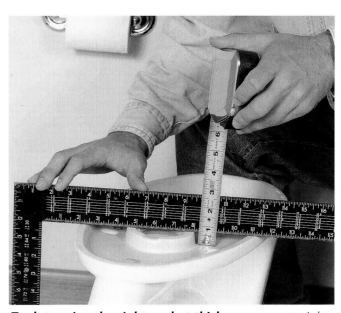

To determine the right gasket thickness use a straightedge and ruler to measure the toilet horn.

seal. There's often enough wax to create a new seal—but only if you can draw the toilet and floor flange together.

Start by popping the caps from the closet bolts at the base of the toilet. Pry under them with a screwdriver or putty knife. With the caps removed, use a small wrench to test the tightness of the nuts. If they turn easily, tighten them only until they feel snug, and then watch the base of the toilet carefully over the next few days. If the floor stays dry, you've solved the problem.

Replacing the Gasket. If water reappears or if the bolts were snug in the first place, you'll need to take up the toilet and install a new wax gasket and closet bolts. (See "Taking Up and Resetting a Toilet," page 121.) If your toilet has been in place for years, don't expect a quick fix to work. Replace the wax gasket at the first sign of trouble.

Broken Flanges

Plastic toilet flanges are sturdy and seldom fail under normal conditions. Flanges made of cast iron and cast brass, on the other hand, are more vulnerable. The slotted portion of a flange is fairly narrow, so the slightest casting flaw will weaken it further. It's easy to break a flange by overtightening the closet bolts, but in time, even normal use can break a weak flange. **1.** When a flange breaks, the bolt on that side drifts outward, losing its grip on the flange. The toilet begins to feel loose, rocking in place when you sit on it. This movement soon breaks the gasket seal, and the toilet leaks with every flush.

If this happens, don't panic, because there's a fairly easy solution. Replacing the entire flange is the most professional repair, but doing so requires cutting and splicing drainpipe or replacing cast-iron fittings—a big job. The easier solution is a repair strap that works surprisingly well. The crescent-shaped strap mirrors the shape of a flange and has an opening for a closet bolt. To use this strap, first remove the toilet. (See "Taking Up and Resetting a Toilet," next page.) Insert a closet bolt through the repair strap; slide the strap under the old flange, next to the break; and install a wax gasket. **2–3.** If the strap won't slide under the flange, loosen the floor screws and lift the flange slightly with a pry bar. When you get the strap in place, retighten the screws.

Flange breaks involve small sections of metal, so there's usually enough flange left to support the repair strap. It's a neat trick, and one that saves hours of work.

Repairing a Cast-Iron Flange

Tools and Materials

- Tools and materials for removing a toilet   **TIME NEEDED: 1–1½ HRS.**
- Flange repair kit
- New wax gasket

PLUMBING TIP: *Before replacing or repairing a broken cast-iron flange, check with your plumbing outlet. New retrofit flanges are being developed all the time.*

1 *After removing the toilet, lift the wax-and-plastic toilet flange insert from the drain, and scrape away any wax that's left on the flange.*

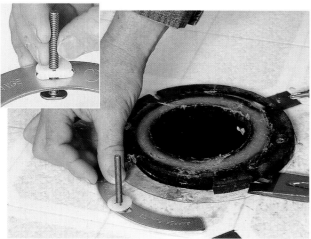

2 *Insert a closet bolt into the repair strap (inset), and slide the strap under the broken section of the toilet flange.*

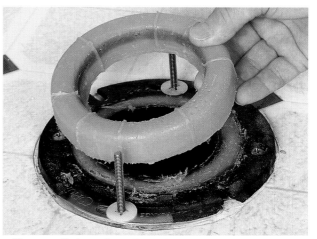

3 *Install the other closet bolt, and press a new bowl gasket over the flange. A wax-over-neoprene gasket is shown.*

Taking Up & Resetting a Toilet

Start by shutting off the water. Flush the toilet, holding the handle down to drain as much water as possible from the tank. Use a paper cup or other small container to scoop the water from the bowl, and use a sponge to soak up the remaining water in the bowl and tank.

Loosen the coupling nut that joins the water supply tube to the fill valve. **1.** Pry the caps from the closet bolts at the base of the bowl, and remove the nuts and washers from these bolts. If the bolts spin in the flange slot, keeping the nuts from threading off, try jamming them to one side so that they bind in the flange slot or against the toilet base. If this doesn't work, use needle-nose pliers to grip the top of the bolts while backing the nuts off. **2.** If all else fails, use a miniature hacksaw to cut through the bolts, just under the nuts.

With all connections undone, put down several layers of newspaper to protect the floor from the wax clinging to the outlet. Before moving the toilet to the newspapers, consider how you'll lift and carry it. A toilet is not terribly heavy, and one person can lift it with the right approach. Because the tank will make the toilet back-heavy when it clears the floor, the best place to grip the bowl is just in front of the tank. This deck area will have a lip, making it easy to grip. (Never lift a toilet by its tank.) Straddle the bowl, and with your feet just forward of the tank, tip the toilet up on one side. **3.** This will break the wax seal. Still straddling the bowl, carefully

Taking Up and Resetting a Toilet

Tools and Materials

TIME NEEDED: 1–1½ HRS.

- Adjustable wrenches
- Needle-nose pliers
- Newspaper
- Hacksaw
- Plumber's putty
- Putty knife
- New wax gasket kit
- Water supply tube
- Groove-joint pliers

PLUMBING TIP: *Toilets with the tank in place are heavy, so unless you take yours apart you may want to ask for help.*

1 Unscrew the compression nut from the toilet shutoff valve. Then loosen the coupling nut at the top of the supply tube.

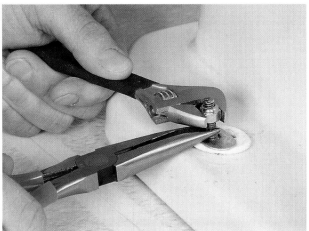

2 If the closet bolt spins in place, you probably have a broken flange. Hold the bolt with needle-nose pliers.

3 Grip the toilet just in from of the seat hinges; carefully lift using your legs; and carry the toilet to several layers of newspaper.

Sequence continues on next page

6 Toilet Repairs & Installations

Continued from previous page

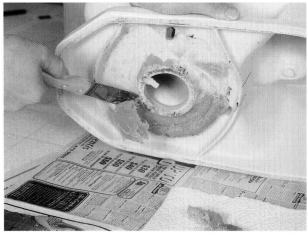

4 Gently tip the toilet on its side, being careful not to disturb the water tank, and use a putty knife to scrape away any old wax.

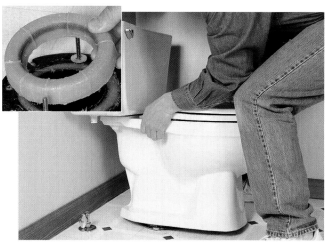

5 Install the new closet bolts and wax gasket. Carefully set the toilet over the bolts, and press the base into the wax.

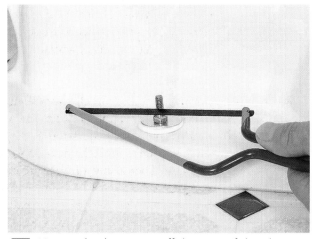

7 Using a hacksaw, cut off the part of the closet bolts extending just above the nuts; retighten the nuts; and snap on the decorative caps.

8 While backholding the shutoff valve with one wrench, tighten a new supply tube in place with another.

raise the toilet several inches and walk (duck-walk) it over to the waiting newspapers. (Rest your elbows on your knees when walking a toilet several feet.) Carefully lay the toilet on its side, and use a putty knife to scrape away any wax clinging to the bottom of the toilet. **4.**

Scrape the remaining wax from the surface of the flange, and slide the old closet bolts from their slots. Each slot has a large opening at one end where you can free the bolt head and remove the bolt. If you've cut off the old bolts, buy two bolts, nuts, and metal washers (usually as a kit), as well as a new wax gasket for the bowl. When shopping for a wax gasket, match your piping system's flange size, either 3 or 4 inches.

Set the Toilet. Slide the bolts into their slots, and center them across the outlet opening from each other, typ-ically 12 inches from the wall. Then press the wax gasket onto the flange. **5** (inset). Some sources suggest stick-ing the new gasket to the toilet, but when it's installed on the flange, the gasket keeps the bolts in place. In fact, you should make sure that each bolt is stuck to the wax gasket in an upright position. These bolts guide the toi-let onto the flange, so it's important that they remain upright and centered.

To set the toilet, grip it near the hinge deck as before, and walk it over to the flange. Lift it just enough to clear the waiting closet bolts. Maneuver the toilet until you can see the closet bolts through the holes in the base of the bowl. When the bolts are visible, slowly lower the toilet onto the wax gasket. **5.** Check the alignment of the tank: the back of the tank should be parallel with the wall. If it isn't, rotate the toilet left or right until it is

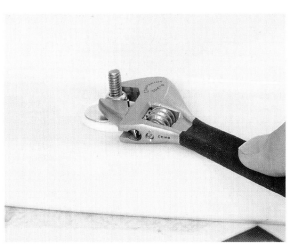

6 Tighten the closet-bolt nuts with a small adjustable wrench (for a better feel), and stop when they feel moderately snug.

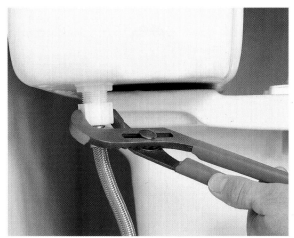

9 Finish by tightening the coupling nut using pliers. Stop when the nut feels snug and begins to squeak.

SMART TIP

Changing Floor Height

If you've taken up the toilet to install new flooring, you may need to alter your approach when resetting the toilet. If all you've done is lay new vinyl over old (not a bad idea considering that asbestos may lurk in old floor coverings and mastics), you'll be able to reset the toilet just as described. If you've installed ¼-inch plywood or cement-based backer board underlayment and/or glazed tile, however, you'll have added to the height of the floor relative to the flange. You'll need to compensate for this increased depth with a thicker bowl gasket.

If the added floor height is less than ¼ inch, you can simply knead and stretch a standard wax gasket to give it a taller profile. With an increase of ¼ inch up to about 1 inch, stack one standard wax gasket on top of another.

straight. Then press down on the rim of the bowl with all your weight. This will compress the wax enough for you to install the nuts on the closet bolts.

Secure the Toilet. If the decorative caps that covered the old closet bolts snapped over plastic retaining washers, install these washers under the metal washers that came with the closet-bolt kit. These plastic keeper-washers are marked "This Side Up." Place the plastic retainers over the bolts first, followed by the metal washers and the nuts. With the bolts ready, draw the nuts down with a 6-inch adjustable or combination wrench, alternating sides every few turns. **6.** Using a small wrench allows you to feel the resistance of the nut.

Continue drawing the nuts down until you feel resistance. Don't overtighten, or you'll break the toilet base.

When the nuts feel snug, stop, and put all your weight on the bowl again. This will probably loosen the nuts enough to gain another turn with the wrench. Repeat this press-and-wrench sequence until the nuts no longer loosen under your weight. Then using a miniature hacksaw, cut the bolts just above the nuts. **7.** This may loosen the bolts, so retighten them as needed. Normally, a plumber would snap the decorative caps over the bolts at this point, but because you live in the house, leave them off for a few days. After some use, the nuts will probably loosen slightly. At this point, tighten them again, and then snap the caps in place. If your bolt caps don't have retainer washers, fill them with plumber's putty and press them over the nuts.

Hook Up the Water. You may be able to reuse the water supply tube. Just coat the washer with pipe joint compound, and tighten the nut over the fill-valve shank. If you've damaged the tube or just want to replace it, use a new stainless-steel mesh tube. Attach and tighten the valve end of the tube first. **8.** Use two wrenches, one to tighten the compression nut and one to backhold the shutoff valve. Then attach the tank end of the tube. Turn the coupling nut onto the fill-valve shank until it's finger-tight; then snug it using a pair of groove-joint pliers. **9.** Don't overtighten the nut.

Finally, turn the water back on, and test your work. As always, look for leaks at the tank bolts. If the bolts are wet, tighten them just a little.

Installing a New Toilet

A new two-piece toilet will come in two boxes, one containing only the bowl and another containing the tank, tank bolts, decorative bolt caps, retaining washers and a large spud gasket, which forms the seal between the tank and the bowl. In addition, you'll need to buy a toilet seat, a set of closet bolts, a bowl wax gasket, and a water supply tube.

Begin by emptying both cartons. Slide the new closet bolts into their flange slots so that they're centered across the opening and are the same distance from the back wall. **1.** Press a new bowl wax gasket onto the flange, and stretch the wax slightly so that the gasket holds the bolts upright. **2.**

Fasten the Toilet in Place. When carrying the new bowl, grip the seat hinge deck with one hand and the front rim with the other. Lift the bowl over the flange until you can see the bolts through the tank holes, and then settle the bowl onto the wax gasket. **3.** As when setting an assembled toilet, this is the time to step back and judge the straightness of the bowl. You won't be able to align the tank with the wall, so eyeball it as best you can. If you're not confident in sighting the unit, measure from the tank-bolt holes to the back wall. Each hole should be the same distance from the wall. If they're not, rotate the bowl accordingly.

When you've aligned the toilet, unpack the cap-retaining washers and place one over each bolt. They'll be marked "This Side Up." Place a metal washer from the

---

SMART TIP

To Caulk or Not To Caulk?

When it comes to caulking around the base of the toilet, opinions vary. Some local codes require it, some forbid it, and others don't address it at all. The advantages of caulking around the base of a toilet are that the caulk 1) has good adhesive qualities, 2) helps preserve the seal by keeping the toilet from moving, 3) keeps the joint free of bacteria and other dirt, and 4) looks better than a dark, soiled perimeter crack (as long as the joint is neatly done).

The disadvantage is that when a leak does occur, it can't be seen, so it does more damage.

There are generally no strong arguments one way or the other, except in two circumstances.

- **Caulking is usually recommended for toilets that are set on concrete. Concrete is never level around a toilet flange, and the added support from the caulked joint helps keep the bowl from rocking.**

- **Caulking is usually not recommended in a bathroom with wood floors (a poor flooring choice). These floors buckle with the slightest penetration of water, and you'll want to see a leak as soon as it starts.**

If codes require caulking around the base of the toilet, use a good-quality mildew-resistant latex or silicone tub-and-tile caulk.

If you choose (and are permitted by local code) to caulk around the base of a toilet, use latex tub-and-tile caulk. Leave the back of the toilet base open for water to escape in case a leak occurs. Start by wetting the floor and toilet base; then apply a liberal bead of caulk in the seam on the three visible sides. Draw a finger all around the joint so that any voids are filled, and wipe away the excess using a damp rag or sponge. Keep in mind that latex caulk will shrink a bit when it cures, so leave a little more in the joint than seems necessary. The caulk will dry to the touch within the hour but will take several days to achieve adhesive strength. In the meantime, feel free to use the toilet.

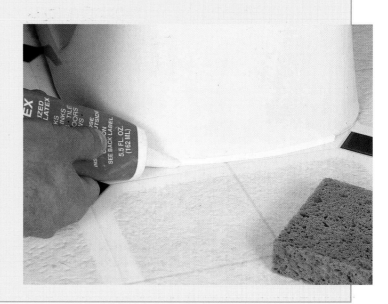

Installing a New Toilet

Tools and Materials

- New toilet
- Water supply tube
- Wax gasket
- Adjustable wrenches

TIME NEEDED: 1 HR.
- Closet bolts
- Pipe joint compound
- Groove-joint pliers

PLUMBING TIP: Use the wax gasket to support the closet bolts when you install the bowl. That way, when you align the bowl with the bolts, the gasket will be precisely positioned for a good seal.

1 Install new closet bolts in the toilet flange. If the bolts come with plastic washers, use the washers to hold the bolts in place.

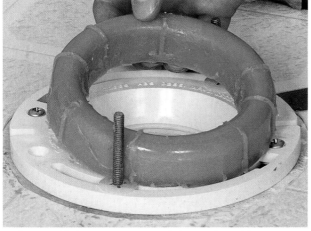

2 Install the new wax gasket on the toilet flange. Press the bolts into the wax to hold them upright.

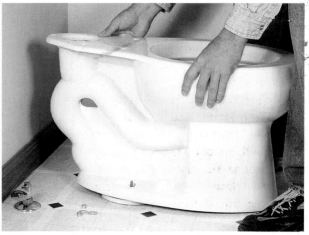

3 Using the closet bolts as guides, set the bowl onto the flange gasket. Site through the china bolt holes.

4 Insert the tank bolts through the bottom of the water tank, and install spacer washers if they are provided.

5 Set the water tank on the bowl deck, and tighten the tank bolts. Level the tank, but don't overtighten the bolt nuts.

6 Toilet Repairs & Installations

closet-bolt kit on top of each plastic retaining washer, and thread the nuts onto the bolts. Tighten the nuts, and cut the tops of the bolts off, as described in "Taking Up and Resetting a Toilet," page 121.

Attach the Tank. With the bowl set, install the tank. The fill valve and flush valve are usually factory installed, but you should always check the tightness of the flush-valve spud nut. Use large groove-joint pliers or a pipe wrench to tighten the nut if necessary. If the nut moves easily, draw it down until it feels snug. If not, leave it alone.

Fit the large rubber spud gasket over the flush-valve threads and onto the tank bolts (along with the supplied rubber washers). **4** (page 125). Lubricate the tank side of the washers with pipe joint compound before installing them. Then lubricate the rest of the washers and the spud gasket with pipe joint compound. Insert the bolts through the tank holes, and set the tank on top of the bowl. **5** (page 125). Some manufacturers use two bolts, and some use three. Some also use additional spacer washers between the tank and the bowl. In these cases, follow the manufacturer's instructions.

With the tank resting on top of the bowl, start a washer and nut on each tank bolt. Tighten these nuts carefully with a small adjustable wrench, alternating from side to side. Focus on keeping the tank level, and stop when the nuts begin to feel snug.

Fixing a Rotted Floor

When you allow a toilet to leak long enough, the underlayment and possibly the subfloor around it swells and rots. The only option then, before replacing the flooring, is to cut out and replace the damaged underlayment area or cut the affected subfloor area back to the nearest joists to replace it. Remove the flooring, and probe the affected area using an awl or screwdriver to determine the extent of the damage and whether it extends past the underlayment to the subfloor.

Replacing Underlayment. When you replace just the underlayment around a toilet, you can leave the toilet flange in place and install the new plywood in two pieces. (The underlayment may be ½-inch or, more likely, ¼-inch plywood over ¾-inch subflooring.) Cut out the damaged area using a circular saw to cut just through the underlayment. Use a utility saw or reciprocating saw to cut through uncut areas in the corners or near walls. Cut the new plywood to size, and then cut it in half, with the cut intersecting the flange opening. Trim the plywood to accommodate the outside diameter of the flange collar (not the flange itself), and slide each half under the flange. (See the illustration below.) Screw and glue the underlayment in place.

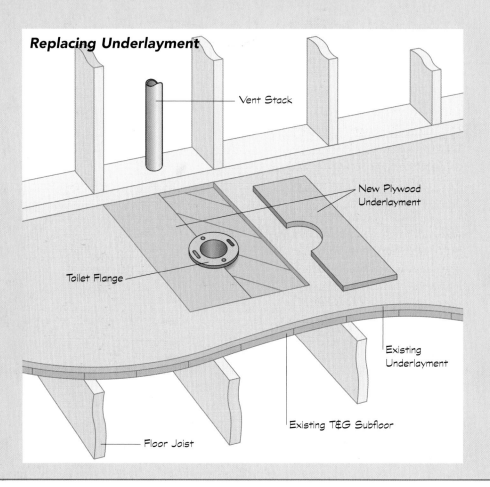

Replacing Underlayment

Vent Stack

New Plywood Underlayment

Toilet Flange

Existing Underlayment

Existing T&G Subfloor

Floor Joist

Final Adjustments. With the bowl set and the tank attached, check to see that the fill tube is connected between the tank's overflow and the fill valve and that the flush lever's chain is connected to the flapper. Attach the chain so that it has approximately 1 inch of sideways deflection.

Install the seat, and connect the supply tube as described in "Taking Up and Resetting a Toilet," page 121. Turn on the water, and with the tank lid removed, watch the toilet closely through several flushes. If the water level is too high, bend the float rod down (or adjust the float cup) until the ballcock (or fill valve) shuts off with the water roughly 1 inch below the top of the overflow tube.

With the toilet working smoothly and the tank and flange seals holding without any leaks, use the toilet for several days. Then check to see whether the closet bolts have loosened. If they have, tighten them one last time, and snap the bolt caps over their retaining washers.

Setting Toilets On Concrete

Setting toilets on concrete presents a few special problems. If anything, a floor should drop down slightly, forming a kind of swale around a drainpipe riser, but they almost always sweep up. The result is a toilet that rides high on its flange, with little of the base touching the floor. This is unworkable, of course, so most toilets that are set on concrete need to be shimmed.

6 Toilet Repairs & Installations

Replacing Subflooring. If the subfloor is damaged, you'll have to replace it. Cut the subfloor back to the nearest joist on each side where there is undamaged subflooring. A reciprocating saw is a good tool for this. Nail two-by blocking around the perimeter of the hole to provide nailing for the new plywood, sized and cut to match the existing subflooring. (See the illustration at right.)

There are two ways to proceed from here. One is to replace the old toilet flange and riser. If you have a cast-iron flange, convert the riser and flange to plastic. (See "Joining PVC to a Cast-Iron Hub," page 63, and "Toilet Flanges," page 117.) If you have plastic pipes, cut off the toilet assembly at the horizontal pipe, and rebuild it exactly the same way using a coupling. Leave the flange off for now. Measure and cut a hole in the new plywood for the riser before installing it. Nail or screw down the subflooring with fasteners around the perimeter every 6 inches on center. Lay down new underlayment and flooring, and then install the new flange.

The second way is to leave the flange in place. Nail two-by blocking between the joists on each side of the toilet riser. Then cut the plywood down the middle the same way as for underlayment (left), and install it, sliding it under the toilet flange. Then lay new underlayment and flooring.

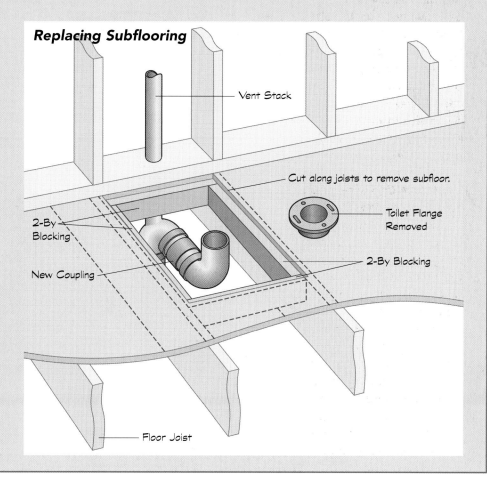

Replacing Subflooring

Vent Stack

Cut along joists to remove subfloor.

Toilet Flange Removed

2-By Blocking

2-By Blocking

New Coupling

Floor Joist

Set the toilet as usual, but draw the closet bolts down only three-quarters of the way. Then level the toilet by sliding cedar or plastic shims under the base. Plastic is best; never use metal shims. Only when you're satisfied that the base is well supported, without any obvious rocking, should you finish tightening the bolts. Continue with the rest of the toilet installation. After testing your work, trim the shims and caulk the base of the toilet to give it more support and to "glue" it down. Caulk also conceals the shims.

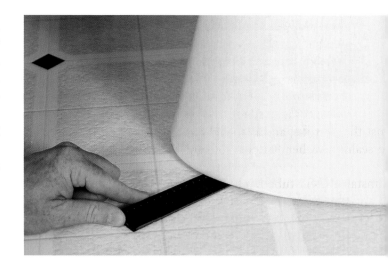

When setting a toilet on concrete, which is hardly ever perfectly level, you'll need to shim the bowl. Plastic shims work best. (Here the concrete is vinyl-covered.)

Replacing an Old Drum-Trap System

As noted earlier, many older plumbing systems (60 years old or more) have hopelessly outdated drum-trap piping configurations serving their bathrooms. In these setups, the sink and tub both flow into a central drum mounted in the floor. The drum trap then drains into the horizontal branch line serving the toilet. This piping cannot be properly vented, and after many years clogs with frustrating regularity.

Unfortunately, drum-trap piping is impossible to reach without tearing out the floor from above or the ceiling from below. If you're planning a bathroom overhaul, make it a point to update this piping. It's not that difficult once you gain access.

Getting Started. Begin by taking up the floor and subfloor in the vicinity of the pipes. Cut out all the lead piping leading to and from the drum trap, as shown in the illustration at right. A reciprocating saw with a metal-cutting

blade is ideal for this work, but a hacksaw will also do. Use a snap-cutter to cut the cast-iron horizontal branch pipe serving the toilet. Make this cut about 3 inches away from the hub of the stack T-fitting so that enough horizontal pipe remains to support new piping.

To rebuild the bathroom drains, first cut a 4-inch stub from 3-inch-diameter PVC drainpipe. Tighten a 4 x 3-inch banded coupling between the cast-iron stub left by the snap-cutter and the plastic stub. Install a 3-inch 90-degree elbow with a 2-

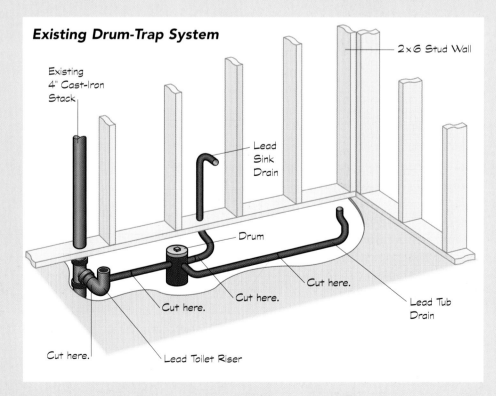

Existing Drum-Trap System

Existing 4" Cast-Iron Stack

2 x 6 Stud Wall

Lead Sink Drain

Drum

Cut here.

Cut here.

Cut here.

Lead Tub Drain

Cut here.

Lead Toilet Riser

SMART TIP

Vent-Related Problems

1. Poorly Vented Toilet. If a toilet flushes so slowly that two or more flushes are needed or additional water must be poured into the bowl to make it flush correctly, suspect a venting problem. A poorly vented toilet will not flush correctly. You'll need to upgrade the piping system. This is mainly a problem in unregulated areas, where unlicensed plumbers rule. For information on vent and drain design, see Chapter 3, "Drains, Vents & Traps," starting on page 34.

2. Frost Closer. During winter, moisture in the air rising through a small-diameter stack may freeze when it meets the cold air. Enough frost can accumulate to form a cap on the stack, causing sink drains to gurgle and toilets to flush slowly. Many northern codes require stacks to be 3 inches in diameter where they pass through the roof, even if the stack below the roof is only 1½ inches. The stack size is typically increased about 1 foot below the roof line, and no stack should extend more than 1 foot above the point of exit from the roof.

---

inch side inlet through which the sink and tub will drain. Check local codes regarding the capacity of a side inlet fitting, however. If this setup is forbidden, install the stub of PVC pipe in the hub of a 3 x 2-inch Y-fitting. Secure the Y-fitting in the banded coupling, with the branch of the Y canted slightly upward. Immediately out of the front of the Y, install a 3-inch 90-degree street elbow to serve as the toilet riser. The riser should be centered 12 inches from the finished wall or 12½ inches from a stud wall. If the fitting space is too tight and the riser falls an inch or two beyond 12 inches, the toilet will still work, though it will sit away from the wall slightly. In worst-case situations, the problem can be remedied by installing a toilet that has a 10-inch rough-in outlet instead of a 12-inch rough-in. Toilets are available to fit 10-, 12-, and 14-inch rough-ins.

Finishing Up. From the side inlet (or branch of the Y-fitting), run 2-inch PVC to a 2-inch Y-fitting. Then, from the branch of the Y, continue up into the plumbing wall to serve the sink. From the top of the sink T-fitting, continue into the attic with a 2-inch vent through the roof or tied back into the main stack. Finally, from the front end of the Y-fitting in the floor, reduce to 1½ inches and continue to the tub trap.

If the floor joists run parallel with the plumbing wall, the piping will be easy to install. If the joists run perpendicular to the piping, you'll need to drill the center of each joist, splicing short sections of pipe together with couplings. **Caution:** *Don't notch the tops or bottoms of these joists.*

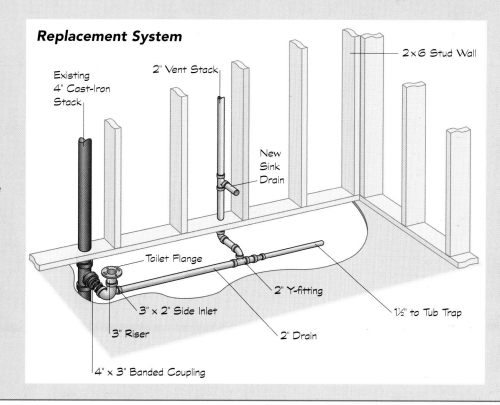

Replacement System

Existing 4" Cast-Iron Stack

2" Vent Stack

2×6 Stud Wall

New Sink Drain

Toilet Flange

3" × 2" Side Inlet

3" Riser

2" Y-fitting

2" Drain

1½" to Tub Trap

4" × 3" Banded Coupling

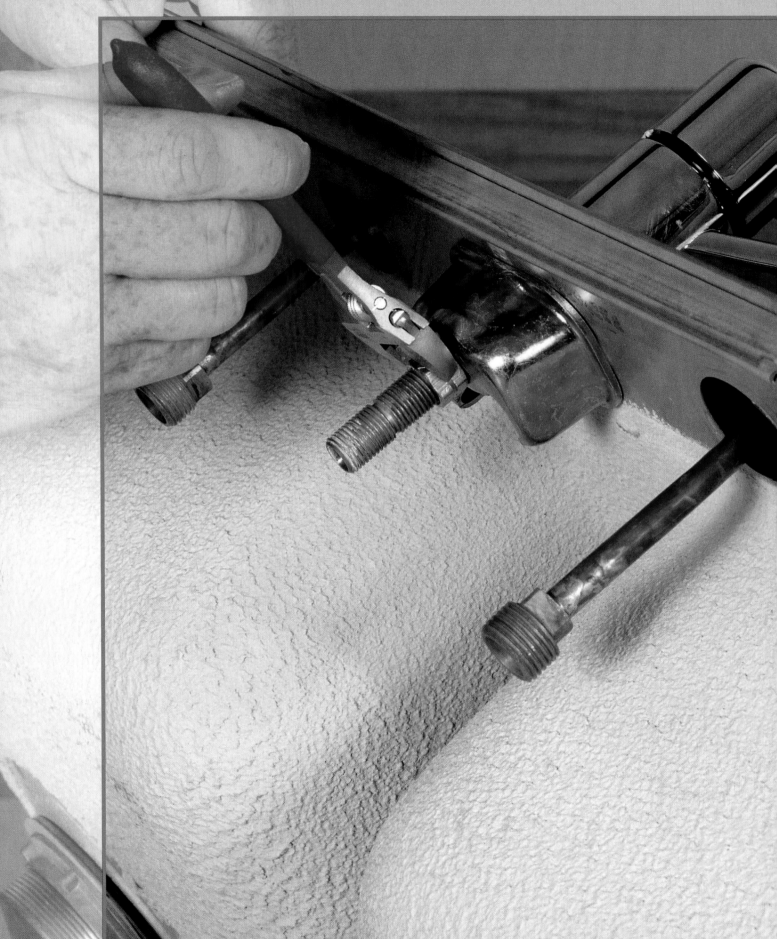

CHAPTER 7

Installing Sinks & Related Equipment

here comes a time when those old faucets and sinks just have to go. And given the range of products on home center shelves these days, you're sure to find something you'd like to take home.

Product options range from simple faucet or drain replacement to complete sink and fixture upgrades. In the bathroom, you might also want to add a new vanity cabinet and top, which in many cases are almost of a piece with the sink. In the kitchen, you might want to add or replace an automatic dishwasher, a waste-disposal unit, or perhaps an instant hot-water dispenser. These days, you'll find dishwashers (and often waste-disposal units) installed in nearly every new home as original equipment, and instant hot-water dispensers are becoming ever-more-popular kitchen add-ons. Besides covering the removal and installation of these fittings, fixtures, and appliances, this chapter explains how careful

maintenance and judicious use can add to the efficiency and longevity of important household products such as dishwashers and waste-disposal units.

Sink-Connection Basics

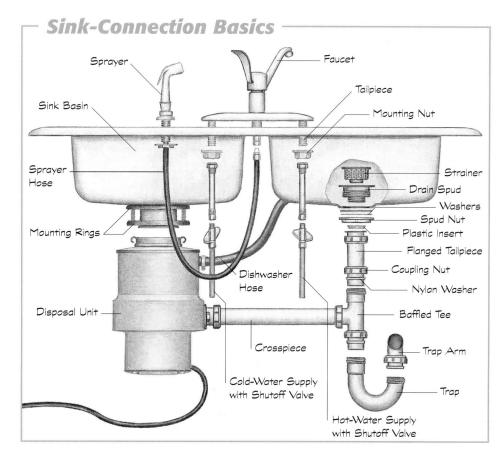

- Sprayer
- Faucet
- Sink Basin
- Tailpiece
- Mounting Nut
- Sprayer Hose
- Strainer
- Drain Spud
- Washers
- Spud Nut
- Mounting Rings
- Plastic Insert
- Flanged Tailpiece
- Coupling Nut
- Dishwasher Hose
- Nylon Washer
- Disposal Unit
- Baffled Tee
- Crosspiece
- Trap Arm
- Cold-Water Supply with Shutoff Valve
- Trap
- Hot-Water Supply with Shutoff Valve

Water- and Waste-Connection Basics

Almost all kitchen and bathroom sink faucets are connected to water piping through flexible supply tubes. In just about every case, you make the riser-to-supply-tube conversion with a compression fitting. While some codes require shutoff valves only on the toilet supply, allowing simple compression adapters on other supply connections, the general trend is toward requiring shutoffs on all fixtures fed by supply tubes. Even when shutoffs are not required, they're a good idea. You'll thank yourself for installing them the first time a fixture or appliance needs servicing.

As for supply tubes, you can choose soft-copper tubes, which are extremely inexpensive, or stainless-steel enmeshed polymer tubes, which cost substantially more but are prefitted and almost foolproof. Stainless-steel mesh tubes are perfect for the poorly equipped and the mechanically timid. At this writing, many codes do not allow plastic supply tubes.

Sink Drains

When it comes to joining a kitchen sink to permanent drain piping, use 1½-inch tubular waste kits and P-traps. Waste kits for double sinks are sold with or without waste-disposal-unit connections. One is called a sink-waste kit and the other, a disposal-waste kit. These kits usually include all the pieces needed to drain both compartments of a sink into a single P-trap. Traps are usually sold separately. Use a 1½-inch flanged tailpiece and P-trap to drain a single-compartment sink.

Bathroom sink drains are always 1¼ inches in diameter, but you can fit them with either a 1¼- or 1½-inch trap. You'll find a special reducing washer packaged with each trap to make the conversion. All waste kits and traps are available in PVC plastic or chrome-plated brass. Plastic is much easier to cut and assemble. It's less expensive, and unlike brass, it doesn't corrode. This is one case where plastic beats metal, hands down. Use chrome traps only when the trap will be visible, as under a wall-hung bathroom sink. You can cut both materials with a hacksaw or wheel cutter.

This sink-drain connection is made using a ground joint adapter, which has a nylon compression washer.

Dishwashers

When hooking up a dishwasher, use ⅜-inch soft copper water piping and compression fittings. Run this line from the hot-water shutoff (or dual stop) under the sink, through the side of the sink cabinet, near the back, to the inlet on the dishwasher's solenoid valve.

Dishwashers usually come with more than enough discharge hose attached. The hose will be made of ribbed plastic or heat-resistant rubber. If you need to extend a rubber discharge line, automotive heater hose is a good choice. You can make all connections using conventional hose clamps. If the sink has no waste-disposal unit attached, connect the free end of the hose to a disposal unit T-fitting under the sink, just above the P-trap. If the sink is equipped with a waste-disposal unit, connect the hose to the discharge nipple cast into the metal body of the unit.

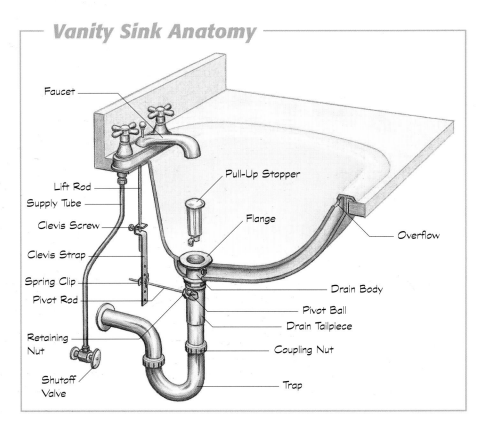

Vanity Sink Anatomy

- Faucet
- Lift Rod
- Supply Tube
- Clevis Screw
- Clevis Strap
- Spring Clip
- Pivot Rod
- Retaining Nut
- Shutoff Valve
- Pull-Up Stopper
- Flange
- Overflow
- Drain Body
- Pivot Ball
- Drain Tailpiece
- Coupling Nut
- Trap

How To Replace a Bathroom Faucet & Drain

Bathroom faucets are sold with and without drain assemblies. Because the lift rod that operates the drain's pop-up plug is installed through the faucet-body cover, it's a good idea to replace both when changing out an old faucet. The procedure described here assumes that your sink is installed in a vanity cabinet.

First, remove the old faucet and drain assembly. Shut off the water, and drain the faucet lines. If you have to shut off the main valve and you have plumbing fixtures on the floor above this bath, open those fixtures as well. Otherwise, water from upstairs will drain onto you as you lie beneath your work.

Removing the Drain

With the lines bled, slide a pan or shallow bucket under the old sink trap, and loosen the trap nuts. **1.** Use a padded pipe wrench or groove-joint pliers on chrome traps. The nuts on plastic traps should be only hand tight. Drop the trap, and empty it into the pan or bucket. Next, loosen the nut at the wall fitting (or floor fitting if you have an old S-trap), and pull the trap arm from the drainpipe. **2.**

Move to the sink's pop-up assembly. You should see a horizontal pop-up lever extending from the back of the drain's tailpiece. The vertical lift rod will be connected to this lever by means of a clevis and tension clip. Squeeze the clip, and pull the clevis from the lever. **3.** Then loosen the nut holding the pop-up lever in the

Removing the Drain

Tools and Materials

- Groove-joint pliers
- Bucket or shallow pan
- Putty knife

TIME NEEDED: 40 MIN.

PLUMBING TIP: *The flat washers used with chrome traps need to be lubricated. If you don't have pipe joint compound, liquid dish detergent is an acceptable substitute.*

1 To remove a sink-basin drain, loosen the two P-trap nuts and remove the trap. Keep a bucket under the trap to catch wastewater.

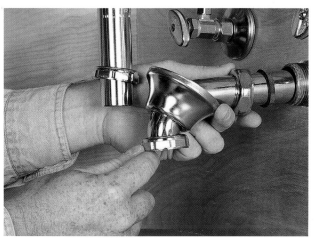

2 To remove the P-trap arm, disconnect the friction nut at the wall and pull the arm straight out from the drainpipe.

3 To disconnect the sink drain's pop-up linkage, squeeze the tension clip and slide the clevis from the lever.

Sequence continues on next page

Continued from previous page

4 *Use groove-joint pliers to loosen the nut that holds the sink drain in place. Backhold the drain with a second pair of pliers if it spins.*

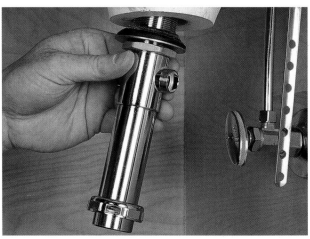

5 *Unscrew the basin flange from the sink drain (working from above), and pull the drain out of the basin from below.*

tailpiece, and pull the lever from the tailpiece to release the pop-up plug in the drain. You'll see a swivel ball in the end of the lever that allows it to pivot up and down, controlling the pop-up, and the pop-up should be free.

To remove the drain from the sink basin, loosen the large fastening nut that holds the drain in place. This hex-shaped nut is threaded over the drain extension at the bottom of the basin. Grip the nut with a wrench or a pair of groove-joint pliers, and back it down the threaded extension about 1 inch. **4.** Then push up on the drain to break the flange seal inside the sink basin. Reach into the sink, and unscrew the flange from the threaded extension. Pull the drain out, and scrape any old putty or pipe joint compound from the basin. **5.**

Removing Old Bathroom Faucets

How you remove the old faucet depends on whether it's a top-mounted or bottom-mounted faucet. Top-mounted faucets are the most common.

Top-Mounted Faucets. A top-mounted faucet is held in place from below by threaded shanks or fastening bolts, which fit through the basin's deck holes. If the faucet is a two-handle model, expect to find jamb nuts tightened onto the shanks from below. In this case, you'll connect the supply tubes to the ends of the shanks. If your faucet has copper tubes instead of brass shanks—usually the case with single-control faucets—the faucet will be held in place by threaded bolts. One

SMART TIP

Drain Variations

The drain assembly described in "Removing the Drain," page 133, is the most common type, but it's not the only one available. Some drain assemblies don't have a threaded flange at the top. In this case, the top of the extension tube is flared to form a flange, which means that you'll need to back the fastening nut completely from the extension. To do that, you'll first need to unscrew the lever housing from the extension. When you have both removed, you'll be able to lift the extension out from above.

Water Connections for Faucets

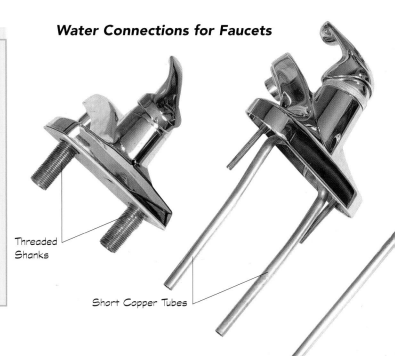

Threaded Shanks

Short Copper Tubes

Removing Faucets

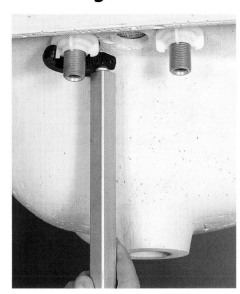

To remove a top-mounted faucet, use a basin wrench to unscrew the jamb nuts from the faucet shanks.

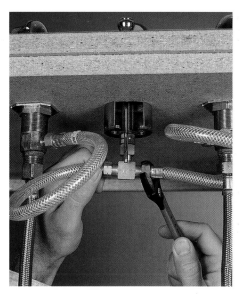

To remove a bottom-mounted faucet, undo the connecting tubing and remove the jamb nuts.

look under the sink, and you'll know the type you have.

When working within the cramped spaces behind a sink, you'll find loosening and tightening nuts a lot easier with a basin wrench. A basin wrench is really just a horizontal wrench on a vertical handle. Lay its spring-loaded jaws to one side, and the wrench loosens, lay it to the other, and it tightens. The extended handle allows you to work high up under a basin or sink deck without having to reach.

Loosen the two coupling nuts that secure the supply tubes to the faucet. Then, using a standard adjustable wrench, disconnect the lower ends of the tubes from their compression fittings. Set the supply tubes aside, and use the basin wrench to remove the fastening nuts

Long Copper Tubes

Tubes with Coupling Nuts

from the faucet shanks or fastening bolts. Finally, lift the old faucet from its deck holes.

Bottom-Mounted Faucets. If the old faucet is a bottom-mounted model, with the body of the faucet installed below the sink deck, the initial approach is from above. Leave the supply tubes in place until after you've completed your work on top. Start by prying the index caps from the faucet handles. Remove the handle screws, and lift the handles from their stems. This will give you access to the flanges (or escutcheons) threaded onto the stem columns. Thread these flanges off, disconnect the supply tubes, and drop the faucet from its deck. Some bottom-mounted faucets consist of three isolated components, including two stems and a spout. These components are joined with tubing and are easy to disassemble from below.

Installing a New Bathroom Faucet

Installing a new faucet is not particularly difficult. If the faucet comes with a plastic or rubber base-plate gasket, put the gasket on it before setting it in place. **1** (page 137). If the new faucet has threaded brass shanks, insert the shanks through the deck holes, center the faucet, and align the back of the base plate with the wall. Then thread a jamb nut onto each shank from below, and tighten the nuts with a basin wrench. While you're tightening these nuts down, try to have a helper keep the faucet straight and centered. If you're working alone, tighten the nuts only until they begin to bind and then recheck the alignment from above. If you find that the faucet has moved, make the necessary adjustments and then tighten the jamb nuts until they feel snug.

If the faucet does not have threaded brass shanks (as most single-control faucets do not), expect to find two bolts alongside two copper tubes. When you have inserted the tubes and bolts through the deck and positioned the faucet, install an extended locking washer and a nut on each bolt, and tighten it all down. **2.** (To connect the water supply tubes, see "Connecting the Water," page 153.)

Installing the New Drain

To install the drain assembly, first find the drain flange ring. Roll plumber's putty between your hands until you've made a soft, pliable rope approximately 5 inches long and ¼ inch in diameter. Stick the putty to the underside of the flange, and set the flange aside for the moment. **3.**

The drain tube should come with its hex nut, brass washer, and rubber gasket already in place. Apply a thin coating of pipe joint compound to the rubber gasket. **4.** Push the drain up through the bottom of the sink basin with one hand, and working from above with the other, thread the flange onto the drain. **5.**

With the two halves joined, orient the opening for the pop-up lever to the back of the sink, and tighten the hex nut, using large groove-joint pliers or a pipe wrench. **6.** Stop when the nut feels snug and the rubber washer is compressed against the basin outlet. Return topside, and trim the excess putty from around the flange using a knife. Then drop the lift rod through the opening in the top of the faucet. **7.** Next, insert the pop-up plug into the drain so that its offset slot faces the back of the basin. It should rest on top of the lever, slightly above the closed position. (If you want a pop-up that is removable, turn the offset toward the front of the basin.)

To engage the pop-up plug with the lift lever, loosen the nut that secures the lever in the drain tube. Withdraw the lever slightly, until you hear the pop-up plug drop, and then push the lever forward, into the plug's slot. **8** (inset). Screw the lever's nut back into place, but stop when you begin to feel resistance. The nylon seals in the drain body won't survive overtightening. For the best lift-rod position, slide the clevis bracket onto the lift rod and push the lever all the way down. Connect the lever to the second or third clevis hole from the bottom, and squeeze the clip onto the lever. **8.** Finally, with the lever and lift rod both in a lowered position, tighten the clevis screw against the rod.

Installing a New Bathroom Faucet and Drain

Tools and Materials

- New faucet
- Plumber's putty
- Pipe joint compound

TIME NEEDED: 1 HR.
- Adjustable wrench
- Groove-joint pliers

PLUMBING TIP: *Most new faucets come with a baseplate gasket to prevent water from seeping under the faucet. If yours doesn't, you can fill the base of the faucet with caulk before securing the faucet to the sink deck.*

3 *With the faucet installed, press a roll of plumber's putty around the underside of the drain flange.*

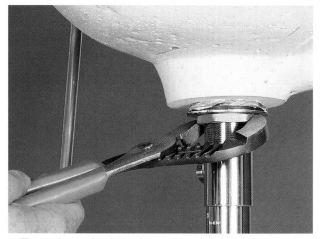

6 *Tighten the hex-shaped jamb nut with groove-joint pliers until it feels snug; then trim away the excess putty from above.*

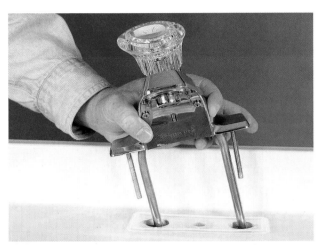

1 With the old faucet removed, set the base-plate gasket in place and insert the faucet's water lines through the deck holes.

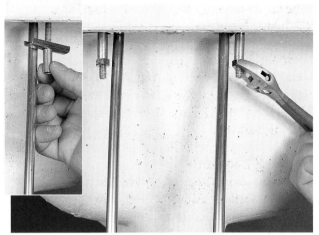

2 Install the extended washers and the spacers (inset), and thread the nuts onto the faucet's fastening bolts.

4 If it's not already in place, slide the cone-shaped gasket onto the drain and coat it with pipe joint compound.

5 Insert the drain through the basin's drain opening from below, and thread the flange ring onto it from above.

7 Lower the faucet's drain-plug lift rod through the hole in the top of the faucet until it bottoms out.

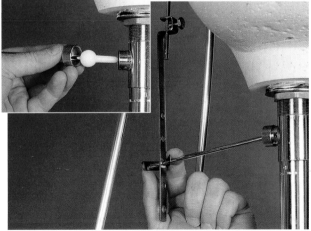

8 Insert the pop-up assembly (inset), connect the clevis through one of the lower holes (with the lever pointing down), and install the clip.

7 Installing Sinks & Related Equipment

How To Replace a Wall-Hung Bathroom Sink with a Vanity & Molded Top

Replacing a wall-hung bathroom sink with a vanity cabinet, a new faucet, and new basin is something you can do in a weekend.

Vanity Cabinets. Vanity cabinets come in a variety of standard widths and depths. They range from 18 to 60 inches wide and 16 to 24 inches deep. Unless your bathroom is unusually small or oddly shaped, you're sure to find one that will fit. You'll find everything from well-built hardwoods to unassembled particleboard. If all else fails, you might consider having one built, though that's an expensive option.

Sinks and Vanity Tops. When it comes to sinks and vanity tops, you'll find several choices in two basic categories. You can choose a molded top with an integral sink basin or a plywood top that is finished in tile or plastic laminate. In the latter case, you buy the basin separately and fit it into a hole cut into the top. (See "Installing a Sink in a Plywood Top," page 141.)

Removing the Wall-Hung Bathroom Sink

Wall-hung bathroom sinks hang from a steel or cast-iron bracket that is screwed to the wall. The bracket lies just under the deck of the sink basin. The sink may also

Removing the Wall-Hung Bathroom Sink

Tools and Materials

- Screwdriver
- Groove-joint pliers
- 4-to-6-in. taping knife
- Drywall joint compound
- Utility knife
- Sandpaper

TIME NEEDED: 1 TO 2 HRS.

PLUMBING TIP: *Before pulling any fixture from a wall, cut the caulk or paint seal with a utility knife, and then bump the fixture loose before lifting.*

1 Begin by removing the fastening screws just under the sink deck; then cut the basin's caulk or paint seal.

2 Grip the basin at the sides, and carefully lift up off the hanger and out from the wall. Then unscrew the hanger from the wall.

3 With minor wall damage, cut out the caulk, knock down the high spots, and apply at least two coats of drywall joint compound.

be screwed to the wall. These two screw holes can be found at the lower corners of the deck apron. When removing a sink, start by turning off the water at the shutoff valve and removing the trap. Then loosen the compression nuts that secure the supply tubes to the shutoff valves or adapters. With the plumbing disconnected, remove the two screws from the apron. **1.** If the sink is caulked to the wall along its deck, slice through the caulk with a utility knife. Grip the sink on each side, and carefully lift it from the hanger bracket. **2.** Remove the bracket, and scrape away any caulk on the wall.

Wall Repair. You may see some minor wall damage, ranging from torn drywall paper to screw holes to a gaping hole in the wall. To repair drywall, start by knocking down any high spots, including those around screw holes. Use a hammer or the end of the knife handle to batter high spots into slight depressions. Wipe on a thin coat of drywall joint compound with a 4-inch taping knife. **3.** This first application is just a base coat, so don't worry about the finish. Just put it on, and walk away. Better to apply three or four skim coats, which dry quickly, than one or two thick coats. After the first coat dries, knock down any high spots with a sanding block and give it at least one more skim coat, feathering the edges around the perimeter. When the final coat has dried, sand it lightly. Finally, paint the area with primer and a top coat.

At this point, you'll also need to remove the base trim from the wall where the new cabinet will go. Pry the base moldings loose using a pry bar. Place a small square of plywood under the bar to protect the wall.

Installing the Cabinet and Top

When walls and floors are plumb and level, vanity installations are easy. First, locate the wall studs behind where the cabinet will be. An electronic stud finder works best. Set the cabinet in place, and screw its back brace to the wall studs. Use 3-inch drywall screws, and predrill holes through the brace to clear the screw threads. You'll need to hit at least one stud. You may also want to trim out the toekick with cove or baseboard.

Unfortunately, though, most floors and walls are a little out of square, either because the house has settled or because it was built that way. To check, move the cabinet into position and look for gaps along the wall. If

7 Installing Sinks & Related Equipment

Fixing Plaster

If a wall-hung sink is mounted on a plaster wall, the final coat of plaster may have been applied after the sink was installed. Expect to break a little plaster in the sink-removal process. You can fix minor plaster damage with standard drywall joint compound, but deeper damage, including missing chunks of plaster, require some perlite plaster or quick-setting drywall compound. Avoid filling deep holes with standard joint compound; it may take days to cure, shrinking as much as 30 percent.

Where plaster is loose or missing, carefully break out the loose material without enlarging the hole any more than necessary. Use a surface-forming plane or a rasp to knock down the perimeter of the hole. Mix plaster for the job in a plastic bucket, using enough cold water to bring the mixture to the consistency of toothpaste. Wait a few minutes for the plaster to stiffen; then stir and apply it directly over the wood or metal lath. Trowel on enough perlite plaster to bring the surface to within ⅛ inch of finish, and let it dry completely. Follow with several skim coats of drywall joint compound; then prime and paint the new surface.

1 Water-spray the area before applying the rough plaster.

2 Follow the plaster with several coats of drywall mud.

3 Seal the area with primer and a coat or two of paint.

you see a gap near the top, shim the bottom of the cabinet. Slide pine or cedar-shingle shims under the cabinet until you've closed the gap. Then mark the shims where they meet the cabinet, and pull them back out. **1.** Cut the excess from each one, and apply a spot of construction adhesive to the top side. Finally, slide the shims back in place, and screw the cabinet's back brace to the wall studs using 3-inch drywall screws. **2.** When you're finished, trim around the bottom of the vanity using baseboard or vinyl cove.

Attach the Top. Always install the faucet and drain assembly in the sink basin portion before setting a molded top. In fact, you can even install the supply tubes if you'd like. With the faucet and drain attached,

lift the molded top over the cabinet, and set it in place. If the vanity sits out in the open, center the top on the cabinet and push it back against the plumbing wall. When it looks right, hook up the drain and the water supplies, and turn on the water for a test. If you don't find any leaks, secure the counter to the cabinet. With a cultured marble top, it's best to glue it down with construction adhesive. Lift the front of the top about ¼ inch, and pump several daubs of adhesive between the top and cabinet along each side.

Dealing with Out-of-Square Wall Corners. What if your vanity is supposed to go into a corner and the corner isn't square? There are actually three practical solutions here, depending on the severity of the problem.

Installing the Cabinet and Top

Tools and Materials

- Vanity cabinet
- Cultured-marble top
- Level
- Shims, pencil

TIME NEEDED: 2 HRS.
- Saw or utility knife
- Variable-speed drill
- Belt sander

PLUMBING TIP: Floors and walls are seldom perfectly level and square. Expect to have to shim and trim. Everything fits better when you do.

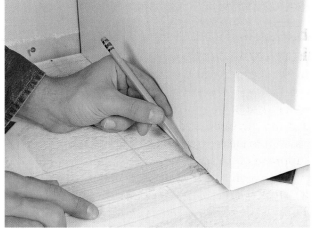

1 Slide a shim under a high corner of the vanity cabinet to level it, and mark the shim with a pencil. Cut and glue the shim in place.

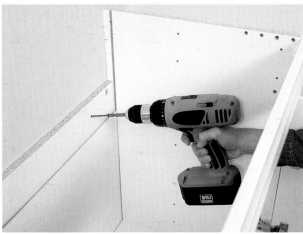

2 Locate the wall studs, and then use a variable-speed drill-driver and drywall screws to fasten the cabinet to the wall.

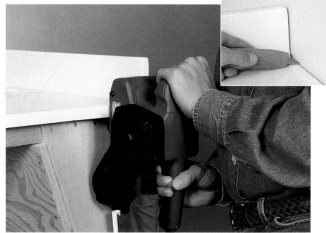

3 If an out-of-square corner makes for a bad fit, sand down the cultured-marble top or cut a recess in the drywall with a utility knife (inset).

With a minor gap of ⅛ inch or so, tub-and-tile caulk will disguise the joint. More serious gaps can be handled by shaving the top to fit the space or by notching the drywall to accept the top.

A belt sander works best in shaving one side of the top. Test-fit the top, mark the estimated stock removal, and sand the edge of the counter to this mark. **3.** You may have to sand and test-fit several times, but with patience, you're sure to find an acceptable compromise.

If you don't have a belt sander or if the top is made of a material that doesn't sand well, you can notch the drywall. Set the top in place, and push it tight against the corner. Using the top as a guide, draw or score a line on the wall indicating the upper limit of the notch. **3** (inset). Remove the top, and cut neatly along this line. Make a corresponding cut along the top of the cabinet, and dig out enough paper and gypsum to accept the edge of the top. Slide the top into the notch, fasten it to the vanity, and caulk the joint between the top and the wall.

Installing a Bathroom Sink in a Plywood Top

Plywood or high-density-particleboard tops are finished with plastic laminate or tile. You can buy them pre-laminated or install your own laminate or tile. Unlike a molded top, plywood and particleboard tops can hold screws, so it makes sense to screw them down. The standard approach is to screw from the bottom up, through the cabinet's corner brackets. (See the photograph above, right.) These brackets may be wood, plastic, or metal.

Choose your screws carefully, however. (Don't use a screw long enough to pierce the laminate glued to the

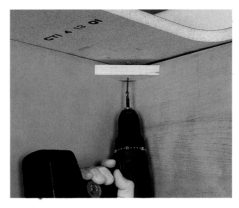

Use deck screws to secure the countertop to the cabinet. Measure carefully for the right screw length.

top of the counter.) Set the top in place; then measure from the bottom of the bracket to the bottom of the counter. Add the depth of the countertop (not the edge band) to this measurement, and subtract ⅜ inch to determine an overall length. If the brackets are made of plastic, remember that plastic can arch upward when you draw the screw tight. This lets the screw travel too far, which may put the laminate at risk. Stop when the screws begin to bind.

Cut the Sink Opening. If you have a new plastic-laminate top and would like to install a china, steel, cast-iron, or plastic-resin sink, don't be intimidated by the prospect of cutting an opening. (To cut an opening in a plywood countertop that you plan to tile, cut the opening before installing the tile.) You'll need a saber saw and a drill. If the new sink comes with a paper template, tape the template to the top, and cut along its dotted line. If you don't have a template, turn the sink upside down on the top, center it, and trace around it with a pencil. **1.**

7 Installing Sinks & Related Equipment

Installing a Sink in a Plywood Top

Tools and Materials

- New sink
- Countertop
- Pencil
- Saber saw

TIME NEEDED: 1–1½ HRS.

- Tub-and-tile caulk
- Sponge

PLUMBING TIP: *Uninstalled countertops can be cut from the top or bottom. Both methods work, but cutting from the bottom reduces chipping.*

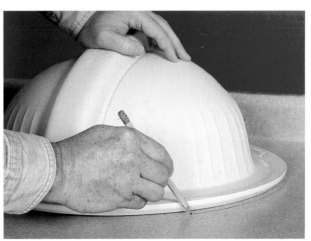

1 Set the basin upside down on the laminated countertop, and center it. Trace around it using a sharp pencil.

Sequence continues on next page

Continued from previous page

2 Draw a second line approximately ½ in. inside the traced basin outline, and cut along it with a saber saw. Set the basin into the cutout.

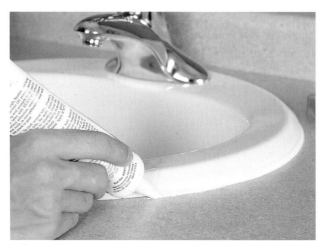

3 Install and connect the faucet and drain, and apply a bead of latex tub-and-tile caulk around the basin's rim.

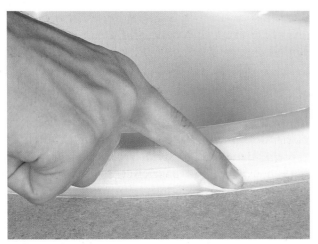

4 Use a finger to force the caulk under the basin's rim. There's no need to take great pains to be neat.

5 Use a wet sponge to smooth the joint and remove excess caulk. Leave only a thin line of caulk behind.

Remove the sink, and draw a second line roughly ½ inch inside the first. You'll cut along this interior line.

Drill a ⅜-inch hole through the top, just inside the line. Install a medium-course blade in a saber saw, and lower the blade into the hole. Cut along the line until you're within 6 inches of completing the circle. **2.** At this point, have a helper support the cutout. Just a little support from below will keep the cutout from falling abruptly and perhaps breaking the laminate in the process. (If the top's backsplash interferes with your saber saw, finish the cut using a utility saw from above or the saber saw from below.)

When you set the sink, adhere it with latex tub-and-tile caulk. In addition to having great adhesive qualities, latex caulk comes in a variety of colors.

Start by squeezing a liberal bead of caulk all along the joint. **3.** Draw a finger along the bead, smoothing it and forcing it into the joint. **4.** Finally, wipe away the excess caulk using a damp sponge or rag. Continue wiping until the joint appears uniform all the way around. **5.**

How To Replace a Kitchen Sink

Kitchen sinks come in several rim styles: self-rimming (cast iron, porcelain, solid-surface resin, and stainless steel), metal-rim (enameled steel and cast iron), and rimless (stainless steel, cast iron, and solid-surface resin).

Self-Rimming Sinks. The most popular is the self-rimming variety. A self-rimming sink has a rolled lip, which

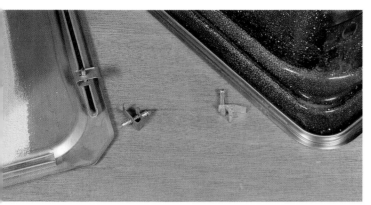

Fastening clips are used in both stainless-steel self-rimming sinks (left in photo) and metal-rim sinks.

rests directly on the counter. All that holds the cast-iron and solid-surface sinks steady is a bead of latex tub-and-tile caulk. Stainless-steel self-rimming sinks have a slightly different rim style. The sink rests on its rim, but special clips secure it from below. These clips slide into channels welded to the bottom of the sink rim. (See the photo above.) While this rim style is popular, a common complaint is that the rolled edge doesn't allow you to sweep food crumbs directly from the countertop into the sink.

Metal-Rim Sinks. The second rim style is more traditional. In this case, a separate metal support rim allows the sink to lay almost flush with the countertop. This rim, which is usually made of stainless steel, clamps over the unfinished edge of the sink. You place the entire assembly into a counter opening and use a series of metal clips to bind the rim to the counter. A metal-rim sink requires a more precisely cut opening. Most of these sinks are inexpensive enameled-steel models.

Rimless Sinks. And finally, there are rimless cast-iron, stainless-steel, and solid-surface resin sinks made to be installed in tiled or solid-surface countertops. Cast-iron sinks are installed similarly to self-rimming sinks. The depth of the sink perimeter lip approximates the thickness of ceramic tiles. This makes for a more uniform appearance, especially when you match the tile and cast-iron sink colors. Under-mount stainless-steel sinks and solid-surface resin sinks are attached from below, with the finished joint all but invisible in solid-surface installations. This makes for an integral solid-surface look because sink and countertop are the same material. Note that, to maintain the manufacturer's warranty, a professional must install solid-surface countertops.

Removing the Old Kitchen Sink

Tearing out the old sink is well over half the battle. How you proceed will depend on how the sink is mounted and whether you'll be leaving the countertop in place. If the old countertop is headed for the dumpster, don't bother separating the sink. Pitch it all. But if you plan to save the old countertop, you'll need to remove the sink and its components carefully.

Stubborn Drain Fittings. When all goes well, it's easy to remove a kitchen sink drain. Just disconnect the tailpiece, grip the spud nut with large groove-joint pliers or a spud wrench, and unscrew the nut from the drain spud. (See the photo below, left.) But if the drain is old, the pot-metal spud nut may be fused to the brass with corrosion. If a spud wrench or large pliers won't do the trick, spray the nut with penetrating oil. Give the lubricant 10 minutes to work, and try it again. If lubrication doesn't help, try driving the nut loose with a hammer

7 Installing Sinks & Related Equipment

Removing Stubborn Drain Fittings

Use a spud wrench or large pliers to remove a drain's spud nut.

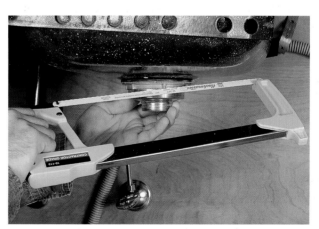

If the spud nut won't budge, remove it by cutting it in two using a hacksaw.

and cold chisel. Set the chisel against one of the tabs on the nut, and drive it in a counterclockwise direction. This will usually break the nut free, allowing you to finish with pliers or a wrench. If that doesn't work, switch to a hacksaw. Position the saw at a slight angle across the nut, and cut until you break through it. (See the photo on page 143, bottom right.)

Stubborn Sink Faucets. A similar approach works on old faucets whose fastening nuts won't break loose. Try a basin wrench and penetrating oil first; if they don't work, saw through the fastening bolts or the inlet shanks. A hacksaw won't fit in these cramped spaces, so use a hacksaw blade by itself. If you're the impatient type, a reciprocating saw fixed with a long metal-cutting blade will slice through faucet components in no time. Reciprocating saws are common rental items.

The Sink Itself. If the old sink is a self-rimming cast-iron or porcelain model, undo the water and waste connections and slice through the caulk between the sink and countertop. A sharp utility knife works best. Then just lift out the sink. If the old sink is a self-rimming stainless-steel unit or a rim-style model, you'll first need to remove the rim clips. (See the photo opposite, right.) The easiest way to remove clips is with a special sink-clip wrench, called a Hootie wrench, though a long screwdriver or nut driver will also work. If the old sink is made of cast iron, take note of the sink rim's corner brackets. These brackets are all that keep an extremely

Attaching Drain Fittings to the New Sink

Tools and Materials

- Drain kit
- Plumber's putty
- Spud wrench

TIME NEEDED: 30 MIN.

PLUMBING TIP: New drains tend to spin in place when you tighten them, which can ruin the paper gasket and squeeze out too much putty. It helps to lubricate the threads lightly with light machine oil.

1 Form plumber's putty into a ½-in. roll several inches long, and press it against the underside of the drain flange.

2 Insert the drain through the sink opening, and install the rubber gasket, paper gasket, and spud nut in that order.

3 Use a spud wrench or large pliers to tighten the spud nut. Trim any excess putty from around the flange in the sink, and tighten the nut again.

heavy sink from falling into the cabinet space. Leave the brackets in place until you've removed the sink. In fact, it's good practice to prop up the sink with a short piece of lumber when undoing the clips from a cast-iron sink. Stainless-steel sinks are much lighter and don't present a problem.

To remove the rim clips, unscrew the hex-head bolt from each one. When lifting a cast-iron sink, you may have difficulty getting a starting grip. Try lifting by the faucet column until you can get a hand under the rim. If that feels too awkward, remove the drain fittings and reach through the openings.

Attaching Drain Fittings to the New Sink

You will need to install a basket-strainer drain in each of the sink's drain outlets, unless you plan on putting in a waste-disposal unit. (See "Waste-Disposal Units," page 156.) Drain kits come with a removable basket strainer and a drain body, large spud nut, paper washer, rubber washer, and coupling nut. You will also need plumber's putty to seal the flange on the drain body.

Begin by setting the new sink on a worktable or on the kitchen floor near the sink cabinet. To keep from damaging the table or floor, place the sink on a piece of cardboard. Separate all drain components. Then roll a handful of putty between your hands until you form a rope roughly ½ inch thick and 10 inches long, and stick the putty to the underside of the drain flange. **1.**

Insert the drain through the sink opening, and press it into place. Working from the underside, slide the rubber washer onto the drain spud, followed by the paper washer and the large spud nut. **2.** Using a spud wrench

Rim clips like these hold metal-rim-style steel sinks in place. You must detach them before attempting to remove the sink from its opening.

or large groove-joint pliers, tighten the nut until much of the putty is squeezed from the flange inside the sink. **3.** Trim away the excess putty with a knife, and tighten some more. Trim the excess putty again, and continue to tighten. When the nut feels tight or the drain begins to spin, stop. For a double sink, install the remaining drain in similar fashion.

Attaching the Faucet

Faucets from different manufacturers differ slightly in the way you mount them, but the basic connections remain the same. You may have to vary some aspects of your installation, depending on your faucet design.

Place the faucet's base plate over the sink's deck holes, and insert the mounting shanks on each side. **1.** From underneath, slide a large washer onto each fastening shank, followed by a jamb nut. Turn the nuts until

7 Installing Sinks & Related Equipment

Attaching the Faucet

Tools and Materials

- New faucet
- Screwdriver
- Groove-joint pliers
- Latex tub-and-tile caulk

TIME NEEDED: 20–30 MIN.

PLUMBING TIP: *Sinks and faucets are often expensive, so do all you can to keep from damaging them—and the floor or countertop— during installation. Do the assembly on a sheet of cardboard or other protective material.*

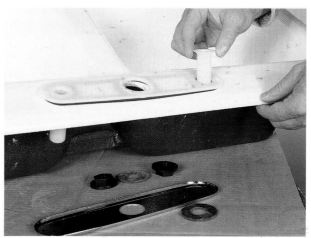

1 Center-column faucets work on sinks with one or three holes. For a multi-hole sink, install a base plate.

Sequence continues on next page

Continued from previous page

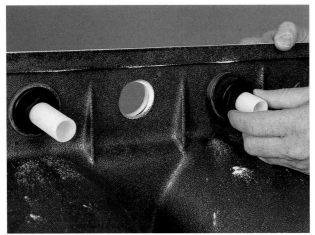

2 *Fasten the plastic base-plate support/gasket from below with plastic jamb nuts. Make them finger-tight.*

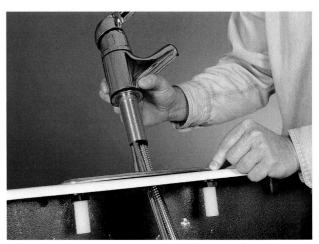

3 *Snap the decorative base plate in place over the plastic support, and insert the faucet's column through the center hole in the sink deck.*

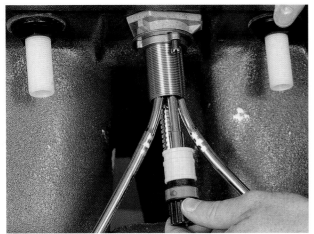

6 *Install the supply adapter on the faucet nipple. Most faucets use a slip fitting with an O-ring seal, as shown.*

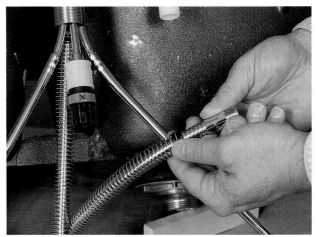

7 *Pull back the spiral tension spring at the bottom end of the spray hose to expose the male attachment threads.*

they're finger-tight. **2.** As you draw down the nuts, make sure the faucet's base plate is parallel with the back edge of the sink.

If the faucet is a single-handle type with central copper inlet tubes, straighten the tubes, position the decorative deck plate over the base plate, and insert the tubes through the center deck hole. **3.** Slide the mounting hardware (either a nut or a screw plate) onto the faucet shaft, and fasten the faucet in place. **4–5.** If the faucet has a pullout spout, connect the spout hose now. Attach the supplied adapter to the faucet nipple. **6.** Pull back the spring housing to reveal the male threads of the hose inlet end, and screw the hose into the adapter. **7–8.** Attach the outlet end of the hose to the faucet at the top of the spout housing to complete the connection. **9.**

Sinks come with either three or four deck holes. The fourth hole is for accessories like a separate hose sprayer, an instant hot-water dispenser, a soap dispenser, and the like. When codes require a backflow preventer in the dishwasher discharge hose, the fourth deck hole can also hold the backflow preventer. If you can't think of an add-on you'd care to own, plug the opening with a chrome or brass-plated sink-hole cover. Some snap in place, while others have a threaded fitting. The plug will need to be watertight, so caulk around it very lightly. The bead should be all but invisible.

Installing a Metal-Rim Sink

Sinks that require separate metal rims have the advantage of a neat, flush-fit appearance. The rim is T-shaped, with a horizontal support flange and a vertical extension. The bottom of the vertical extension is rolled over

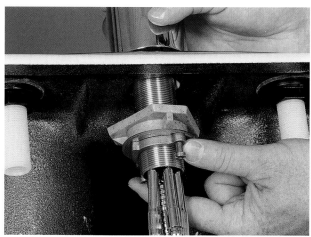

4 Slide the mounting hardware onto the column and tighten it. The unit shown has a plastic spacer, steel washer, and brass nut.

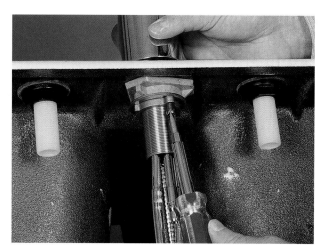

5 Use a screwdriver to drive the setscrews against the large washer. Stop when the screws feel snug.

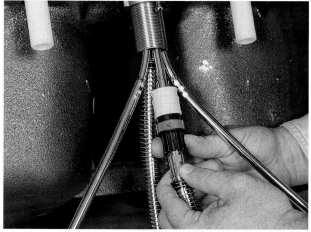

8 Tighten the male threads into the bottom of the faucet's supply adapter. Stop when it feels snug. Don't overtighten it.

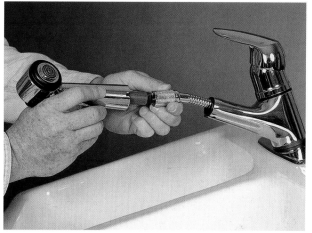

9 From above, thread the outlet end of the hose into the spray head. Pull the hose out several times to test it for ease of use.

7 Installing Sinks & Related Equipment

to form a lip. You need to cut a more precise opening in the countertop, and you'll have a dozen or so rim clips to install. As noted earlier, the easiest way to install clips is with a special clip wrench. Lacking such a wrench, a long, slotted screwdriver or nut driver will work.

Lay Out and Cut the Opening. When laying out the countertop opening, you won't need a paper template. Instead, the vertical extension of the rim serves as a template. Just position the rim on the countertop, with the flange on top, and trace around the outside of the vertical portion of the rim. **1** (page 148). Then cut carefully on this line using a saber saw. **1** (inset, page 148).

Install the Sink Rim. Sink rims are made to work on cast-iron sinks and on enameled-steel sinks. (Stainless-steel sinks have built-in clip channels.) As you inspect the rim, you'll notice that it has two sets of knock-in tabs running around its vertical band. These tabs, when folded in, support the rim of the sink before the clips are installed. The row of tabs closest to the flange are for steel sinks, while those farther from the flange are for thicker cast-iron sinks.

When buying a rim for a cast-iron sink, choose one that has separate corner brackets. Unlike steel sinks, cast-iron sinks are too heavy to be supported safely by thin metal tabs. If you can't find corner brackets, make a homemade support. (See "Supporting a Heavy Sink," page 152.)

To install a sink rim, set it over the sink and use a screwdriver to punch in all the perimeter tabs. **2** (page 148). Lift the sink into the opening, and settle it on its rim.

Install the Sink Clips. The sink clips and bolts will come unassembled in a plastic bag. Thread a bolt into each clip, and lay the clips within reach on the cabinet floor. Look closely, and you'll see that the clips have one hooked end and one flat end. Install the clips so that the hooked end fits into the rolled edge in the sink rim and the flat end grips the bottom of the counter. Tighten each bolt until the clip drives the sink up against the rim flange and pulls the flange down against the counter. **3.** A typical installation requires about a dozen clips, spaced roughly 8 inches apart. If the corners of the sink do not draw down completely, use an additional clip at each corner.

Installing sink clips is usually fairly straightforward. In some cases, however, the standard ¾-inch spacers that

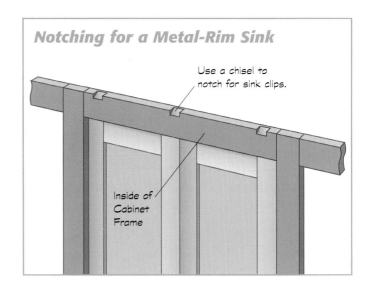

Notching for a Metal-Rim Sink

Use a chisel to notch for sink clips.

Inside of Cabinet Frame

Installing a Metal-Rim Sink

Tools and Materials

- Sink and rim
- Pencil
- Saber saw
- Screwdriver
- Rim Clips
- Sink-clip wrench

TIME NEEDED: 1–2 HRS.

PLUMBING TIP: *Plumber's putty has long been used to seal rim-style sinks. But putty grows black and brittle with age, so a better choice today is latex tub-and-tile caulk.*

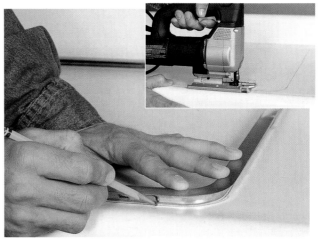

1 Position the sink rim on the countertop, centered over the sink base and parallel with the back wall, and trace around it.

2 Use a screwdriver to bend the tabs inward on the sink rim. With a cast-iron sink, install supporting corner brackets as well.

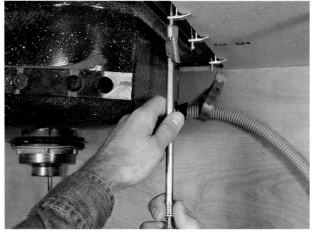

3 Use a sink-clip wrench (or a long nut driver or screwdriver) to drive the clip bolts against the underside of the counter.

Installing a Spray Attachment

If your faucet has a separate hose spray attachment, hook it up while you're installing the faucet. After attaching the faucet to the sink, fit the sprayer's deck fitting through the sink's fourth deck hole, slide the jamb nut onto the fitting's shank, and tighten it. **1–2.** Wrap two to three layers of pipe-thread sealing tape clockwise around the male threads of the faucet's center diverter nipple. **3.** Lacking tape, a small dab of pipe joint compound will work. If the hose has male threads and the faucet diverter nipple has female threads, apply tape or pipe joint compound to the male side. Thread the hose fitting onto the faucet's diverter fitting, and tighten it with an adjustable wrench. **4.** Then finish the faucet hookup by attaching the supply tubes. **5.**

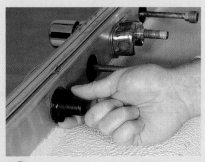

1 Insert the faucet, tightening the center nut with a wrench.

2 Install the spray attachment's deck fitting.

3 Wrap pipe sealing tape around the diverter nipple.

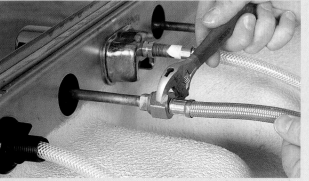

4 Feed the hose through the deck fitting and tighten it over the diverter nipple.

5 Install supply tubes onto the faucet stubs. Backhold the stubs on the final turn.

7 Installing Sinks & Related Equipment

separate the counter from the cabinet rails or the rails themselves will block a portion of the clip space along the front of the sink. If you find yourself unable to fit clips along the front of the sink, chisel a few clip slots in the rail or spacer material. (See the illustration on page 148, top right.)

Installing a Self-Rimming Cast-Iron Sink

Cast iron is heavy and expensive, so call a friend if you think you need help. With one of you on each side, lift the sink over the counter and into the sink opening. When it's set, carefully move it around until you have it centered and straight, relative to the backsplash. Don't be too concerned if the sink rocks in place. Some sinks become a little warped in the firing process. A warp of ¼ inch is acceptable, because when you've balanced and shimmed the sink corner to corner, you'll be able to fill the two ⅛-inch gaps with caulk. A warp greater than ¼ inch is too much. Insist on a replacement. In any case, wait until the sink is hooked-up and tested before doing any caulking.

Connecting the Traps

With two sink basins (each with a strainer-drain), you'll need a plastic sink waste kit and a plastic P-trap to complete the waste hookup. Depending on the rough-in position of the permanent piping, you may also need a tailpiece extension, one that has a female hub and compression fitting at one end.

The new sink waste kit will consist of two flanged

tailpieces, a baffled T-fitting, a 90-degree extension tube, and assorted nuts and washers. Two of the washers will be insert washers with an L-shaped profile. Insert one of these into the top of each flanged tailpiece. **1** (inset). Then slide metal coupling nuts onto the tailpieces, and thread the nuts onto the drain spuds. **1.** Next, install the baffled T-fitting on the tailpiece nearest the permanent drain piping. Connect the fitting and all subsequent joints with nylon compression washers and slip nuts. **2.**

Connect the Sink Basins. With the T-fitting in place and its branch inlet facing the drain on the other sink basin, hold the 90-degree extension tube between the tailpiece and the T. Mark it for length. **3.** Cut the tube with a hacksaw, making sure that you allow for the depth of the T's hub, and attach it to the remaining drain on the 90-degree end and to the T-fitting on the other. **4.** Next, hold the assembled P-trap in place so that the trap arm meets the piping outlet in the wall. If the trap will fit between the T-fitting and the drain outlet, hook it up directly. If you see a gap between the top of the trap hub and the bottom of the baffled T-fitting, you'll need to lengthen the drain using a fitted tailpiece extension. These extensions come in various lengths and can be cut to fit. If the T-fitting is too long, mark and cut it. **5.**

New-Construction Drainpipes. With all the piping ready, connect the trap to the permanent waste pipe in the floor or wall. In a new installation, where a 1½ inch PVC pipe exists in the wall, you'll need to fit this pipe with a ground-joint trap adapter. If you've purchased a plastic P-trap, the adapter will be included. Cut the PVC drainpipe (if needed), and glue the adapter to the pipe. **6.** Then connect the trap to the adapter using a compression washer and nut. **7A.**

Existing Drainpipes. If you're connecting the new trap to an existing drain fitting, expect one of two trap-to-drain arrangements. If the drain line was installed within the past 30 years, you may luck out and get a plastic ground-joint trap adapter. Slightly older homes may have copper or brass adapters. In all three cases, standard compression washers and nuts will make the transition.

But if the permanent piping is made of galvanized steel, expect a friction fit. In this case, substitute a flat rubber washer for the beveled nylon washer included with the trap. Flat washers, called

Connecting the Trap

Tools and Materials

- Hacksaw
- Sink trap kit
- Marker or pencil

TIME NEEDED: 30 MIN.

- Groove-joint pliers
- PVC primer, cement

PLUMBING TIP: When connecting a new sink trap to a corroded metal drainpipe, you'll sometimes have trouble making the seal with a rubber washer. If a leak here persists, discard the friction nut and washer, and join the trap and old drainpipe with a 1¼ x 1½-inch banded coupling.

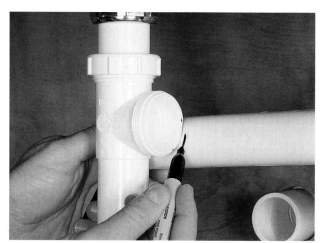

3 Hold the horizontal extension tube up to the baffled waste T-fitting, and mark the tube to length.

6 Apply PVC primer and cement to the outside of the drainpipe and the inside of the ground-joint adapter, and cement them together.

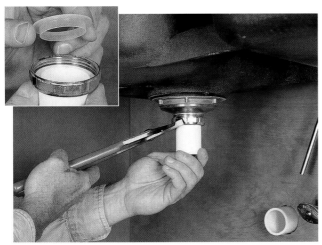

1 Press the nylon insert washer into the flanged tailpiece (inset), and tighten the tailpiece onto the drain spud.

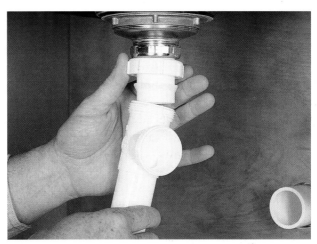

2 Slide a compression nut and beveled, nylon washer onto the tailpiece, and install the baffled T-fitting.

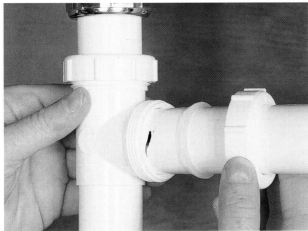

4 Install a compression nut and washer onto the horizontal extension tube, and tighten the tube in the T-fitting.

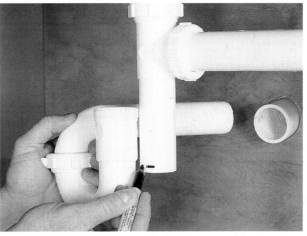

5 In similar fashion to Step 3, hold the trap in place and mark the T-fitting to length. Cut the T-fitting with a hacksaw.

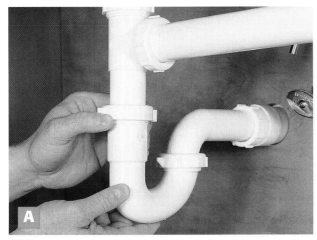

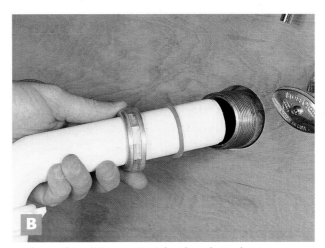

7 How you make the trap-to-drainpipe connection depends on the piping material at hand. A plastic ground-joint adapter (A) is best with plastic pipe and a flat, rubber washer and metal nut (B) are best when the drain is made of galvanized steel. A banded coupling is another option, but it costs much more.

7 Installing Sinks & Related Equipment

SMART TIP

Supporting a Heavy Sink

If you're planning to install a metal-rim cast-iron sink and can't find a rim with corner brackets, rig your own support using a 2x4 and ¼-inch rope. After installing the rim, lay a 36-inch 2x4 across the sink. Run the rope down through one drain opening and up through the next (or around a second, smaller, 2x4 set across the drain with a single-basin sink). Tie off the rope tightly around the 36-inch 2x4, and set the sink in the opening. After securing the clips and connecting the plumbing, undo your homemade support.

Installing a Cast-Iron Sink

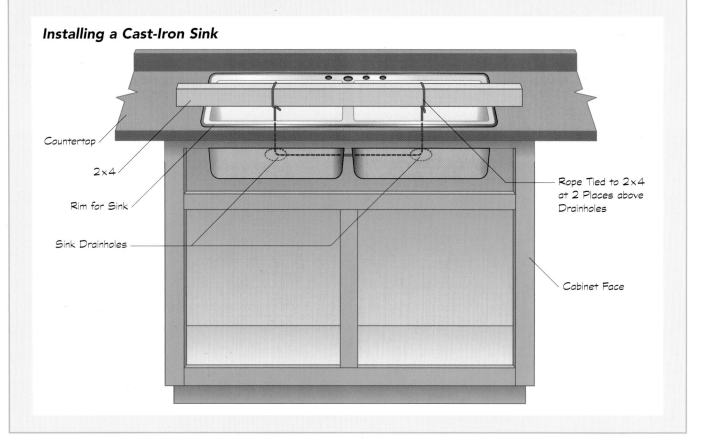

Countertop

2x4

Rim for Sink

Sink Drainholes

Rope Tied to 2x4 at 2 Places above Drainholes

Cabinet Face

friction washers, are those used on chrome traps. Every hardware store has them. To make a friction connection, slide a slip nut onto the trap arm, followed by a flat washer. Lubricate both sides of the washer with pipe joint compound, and then clean the end of the drain-pipe with sandpaper. Insert the trap arm into the drain, and slide the nut and washer forward. **7B** (page 151). Finally, tighten the nut onto the pipe's threads.

If you can't make a leak-proof connection with a friction washer and plenty of pipe joint compound, remove the nut and washer entirely and substitute a banded coupling. Choose a reducing coupling designed to join 1½-inch Schedule 40 PVC pipe to 1½ inch copper pipe.

Connecting the Water

Almost all water pipe-to-supply-tube connections these days are made with compression fittings, either adapters or valves. Only older homes have friction (cone) washer connections, and even these are easy to convert to compression fittings. Just clean the supply-pipe threads with a wire brush, coat them with pipe joint compound, and screw on new compression valves.

Connection Types. The kind of supply tube you use will depend, in part, on the type of connection on the faucet. Some faucets come with threaded shanks. Others have copper tubes fitted with threaded adapter nuts, and still others have copper tubes with no fittings. For those with threaded fittings, choose a ball-head supply tube or a prefitted stainless-steel-and-polymer tube. If your faucet has threaded adapters on copper tubes, be sure to backhold the adapters when tightening the coupling nuts.

Of the faucets that come with simple copper inlet

tubes, some have short tubes—about 6 inches long—and others have longer ones. The longer ones are usually long enough to reach water stub-outs in the wall. In that case, no supply tubes are needed. Just trim the inlet tubes to length, and join them to compression fittings or valves. If the copper inlet tubes are not long enough, the best approach is to buy supply tubes that have a ⅜-inch compression fitting at one end. Join the supply tube to the inlet tube with this fitting, and join the bottom end to the shutoff valve's compression fitting.

Leakproof Connection. To make a trouble-free connection at the shutoff valve or adapter, measure the water supply tube carefully. Make sure you factor in the depth of the fitting's hub. **1.** Then slide the compression nut onto the tube, followed by a brass compression ring, or ferrule. Coat the ferrule and fitting threads with pipe joint compound. **2.** Insert the tube into the valve port so that the tube meets the port head on. Even a slight angle can make the nut hard to start or cause it to bind once started. Turn the nut onto the threads, and continue to turn it until it's finger-tight. To make sure that the tube has not caused the nut to bind, wiggle it slightly and try to tighten the nut more. If you're satisfied that the nut is really finger-tight, give it an additional full turn with a small open-end or adjustable wrench. **3.** As always with compression fittings, the greater danger is that you'll overtighten. Better to have to tighten it a little more if it happens to leak than to ruin the connection at the start.

Connecting the Water

Tools and Materials

- Water supply tube
- Tubing cutter
- Pipe joint compound
- Adjustable wrench

TIME NEEDED: 30 MIN.

PLUMBING TIP: The trick to good compression connections is to have the supply tube enter the fitting exactly straight on. If it's off to one side, even a little, you'll have trouble getting the nut started. So if it isn't working, view the connection from another angle. Bend the tube or rotate the fitting as needed.

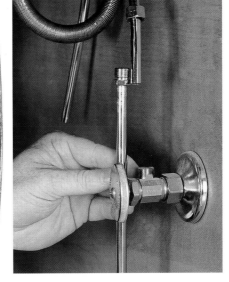

1 Hold the water supply tube between the faucet stub and the shutoff port, and mark it for length. Account for the depth of the fitting hub.

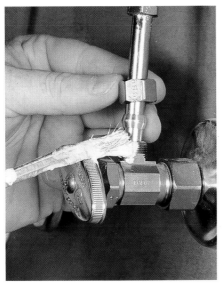

2 Connect the tube, and install the compression nut and ferrule. Coat the threads and ferrule with pipe joint compound.

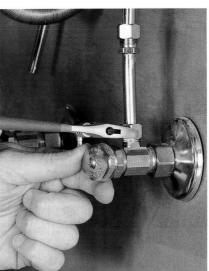

3 Tighten the compression nuts at both ends of the supply tube. Backhold the upper fitting.

How To Install a Laundry Sink

Plastic and fiberglass laundry sinks come in several forms. Some are freestanding, some are wall-hung, and some are counter-mounted. Counter-mounted sinks are made to drop into cabinets, like self-rimming kitchen sinks. Fiberglass is sturdier than plastic.

Laundry sinks require lower piping connections than bathroom and kitchen sinks. While a kitchen sink drain is roughed-in 18 inches above the floor, a laundry sink's connection shouldn't be higher than 13 inches, measured from the center of the drainpipe. You can install the water-pipe stub-outs 15 to 16 inches off the floor.

Other differences involve the drain fittings and mounting methods. Drop-in models require that you install a basket-strainer drain, like those used on kitchen sinks, while wall-hung and freestanding models usually come with a drain fitting molded right into the bottom of the sink. These drains come with a rubber stopper, like those used in older bathtubs.

Installing a Freestanding Laundry Sink

The deck holes on laundry sinks have 4-inch center spreads, so kitchen faucets, which have 8-inch spreads, won't work here. Many people use lavatory faucets on laundry sinks because they're affordable, but special 4-inch-spread utility faucets are a better choice. They're often made of heavy brass and have spouts fitted with hose threads.

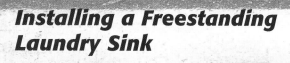

Installing a Freestanding Laundry Sink

Tools and Materials

- Laundry sink kit
- Screwdriver
- Hacksaw
- Adjustable wrench

TIME NEEDED: 1 HR.

PLUMBING TIP: *Freestanding laundry sinks are easy to bump out of position, which can cause both water- and drain-connection leaks. In addition to anchoring the legs to the floor, attach the sink to the wall with latex caulk.*

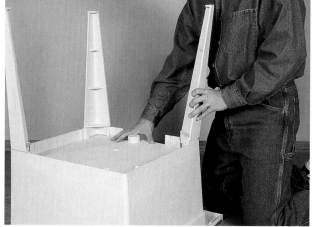

1 Turn the sink upside down to make it easier to install the legs. Just snap each leg into its molded slot.

2 Install a nylon insert washer in a flanged tailpiece, and connect the tailpiece with a slip nut. Attach the trap once the sink is in place.

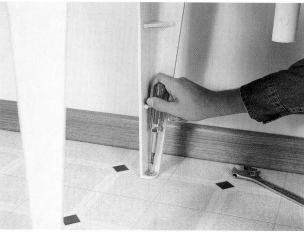

3 Use wood or utility (deck) screws to anchor the legs to the floor. On concrete, use screws and plastic anchors.

Install the faucet just as you would in a kitchen or bathroom sink. (See "Installing a New Bathroom Faucet and Drain," page 136.) Install the sink legs by snapping them into the molded slots on the bottom of the sink. **1.**

To hook up the trap and drainpipes, use a flanged tailpiece extension and the nylon-insert washer that comes with the sink. Set the washer on the drain; slip the tailpiece over the washer; and tighten the slip nut. **2.** Then trim the plastic tailpiece to length, and install a P-trap between the tailpiece and the permanent piping in the wall. Make the water connection with supply tubes, just as you would a kitchen-sink installation. (See "Connecting the Water," page 153.)

Each sink leg will have a hole in its base. Position the sink against the wall, and mark the floor through these openings. Then drill holes in the floor for screws. With a wooden floor, screw directly through the legs and into the floor with deck screws. **3.** On concrete, install plastic anchors in the floor and then screw into the anchors. Securing the legs is an important step, as it keeps the sink from getting bumped out of position.

If your freestanding sink has screw holes at the outer edges of its deck, screw the sink to the wall as well. This will make the fixture rock-steady.

Wall-Hung Laundry Sink. A wall-hung sink will come with a mounting bracket and two side covers. The trick is to screw the mounting bracket to a sturdy support feature. In new construction or a complete remodel,

---

How To Replace an S-Trap

As discussed in "Trap Variations," page 50, Chapter 3, a sink that is drained through the floor via an S-trap is no longer legal, because the trap can't be vented. If your fixtures now drain through S-traps, you won't be required to change them, however, because they're covered by the grandfather clause. (And besides, an S-trap is just the most visible symptom of an outdated system. Ideally, the entire drainage system should be rebuilt to meet current standards, although that's an expensive option that most people can't afford.)

Still, if you're replacing a sink that has an S-trap, you may as well do all you can to improve the way that new fixture performs and replace the trap. The solution is surprisingly easy and costs just a few dollars. It consists of installing an automatic vent device inside the sink cabinet. For more on automatic vents, see "Automatic Vent Device," page 44, Chapter 3.

Begin by attaching a banded coupling to the drain at floor level. (Or if possible, thread a 1½-inch PVC female adapter onto the drain's threads. These are the same threads used to connect the S-trap.) From the top of the coupling (or adapter), use two 45-degree PVC elbows to offset a riser to the back wall of the cabinet, about 4 inches left or right of center. Bring the riser up to trap level, about 18 inches off the floor, and install a sanitary T-fitting. Using a PVC ground-joint trap adapter, pipe the trap into the riser. Out of the top of the

T, extend the riser up 6 inches, ending with another 1½-inch female adapter. Thread an automatic vent device into this adapter.

Automatic vent devices don't last indefinitely, so remove the vent every couple of years and check its operation. With the vent in hand, its spring-loaded diaphragm should be held firmly against its seat. If the diaphragm is down even slightly or if the rubber has deteriorated, install a whole new unit.

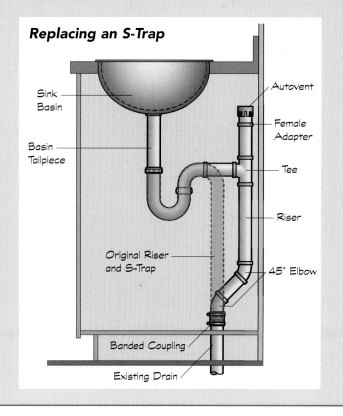

Replacing an S-Trap

Sink Basin

Basin Tailpiece

Autovent

Female Adapter

Tee

Riser

Original Riser and S-Trap

45° Elbow

Banded Coupling

Existing Drain

7 Installing Sinks & Related Equipment

you'll be able to provide 2×6 lumber backing in the wall. Position the top of the backing 32 inches off the floor. In a retrofit installation, position the mounting bracket so that you can anchor firmly into at least one stud. Use drywall anchors through the bracket on either side of the stud. Standard sink height is between 32 and 34 inches off the floor. With the bracket mounted, hang the sink on the bracket and install the side covers. These covers, which may be plastic or steel, also provide support to keep the sink from tipping down in front. Finally, make the water and waste connections, and caulk the joint between the sink deck and wall.

Waste-Disposal Units

The first thing to know about waste-disposal units is that they're not substitutes for trashcans. Despite the claims of some manufacturers, the list of things that a disposal unit can safely handle is fairly short. Soft food items like boiled potatoes and oatmeal or crispy vegetables such as lettuce, carrot or potato peels, and the like are easily ground into a pulp that can be flushed away with enough water. Hard or stringy food items, on the other hand, are troublesome. Celery, egg shells, coffee grounds, and even apple seeds are common sources of trouble. And of course, you should keep trash such as paper, plastic, twist-ties, and so on from making its way into a waste-disposal unit.

General Repairs and Maintenance

When a waste-disposal unit won't work, the problem is most likely either a jammed drum or a burned out motor. It's easy to clear a jammed drum, but unless the motor is still under warranty, it may not be worth repairing. The labor cost to diagnose and fix a used unit is often almost as much as the cost of a new unit.

Restarting a Jammed Waste-Disposal Unit. Manufacturers expect their units to stop once in a while, so they build in two useful features. One is a wrench slot in the unit's motor shaft; the other is an electric restart button. Both are located on the underside of the motor housing.

If you can't see or feel the obstruction from above, find the wrench that came with your waste-disposal unit or a large Allen wrench, and move to the bottom of the unit. Unplug the disposal and insert the wrench into the shaft at the bottom-center of the unit, and crank the motor back and forth. **1.** This will almost always clear the obstruction. You'll know you've made progress when the motor spins freely, without continuous resist-

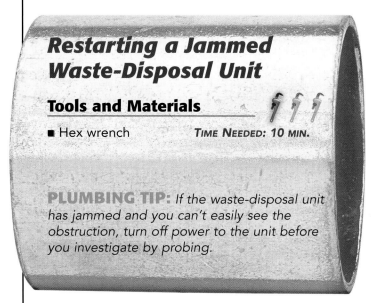

Restarting a Jammed Waste-Disposal Unit

Tools and Materials

- Hex wrench   TIME NEEDED: 10 MIN.

PLUMBING TIP: *If the waste-disposal unit has jammed and you can't easily see the obstruction, turn off power to the unit before you investigate by probing.*

ance. Plug in the unit and press the reset button to allow it to run again. **2.** Once the unit starts up again, test it. But make sure you use plenty of running water.

Routine Maintenance. Use cold water when grinding food scraps. To sharpen impeller blades, fill the waste-disposal unit with ice cubes and turn it on. Do this every couple of months. To keep a unit from developing a bad odor, use it often and with lots of running water. If your unit already smells, pour lemon juice into the drum and let it stand for a few minutes; then flush it. Run the unit with plenty of water thereafter. To clean the inner work-

Removing a Waste-Disposal Unit

Tools and Materials

- Screwdriver   TIME NEEDED: 30 MIN.
- Groove-joint pliers

PLUMBING TIP: *If you're not up to wiring a first-time disposal unit, pull the cable and install the boxes, then hire an electrician to install the breaker and switch.*

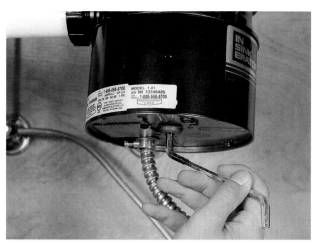

1 *Insert a hex wrench (either a regular Allen wrench or one supplied with the unit) into the motor shaft and spin the motor right and left.*

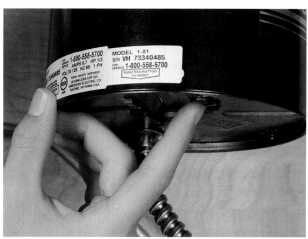

2 *When the motor seems to spin freely, press the reset button to restart the stalled motor. Do this several times, if needed.*

ings, quarter a potato, toss it in, and run the unit with cold water. When the drum is empty, run the unit with lots of hot water. And finally, avoid pouring your left-over sodas into the unit. Carbonated drinks contain carbonic acid, which is corrosive.

Removing a Waste-Disposal Unit

Unlike drain fittings, waste-disposal units don't become hopelessly stuck to sinks. The reason has to do with the mounting mechanisms, which range from simple hose-clamp fasteners to threaded-plastic collars to triple-layer bolt-on assemblies. The triple-layer mechanism

described here is the most common—and the most complicated.

To remove an old waste-disposal unit, start by shutting off the electrical power to the unit, either within the sink cabinet or at the main service panel. If your disposal unit also drains a dishwasher, loosen the hose clamp that secures the dishwasher discharge hose and pull the adapter from the waste-disposal-unit nipple. **1.** Next, loosen the horizontal waste tube's slip nut at the waste T-fitting, and undo the bolt or compression nut that secures the tube to the side of the disposal unit. **2.** Remove this tube.

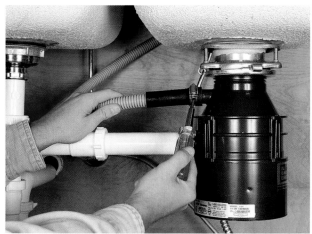

1 *Unscrew the hose clamp on the dishwasher discharge hose. Pull the hose from the disposal unit's inlet nipple.*

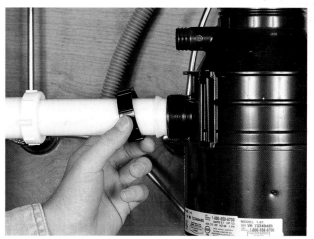

2 *Remove the waste connection at the side of the disposal unit. Some are bolted in, and some have compression nuts.*

Sequence continues on next page ➤

7 Installing Sinks & Related Equipment

Continued from previous page

3 Insert a screwdriver into one of the tabs of the retaining ring as shown, and rotate the ring counterclockwise.

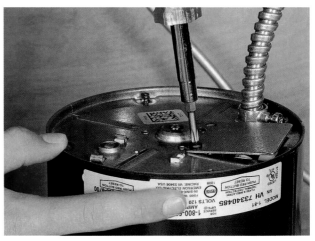

4 Once you have disconnected the disposal unit, lower it and turn it over. Use a screwdriver to remove the electrical box cover.

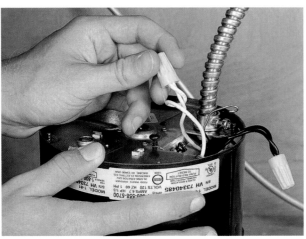

5 With the power shut off at the main panel, reach into the box and pull out the wires. Remove the twist connectors.

6 Disconnect the ground wire, and loosen the box connector. Pull the conduit and wires from the connector.

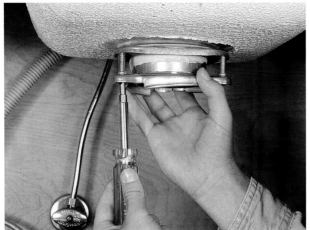

7 To remove the waste-disposal-unit drain fitting from under the sink, loosen the three bolts in the retaining ring.

8 With the pressure removed, slide the retaining ring up and use a screwdriver to pry off the snap ring to release the components.

To release the waste-disposal unit, look for three rolled-edge slots on the mounting ring. The ring is mounted at the top of the unit and has three such slots. Insert a screwdriver into one of the slots, and rotate the ring counterclockwise. **3.** If it won't budge, tap it with a hammer. As soon as the unit breaks free, support its bottom with one hand and rotate the nut about 2 inches until the unit falls away. This will leave only the bolted drain fitting in place.

With the disposal unit out, loosen the screw that holds the cover plate to the unit's electrical box. **4.** Pull the wires from the box, and undo the twist connectors and grounding screw. **5.** Then remove the fastening nut from the threaded box connector. This nut is located just inside the box, and you can turn it with your fingers as soon as you knock it loose with the screwdriver. With the nut removed, pull the connector and wires from the unit. **6.**

To undo the drain assembly, use a slotted screwdriver to loosen all three bolts separating the layers of the drain. **7.** With the bolts unscrewed about ½ inch, push the mounting flange up to reveal the locking ring. Pry this ring from its groove, and all the under-sink components will fall away. **8.** Lift the drain from the sink, and scrape away any old putty you find clinging to the basin under the flange.

Installing a Waste-Disposal Unit

In a simple one-for-one swap, just install the new waste-disposal unit in reverse order of removal of the old one, using existing wiring and waste fittings. If you're installing your first unit, start with the drain assembly.

SMART TIP
When To Replace a Waste-Disposal Unit

If, when using a wrench to free up a jammed waste-disposal unit, you can feel or hear a bearing grind or see lateral movement in the shaft, it is probably time to replace the unit. Also, if after pressing the reset button your unit makes a low humming noise and then trips again, you should replace it. As a last-ditch effort, you might drop the unit out of the sink and remove the large rubber gasket at its top. This allows you to see directly into the drum. You might find a piece of string or some other object binding one of the impellers. In most cases, however, the symptoms just mentioned signal a dead or dying unit.

Install the Drain Assembly. As with conventional kitchen sink drains, the drain that goes from a sink to a waste-disposal unit needs to be sealed with plumber's putty. Roll fresh room-temperature putty between your hands until you have a rope of it about 10 inches long and ½ inch thick. Press the putty around the underside to the drain flange, and press the flange onto the bottom of the sink at the outlet. **1.**

The drain assembly that attaches underneath the sink consists of a gasket, a sealing flange, a bolted flange (with a tapered edge to accept the mounting ring), and

7

Installing Sinks & Related Equipment

Installing a Waste-Disposal Unit

Tools and Materials

- Waste-disposal unit
- Plumber's putty
- Screwdriver
- Hacksaw
- Electrical cable

TIME NEEDED: 1 HR.
- Switch, box, pencil
- Utility saw
- Wire stripper
- Wire connectors

PLUMBING TIP: Assembling the under-sink drain connectors in a confined space is probably the most difficult part of this project.

1 Roll plumber's putty in your hands to make a 10-in. length with a diameter of about ½ in. Press it under the drain flange.

Sequence continues on next page

Continued from previous page

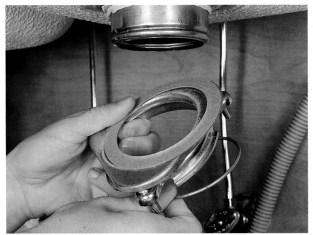

2 Slide the mounting assembly (gasket, sealing flange, mounting flange, and split ring) onto the drain spud.

3 Install the split ring at the bottom, and turn the flange bolts clockwise with a screwdriver, each in turn a little at a time, until they're snug.

5 Install the horizontal tailpiece extension between the existing second-sink T-fitting and the disposal unit.

6 If you want to hook up a dishwasher, drive the plug from the disposal unit's dishwasher nipple and connect the discharge hose.

a split retaining ring. **2.** Turn the flange bolts counter-clockwise until they're backed out of the bolted flange most of the way. Next, slide the gasket and the sealing flange onto the drain spud so that the sealing flange's smooth surface faces the sink. Then slide the bolted flange up against the sealing flange, with its slotted-taper facing down. While holding both flanges against the bottom of the sink, slip the retaining ring over the drain spud until it seats in its groove.

With the retaining ring in place, let the flanges down and rotate them until the bolts seat against the sealing flange. Tighten all three bolts, a little at a time, until you've drawn the components together and squeezed most of the putty from the in-sink flange. **3.**

With the drain assembly in place, lift the waste-disposal unit up to the drain and engage its mounting ring.

Rotate the ring clockwise until you feel stiff resistance. Then insert a screwdriver into one of the rolled-edge slots, and tighten the ring until it stops. **4.**

Connect the Waste Kit. Next, you must connect the waste kit. All waste-disposal units come with a 90-degree waste L-fitting. When installing the unit in a single-compartment sink, use the L-fitting to join the P-trap.

With a double sink, however, you don't need the L-fitting. Instead, buy a disposal-unit waste kit, which comes with a straight flanged tailpiece extension instead of the 90-degree waste L-fitting. The kit's assembly procedure is similar to that for installing a conventional sink waste kit. (See "Connecting the Trap," page 150.) The only difference is in how the flanged tailpiece joins the waste-

4 Lift the disposal unit to the drain fitting, and engage the mounting ring. Rotate the ring clockwise to secure the unit.

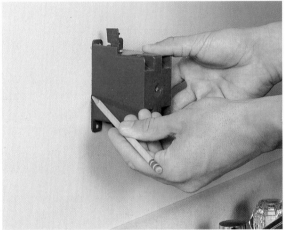

7 Hold a cut-in retrofit electrical box against the wall above the unit, and trace around it. Stay at least 1 in. away from studs.

Sequence continues on next page

disposal unit. All the parts you'll need, including a flange, a rubber gasket, and one or two bolts, come with the new unit. To make the connection, once you've assembled the rest of the kit, slide the compression washer and slip nut onto the tailpiece. Next, fit the gasket into the waste-disposal unit's outlet, slide the flange onto the tailpiece, and bolt the flange into the unit. Now slide the compression washer and slip nut toward the flange, and tighten the nut. **5.** The other end of the tailpiece joins the branch of the kit's waste T-fitting. Finally, remove the dishwasher knockout plug and attach the dishwasher drain hose if you have one. Tighten the supplied hose clamp to complete the connection. **6.**

Install the Wiring. Local building codes vary, but don't expect to be able to pull electricity from an existing

---

SMART TIP

Switching Options

If cutting a new switch box into a kitchen wall sounds like more of a project than you'd care to tackle, you might consider surface-mounting a switch box in the cabinet, just inside one of the cabinet doors. If this sounds like a great idea now, keep in mind that reaching into a cabinet several times a day won't be very handy.

Another way to avoid cutting a switch into a wall is to buy a batch-feed waste-disposal unit. To activate this type of unit, you press the stopper into the drain and give it a twist. These units can be ordered with three-prong plugs, so all you'd need to provide is a grounded receptacle inside the cabinet. This arrangement still requires a new circuit, however, so you may as well opt for the more convenient wall-switch option.

---

kitchen circuit to power your new waste-disposal unit. Most kitchen circuits are stretched to the limit already, and circuits with ground-fault circuit-interrupter (GFCI) protection won't be able to handle the startup overcurrent generated by these units. While a disposal unit and instant hot-water dispenser may be able to share a circuit, a disposal unit and dishwasher may not. You should bring a new circuit into the kitchen for a new waste-disposal unit.

Shut off the power at the main electrical service panel, and install a new 15-amp circuit breaker. (If you're not comfortable installing a circuit breaker, then run the cable between the panel and the waste-disposal unit, make the connection at the unit, and hire a licensed electrician to install the breaker. The job won't cost much this way, and you won't be exposing yourself to 100 amps or more of electricity. Leave at least 4 feet of cable hanging near the panel.) Extend 14/2G cable between the panel and the cabinet wall. Each house will present it's own barriers, but look for a basement or attic route of delivery. When you reach the kitchen wall behind the cabinets, drill into the wall, either through its sole plate or top plates. Choose a stud space behind the sink cabinet.

Install the Switch. To install a new switch box above the counter, locate the wall studs. Staying at least 1 inch away from the nearest stud, place a retrofit box against the drywall, and trace around its flange with a pencil. **7.**

Continued from previous page

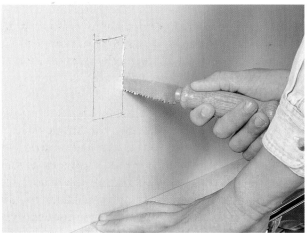

8 Use a utility saw to cut out the opening for the electrical switch box. Work carefully, and try for a tight fit.

9 Pull the cables into the cut-in box, and press the box into the wall. Engage the attachment tabs by tightening the screws.

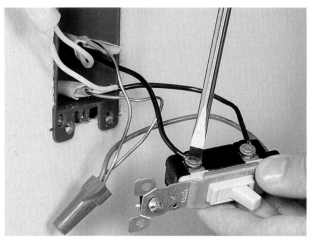

10 Wire the switch with black wires and a grounding pigtail; join the white wires and the grounding wires in separate connectors.

11 Use flex conduit between the wall and disposal unit, and join like-colored wires using twist connectors.

SMART TIP

Guidelines for Running Cable

When running cable across floor or ceiling joists, drill the center of each joist, and pull the cable through. Whatever you do, don't notch any joists. Notches weaken joists. When running cable along a joist, secure the cable using special cable staples every 4 feet. When possible, staple the cable within 8 inches of each outlet box. This won't be possible when using a retrofit box, of course. Any splices must be made in a permanently accessible junction box using wire connectors. New wiring requires a permit and inspection.

Cut along these lines with a utility saw. **8.** After cutting the box opening, bore a 1-inch hole below the countertop into the wall of the cabinet in which you'll install the waste-disposal unit.

Using electrical fish tape, feed the new cable into the stud space from the attic or basement, and pull at least 12 inches of cable into the kitchen through the new box opening. Again using fish tape, feed a second length of cable down through the switch opening, and pull it into the sink cabinet through the hole you bored. Leave at least 30 inches of cable showing in the cabinet and about 12 inches at the switch-box opening. Push the two cables into the retrofit box, strip the sheathing from the cable, and press the box into the wall. **9.** Tighten the bracket screws on the face of the box until the bracket grips the back side of the drywall.

To wire the switch, strip ⅝ inch of insulation from each wire. Join the white wires using a wire connector, and connect both grounds with a 6-inch pigtail to the green screw on the switch. Then connect the black wires to the screws on the side of the switch. **10.** Mount the switch in the box, and install the cover plate.

Before making the connection to the waste-disposal unit, slide about 24 inches of flex conduit over the cable in the cabinet, and push the conduit through the wall opening several inches. Then install a conduit box connector on the waste-disposal-unit end of the conduit, and strip the sheathing from the cable extending beyond the box connector.

To wire the new waste-disposal unit, remove its cover plate. Install a cable connector in the box. Trim the cable wires to length, and strip ⅝ inch of insulation from each wire. Feed the wires through the box connector, and with yellow twist connectors, join the unit's lead wires to the new circuit wires, white to white and black to black. **11.** Attach the circuit's bare wire to the grounding screw in the unit, and reattach the cover plate.

SMART TIP

Choosing a New Waste-Disposal Unit

As you shop, you'll notice a great range of prices. What's the difference? Materials and features. The inexpensive models may have only one impeller inside a steel drum, driven by a single-direction ⅓-hp motor. The higher-dollar models will likely have corrosion-proof stainless-steel upper bodies and ½-hp motors that are capable of driving in both directions. (A reversing motor alternates directions each time it is turned on.) These waste-disposal units are not as prone to the sort of one-way bind that an apple seed or fruit stem can cause. A reversing motor does automatically what you might have to do with a wrench.

Is a $200 model worth that much more than a $60 model? The answer depends on your expectations. The more-expensive waste-disposal units are less prone to stoppage and certainly have better components and a longer life span. But if you don't mind wrenching a stuck unit a couple of times a year, then something in the midrange ($80 to $100) will probably work fine.

Built-In Dishwashers

The best thing you can do for a dishwasher is to use it. If you don't for weeks on end, the water held in the pump may evaporate, allowing the seals to dry out and leak the next time you use the machine.

Maintenance. Check for a slimy dirt buildup on the lower section of the door seal at least once every few months. It's hard to see this accumulation from above, so use a pocket mirror. If you see signs of a buildup, clean the seal with detergent. While you're at it, lift the float from the bottom of the unit to check for dirt. A dirty float can increase the water level enough to cause a leak. And finally, check the spray arms for bits of plastic and other debris. If you see any debris in these holes, pick it out with tweezers.

Installation Requirements. A dishwasher requires hot water and electricity in order to function. Most often, the unit is located as close as possible to the kitchen sink for access to water. Location doesn't have much of an effect on electrical needs.

To wire the dishwasher, your minimum electrical requirements will be a dedicated 15-amp circuit run in 14/2G NM-B cable (14-gauge, two-wire-with-ground nonmetallic cable). If the dishwasher has a preheater, which boosts the temperature of the water, you may need a 20-amp circuit with heavier 12/2G cable. Check the manufacturer's specifications carefully. Some local codes allow a direct connection, in which the cable is brought into the opening through the back wall or the floor and is connected directly to the dishwasher's electrical box through a standard box connector. In this case, no conduit is needed. Other codes require a disconnect switch inside the sink cabinet. Any cable that you install in a cabinet needs to be encased in flexible conduit.

Removing an Old Dishwasher

If you're replacing a worn-out dishwasher, you'll need to remove the old unit before you can install a new machine. Turn off the dishwasher electrical circuit at the main breaker panel, and turn off the water at the shutoff valve.

You'll see a small access panel on the lower front portion of the dishwasher. Look around the perimeter of the panel for screws that hold it onto the frame of the machine. Remove the screws, and pull off the panel. **1** (page 164).

Next, you'll have to disconnect the water supply, the drain, and the electricity. Get a bowl or small pan, and place it under the 90-degree elbow of the water supply. Using an adjustable wrench, unscrew the compression nut holding the water supply tube to the elbow, and disconnect the tube. Hold the tube over the bowl or pan, and pull it back and down, free from the front of the dishwasher. **2.** Next, disconnect the drain hose just to the right of the water fitting, and allow any excess water to drain into the bowl. Finally, remove the cover of the machine's electrical box, and disconnect the wiring by unscrewing the wire connectors. Pull the circuit cable free of the machine.

With the water, drain, and power disconnected, carefully pull the old machine out and away from the cabinets. **3.** You may have to shimmy the machine out of the opening little by little until it's free.

SMART TIP

Hose Alternative

Many dishwashers come with a discharge hose already attached. If you buy one that does not or if your installation has the dishwasher farther away from the sink than is normal, you'll need to bring some of your own hose to the project. If you can't find a discharge hose locally, automotive heater hose is a reasonable substitute. It can easily handle prolonged exposure to heat and detergent. Take a piece of your discharge hose (or the size you need) to the store.

Removing an Old Dishwasher

Tools and Materials

- Screwdriver
- Nut driver
- Adjustable wrench
- Bowl or pan

TIME NEEDED: 30 MIN.

PLUMBING TIP: *It's easy to scratch hardwood or tear floor covering when pulling an old dishwasher from it's cabinet space. To prevent damage, tape cardboard to the floor before you move the dishwasher.*

1 *Begin by removing the old dishwasher's front access panel. Look for several hex-head or slotted screws holding it.*

2 *Have a pan or bowl handy when you disconnect the water and discharge lines. Drain the lines into the bowl.*

3 *Disconnect the brackets screwed to the underside of the countertop, and carefully pull the dishwasher out by the door.*

Installing a New Dishwasher

New dishwashers normally come boxed and mounted on a wooden frame. Carry the boxed unit into the kitchen, near the cabinet opening, and cut away the box. To keep from damaging the floor, save two of the cardboard panels. Place one directly behind the dishwasher, and tip the appliance on its back. Remove the lag bolts from the wooden frame, and then screw the leveling legs in at least half-way. This will shorten the dishwasher's overall height and allow you to slide it under the countertop's edge band. Remove the screws from the front access panel, as well. Set the panel aside.

Preliminary Connections. If your dishwasher did not come with a discharge hose, attach about 6 feet of hose to the purge pump's nipple, and secure it with a hose clamp. **1.** Feed the hose through the back of the unit's frame, and let it lay for the moment.

Next, you'll need the water connector, a 90-degree elbow with ½-inch MIP threads on one side and a ⅜-inch compression fitting on the other. Wrap three rounds of pipe-thread sealing tape counterclockwise around the threads of the fitting's ½-inch side, and start the elbow into the threaded port of the solenoid valve. **2.** Tighten the fitting until it feels snug. Stop when the ⅜-inch side points toward the dishwasher's purge pump.

If local codes allow a direct electrical connection, install a cable connector in the unit's electrical box and pull the wires out of the box. If the codes require a flexible conduit hookup, make this a conduit connector. **3.**

Installing a New Dishwasher

Tools and Materials

- Dishwasher, fittings
- Nut- and screw-driver
- Needle-nose pliers
- Adjustable wrench

TIME NEEDED: 2 HRS.
- Wire strippers
- Wire connectors
- Pipe sealing tape

PLUMBING TIP: *Dishwasher leaks are not always visible, so they can do a lot of damage. Install a battery-operated water alarm in the cabinet. Place the sensor under the dishwasher.*

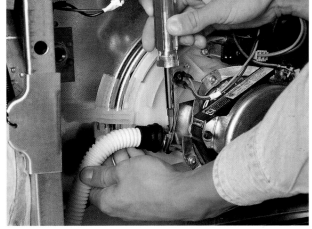

1 *Attach the discharge hose to the dishwasher's pump, and lock it firmly in place using the supplied hose clamp or grip ring.*

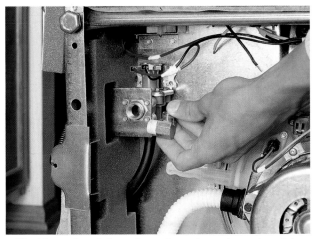

2 *Thread a dishwasher elbow into the solenoid valve. Use pipe-thread sealing tape, and wrench it until it's snug.*

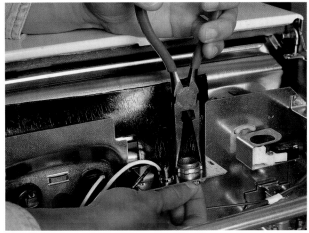

3 *Install a cable or conduit box connector in the unit's electrical box. It is required by the National Electrical Code.*

Sequence continues on next page

7 Installing Sinks & Related Equipment

Continued from previous page

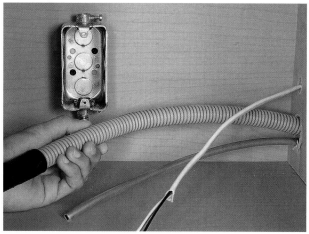

4 Attach a box in the cabinet (if needed), drill a hole in the cabinet side, and pull the water and discharge lines and electrical cable through.

5 Remove the existing hot-water compression valve (or adapter) from under the sink, and install a new dual stop valve.

8 With the unit positioned and leveled, screw the fastening brackets to the bottom of the counter-top's edge band.

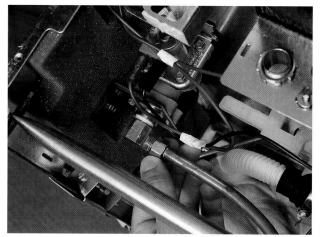

9 Slide a compression nut and ferrule onto the ⅜-in. copper water supply line, and connect the line to the dishwasher elbow.

Utilities. Leaving the dishwasher for a moment, drill water, waste, and power access holes through the side wall of the adjacent sink cabinet, just above the floor. Position the holes vertically, tight against the back wall. You'll need a 1½-inch hole for the water and drain lines. If the electrical feed line will pass through the sink base, you'll also need a ¾-inch hole for the conduit. **4.** (If you need to run a new circuit to this location, see "Installing a Waste-Disposal Unit," page 159, for instructions on running cable.)

Push a 5-foot length of ⅜-inch soft copper through the hole, and center the tube in the dishwasher opening, flat against the floor. Lay the electrical cable next to it.

You won't need to alter any permanent piping to make the water connection. Just tap into the existing faucet piping by replacing the existing hot-water shutoff valve (or compression adapter) with a ⅜ × ⅜-inch dual-outlet valve. Shut off the water main, and drain that part of the system. Remove the faucet supply tube, loosen the compression nut securing the existing valve (or adapter), and remove the valve. Lubricate the compression ferrule left on the riser using pipe joint compound, and install the new dual-outlet valve using the existing compression nut and ferrule. **5.** Then use the valve's ⅜-inch port to feed the faucet and the other to feed the dishwasher.

If you plan to hook up the dishwasher's drain to a waste-disposal-unit nipple, use a screwdriver or punch to break the plug from the nipple. Then reach into the waste-disposal unit, and retrieve the pieces.

If your sink does not have a waste-disposal unit, disconnect the sink's P-trap, and cut a dishwasher drain T-

6 Slide the dishwasher into the space. Stop several times to pull more cable and pipe into the cabinet as you proceed.

7 With the dishwasher in place under the countertop, thread the leveling legs down with an adjustable wrench and level the unit.

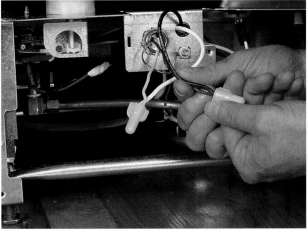

10 Join like-colored wires in twist connectors. Bond the grounding wire under the green ground screw.

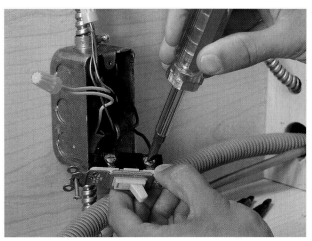

11 Attach the black wires to the switch (if you're using one). Join the white wires in a connector, and bond the ground to the box.

Sequence continues on next page

7 Installing Sinks & Related Equipment

fitting into the waste-kit assembly. This fitting (plastic or chrome) usually goes between the drain assembly's T and the trap, but if it won't fit there, you can splice it into the horizontal tube that joins the two sink drains.

Position the Dishwasher. With the water, drain, and electrical hookups prepared, place a cardboard panel in front of the dishwasher and return the unit to its upright position. Orient the back of the dishwasher to the front of the opening; then pull as much of the discharge hose as possible through the largest hole in the cabinet's side wall. Slowly push the dishwasher into the cabinet opening. **6.** Stop periodically to pull more of the hose into the cabinet.

Remove the cardboard, and adjust the leveling legs using an adjustable wrench. **7.** Raise the dishwasher until its fastening brackets come to rest against the bottom of the cabinet's upper rail or the countertop's edgeband and the unit is level. With all four legs touching the floor, the front sides of the dishwasher should run parallel with the cabinet stiles. When the dishwasher is level, screw the front brackets to the cabinet rail or countertop edge band. **8.**

Hook Up the Dishwasher. To make the water connection, bend the soft-copper supply tube to meet the dishwasher's elbow. Slide the compression nut and ferrule onto the tube, lubricate the ferrule with pipe joint compound, and thread the nut onto the elbow. Tighten it one turn past finger-tight. **9.**

To complete the electrical connection on the unit, attach the conduit to the box connector, strip about 6

Continued from previous page

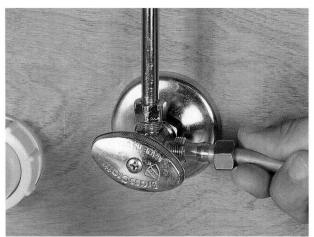

12 Install the dishwasher water supply line in one port of the dual stop valve, and connect the faucet supply tube to the other.

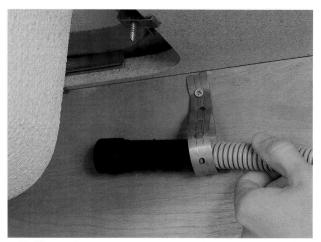

13 The discharge hose must connect to a backflow preventer or loop up to the top of the cabinet, secured with hole strap as shown.

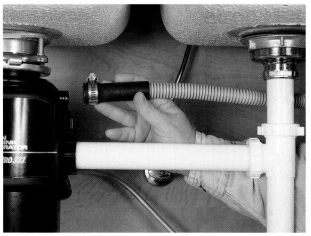

14 Attach the discharge hose to the waste-disposal-unit nipple (if applicable). Be sure to punch the plug from the nipple.

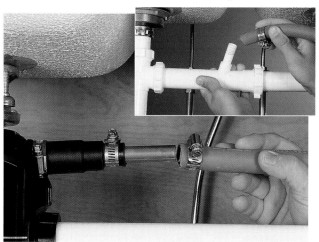

15 With heater hose, connect to the disposal unit using an adapter. If you don't have a disposal unit, use a waste T-fitting (inset).

inches of sheathing from the cable, and strip about ⅝ inch of insulation from the wires. Tighten the bare grounding wire under the ground screw in the box, and using wire connectors, join the dishwasher lead wires to the circuit or switch-leg wires, black to black and white to white. **10.** Then replace the box's cover plate.

Electrical and Water Connections. Moving back into the sink cabinet, hook up the electrical single-pole switch if you're using one. Connect the conduit and cable to the box, and strip the wires. Join the wires using wire connectors, and pigtail the grounding wires to the box. Attach the black wires to the switch: circuit wire to the brass screw and switch-leg wire to the silver screw. **11.** Then fasten the switch to the box using screws, and attach a cover plate.

Trim the copper water supply tube to length, and join it to the remaining port of the dual valve using a compression nut and brass ferrule. **12.** Turn on the water so that the connections are under pressure while you finish the job. Any leaks should appear within the next 10 minutes.

Codes require one of two backflow prevention methods for the discharge hose. Either install a backflow preventer or bring the hose up near the countertop level and secure it there. If a backflow preventer is mandated, you can install it in the fourth deck hole of the kitchen sink or in a new hole drilled through the countertop, near the sink deck. If an elevated loop will suffice, clamp it just beneath the countertop using a conduit strap: bring the hose up in a loop, pass it through the strap, and screw the strap to the bottom of the countertop or the back of the cabinet. **13.** A ⅝-inch wood or drywall screw is long enough to do the job and short enough to avoid piercing the laminate. In any case, don't just run the free end of the hose into the waste-disposal unit or the sink's waste T-fitting. If you do and the drain backs up, the overflow will spill into the dishwasher.

Waste Connection. If the discharge hose is a factory-supplied, ribbed-plastic version, it will fit right over the drain nipple on the waste-disposal unit. **14.** Just slide it on and secure it with a hose clamp.

If the discharge hose is ⅝-inch heater hose or a factory version very much like it, you'll need a dishwasher waste adapter. These rubber couplings are sized to fit the waste-disposal-unit nipple on one end and are stepped through several sizes on the other. To make the hose-to-adapter connection, trim off several steps with a knife so that the discharge hose fits inside the rubber adapter. Then secure it with a hose clamp.

While this method usually works, the adapter is pliable enough to allow a kink, so a better way is to splice a 3-inch piece of ½-inch copper pipe between the discharge hose and the adapter. The outside diameter of the pipe fits perfectly inside the hose and the smallest adapter size. **15.** Hose clamps hold it all together and keep the adapter from kinking.

If you don't have a waste-disposal unit, install a drainpipe with a dishwasher T-fitting and attach the drain hose to it. **15** (inset).

Final Check. With all connections made, turn the dishwasher on and run it through a complete cycle. Watch for leaks in the discharge and water lines. If a drip appears around a compression fitting, tighten it just enough to stop the leak. If water appears around the stems of the dual valve, tighten the packing nut in like fashion. Also, watch for excessive vibration. If the unit vibrates at all, look for a leveling leg that doesn't quite touch the floor. Adjust the leg accordingly. When everything checks out, install the access panel and put your new dishwasher to work.

A final note of caution: If this is your older home's first dishwasher, watch for a clogged kitchen drain line. A dishwasher's high-volume, hot-water purge often breaks up years of solid accumulation. This debris can gather at a choke point and clog an already slow drain. If this happens, cable the entire line and flush it with plenty of hot water.

The good news is that dishwashers keep kitchen drain lines squeaky clean. Cable the line once, and you won't need to do it again. Still, watch things closely during the first few load cycles.

Adding a Built-in Dishwasher

What if your kitchen wasn't designed with a built-in dishwasher in mind? With custom cabinets, it's going to be tough to create an opening. But if your kitchen has stock cabinets, with standard-sized units screwed together to make a continuous run, it's possible to remove one of the base units to make room for a dishwasher.

A conventional dishwasher requires a cabinet opening 24 inches wide, 24 inches deep, and at least 34½ inches tall, as measured to the underside of the countertop's edge band. (Most companies also make compact 18-inch models, which fit 18-inch-wide cabinet spaces.) The target cabinet should be a door unit. A drawer unit would work, but most kitchens have too few drawers for convenient storage already.

In conventional installations the dishwasher sits next to the sink cabinet, but this is not the only possibility. If you need to, you can skip a cabinet's width, but don't place the dishwasher more than 6 feet from the drain outlet. Not only will it be a hassle moving dishes from the sink to the dishwasher, but the unit's purge pump may not be up to the distance. If you do skip a cabinet's width, drill the side walls of the intervening cabinet, and pipe the water and discharge tubes straight through, tight against the back wall.

To free a cabinet, you'll have to remove three sets of screws, plus the toekick trim. One set of screws joins the cabinet stiles (the vertical hardwood framework). If you don't find them in the target cabinet, look at the stiles in the adjoining cabinets. The next set of screws will be in the corner brackets at the inside top of the cabinet. These secure the countertop to the cabinet. The final few will be in the back brace. These secure the cabinet to the wall studs. Toekick trim can be made of wood, hardboard, or vinyl. Work it loose using a pry bar.

Hot-Water Dispensers

Instant-hot-water dispensers are custom made for busy lives. At 190 degrees F, the water that these pint-sized appliances serve up is most likely at least 40 to 50 degrees hotter than that delivered by your water heater. (Water heaters are dangerous when used above 140 degrees F.) Water at a temperature of 190 degrees F is just right for blanching vegetables, making instant soups, and brewing real coffee, one cup at a time. Most units deliver 40 to 60 cups of hot water a day. The operating costs are about the same as a 40-watt lightbulb. Dispensers range in price from $90 to $250. The more expensive ones are better insulated and produce more hot water.

Basic Considerations. Hot-water dispensers are easy to install and don't require a dedicated water line. If you have copper pipes, you can steal water from the cold-water riser under the sink through a self-piercing saddle valve. This is the same kind of valve used to supply icemakers. (If your piping is made of brass or galvanized iron, you can still use a saddle valve, but you'll need to shut the system down and drill a tap hole into the riser.) If your cold-water riser ends at floor level or the back wall, keeping you from installing a saddle tap, you might consider splicing into the supply tube using a T-fitting and a ⅜-to-¼-inch reducing coupling.

Most units come with three-prong plugs, so a grounded receptacle inside the cabinet will do. Although a shared small-appliance circuit can power the dispenser, a dedicated circuit is a good idea. Expect the unit to consume between 4 and 5 amps of power. That's roughly one-third the capacity of a 15-amp waste-disposal-unit circuit or one-fifth of a 20-amp kitchen circuit. If you decide to run a new circuit, follow the same procedure and guidelines discussed in running circuits for waste-disposal units. (See "Installing a Waste-Disposal Unit," page 159.)

Installing an Instant Hot-Water Dispenser

Begin the installation of an integral-tank-and-faucet instant hot-water dispenser by installing the self-piercing saddle valve on the cold-water riser pipe. Back the tapping pin out as far as it will go, and with the rubber tapping seal in place, bolt the two halves of the assembly together over the riser. **1.** Draw the two bolts down alternately, a little at a time, until they feel snug.

Next, install the tank. Feed its threaded shank up through the fourth sink-deck hole, and screw the

mounting nut onto it from above. **2** (inset). This will leave the unit hanging loosely from the deck. To secure it firmly, turn the jamb nut clockwise until it contacts the deck, and then tighten it with a basin wrench. **2.** With the unit in place, insert the chromed spout into the port atop the shank, and tighten the setscrew. **3.**

To make the water connection, carefully bend the unit's ¼-inch copper supply tube down to meet the saddle valve, and trim it to length. Then join the tube to the valve's compression fitting. **5.**

Make sure all the fittings are tight, plug in the unit, and test it for leaks. If the water doesn't seem hot enough, hold a thermometer under the running water. It should read 190 degrees F. If it doesn't, adjust the temperature by turning the adjustment screw counterclockwise. **6.**

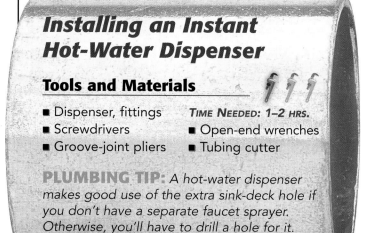

Installing an Instant Hot-Water Dispenser

Tools and Materials

- Dispenser, fittings
- Screwdrivers
- Groove-joint pliers

TIME NEEDED: 1–2 HRS.
- Open-end wrenches
- Tubing cutter

PLUMBING TIP: A hot-water dispenser makes good use of the extra sink-deck hole if you don't have a separate faucet sprayer. Otherwise, you'll have to drill a hole for it.

3 Install the spout in the sink-deck fitting, and tighten the faucet's setscrew to secure it. The spout seals with an O-ring.

A Home for the Dispenser

Instant-hot-water dispensers are designed to be installed in the fourth deck hole of a kitchen sink. If you have a deck hole that is now plugged with a cover, remove the cover. If you have a stainless-steel sink without a fourth hole, you can cut a hole with a knockout punch. If you have a solid-surface sink, you can bore a 1¼-inch hole. You can't drill porcelain cast-iron or enameled-steel sinks, however. Your only choice here is to drill the countertop next to the sink. Make this 1¼-inch hole near the back of the countertop, beyond the reach of small children. Water from a hot-water dispenser (approximately 190 degrees F) can cause third-degree burns instantly. You'll also need to position the spout as close as possible to the sink, so its spout is near the basin. Before drilling a countertop, check the clearance under the sink. If the cabinet side wall is too near, a dispenser won't fit. Of course, you'll need a 120-volt receptacle in the cabinet as well. Check local codes to see whether a hot-water dispenser can share a circuit with a waste-disposal unit.

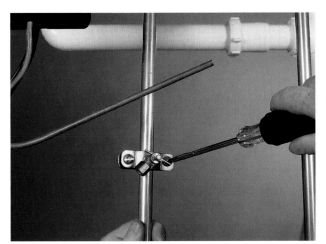

1 Make the water connection using the supplied saddle valve. All you have to do is clamp the valve onto the cold-water line.

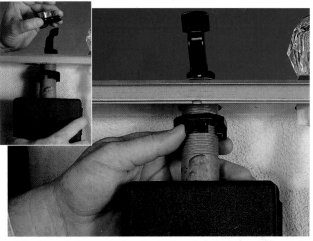

2 Feed the unit through the sink hole, and install the mounting nut from above (inset). Tighten the jamb nut below.

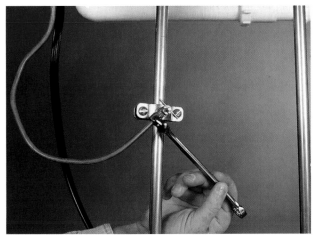

4 Connect the ¼-in. heater water line to the saddle valve using the supplied compression nut and ferrule. Use an open-end wrench as shown.

5 If the heating unit delivers water above or below 190 deg. F, adjust the temperature setting using a flat-blade screwdriver.

7 Installing Sinks & Related Equipment

CHAPTER 8

Faucet Repairs

aucet repair is an ideal do-it-yourself project. It's light work, and the parts are affordable—often less than $5 for a complete repair. With compression faucets, the material costs can run closer to 5¢ if you just have to replace a washer. (Hire a professional plumber to repair a faucet, and you will find that labor accounts for most of the bill.) But the longer you wait to fix a faucet, the more expensive a repair will become. A steady drip will eventually destroy important parts in the unit, requiring complete replacement (at a much higher cost than a repair) and wasting hundreds of gallons of water in the process.

Faucet Overview

Old fashioned single-inlet faucets could turn a supply of water on and off, but they provided only cold or hot water. To get warm water, you had to mix the hot and cold water in a basin. Dual-inlet faucets, now universally standard, can mix hot and cold water before sending it through the spout. You'll find dual-inlet faucets with four kinds of water-control mechanisms.
- Compression valve
- Cartridge
- Ball valve
- Ceramic disk valve (also usually in a cartridge)

8 Faucet Repairs

Cartridge Faucet. *With a cartridge faucet, repair usually consists of merely replacing the cartridge.*

Compression Faucet. *Compression faucets are fitted with a replaceable stem washer for low-cost repair.*

Washerless Faucet. *Many modern faucets use washerless technology in which handles pivot just one-quarter turn.*

Leakproof Water Control. To make a positive seal against continuous water pressure, one of two things is required: 1) some form of resilient gasket material to fill the gaps between sealing surfaces or 2) companion sealing surfaces that are rock hard and precisely machined for a tight, leakproof fit. Compression, ball-type, and many cartridge faucets use metal or nylon moving parts with neoprene-rubber washers, seals, or O-rings. Other cartridge designs use ceramic disks, which have an extremely hard, smooth surface. Many top-of-the-line faucets use ceramic-disk technology for water control.

There are hundreds of faucet makes and models in use today, each with its proprietary twist. In fact, when working on some older models you might wonder why anyone would clutter such a simple device with so many extra gaskets, spacers, and sleeves. If you come across one of these faucets, don't be overwhelmed. Just replace the

extra parts in reverse order of removal, and concentrate on the basics. Discussion of the four basic faucet designs follows. In some cases you may be able to identify your faucet type by looking at the faucet or identifying its brand. In others, you'll have to take the faucet apart.

Washer-Equipped Compression Faucets

The most familiar faucet may be the washer-equipped compression-type faucet, sold under many brand names. Compression faucets control water by means of threaded, washer-fitted stems that move up and down over brass seats. Every compression faucet consists of a handle, a packing nut and/or bonnet nut, a threaded stem with washer, a washer screw, and a brass seat. The washer fits into the seat to shut off the water.

In two-handle dual-inlet faucets, each inlet port has its own stem. (The compression design doesn't allow for single-handle dual-inlet faucets.) Single-stem compression faucets, including hose bibcocks, sillcocks, boiler drains, and old-fashioned single-inlet faucets are not mixing valves.

Washerless Faucets

When cartridge faucets first appeared in the late 1950s, they were touted as "washerless" at a time when virtually everyone was familiar with leaky washer faucets. Since then, other washerless designs have been developed, namely, ball-type and ceramic-disk faucets.

Virtually all washerless faucets operate according to the same design principle: inlet ports are moved into or out of alignment with companion ports in the faucet body. When the openings are aligned, water flows from pipes to spout. When rotated out of alignment, the flow

---

Washerless Faucets

Cartridge. *The stem in this faucet's cartridge travels vertically.*

Ball-Type. *The ball mechanism in this faucet arches and rotates.*

Ceramic Disk. *This faucet uses a hard ceramic disk to control flow.*

is sliced off. The degree and angle of rotation dictates the volume of the flow and the temperature of the mix. These faucets tend to work trouble-free longer than compression faucets for one very good reason: you can't over-tighten a cartridge faucet. While those who grew up with leaky compression faucets instinctively give faucet handles an extra twist, which hastens the destruction of the washer and results in a dripping faucet, washerless faucets can only be tipped or lifted (single-handle models) or rotated one-quarter turn (dual-handle models).

Cartridge. A cartridge faucet may have two handles, like compression faucets, or a single handle. If your faucet is an Aqualine, Moen, Price Pfister, or Valley brand single-handle model, it is probably a cartridge type. If it is a dual-handle model, you'll have to take it apart to tell what kind it is. For repairs, see pages 185 to 189.

Ball-Type. Ball-valve faucets are always single-handle units. The ball contains inlet ports that align with faucet-body ports to allow water flow. Movement of the ports alters the flow rate and hot-cold mixture. Delta and Peerless are the major ball-type faucet brands. For repairs, see pages 183 to 184.

Ceramic Disk. Another single-handle or two-handle design, ceramic-disk faucets contain a cylinder that houses two mating ceramic disks, one with inlet and outlet ports and one without. The disks slide into and out of alignment with each other to control water flow and temperature. If you have an American Standard or Reliant unit, it is likely a ceramic-disk faucet. For repairs, see pages 189 to 192.

Repairing Compression Faucets

Compression faucets have three basic problem areas, each with its own symptom.

- If the faucet drips from the end of the spout, you'll have to replace the seat washers and frequently the seats themselves. (See below.)

Compression Faucet Anatomy

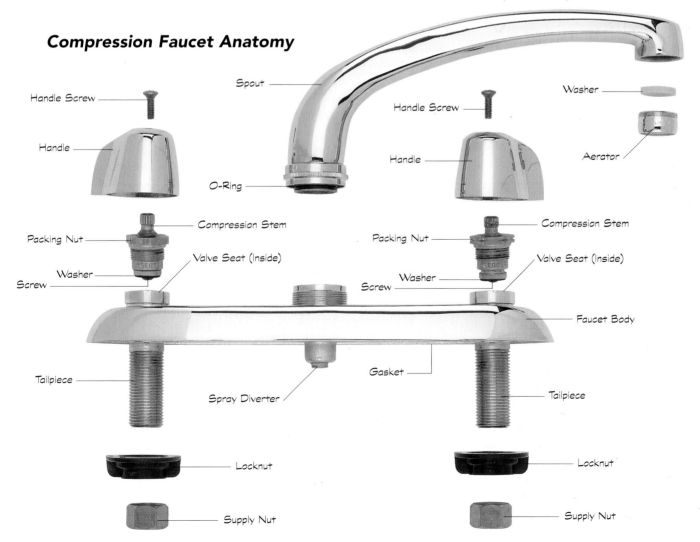

Handle Screw · Spout · Handle Screw · Washer · Handle · Handle · Aerator · O-Ring · Compression Stem · Compression Stem · Packing Nut · Packing Nut · Washer · Valve Seat (Inside) · Valve Seat (Inside) · Washer · Screw · Screw · Faucet Body · Gasket · Tailpiece · Tailpiece · Spray Diverter · Locknut · Locknut · Supply Nut · Supply Nut

8 Faucet Repairs

• If the faucet leaks around its handles when the water is turned on but not when the water is shut off, the stem packing is worn, and you should replace it. (See pages 180 to 182.)

• If a kitchen or bar faucet leaks around the base of its spout, replace the spout collar seals. (See page195.)

Replacing a Seat Washer To Fix a Leak

Compression faucets and valves need repair as soon as you notice them dripping or when their neoprene-rubber washers become old and brittle.

Handles First. To service the faucet, remove the handles after you turn off the water supply at the shutoff valves. Some older faucet models have exposed handle screws. If you don't see handle screws, either in the tops of the handles or on the sides of the handle collars, they are probably hidden under decorative index caps. Index caps are usually marked "H" and "C." To gain access to the handle screws, pry under the index caps with a sharp knife, and set them aside. **1.** To keep from reversing the hot- and cold-side stems, work on only one side at a time.

Remove the screw, and lift the handle from the first stem. **2.** If the handle won't budge, gently pry under it with a screwdriver or pry bar, padded with cardboard or fabric. If it still won't budge, stop prying.

Stuck Handle. Any handle can stick, but those made of inexpensive pot metal are the most difficult to release. Steady contact between the pot metal and the brass in the faucet stem causes electrolytic corrosion, fusing the dissimilar metals. When faced with really stuck handles, you'll have two choices. You can cut the handle with a hacksaw, slicing along one side to release its grip. After overhauling the faucet, install universal handles. You'll find them at home centers and retail plumbing outlets.

Another option is to buy an inexpensive handle puller, available at hardware stores. A handle puller looks and works a bit like an automotive wheel puller. It consists of a threaded stem, a T-handle, two side clamps, and a sliding collar. Insert the stem into the handle's screw hole until it bottoms out in the faucet stem. Press the side

Replacing a Seat Washer

Tools and Materials

■ Utility Knife ■ Screwdriver ■ Handle puller ■ Adjustable wrench ■ Repair kit

TIME NEEDED: 30 MIN.

PLUMBING TIP: If you can't break the faucet handle loose from the stem by prying with a screwdriver, buy or borrow a handle puller. They are not terribly expensive.

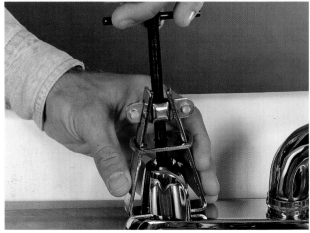

3 If you can't lift off the handle, it's best to use a handle puller. Drive the stem of the puller into the screw hole.

clamps under the handle, and slide the collar down to lock the clamps in place. Then twist the stem in a clockwise direction until you feel the handle break free. **3.**

Getting at the Washer. With the handle removed, look for the hex-head bonnet nut that locks the stem into the faucet. If you see two nuts, the smaller top nut will most likely be the packing nut and the nut threaded into or over the body will be the bonnet nut. Loosen the bonnet nut. **4.** If it binds before you can remove the stem, rotate the stem up or down. This should free the nut, allowing you to lift the stem from the faucet.

Expect to find a worn or broken rubber seat washer attached to the stem. **5.** Put the handle back on the stem to make it easier to work on. To remove the washer, back

the screw off the end of the stem. **5** (inset). Carefully pry the washer from the stem using a sharp knife.

Before replacing the seat washer, decide whether you should use a flat or beveled one. (The person before you may have installed the wrong type of washer, so don't assume the one you took out is what your faucet needs.) Examine the brass seat. (This is also a good time to check the seat for damage.) If the faucet's seat has a raised rim, approximately 1/16 inch tall, use a flat washer. If the seat is concave, without a pronounced rim, use a beveled washer.

The washer you install needs to fit the stem perfectly, so it's best to take the stem with you to your local hardware store. You can also buy a washer assortment kit. These kits usually include a variety of washer screws as well. Look for a kit with a dozen or more washer sizes.

1 After shutting off the water supply at the shut-off valve, pry the index cap from the handle with a sharp tool like a utility knife.

2 Use a screwdriver to remove the handle screw from the handle. The screw is most likely to be a Phillips-head type.

4 Use an adjustable wrench to loosen the bonnet nut. If the nut binds, turn the stem counter-clockwise as far as it will go and try again.

5 Lift the stem to expose the seat washer and screw. Reattach the handle to make working on the stem easier, and remove the washer screw.

8 Faucet Repairs

Sequence continues on next page

Continued from previous page

6 Choose the correct size and shape replacement washer for your faucet (by examining the valve seat), and press it into the stem's retainer.

7 Tighten the washer screw in place, and coat the washer and stem threads with heat-proof faucet grease before reinstalling the stem.

Installing the Washer. When you've located the right washer, press it into the stem's retainer, and tighten the screw through it. **6.** Before returning the stem to its faucet port, lubricate the washer with heat-proof or food-grade plumber's grease, available at hardware and plumbing outlets. **7.** Grease can sometimes double the life of a washer, especially if the seat is a little rough. Apply a dab of grease to the stem threads and to the top of the stem as well. Lubricating the coarse stem threads keeps the stem operating smoothly, and lubricating the stem keeps the handle from sticking. Don't grease the threads of the washer screws, however.

With the new seat washer installed on the stem and lubricated, thread the stem back into its port about halfway. Then thread the bonnet nut into the faucet or over the faucet port. At some point, the stem may cause the bonnet nut to bind. Thread the stem up or down a little to release the bind. Continue tightening the bonnet nut until it feels snug and the stem turns freely. Finally, replace the faucet handle, and repeat the process with the remaining stem.

Replacing Faucet Seats

When the valve seat in a compression faucet appears pitted or feels rough, replace it if possible. New washers installed over damaged seats won't last long, and each subsequent leak will worsen the seat condition. Replacing a seat is not difficult, but finding a replacement can be time consuming.

First, determine whether the faucet has replaceable seats. Most kitchen and bathroom faucets do, but some

Replacing Faucet Seats

Use a seat wrench to remove a damaged replaceable faucet seat.

Slide the new seat onto the wrench, and install it in the faucet, turning clockwise.

tub faucets do not. Shutoff valves and hose bibcocks almost never have replaceable seats. To determine whether a seat is replaceable, use a flashlight to illuminate the inside of the faucet and look for a wrenching surface in the throat of the seat. If the inner surface of the inlet is hex shaped or has four deep grooves, the seat is replaceable. If it's smooth, the seat was machined into the faucet body and is not replaceable. (To refurbish a permanent seat, see "Grinding Faucet Seats," at right.)

Removing the Seat. To remove a defective seat, you'll need a seat wrench—an inexpensive L-shaped tool with two tapered ends, one large and one small. The wrenching surface on some models is a continuous taper; on others, it's stepped, small to large. Both types work. Just insert one end of the wrench through the throat of the seat, and press down firmly. While bearing down on the wrench, rotate it in a counterclockwise direction. When the seat breaks free, spin it out. If a seat refuses to budge, position the wrench squarely in the seat and tap the wrench lightly with a hammer. The seat-to-faucet connection is brass to brass, so the seat should break free with little effort.

Faucet seats come in many shapes and sizes, so take the old one with you to a well-stocked plumbing store to be sure you get an exact replacement. The profile of the replacement may appear slightly different, but its threads, height, and rim size should match those of the seat you've removed. When you get it home, wedge the new seat onto the wrench and tighten it into the faucet port (photo at bottom right, opposite). Assuming the stem is in good condition, the new seat should give the faucet years of new life.

Grinding Faucet Seats

You should refurbish faucet or valve seats when the seats are not replaceable, of course, or when obtaining replacement seats is too difficult.

You'll need a seat-dressing tool. You can rent a professional model or buy an inexpensive version, such as the one shown below, at most hardware stores. Inexpensive seat dressers include a threaded stem with a T-handle and several grinding blades. The blades are flat disks with cutting or burnishing surfaces stamped into them. A typical kit has one coarse cutting blade, a medium-coarse blade, and a burnisher. The working progression is always from coarse to fine.

To dress the seat, turn off the water at the shutoff valves and remove the stem from the faucet. Attach the coarsest blade to the seat dresser, and insert the tool into the faucet port (top photo, below). With the blade resting squarely on the rim of the faucet seat, press down firmly and rotate the tool clockwise (bottom photo).

Grinding Faucet Seats

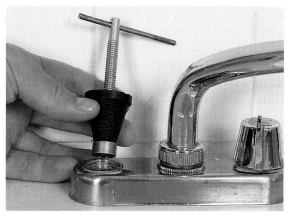

Start with a coarse blade in the seat dresser, and feed it into the faucet port.

Hold the seat dresser straight, press down on it, and twist it clockwise.

SMART TIP

"H" Is for Left

The hot-side faucet handle, usually marked "H" somewhere on the handle, should always be on the left as you face the faucet. If it's not, the faucet may have been installed backward or the water lines under the sink may be reversed. To see whether the faucet was installed backward, check the stems. They may look alike, but they don't rotate the same. With compression faucets, you turn the water on by rotating the hot-water handle counterclockwise and the cold-water handle clockwise. If your faucet doesn't work that way, someone reversed the stems. A repair is your chance to correct them.

Each twist of the blade will remove a little brass from the seat surface. The goal is to reduce the height of the seat uniformly to a depth just below the deepest void in the rim. This is usually only ¹⁄₃₂ to ¹⁄₁₆ inch, so it doesn't take much. When you reach this point, switch to a medium-coarse blade to remove the roughness. Finally, attach the burnishing blade, and smooth the seat surface.

Repairing Worn Stem Packing

When you rotate a faucet stem up into the "On" position, water rushes past the seat and into the spout. It also rises against the top of the stem, where it is held in check by an O-ring or, in older faucets and valves, a soft filler material called packing string. The packing is compressed between the stem and packing or bonnet nut, and the packing seal is completed with a cone-shaped leather or graphite washer.

When O-rings are used, the stem will usually not have a separate packing washer; rather, the O-ring fits between the stem and a brass sleeve, or stem nut, and is held in place by the bonnet nut. (See "Replacing O-Ring Packing Seals," page 182.) In some faucets, the stem nut replaces the bonnet nut entirely. On faucets and valves where stem nuts have male threads, a thin nylon or composition washer seals between the nut and the faucet.

Simple Fixes. When dealing with valves and faucets that have separate packing nuts, try tightening the nut about one-half turn. This will usually compress the existing packing material enough to stop the leak. Several threads showing beneath the nut are a good indication that additional tightening will help. While you may

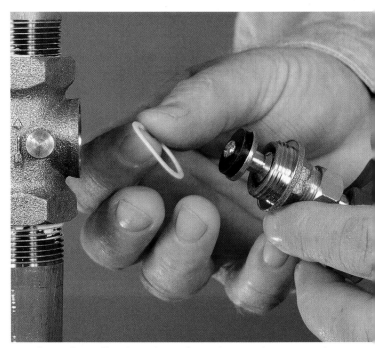

Modern shutoff valves *have flat nylon washers to seal the stem against the fitting body.*

need to remove the faucet handle to get to this kind of packing nut, you won't need to turn the water system off. Just tighten the nut until the leak stops.

If the leak persists, turn off the water at the shutoff valves, undo the nut, and raise it enough to clear the threads. Wrap packing string around the stem, just above the old packing washer, and retighten the nut. The added material will compress the old packing enough to create a new seal. While packing string works in most cases and will save your having to find a perfectly matched replacement washer, don't overdo it. Two turns around the stem are usually plenty. Add too much string, and you won't be able to get the nut started.

Replacing the Packing Washer. If a little packing string won't stop the leak, you might try adding more, but the better choice is to replace the packing washer. Turn off the water, loosen the packing nut, and lift it off the stem. **1.** Dig out the old packing, and slide a compatible replacement washer onto the stem. **2.** Slide it down, until it comes to rest against the stem washer or packing gland. A gland is a recessed area, usually in the top of a larger nut. Where a packing gland is in place, press the packing washer into the gland. Wrap packing string around the stem on top of the packing washer. **3.** Then tighten the packing nut until it feels snug. Turn the water back on, and test your work. If water seeps around the stem, continue to tighten the packing nut only until the leak stops.

Fixing O-Ring Stem Leaks

Over the years, most faucet and valve companies have gone to O-ring packing seals. The O-ring is held against the stem by a bonnet or stem nut. This nut may have male threads turned into a recessed body port. A large, flat washer made of nylon or a composition material seals the joint between the nut and faucet body. These assemblies are less susceptible to wear than graphite or leather packing washers, but both the O-ring and flat washer can fail. When they do, water appears under the handle, just as it does with older packing assemblies.

Neither O-rings nor flat washers are hard to replace, but you'll need a close replacement match. Take the stem to a well-stocked plumbing outlet.

SMART TIP

Turn Off the Water

The first step in servicing any faucet is to turn off the water, usually at the shutoff valves under the sink, and open the faucet to relieve any remaining water pressure in the supply lines. If you don't find valves under the sink, shut off the water at the meter (municipal water) or pressure tank (private well). And if you have plumbing fixtures on a floor or two above the sink on which you're working, open all upstairs faucets and drain the system.

Repairing the Packing Washer

Tools and Materials

TIME NEEDED: 30 MIN.

- Screwdriver
- Adjustable wrench
- Packing materials

PLUMBING TIP: If you have a single faucet that's in really bad shape, replace it with another. These simple compression faucets are still available, and most are very well made.

1 To repair a leak coming from the area of the packing washer, shut off the water and remove the handle and bonnet nut.

2 Pry off the old graphite packing washer using a flat-blade screwdriver, and slide a new washer onto the stem.

3 Wrap packing string around the stem to finish the job. For a quick fix, you can instead add packing string to the packing in an old faucet.

8 Faucet Repairs

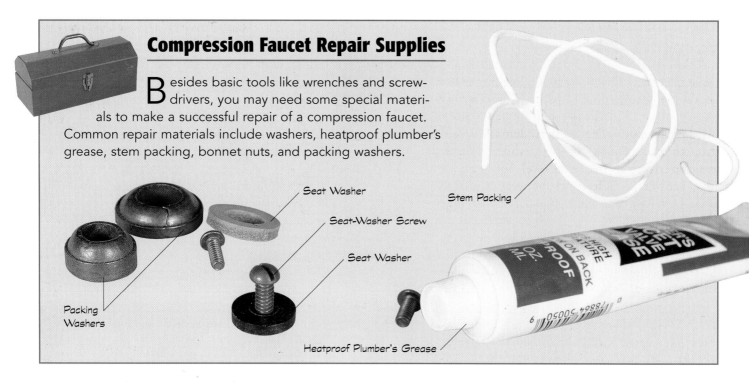

Compression Faucet Repair Supplies

Besides basic tools like wrenches and screwdrivers, you may need some special materials to make a successful repair of a compression faucet. Common repair materials include washers, heatproof plumber's grease, stem packing, bonnet nuts, and packing washers.

Stem Packing

Seat Washer

Seat-Washer Screw

Seat Washer

Packing Washers

Heatproof Plumber's Grease

Replacing O-Ring Packing Seals. To deal with O-ring stem leaks, shut off the water and drain the faucet or valve. Then remove the handle, and loosen the stem nut. Lift the stem from the port, and pull the nut from the stem. (See the photo below, left.) Roll or cut the old ring from the stem, and slide an exact replacement in place. If the old O-ring was seated in a groove in the stem, make sure the new ring seats as well. Lubricate the O-ring lightly with plumber's grease. (See the photo below, right.) Then press the stem nut back over the stem. As always with O-rings, try to find one that is made or at least recommended by the faucet manufacturer.

Although you won't usually need to, it's a good idea to replace the flat washer as a preventive measure, especially if one is included in the O-ring kit. If you find that the flat washer is leaking and don't have a replacement, you may be able to fortify the old washer with a thin layer of nonstick plumber's pipe-thread sealing tape. It works best if you stretch the tape around the washer, lapping it in the direction of the nut's rotation. Drop the washer into the recessed rim of the port, tighten the nut, replace the handle, and turn the water back on.

Replacing O-Ring Packing Seals

Expose the O-ring by lifting the bonnet nut from the faucet stem.

Roll a new O-ring onto the stem, and lubricate it using plumber's grease.

Fixing Ball-Type Faucets

Delta Faucet Company is one of the pioneers in alternative faucet design, with its proprietary ball-and-cam mechanism, and actually offers two name brands. The Delta trademark is sold through professional plumbers, while the Peerless line is sold at the retail level. You'll notice slight cosmetic differences between the two lines, but both use the original ball-and-cam mechanism.

What traditional ball-type faucets have going for them is affordable repair parts. You don't usually discard the entire mechanism. Instead, you can replace only those parts that are worn, which in many cases, are the springs and rubber seals. Several repair kits are available. Some include only the inlet springs and seals; some include seals, springs, and cam cover; and some include all mechanical components, including a stainless-steel or plastic control ball and a special wrench needed to remove the old ball.

How to Repair a Leaky Ball Faucet

To gain access to a ball-type sink faucet, turn off the water at the shutoff valves and tip up the handle. Loosen the Allen screw in the lower-front section of the handle, and lift off the handle. **1.** Where the handle had been, you'll find a large chrome cap with either wrenching surfaces or a

Ball-Type Faucet Anatomy

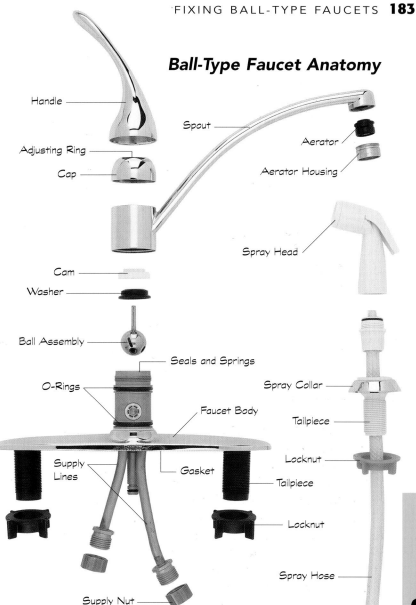

Handle
Spout
Adjusting Ring
Cap
Aerator
Aerator Housing
Spray Head
Cam
Washer
Ball Assembly
Seals and Springs
O-Rings
Faucet Body
Spray Collar
Tailpiece
Locknut
Supply Lines
Gasket
Tailpiece
Locknut
Spray Hose
Supply Nut

Repairing Ball-Type Faucets

Tools and Materials

- Screwdriver   **TIME NEEDED: 30 MIN.**
- Groove-joint pliers
- Allen wrench
- Ball-type faucet repair kit

PLUMBING TIP: *It's hard to tell the difference between old and new springs and seals, so throw out the old ones as soon as you remove them to avoid mixing them up.*

1 To reach the handle screw, shut off the water and tip back the handle. Insert an Allen wrench or faucet tool, and remove the screw.

Sequence continues on next page

Continued from previous page

2 Loosen the cam nut to gain access to the ball assembly. Delta faucets have slotted nuts (inset); Peerless units have wrenching surfaces.

3 Lift the plastic cam to expose the ball assembly below. Plan at least to replace the cam and the faucet seals.

4 Lift the ball from the faucet body, and set it aside. Some kits come with replacement balls and some do not, so choose accordingly.

5 Use an Allen wrench or thin screwdriver to lift the rubber seals and springs from the inlet and outlet openings. Replace them all.

knurled rim. If the nut you see has wrenching surfaces, loosen the nut with smooth-jaw pliers or an adjustable wrench. **2.** If the cap has a knurled rim, use either the Delta wrench that comes with each repair kit or large adjustable pliers padded with cloth or duct tape. **2** (inset).

With the cap removed, lift the nylon and neoprene cam that covers the top of the ball. **3.** Then remove the ball. **4.** Set both aside. Reach into the faucet body, and using the Allen wrench or a small screwdriver, lift the cold-water rubber seal and its spring from the inlet port. Then lift the hot-water seal and spring. **5.** There's little noticeable difference between old and new seals and springs, so it's easy to get them mixed up. Throw out the old ones immediately. If you plan to replace the cam, discard it as well. If your faucet is more than 10 years old or has dripped for several months, replace the ball, too.

Reassembly. Assuming you'll be replacing everything except the ball, press each rubber seal onto its spring. Slide the seal and spring onto an Allen wrench or screwdriver, with the seal facing up. With an index finger holding the assembly in place, insert the spring and seal into the inlet. Install the remaining seal and spring in the same way.

With the new seals installed, press the ball into the body. The ball will have a peglike key on one side that matches a slot in the body, so there's no chance you'll get it wrong. Press the new cam cover over the ball, and align its key with the keyway on the faucet body. Push it down until the key engages, and then thread the cap over it. Tighten the cap until it feels snug, but don't overdo it. Replace the handle, and test your work. If the faucet drips or water appears around the handle, remove the handle and tighten the cap a little more.

Repairing Cartridge Faucets

Repair of a cartridge-type faucet usually consists of merely replacing a long, self-contained cartridge.

Cartridge faucets offer an important benefit: if the water piping was installed backward, you can still have the hot water on the left. All you do to reverse the hot and cold sides is rotate the stem 180 degrees. This is a handy feature in back-to-back bathrooms, where a shared set of risers leaves one bath with reversed piping. A reversible faucet saves pipe and aggravation. But you must also make sure you replace the cartridge in the same orientation.

Repairing a Single-Handle Kitchen Faucet

Begin by turning off the water at the shutoff valves. The faucet handle may or may not have a chrome or plastic index cap. If it does, pry under the cap with a utility knife to gain access to the handle screw. If it doesn't, like the one shown in the photo, just pull off the cover. **1.**

Remove the screw from the handle, and tip the handle up and back. **2** (page 186). The handle's cam slot fits

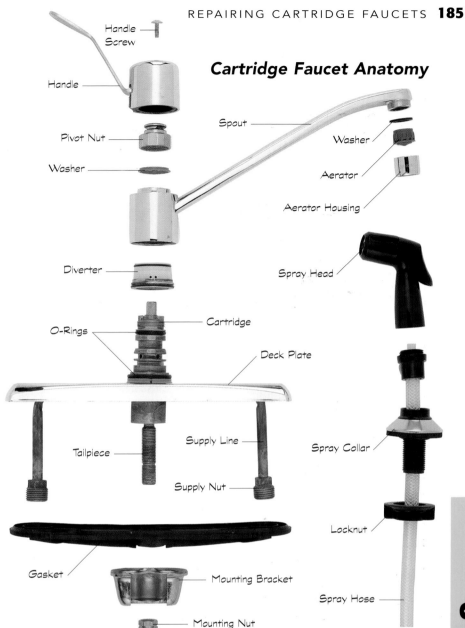

Cartridge Faucet Anatomy

Handle Screw
Handle
Pivot Nut
Washer
Diverter
O-Rings
Tailpiece
Gasket
Mounting Nut
Mounting Bracket
Supply Nut
Supply Line
Cartridge
Deck Plate
Spout
Washer
Aerator
Aerator Housing
Spray Head
Spray Collar
Locknut
Spray Hose

Repairing a Kitchen Cartridge Faucet

Tools and Materials

TIME NEEDED: 30 MIN.

- Screwdriver
- Needle-nose pliers
- Adjustable wrench
- New cartridge

PLUMBING TIP: *Sometimes, mineral buildup makes cartridges hard to remove from the faucet. Pour a little vinegar into the cavity, and wait a few minutes. The cartridge should break free when you next pull on it.*

1 *To get access to the handle screw, lift the decorative cap from the column. If there's no lift-off cap, pry up the index cap.*

Sequence continues on next page

Continued from previous page

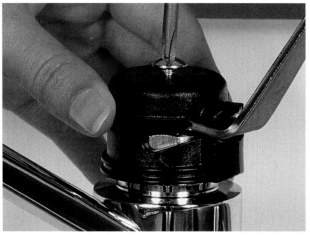

2 Remove the handle screw using a Phillips-head screwdriver. The screw is threaded into the stem of the cartridge.

3 Lift the handle and hood from the faucet to reveal the pivot nut. The hood covers the top of the cartridge.

4 Use an adjustable wrench to remove the pivot nut. Rotate the nut counterclockwise to unscrew it from the faucet body.

5 Using needle-nose pliers, withdraw the retainer clip to remove the cartridge (inset), and lift out the cartridge by the stem.

into a deep groove in the pivot nut, so expect to have to wiggle and coax it a bit. When the lever clears the pivot nut, lift it and its plastic hood from the faucet column. **3.** Loosen and remove the threaded pivot nut to reveal the top of the cartridge. **4.** Looking closely, you'll see that the cartridge is locked in place by a small U-shaped clip, positioned horizontally across the top of the cartridge. Use needle-nose pliers or a screwdriver to remove this clip. **5** (inset). Then grasp the cartridge stem, and pull straight up. **5.** If it feels stuck, grip it with pliers and pull a little harder: it will break free and come out.

Replacing the Cartridge and Handle. To make the repair, insert a new cartridge into the port, and press it down as far as it will go, aligning the flat notches in the stem with the brass-body slots. Insert the retainer clip. If it won't go in all the way, rotate the stem to correct a slight misalignment. Push the clip into its slot until it bottoms out. With the new cartridge locked in place, thread the pivot nut back onto the column and replace the handle.

Replacing the handle can also be tricky. The cam opening in the handle must engage the groove of the pivot nut. If it doesn't, the handle won't operate through its full range. You'll be able to turn the water on and off, but just barely. To avoid the problem, tip up the handle as high as it will go within its plastic hood. Carefully engage the back of the lever in the pivot nut's groove. When you feel it engage, press the handle down, install the stem screw, and replace the decorative cover. Turn the water back on, and test your work. If you find that the hot water is now on the right side, remove the handle and rotate the stem 180 degrees.

Repairing a Single-Handle Bath Cartridge Faucet

To repair a cartridge faucet for the bathroom sink, turn off the water at the shutoff valves and tilt back the handle. Using a utility knife, pry the red-and-blue index cap from the underside of the handle. **1.** Loosen the screw under the cap with an Allen wrench, and set the handle aside. With the handle removed, you'll see a brass or cast-metal cover screwed in place. Remove the screw and cover to reveal a plastic (usually gray) retaining ring. **2.** Rotate the ring counterclockwise until it lifts off, revealing a white nylon retaining nut. **3.** Pull the U-shaped (usually brass) retaining clip from the back of the nut, and remove the nut. **4** (page 188). Pull the cartridge from the faucet body using slip-joint pliers. **5** (page 188). Replace the entire cartridge, and assemble the remaining components in reverse order of removal.

Repairing Two-Handle Cartridge Faucets

Many manufacturers offer two-handle cartridge faucets, usually as low-cost alternatives to their single-control models. They are modestly priced and perfect for the mechanically timid because anyone can overhaul them.

Repairing a Single-Handle Cartridge Faucet

Tools and Materials

- Utility knife
- Allen wrench
- Screwdriver
- Slip-joint pliers
- New cartridge

TIME NEEDED: 30 MIN.

PLUMBING TIP: *If you can't get the cartridge out of the faucet and vinegar (to loosen minerals) doesn't work, buy a cartridge-extraction tool from a plumbing-supply store.*

1 Tip back the faucet handle as far as it will go. Pry out the decorative index plug using a utility knife, and remove the handle's Allen setscrew.

2 Loosen the fastening screw that secures the metal cover to the top of the faucet. Remove the screw and cover.

3 Rotate the plastic ring counterclockwise, and remove it to expose the nylon nut and cartridge retaining clip.

8 Faucet Repairs

Sequence continues on next page

Continued from previous page

4 *Pull out the U-shaped clip at the back of the assembly to free the nut and cartridge. Remove the nut, and set it aside.*

5 *Use pliers to pull out the old cartridge. If it won't budge and minerals don't seem to be the problem, buy a cartridge-extraction tool.*

To fix a leaking faucet, shut off the water and pry the index cap from the handle. **1.** Remove the handle, and loosen the cartridge nut using an adjustable wrench, smooth-jaw pliers, or groove-joint pliers with the jaws wrapped in duct tape. **2.** Lift the original cartridge from the faucet body, throw it away, and stick a new one in its place. **3.** Restore the nut and handle. Be sure to work on only one

SMART TIP

Getting Rid of a Faucet Sprayer

If the faucet spray attachment doesn't work properly and you'd rather be rid of it entirely, you can remove it and in the process free up the sink deck hole for a soap dispenser or hot-water dispenser. You'll have to close off the faucet nipple with a threaded cap, however. (Some nipples are threaded inside as well, so you can buy a threaded plug to close it off instead.) To eliminate the hose spray, remove it, apply pipe joint compound to the faucet nipple threads, and tighten the plug or cap onto the nipple.

Repairing a Two-Handle Cartridge Faucet

Tools and Materials

TIME NEEDED: 30 MIN.

- Utility knife
- Screwdriver
- Pliers
- New cartridge
- Plumber's grease

PLUMBING TIP: *Using plumber's grease, lubricate the O-rings on the replacement cartridge to make it easier to remove in the future and to minimize calcification problems.*

1 *Use a knife to pry the index cap from the handle. ("Hot" should be on the left.) Then remove the retaining screw, and lift off the handle.*

SMART TIP

Watch the Sleeve

Many single-handle cartridge sink and tub-shower faucets require an extra step before you can remove the retaining clip. With the handle off the faucet, you may see a stainless-steel sleeve installed over the cartridge and column. This sleeve is decorative, but it also keeps the clip from backing out. Pull the sleeve from the column, remove the clip, and replace the cartridge. As is the case with many single-handle cartridge faucets, reversed hot and cold sides can be corrected by rotating the stem 180 degrees.

With single-handle cartridge faucets, you might find stem sleeves that you must remove before you can reach the retainer.

side at a time to keep from accidentally reversing the cartridges. When you're finished, turn on the water to test your work.

Most dual-handle cartridge faucets have disposable cartridges similar to those just described. But some have spring-loaded rubber seals in the inlet ports like those you find in ball-type single-handle faucets. If upon lifting the cartridge you notice these accessible seals, keep the cartridge and replace only the seals and springs.

If you find that your faucet cartridges are hard to remove, hard-water calcification over the years may have stuck them in place. Some faucet manufacturers offer cartridge extraction tools, but it also helps to pour warm vinegar into the faucet port and around the cartridge. Give the vinegar a few minutes to work, and try pulling the cartridge again.

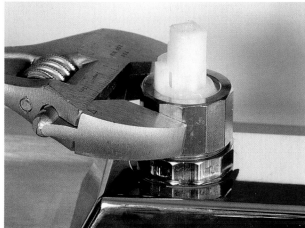

2 Using an adjustable wrench, turn the chrome retaining nut counterclockwise to remove it from the cartridge.

3 Lift out the old cartridge, and install an exact replacement. Before inserting the new cartridge, lubricate the O-rings with plumber's grease.

8 Faucet Repairs

Repairing Ceramic-Disk Faucets

Ceramic-disk faucets are particularly vulnerable to sediment accumulations. For this reason, don't assume that a dripping faucet needs a complete overhaul. When a ceramic-disk faucet develops a steady drip, remove the aerator and move the handle through all positions several times. If sediment was the culprit, this should clear it. In general, a ceramic-disk faucet is not a good choice if you experience sediment problems with your water, especially if they are so severe that you require a filter.

Fixing a Leak in a Ceramic-Disk Faucet

If you have a newer-style ceramic-disk faucet and you can't seem to clear the sediment by rotating the handle, you'll need to check the cartridge. Shut off the water, tip back the handle, and loosen the setscrew. **1.** Remove the handle, and lift off the decorative cartridge cap. **2.** Use a small flat-blade screwdriver to remove the retaining screws. **2** (inset). Then lift the cartridge from the

Ceramic-Disk Faucet Anatomy

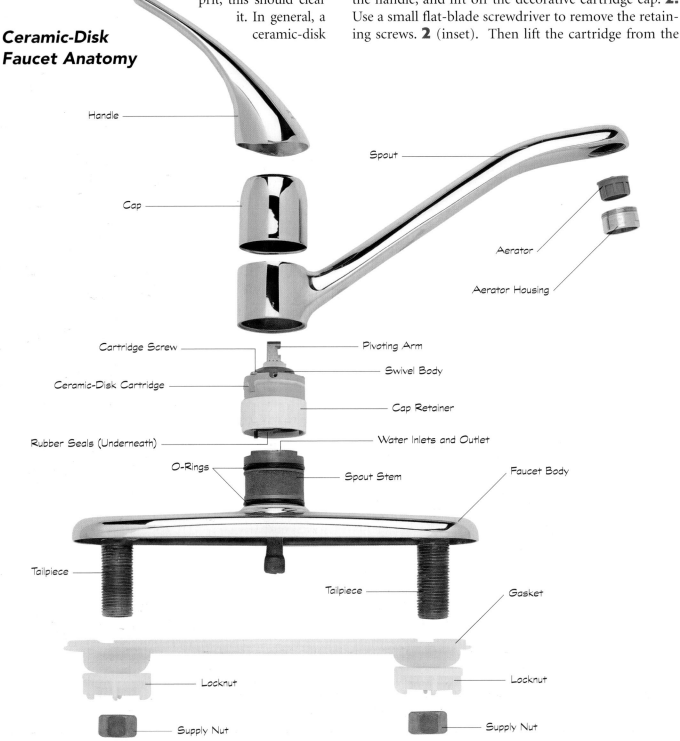

- Handle
- Spout
- Cap
- Aerator
- Aerator Housing
- Cartridge Screw
- Pivoting Arm
- Ceramic-Disk Cartridge
- Swivel Body
- Cap Retainer
- Rubber Seals (Underneath)
- Water Inlets and Outlet
- O-Rings
- Spout Stem
- Faucet Body
- Tailpiece
- Tailpiece
- Gasket
- Locknut
- Locknut
- Supply Nut
- Supply Nut

SMART TIP

Don't Shatter the Ceramic

Ceramic disks are extremely durable, but they have a weakness. When you drain a piping system for repairs and then turn the water back on, the air in the system escapes through the faucets in bursts and surges. These pressure shocks can shatter a ceramic disk, preventing the faucet from shutting off completely. To avoid ruining your ceramic-disk faucet, turn the water back on slowly after a plumbing repair. Allow the air to be pushed from the system gradually before turning the shutoff valve to its full-open position.

faucet. **3.** If you see sediment in the inlet ports, clean it out using tweezers. You can also remove the neoprene seals (visible in photo 3) to look for sediment. Clean them if you find sediment, but if you don't find any, the problem is likely in the cartridge. Most ceramic cartridges are not serviceable, so replace the cartridge, and reinstall the handle.

Repairing Two-Handle Ceramic-Disk Faucets

Dual-control ceramic-disk faucets are more substantial, but the repair sequence is similar to that for single-handle models. Turn off the water at the shutoff valves below the sink. Remove the first handle, and use a screwdriver to remove the cartridge

Fixing a Leak in a Ceramic-Disk Faucet

Tools and Materials

- Allen wrench   TIME NEEDED: 30 MIN.
- Flat-blade screwdriver
- Groove-joint pliers
- New cartridge   ■ Tweezers

PLUMBING TIP: Sometimes you can refurbish a ceramic-disk cartridge by cleaning or replacing its neoprene seals, but more often you'll have to replace the entire cartridge.

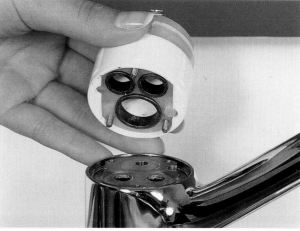

1 To locate the handle screw, shut off the water and tip the handle back. Use an Allen wrench to remove the screw.

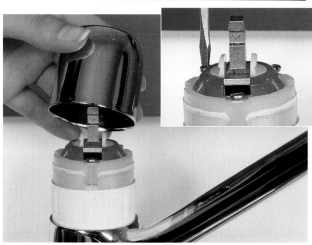

2 Lift off the decorative cap to expose the cartridge. Using a flat-blade screwdriver, loosen the screws at the top of the cartridge (inset).

3 Look for sediment near either or both of the inlet ports. Clear the sediment and clean the seals, or replace the cartridge.

cap. **1.** Use an adjustable wrench or smooth-jaw pliers to loosen the retaining nut. **2.** Lift out the ceramic-disk cylinder, and install an exact replacement. **3.** Repeat the sequence with the remaining cylinder.

Faucet-Related Repairs

Besides the annoying drip-drip-drip of a leaky faucet, you may be faced with other faucet problems: leaking spray attachments, erratic or uneven water flow from an aerator, and leaks at the base of the faucet spout.

Dealing with Leaky Spray Attachments

The hose spray attachment is the weakest part of any faucet. It's not unusual for homeowners to replace one three or four times before the faucet wears out. In households with hard water, mineral deposits form in and around the spray nozzle. With enough calcification, the stop mechanism in the nozzle won't shut off completely, and the spray pattern becomes irregular.

With many troublesome attachments, the entire hose and nozzle assembly needs to be replaced, but when hard water is clearly the culprit, you might try cleaning the nozzle first. Heat about two cups of vinegar, and place the entire nozzle in a container with the vinegar. (See the photo opposite.) To hold the nozzle open, slip a rubber band over the release lever. After an hour or so, operate the nozzle under pressure, squeezing and releasing it repeatedly. You might also try rapping the nozzle on the counter. If you've cleared the stop mechanism

Repairing a Two-Handle Ceramic-Disk Faucet

Tools and Materials

TIME NEEDED: 30 MIN.

- Utility knife
- Screwdriver
- Adjustable wrench
- Slip-joint pliers
- New cartridges

PLUMBING TIP: *Work on only one side of the faucet at a time to avoid mixing up the hot- and cold-water parts.*

1 Remove the first handle and use a screwdriver to undo the cartridge cap. Work on only one cartridge at a time.

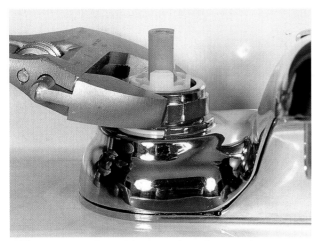

2 Use an adjustable wrench to loosen the cartridge retaining nut. Rotate the nut counterclockwise to remove it.

3 Lift out the old cartridge using slip-joint or groove-joint pliers, and install an exact replacement. Replace both sides of the faucet.

Soak a mineral-hardened spray nozzle in warm vinegar to dissolve calcified minerals and enable it to work properly.

but still have a partially clogged nozzle, unscrew the aerator from the nozzle and poke the mineral particles from the screen with a straightened paper clip.

How to Replace a Spray Attachment. When stopgap measures no longer work, it's time to replace the entire spray assembly. It's best to buy a replacement made by the manufacturer of your faucet, but universal kits will also work. Start by shutting off the water and draining the hose as much as possible. Then reach under the sink, and cut the old hose in two, catching the small amount of water that drains out. Pull the old hose through it's deck fitting, and discard it. Then, from under the sink, unscrew the remaining length of hose from the faucet nipple. Remove the jamb nut from the deck fitting under the sink, and remove the fitting. **1.**

With the old assembly removed, install the new deck fitting, and then feed the hose through it from above. **2.** Apply a small amount of pipe joint compound to the male threads of the faucet nipple, and thread the new hose in place using an adjustable wrench or smooth-jaw pliers. **3.** Don't overtighten the fitting.

How to Replace a Spray Attachment

Tools and Materials

- Screwdriver
- Pliers
- Adjustable wrench
- Spray replacement kit

TIME NEEDED: 30 MIN.

PLUMBING TIP: *If cleaning doesn't bring your sprayer back to proper working order, you need to replace it—a quick and easy project that costs only a few dollars.*

1 *After removing the old spray attachment, slide the rubber gasket onto the new one's fitting shank, and feed the shank through the sink deck hole.*

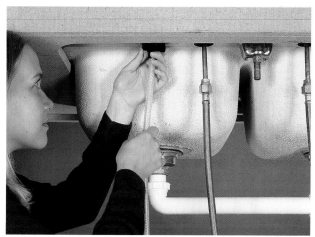

2 *Slide the hose through the deck fitting from above, and install the jamb nut below. Tighten the nut until it's snug.*

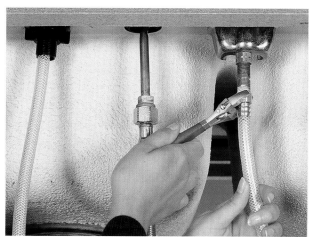

3 *Finish by connecting the spray attachment's hose to the faucet's diverter nipple. Use a light coating of pipe joint compound on the nipple.*

8 Faucet Repairs

Clearing Sediment and Mineral Buildup

Mineral-encrusted aerators are easy to unscrew from the faucet spout for cleaning or replacement.

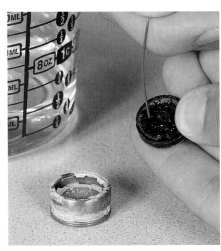

Soak the scaled-over aerator parts in vinegar, and clear the screens with a straightened paper clip.

Correcting Aerator Problems

If a sudden drop in pressure occurs at only one faucet or the water doesn't seem to flow properly, the aerator may be clogged.

All kitchen- and bathroom-sink faucets have spout attachments called aerators. As the name implies, an aerator mixes air into the flow from the spout and keeps the water from spiraling out at an angle or with too much force. Aerators also contain sediment screens. The screens hold a little water after you shut the faucet off, so with hard water they're prone to calcification, but the most common problem is sediment, usually from a line repair or a sandy well. When sediment is caught in an aerator, it shows as a pressure drop. If only one faucet in your home exhibits a pressure drop, suspect a clogged aerator. If all faucets seem to lose pressure, you have a system problem.

Clearing Sediment and Mineral Buildup. Sediment can be easily cleaned from an aerator. Just grip the aerator with your fingers or with padded pliers, and unscrew it from the faucet. (See the photo above, left.) Carefully remove the various screens and disks, and lay them out in order of removal. Use a paper clip to poke through each hole in the plastic disk, and backflush the metal screens. Reassemble the components, and install the aerator. If this doesn't correct the problem, throw the old one out and buy a new one.

If a white crusty buildup from calcification is the problem, remove the aerator and soak it in warm vine-

Repairing an Older Ceramic-Disk Faucet

If sediment in the faucet is not the culprit, you can often stop a leak in an older ceramic-disk unit by increasing tension on the disk. Pry off the index cap, and remove the screw and handle. You'll see a chrome cap concealing the ceramic water-control mechanism. Remove the two small screws that hold the cap in place, and lift the cap. This will reveal a large plastic adjustment nut with series of holes around its rim. The holes correspond to an identical set of holes in the faucet body. Using large pliers, rotate the nut clockwise until the next set of holes aligns. Replace the cap and handle, and test your work. If the faucet still leaks, advance the nut one more hole. Continue this routine until the leak stops or the nut feels too tight to move. If these quick-fix methods don't help, then it's time to replace the cartridge.

Shut off the water, remove any decorative cap and the handle from the faucet, and back the adjustment nut completely out of the faucet. Remove the screws that hold the old disk in place, and install an exact replacement. Thread the adjustment nut back into the faucet until its alignment is roughly the same as it was when you first opened the faucet. Turn the water back on, and test your work. If the faucet drips, continue tightening the adjustment nut, one hole at a time, until the leak stops

gar for an hour or so. If the aerator holes and screens remain partially plugged, poke at them using a paper clip. (See the photo opposite, right.)

Fixing Faucet Spout Leaks

Leaks frequently appear around the base of the faucet spout and from under the spout collar, and they should be fixed as soon as possible. If allowed to leak for long, the water that accumulates around the base of the faucet can work its way under the baseplate. From there, it can drop into the cabinet or seep into the countertop, where it can cause real damage.

Repairing Two-Handle Faucet Spouts. To start, turn off the water at the shutoff valves. Most modern faucets have O-ring spout seals. If your faucet has two handles, the spout is probably held in place by a threaded retaining nut, either exposed or hidden beneath a decorative cap. An exposed nut may be smooth or ridged around the perimeter. Remove this kind using a strap wrench or a pair of groove-joint pliers with thick padding on the jaws. **1–2.** A hidden nut may be a hex type. Remove it using an adjustable wrench or smooth-jaw pliers. With the retaining nut removed, lift and twist the spout until it slips off. **3.** With the spout out of the way, you will see one or more O-rings on the spout stem, which act as water seals. The O-rings are probably worn or broken. Cut them out using a utility knife, and install replacements, lubricating the new O-rings with heat-proof plumber's grease. Then reinstall the spout, and turn on the water.

Repairing a Two-Handle Faucet Spout

Tools and Materials

- Strap wrench
- Utility knife
- Spout O-ring kit

TIME NEEDED: 30 MIN.

PLUMBING TIP: *A faucet spout that has leaked for some time may have a coating of calcified minerals if the water is hard. Should that be the case, soak the affected parts in warm vinegar before reinstalling them.*

1 Use a strap wrench or smooth-jaw pliers, padded with cloth or duct tape, to remove the spout cap.

2 When the cap breaks free, finish unscrewing it by hand. If it's caked over with minerals, soak it in warm vinegar.

3 Grip the spout near it's base, and pull up on it. Cut off the old O-rings, and install and lubricate new ones before reassembling the spout.

8 Faucet Repairs

Repairing Single-Handle Faucet Spouts. If yours is a single-handle faucet, you'll need to remove the handle and a retaining cap nut. Shut off the water. If the faucet handle has an index cap or decorative cover, remove it, back out the screw holding the handle, and remove the handle. **1.** Many faucets have an Allen setscrew holding the control lever/handle in place. If yours does, tip the handle back and loosen this screw. If you find a knurled cap nut just under the lever, unscrew it as well. If you find a pull-off decorative cap, expect to find a retaining nut just under the cap. Loosen the nut, and pull the spout from its post. **2.**

With the spout removed, look for two or three rubber O-rings seated in grooves in the post. Pry or cut these seals off without scratching the post. **3** (inset).

Buy factory replacements from a local plumbing-supply retailer, and roll the new O-rings onto the post until they become seated. **3.** Finally, lubricate the O-rings with plumber's grease, and carefully press the spout collar over the post. Replace the fastening nut or cap and the handle, and turn the water back on.

Repairing Tub & Shower Faucets

While all that stands between you and the inner workings of a typical sink faucet is the handle, bathtub and shower faucets have a deep-set mounting profile, making repairs a little more difficult.

Repairing Single-Handle Faucet Spouts

Tools and Materials

TIME NEEDED: 30 MIN.

- Screwdriver
- Adjustable wrench
- Utility knife
- O-ring kit

PLUMBING TIP: *The retaining nut in a single-handle faucet holds both the cartridge and the spout body. Remove the nut to release the spout.*

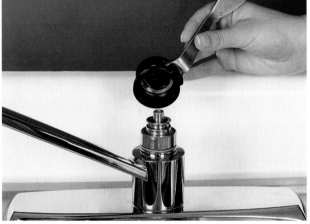

1 Start by removing the handle and retaining nut or pivot nut under it. There's no need to remove the cartridge.

2 Grip the spout near its base; then twist and lift it off the faucet body. The spout should come free with steady pressure.

3 Carefully cut the old O-rings from the spout stem, and roll new ones in place. Lubricate the rings with plumber's grease before reassembly.

Reaching Recessed Faucets

Full-skirt escutcheons or decorative chrome trim plates are indicators of deep-set faucets. You have to remove the escutcheons to reach the bonnet nuts, which hold the faucet stems in place. Escutcheons are easy to remove once you figure out the fastening mechanism. (See "Escutcheon Alternative," on page 199.)

To begin, remove the handles. Working on one side at a time, pry off the index cap to reach the handle screw. If the cap has knurled edges, it is most likely threaded. Unscrew it using needle-nose pliers. **1** (inset). Once you have access to the handle screw, back it out and remove the handle. If you see a knurled stem nut, remove it using an adjustable wrench, smooth-jaw pliers, or groove-joint pliers padded with cloth fabric or duct tape. **1.** (If you don't see a nut, the escutcheon is attached to the faucet stem. See "Escutcheon Alternative," page 199.) If the escutcheon won't let go, check to see whether it's caulked to the wall tile. If it is, slice through the caulk with a utility knife to free it.

The bonnet nut rests beneath the plane of the finished wall. Only a deep-socket faucet wrench will reach it. **2.** You can rent professional versions of these socket wrenches, but homeowner versions are also available at modest cost from hardware stores and home centers. Once you've got past the escutcheons and bonnet nuts, the mechanism is not different from other ordinary compression faucets. **3.** See "Repairing Compression Faucets," page 175, for more information about working with compression faucets.

Reaching Recessed Faucets

Tools and Materials

- Needle-nose pliers
- Adjustable wrench
- Deep-socket faucet wrench
- Screwdriver
- Faucet washers

TIME NEEDED: 45 MIN.

PLUMBING TIP: *The key to working on many wall-mounted tub-shower faucets is using special socket wrenches that are deep enough to reach the recessed bonnet nut.*

1 Start by removing the handle index cover (inset) and screw; then remove the escutcheon nut from the stem or unscrew the escutcheon.

2 Press the deep socket wrench onto the recessed bonnet nut, and remove the nut and stem from the faucet body.

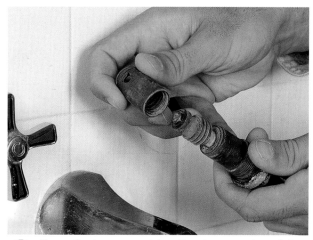

3 If you find a stem with a floating seat (an older design), unscrew the seat from the stem and replace the washer.

8 Faucet Repairs

Fixing Single-Handle Tub and Shower Faucets

Cartridge-type tub and shower faucets with single-handle controls have mechanisms similar to those used in their kitchen and bath counterparts, and the cartridges are held in place by similar U-shaped retaining clips. Gaining access is a little different, however.

Turn off the water at the shutoff valves. Pry the decorative insert from the plastic handle, and remove the handle screw and handle. **1–2.** In some models, a plastic cam fitting or bushing will be in place between the handle and stem. Remove it as well.

With the handle off, you'll see a metal sleeve installed over the cartridge and column. The sleeve is decorative, but it also keeps you from being able to remove the retaining clip. Pull the sleeve from the column. **3.** With the sleeve removed, you can pull the retaining clip using needle-nose pliers. **4.** Slide the cartridge out from the column, and replace it. **5.** Reassemble the faucet, and turn the water back on. As with other cartridge units, you can usually correct reversed hot and cold sides by rotating the stem cartridge 180 degrees.

Working with Scald-Control Faucets

Scald-control faucets have long been installed in hospitals and nursing homes, and in the past few years many codes have been updated to require scald control for residential bath and shower faucets. It takes only a couple of seconds of exposure to 140-degree-F water to produce a third-degree burn—and only one second at

Fixing Single-Handle Tub and Shower Faucets

Tools and Materials

- Utility knife
- Screwdriver
- Needle-nose pliers
- Replacement cartridge

TIME NEEDED: 30 MIN.

PLUMBING TIP: *Some faucet handles have a separate bushing between the handle and stem. Be sure not to damage or lose it during the repair procedure.*

1 To gain access to the handle screw, start by removing the handle's decorative index cap. Pry under it with a knife.

3 Carefully pull the decorative stainless-steel inner sleeve from the valve body and trim plate.

4 Use needle-nose pliers to pull the U-shape retaining clip from the cartridge. Be careful not to bend it or you'll have difficulty replacing it.

150 degrees F. Many homeowners have their water heaters set that high. (A 125-degree-F setting is safer, and your heater will give you longer service at that setting.) Small children, the elderly, and anyone with limited mobility are at greatest risk.

Every manufacturer now makes affordable scald-control faucets for residential use. Most are single-control faucets, but there are a few two-handle models.

Handle-Rotation Stop. Scald control is delivered in two ways. First is a temperature-limit adjustment, in the form of a handle-rotation stop. With a handle stop, you remove the handle and dial in a comfortable water temperature, with the water running, and then lock the setting and replace the handle. Thereafter, when you turn the handle to "Hot," it will rotate only to the stop position. You can reduce the temperature with cold water, but you can't exceed the hot limit. Because ground temperatures change with the seasons, affecting water temperatures, you may need to adjust these settings twice a year.

Pressure-Balance Spool. The second mechanism, a pressure-balance spool, is designed to accommodate a sudden drop in pressure on one side of the piping system. Pressure drops are common. The most familiar scenario: You're taking a shower when someone in an adjacent bathroom flushes the toilet. The toilet diverts half the line pressure from the cold side of the faucet, upsetting the ratio of hot-to-cold water. The result is a sudden blast of hot water.

Balance spools come in several forms, but the most common is a perforated cylinder with a similarly perforated internal slide. The slightest drop in line pressure on one side of the faucet moves the slide over a bit, realigning the perforations and reducing intake from the high-pressure side. When pressure is restored to the

2 Use a Phillips-head screwdriver to remove the handle. Be careful not to lose the plastic inset bushing.

5 Pull the old cartridge from the faucet, and install an exact replacement. Replace the retaining clip, inner sleeve, and handle.

SMART TIP

Escutcheon Alternative

Deep-set escutcheons use two mounting designs. In one, a knurled nut just under the faucet handle keeps the escutcheon in place. (See the inset to photo 1 on page 197.) In the other, the escutcheon has internal threads and is turned directly onto the faucet stem. If you don't see a nut when you remove the faucet handle, grip the escutcheon directly using your hand or, if it's tight, smooth-jaw pliers or a strap wrench to remove it.

Faucet escutcheons without retaining nuts usually have internal threads. They just twist off.

8 Faucet Repairs

Cleaning Sediment from a Pressure-Balance Spool

Some scald-control faucets have integral water stops. Use a screwdriver to shut off the water.

To clear a balancing spool of sediment, pull it out and tap it on the counter. Flush the spool with water, and replace it.

weak side, the slide returns to its original position. These simple devices are so effective that water won't even flow through a faucet when one side is turned off. You'll find pressure-balance spools in two locations. Some are built into the faucet body—with front access—and some are built into the valve cartridge.

As an added benefit, many of these upgraded faucets are built with integral stops, one on each side of the control. Instead of shutting down the entire water system for repairs, you can just close the stops with a screwdriver.

Cleaning Sediment from a Pressure-Balance Spool.

Pressure-balance spools are vulnerable sediment problems. When a spool clogs with sediment, the faucet will deliver only a trickle of water or only hot or cold water.

To deal with a gradual accumulation of sediment in a spool that's installed in the faucet body, remove the faucet handle and escutcheon. Close the integral stops by turning the exposed screwheads clockwise with a flat-blade screwdriver. (See the photo at top, left.) You'll find the stops just behind the faucet's trim plate on each side of the faucet. Use a large flat-blade screwdriver to unscrew the spool from the faucet body, and remove it. (See the photo at top, right.) Tap the spool several times on a hard surface, and then rinse it clean. The internal slide should easily slip back and forth when you tip the cylinder. If it doesn't, you'll need a new spool. Reinstall the spool, open the stops, and reassemble the faucet. Make sure both stops are fully open when you put the faucet back into service. It's easy to mistake a nearly closed stop for a clogged balance spool.

Of course, if the spool is built into the faucet cartridge, you may need a new cartridge. (See "Pressure-Balanced Cartridges," below.) Before replacing it,

Pressure-Balanced Cartridges

Scald-control measures have changed the way you work on familiar cartridge faucets. Many cartridges and faucets look like standard units, but they now contain a balancing spool, and they are installed differently. You can't remove them from the faucet without a special tool, so don't try pulling them out, the way you would a standard cartridge. Either buy a metal twist tool, like the one shown here, or use the little tool that comes with each replacement cartridge. If you need to work on one of these faucets, proceed carefully until you learn how things work. Manufacturers normally provide toll-free numbers and Web sites with their instructions, so there's plenty of help available.

Cartridges with built-in balancing spools often require a special removal tool.

however, try to clear the sediment by rotating the handle through all positions with the water on.

Repairing Freeze-Proof Sillcocks & Hydrants

Freeze-proof sillcocks and yard hydrants can be rebuilt like other compression faucets. But the seats are inaccessible, so be sure to make repairs before seat damage occurs.

Fixing a Freeze-Proof Sillcock.

As soon as you notice a drip, turn off the water at the nearest shutoff valve. Remove the handle using a screwdriver. **1.** Keep it nearby because you'll use it later to pull the long stem from the faucet body. Remove the packing nut using an adjustable wrench. **2.** Before trying to loosen the nut, however, check it or the area around it for a stamped or printed label indicating the direction of the threads. These nuts often have left-hand threads, so you'll need to rotate the nut clockwise to loosen it. If you see no such label, try rotating the nut counterclockwise. Don't force it until you're sure which way you're supposed to turn it.

Some sillcocks have standard seat washers, like those found on kitchen faucets, while others have large rubber stoppers threaded in place. In both cases, expect the stem to resist your attempts to remove it. Start by reattaching the handle and backing the stem from its threads, and then pull the stem straight out. **3.** If it

Fixing a Freeze-Proof Sillcock

Tools and Materials

- Screwdriver
- Adjustable wrench
- Needle-nose pliers
- Sillcock repair kit
- Plumber's grease
- Packing string

TIME NEEDED: 30–45 MIN.

PLUMBING TIP: *Because the valve seats are inaccessible, it's important that you fix a leak as soon as you notice it to avoid persistent leaking problems.*

1 To service a freeze-proof sillcock, begin by removing the handle screw and handle to get access to the packing nut.

2 Before removing the handle, open the faucet; then use an adjustable wrench to unscrew the packing nut from the faucet body.

3 Replace the handle, make sure the faucet is fully open, and pull on the stem to remove it. If it sticks, twist left and pull harder.

8 Faucet Repairs

Sequence continues on next page ▶

Continued from previous page

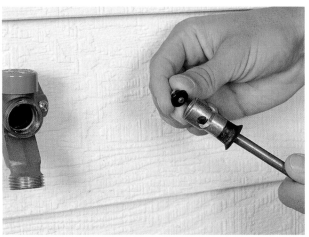

4 *Replace the seat washer, and coat it and the stem threads with plumber's grease. Replace the stem.*

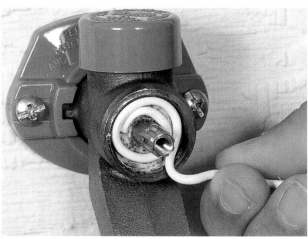

5 *If the stem leaks near the handle, add two rounds of packing string, and tighten the packing nut.*

won't budge, pull harder. As long as the packing nut is loose and the stem has cleared its internal threads, it should break free. When you get the stem out, replace the stopper or seat washer. **4.** Coat the replacement washer with plumber's grease, and reinstall the stem.

Leaking Handle. If you notice a leak around the handle when you use the faucet, loosen the packing nut and pull the stem out partway. You'll see that a brass washer holds the packing against the packing nut. Slide the washer forward a little, and wrap two rounds of packing string around the stem next to the packing. **5.** Slide the

washer back against the packing, and tighten the packing nut in place.

Leaking Vacuum Breaker. If you have a top-mounted vacuum breaker that sprays water, you can repair it with parts from a standard repair kit, available at hardware stores and home centers. To gain access to the breaker, pry off the plastic cap. **6** (inset). You may be able to use just your fingers. If not, use a small flat-blade screwdriver to work the cap off. Using needle-nose pliers, pull out the plastic plate you'll find just below the cap. **6.** You'll see a rubber seal under the plastic plate. Pull it out and replace

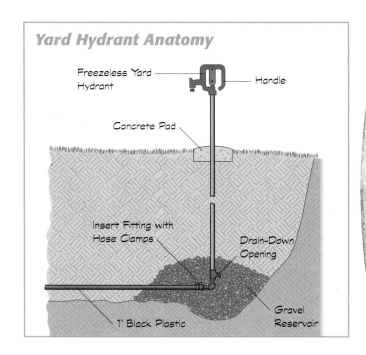

Yard Hydrant Anatomy

Freezeless Yard Hydrant — Handle
Concrete Pad
Insert Fitting with Hose Clamps
Drain-Down Opening
1" Black Plastic
Gravel Reservoir

Repairing a Yard Hydrant

Tools and Materials

- Two pipe wrenches   TIME NEEDED: 30 MIN.
- Hydrant repair kit
- Groove-joint pliers
- Plumber's grease

PLUMBING TIP: *A yard hydrant may seem to be an intimidating piece of equipment; however, it's really a simple mechanical device, and once you know how it works, repairs are not that difficult to make.*

6 To fix a leaking vacuum breaker, pry off the top cap (inset), and lift out the small plastic screen using needle-nose pliers.

7 Install new vacuum-breaker seals from a standard repair kit, and replace the plastic screen and top cap.

it. **7.** Put the plastic plate back in the faucet body, and press the cap back in place. Make sure the faucet is reassembled properly, turn the water back on, and test your work.

Repairing a Yard Hydrant

The repair procedure for in-ground yard hydrants resembles that for freeze-proof sillcocks. The lever-type handle at the top of the hydrant connects to an extended stem that's 3 to 6 feet long. The bottom end of this stem is fitted with a large rubber stopper. To replace this stopper, turn off the water at the nearest shutoff valve, and lift the lever to the "On" position. Then, using two pipe wrenches, backhold the riser pipe with one wrench and grip the wrenching surface at the base of the head with the other. **1.** Rotate the head of the hydrant counterclockwise. When the head clears its threads, lift the stem completely out. You may need the assistance of a helper if the stem is longer than 3 or 4 feet. Remove the old stopper, and install an exact replacement. **2.** Return the stem to its riser pipe. As you tighten the head in place, be sure to backhold the riser to avoid breaking the hydrant away from its underground connection. Finally, lower the handle, turn the water on, and test your work.

1 To gain access to the stem, shut off the water at the nearest shutoff valve, backhold the riser pipe, and rotate the head counterclockwise.

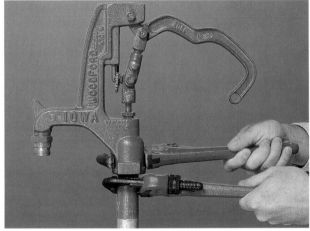

2 Lift out the stem; unscrew the old stopper using pliers; and install a new one. Coat the stopper with plumber's grease, and reinstall the head.

8 Faucet Repairs

CHAPTER 9

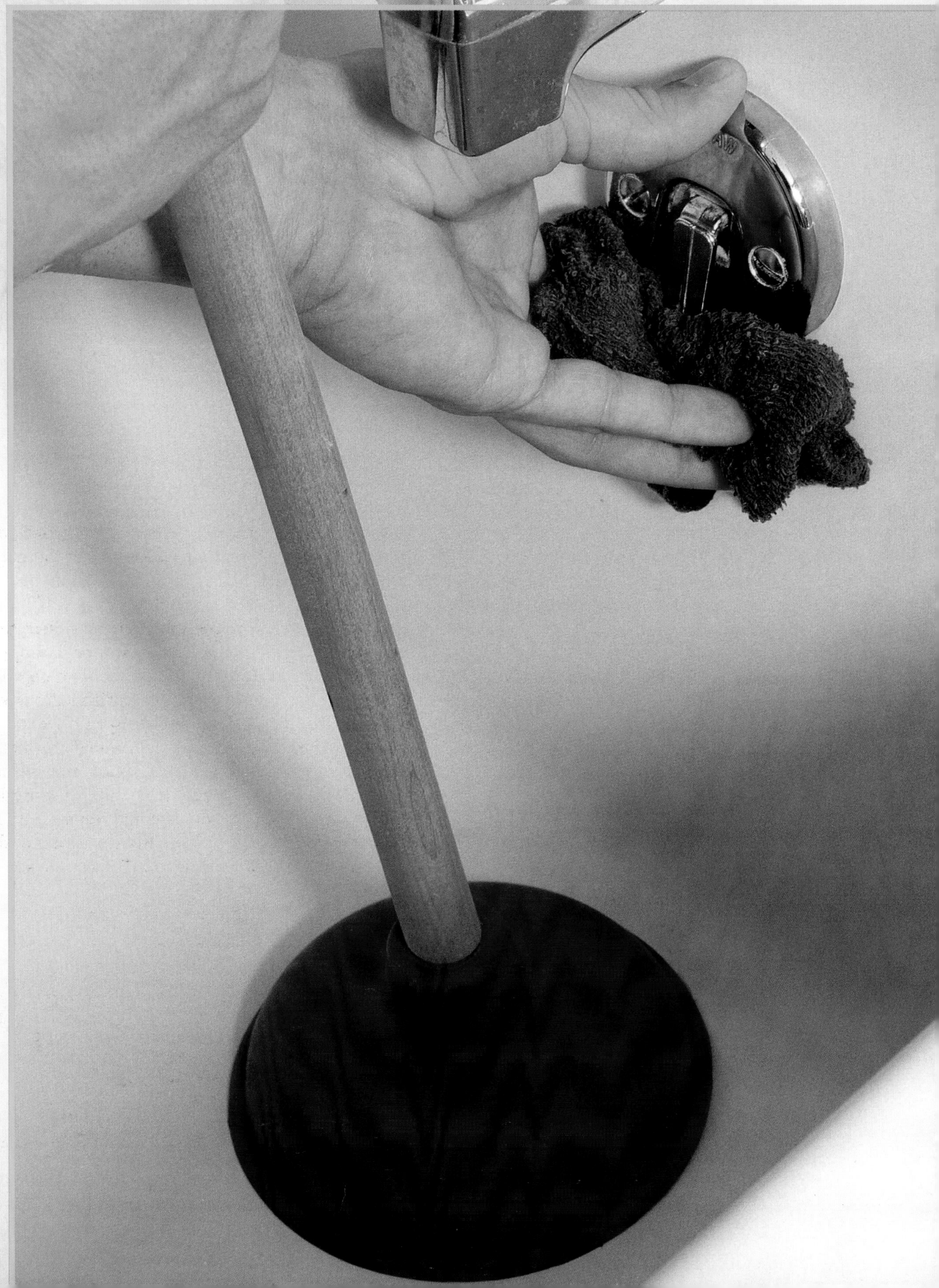

Clearing Drainpipes

here are two basic kinds of drainpipe clogs. The first is a localized obstruction, usually in a fixture trap, in a mechanical waste fixture or appliance, or at an abrupt change of direction in the piping. This kind of clog is the one so frequently depicted in chemical drain-cleaning commercials. It usually comprises a buildup of soap, hair, and cosmetics, or is caused by foreign objects such as toothpicks, cotton swabs, washcloths, or small toys. (See the illustration in "Types of Clogs," below.) This kind of clog is fairly easy to clear. You can often force it with a plunger or retrieve the object using an inexpensive drain auger or even a piece of wire.

The second type of drainpipe clog is an extended, sometimes pipe-length accumulation, which takes years to form. Only a thorough reaming with a blade-head drain auger will clear this type of clog. Enzymatic drain cleaners can help, but nothing is as quick or thorough as a drain auger.

Horizontal and Vertical Clogs. If you were to cut through a pipe with an extended accumulation, you'd see that the clog formed in one of two ways, depending on whether the pipe was installed horizontally or vertically. (See the illustrations below.) In a horizontal line, the clog forms from the bottom up, until the water flows through only the top ¼ to ½ inch of pipe before it becomes completely stopped up. A clog in a vertical line accumulates from the outside in, leaving an ever-smaller drain hole in the center. Either way, a slow drain can abruptly stop flowing, with an object the size of a pea blocking the flow.

Types of Clogs

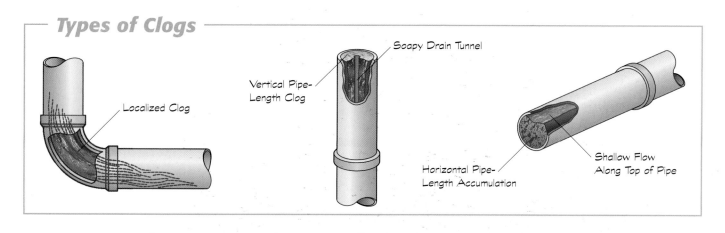

Localized Clog

Vertical Pipe-Length Clog

Soapy Drain Tunnel

Horizontal Pipe-Length Accumulation

Shallow Flow Along Top of Pipe

SMART TIP

Hot-Water Drain Maintenance

Extended drainpipe accumulations usually occur in kitchen and bath lines, most often in the homes of resource-conservative, conscientious homeowners. The operation of an automatic dishwasher might explain why: when a dishwasher is installed for the first time in an older home, it often quickly causes the kitchen drain to back up because the hot water from its wash cycle breaks up existing accumulations, which then gather at a choke point and block the flow of water behind it. Conversely, a new drain line that carries the high-volume hot-water purge of a dishwasher almost never clogs, no matter how many years it's in service. The lesson here is that regular doses of very hot water keep accumulations of grease and cosmetics from forming. So if you take shallow baths or short showers and use the bare minimum of hot water in the kitchen (generally being resource conservative), you increase the chance that grease and cosmetics will congeal against the cool walls of drainpipes. With each use, more grease, hair, and food particles join the slimy aggregate, until the line eventually closes entirely.

To avoid these kinds of problems, run the hottest tap water you have into each fixture, with the stopper closed, every two weeks or so. When the basin or tub is nearly full, open the stopper and follow with 30 seconds of hot tap water.

Drain Cleaners

When you're faced with a stopped-up drain, you'll need to clear it, either by breaking it down and dissolving it chemically or by mechanically removing the obstruction with a drain-clearing tool.

Chemical Drain Cleaners

There are three general varieties of chemically based drain cleaners: alkaline, enzymatic, and acidic.

Alkaline Cleaners. Supermarket products, which you pour directly into a stopped sink or tub, are alkali-based products. These have copper sulfide, sodium hydroxide, or sodium hypochloride as their active ingredients. They work on the simplest of hair and grease clogs, but they'll do little to clear an extended accumulation.

Enzymatic Cleaners. A less hazardous and more environmentally friendly version of drain cleaners uses enzymes to break down clogs. Enzymatic treatments often work, but they take a few days. They are especially good at preventive maintenance. Using an enzymatic drain treatment twice a year will help keep drains clear and will benefit your septic system if your house is not connected to a municipal sewer system.

Acidic Cleaners. Acids, the final group of chemical cleaners, are more troublesome. They can be effective, but they're enormously dangerous in the wrong hands.

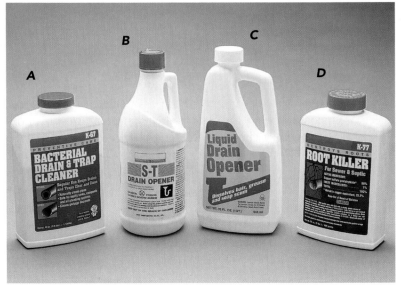

Chemical Drain Cleaners: **A**—*enzymatic,* **B**—*acid-based,* **C**—*lye-based,* **D**—*copper root repellent*

SMART TIP

Repelling Tree Roots

Copper sulfate-based drain cleaners are most effective at keeping tree roots out of sewer lines. Copper repels roots, so if you're lucky enough to have large trees in your yard, a once- or twice-a-year treatment is a good idea. It's interesting to note that old-time plumbers sometimes wrapped copper wire around sewer pipe joints.

Sulfuric and hydrochloric acid will dissolve just about any blockage material commonly found in plumbing systems, including dish rags, diapers, chicken bones, and the like.

However, hydrochloric acid will also damage porcelain, most metals, and just about everything except vitreous china. Sulfuric acid is less likely to damage metal piping but will degrade aluminum, stainless steel, and porcelain. Its rotten-egg stench will also drive you from your home. These are products of last resort, so read labels and proceed extremely carefully. Avoid using them if at all possible.

Mechanical Drain Cleaners

Mechanically clearing a clogged drain or cleaning a slow-running one is not complex work and doesn't require an armful of tools. Using a plunger, a screwdriver, and a piece of wire you'll be able to handle the most common clogs. For those rare occasions where a plunger doesn't seem to work, you'll need additional tools, all of which can be rented. You need not own them unless you live where rental outlets are few and far between.

Plunger. Get the kind of plunger that has a foldout extension cup. When folded in, it works on sinks, showers, and tubs. When folded out, it fits a toilet outlet. Standard plungers have trouble making a seal in toilets, and without a good seal, plunging is not effective.

Drain Auger. A drain auger is a long coiled-wire cable with a springlike head on its working end. You'll see two kinds when you go shopping: one is just a coil of cable with a piece of offset tubing as a crank; the other has its cable spooled in a metal or plastic housing. Buy the one with the housing because its wider cranking arc provides better torque for stubborn clogs. The housing also minimizes the spraying of indelible black drain slime around the room as you retrieve the cable.

Closet Auger. A closet auger is also a drain snake, but its design limits its use to toilets (also known as water closets.) It consists of a 3-foot metal tube that bends at a right angle at the bottom. The tube houses a cable and

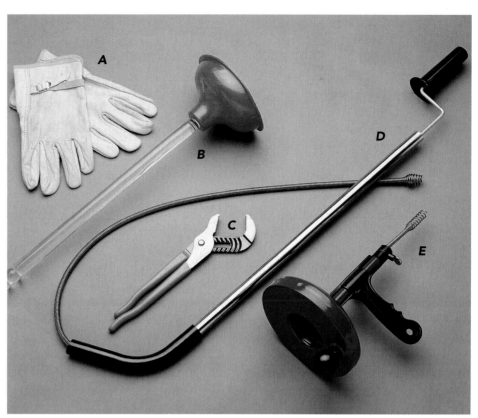

*Mechanical Drain Cleaners: **A**—work gloves, **B**—plunger, **C**—groove-joint pliers, **D**—closet auger, **E**—drain auger*

crank-rod, which total about 6 feet. You insert the bend of the auger into the toilet outlet with the rod pulled back, then push the rod and cable forward while cranking in a clockwise direction. The cable is just long enough to reach through the trap to the drain opening in the floor. A closet auger is about the only effective way of dealing with stubborn toilet clogs.

Power Auger. If you try clearing a problem drain with a plunger or lightweight cable but don't seem to make much progress, you're probably dealing with an extended accumulation. Drain snakes, with their small springlike heads, don't make much of an impression on this type of clog. You may be able to improve the flow for a few weeks, but it won't last. Years of accumulation require a heavier cable with a more aggressive head. The head may be shaped like an arrowhead, or it may have caliper-like blades. While these features can be found on a few hand-crank models, most such snakes are power-driven by either a hand-held drill-like motor or a chassis-mounted motor. There are two basic sizes. The light-duty ones are designed for drains up to about 2 inches in diameter, which carry gray water. The larger heavy-duty ones are designed for sewers. These machines are too costly to purchase for occasional use. If you can't rent them, hire a professional plumber.

Access to Sink Lines

Often the most perplexing part of cleaning a sink drain is gaining access to the line. Snaking directly through a sink opening almost never works because sink drains are designed to keep things out. For example, the flow in a kitchen sink is restricted to three or four openings, roughly ¼ inch in diameter, by the drain grate. Any drain snake with a large-enough head to get the job done won't fit through these openings. Even if it could, you'd have trouble working against the resistance of a fixture trap. If the clog is in the trap, you'll have better luck using a plunger or taking the trap apart.

The only time you will be able to fit a snake cable directly through a sink drain is when the sink is a bathroom basin with a removable pop-up plug. Simply removing the pop-up and lever would likely solve the problem without snaking, though, because this is where most basin clogs occur.

Removing the Trap. Tubs and showers should be snaked from above, but not sinks. Instead, remove the trap. You can remove a sink trap easily, because all the connections are made with friction washers and slip nuts. If your fixture trap is made of plastic, you should be able to loosen the nuts by hand. **1.** If it's made of chrome-plated brass, use groove-joint pliers or a pipe wrench to free the slip nuts. **1** (inset). Place a pail or pan under the trap to catch any spills; then loosen the nuts that secure the trap to the sink and drainpipe.

With the trap removed, push the auger cable directly into the waste pipe in the floor or wall. **2.** When reassembling a chrome trap, replace the rubber washers. Coat the washers with pipe joint compound, and tighten the nuts with pliers or a wrench.

If the old trap is in poor condition, consider replacing it with plastic, which is easy to cut and fit and never corrodes (unless it will be exposed, in which case chrome is more attractive). Tighten plastic nuts only hand tight, and avoid using pipe joint compound.

Dealing with Bath Sink Pop-Ups. Most bathroom-sink clogs occur around the pop-up drain mechanism, when hair gets caught on the lift lever and accumulates until most of the drain is choked off. To check the pop-up mechanism, remove the lift lever to free the pop-up plug. **1.** Just loosen the knurled nut securing the lever to the back of the drain tube under the sink basin, and pull the lever out partway. Don't pull it out all the way if you can help it, as this will let the hair clog fall into the trap. If it does fall, chances are it will be flushed out anyway, but it's always better to remove it. Next, remove

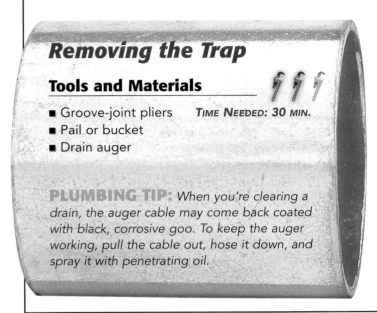

Removing the Trap

Tools and Materials

- Groove-joint pliers   TIME NEEDED: 30 MIN.
- Pail or bucket
- Drain auger

PLUMBING TIP: When you're clearing a drain, the auger cable may come back coated with black, corrosive goo. To keep the auger working, pull the cable out, hose it down, and spray it with penetrating oil.

the pop-up plug. **2.** If you see hair that could be clogging the drain, pull it out using needle-nose pliers or a piece of wire. When you've removed the clog, replace the pop-up.

Access to Cleanout Fittings

If your home's drainage piping is made of cast iron, then removing a cleanout plug will require effort. The problem is that traditional brass plugs and cast-iron fittings

Dealing with Bath Sink Pop-Ups

Tools and Materials

- Groove-joint pliers   TIME NEEDED: 20 MIN.

PLUMBING TIP: Pop-up levers have a tendency to clog. To make yours easier to service, install the lever under the pop-up instead of through it. Thereafter, lift out the plug and snag the clog from above.

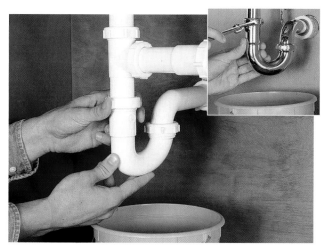

1 To gain access to a sink drain, remove the trap and trap arm. Plastic is hand tight, while chrome takes a wrench (inset).

2 Feed the auger cable into the drain until you feel resistance; then crank through the clog, forward, and back, always cranking clockwise.

9 Clearing Drainpipes

are not compatible. The two metals have different electrical charges, so electrolytic corrosion occurs. (See "Electrolysis," page 84.) Iron, the more-negative side, breaks down, locking the plug in the fitting. The fact that brass is relatively soft and gets softer with age doesn't help: often the wrenching surface crumbles.

It's usually easier to chisel the plug from the fitting. Position a cold chisel against the exposed threads of the brass plug, and drive the plug in a counterclockwise direction. This will force the threads to break free, allowing you to turn the plug the rest of the way with a wrench. The method works on floor-drain cleanouts, too.

When a brass plug won't budge, break it free using a hammer and chisel. Replace the plug with a plastic one.

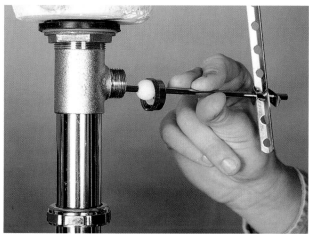

1 To check for a hair clog on the pop-up plug and lever, loosen the nut and slide the lever out enough to free the plug.

2 Lift the pop-up plug. You may see a clump of hair clinging to its bottom. Shine a flashlight into the drain, and retrieve a hair clog with wire.

Clearing Plastic Drainpipes at a Cleanout

A motorized auger works best on really stubborn clogs.

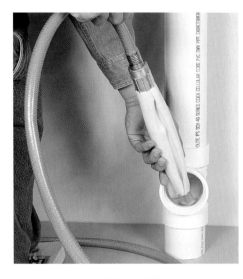

A flush bag forces the clog with water pressure.

When you've completed your drain-cleaning chores, discard the old brass plug and replace it with a plastic plug. If the cast-iron threads are too badly corroded to accept a new threaded plug, buy a rubber expansion plug instead. Insert it into the opening, and tighten the wing nut. The nut pulls a draw bolt, which expands the plug against the fitting.

If the drainage system is made of PVC (white) or ABS (black) plastic or copper and brass, opening a cleanout fitting is easy. Just remove the plug from the T-fitting using a wrench.

With the plug removed, you can use a drain auger to clean out the drain. A motorized auger works best, but a hand-operated model will handle most small drain clogs. With larger pipes you can use a flush bag, sometimes called a blow bag, to clear a clog. Thread the bag onto a garden hose, and insert the bag into the drain. Push the hose into the pipe until you reach the clog, and then turn on the water. Water pressure should dislodge the clog and open the drain. Flush bags can only be used downstream of all branch lines.

Clearing Techniques

Drain-cleaning tools are not particularly difficult to use. Knowing how to apply a few special techniques, however, makes them more effective.

Getting the Most from a Plunger

A plunger works better when you add water. Many slow-draining fixtures already have water in them, of course (that's how you know they're slow), but if yours doesn't, add some. In addition, make sure that all overflow tubes

are blocked. If you don't block these passages, they'll bleed off the pressure created by the plunger.

When plunging a tub, hold a wet rag firmly against the bottom of the overflow plate. With bath basins, stuff a rag into the overflow openings just below the rim. Hold it firmly in place. The same goes for dual-compartment kitchen sinks. When plunging one side, plug the other. But when a sink compartment with a waste-disposal unit backs up, plunge only that side. The problem here is usually a blocked T-fitting in the waste kit just under the sink.

Remember that suction is almost as effective as pressure, so try to maintain a good seal between the plunger and fixture surface through both the up and down motions. If the plunger doesn't seem to be creating enough pressure or suction because of the contour of the fixture, try coating the rim of the plunger with petroleum jelly. Follow every plunging by running hot water for at least a minute or two.

Effective Auger Techniques

Once you've gained access to the drainpipe, pull about 18 inches of cable from the spool and feed it carefully into the line.

Some drains reveal their clogs immediately. As soon as you pull the trap, you'll see it. Other lines appear clean but are clogged somewhere downstream. If you see no apparent obstruction, don't bother cranking the cable into the line. Just feed it in until you feel resistance. At this point, tighten the setscrew and push the cable forward while cranking in a steady, clockwise direction. (See the photo opposite.) When you run out of cable, loosen the setscrew, pull another 12 to 18 inches from the spool, tighten the setscrew, and crank

Plunging to the Max

When plunging a tub, *plug the overflow fitting with a wet rag.*

When plunging a bathroom sink, *cover the overflow hole in the basin with a wet rag.*

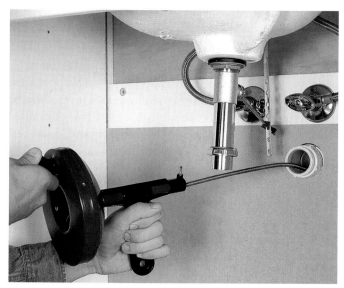

Remove a bathroom sink's trap and trap arm, and feed the auger cable directly into the drainage line. Follow with plenty of hot water once you've reassembled the trap.

SMART TIP

Keep on Course

When you feed an auger cable into a T-fitting in a wall, use a flashlight and make sure the head of the cable points down. Be careful, because it's easy to send the cable in the wrong direction, up a vent pipe. Professional-quality drain augers are fitted with drop heads, which automatically seek the lowest route, but most do-it-yourself homeowner augers are not.

forward again. Repeat this procedure until you break through the clog or reach the next-largest drainpipe. (You'll feel the cable flop around in the larger pipe.)

Meeting the Clog. You will know that you've snagged or forced open a clog when you feel the resistance—or lack of it—in the cable. This is an important consideration, especially with rented power equipment. With motor-driven cables, it's easy to break the cable off in the line when the head snags an obstruction. Always proceed slowly. When you feel sudden resistance followed by the sensation that you've broken through it, retrieve the line completely. This suggests that you've snagged an object, such as a rag. (In a sewer line, this behavior may indicate that you've hooked a bundle of threadlike tree roots.)

To retrieve a foreign object, pull the cable out of the line 1 or 2 feet at a time, feeding the cable into the spool as you go. As you pull back, continue cranking in a clockwise direction. Reversing direction will only release whatever you've snagged.

Push and Pull. If you feel a steady, prolonged resistance after first hitting the clog, try a push-and-pull approach. Push the cable forward 3 feet, then back 2 feet, then forward 4 feet, then back 2 feet, and so on. Stop if you feel the cable flip over when pushing it through stiff resistance. If you keep cranking, the cable will tie itself in knots. Instead, reverse direction gently. When you feel the cable right itself, pull it out and check for damage. If you see no damage, crank the cable into the clog again, working forward and back. Many drain lines require several passes to break up enough of the clog to allow water to flow through.

SMART TIP

Clearing Sewer Lines

Clearing the underground sewer line between your house and street is tricky work—not for most homeowners. A power-operated auger is big and powerful, and the motor is always stronger than the cable. To keep from breaking the cable off inside the sewer service, the operator must listen carefully to the motor, feeling and listening to the resistance of the cable. The operator needs to be able to sense the difference between tree roots, a broken pipe, piping offsets, and the juncture of private sewer service and public sewer main. All things considered, you should probably hire a pro for this work.

Clearing a Stopper Mechanism

Tools and Materials

- Screwdriver
- Drain auger
- Needle-nose pliers

TIME NEEDED: ½–1 HR.

PLUMBING TIP: Expect to feel resistance when the cable enters the tub's trap, about 18 inches down. Crank though the blockage, and then retrieve the cable to check for hair.

Whenever you clear a line, follow up with lots of hot water. It's common for a newly opened line to immediately become clogged again because the loose debris settles into a new mass. To clear the line this time, just use a plunger and lots of hot water.

Clearing Bathtub Drains

The best way to cable a tub drain is through the overflow tube. That's because the piping connection is not under the tub's drain fitting but 6 inches forward, under the overflow tube. If you try cabling the drain opening, you'll hit the drain T-fitting immediately.

To further complicate matters, most tubs that drain slowly do so not because the drain line or trap is clogged but because hair clings to the tripwaste linkage. An out-of-adjustment tripwaste will also cause a tub to drain slowly. Don't assume you have a clogged line until you've checked out the tripwaste mechanism.

Clearing a Stopper Mechanism

If the tub has a screen over the drain opening, then the tripwaste mechanism consists of a cylindrical stopper inside the overflow tube. Hair accumulations often collect just below the screen. Remove the screen, and check for hair clinging to the cross members. Remove all the hair you can see using needle-nose pliers.

If the tub still drains sluggishly, remove the screws from the overflow cover plate. **1** (inset.) Pull the plate, lift wire, and stopper from the overflow tube. These parts are all connected, so expect them to come out

together. Insert a drain auger into the drain line all the way back to the vertical stack, usually 3 to 6 feet away. **1.**

If the drain seems to flow well with the tripwaste removed but slows when it's back in place, you need to adjust the stopper. Years of use can stretch the lift wire or loosen the locking mechanism, leaving the stopper riding too low in the drain in the open position. Pull the tripwaste out, and shorten the wire. The lift wire will be either threaded or attached to a notched clip. If it's threaded, loosen the locknut, thread the wire up roughly ¼ inch, and tighten the locknut. **2.** If you see a clip, raise the wire one notch.

Clearing a Pop-Up Mechanism

Tools and Materials

- Screwdriver
- Slip-joint pliers

TIME NEEDED: 30 MIN.

PLUMBING TIP: Before replacing the pop-up, set the overflow lever to the open position. Insert the linkage and test your work.

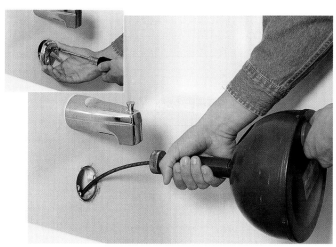

1 *Remove the two overflow screws (inset), and pull out the tripwaste mechanism. Insert the auger cable through the overflow.*

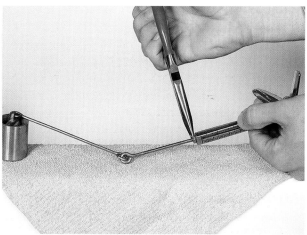

2 *Adjust the tub drain's tripwaste linkage (usually making it shorter), and secure it by tightening the locknut using needle-nose pliers or a wrench.*

Clearing a Pop-Up Mechanism

If the bathtub has a pop-up drain plug, chances are that you'll be able to correct the problem using no tools. Just pull the plug and the linkage attached to it from the drain. **1.** You're likely to find a dense mat of soapy hair clinging to the rocker lever. Remove the hair clog.

If the tub still drains sluggishly, remove the screws from the overflow cover plate, and pull the plate, lift wire, and coil from the overflow tube. These parts are all connected and will come out together. If the large wire coil at the bottom of the lift wire is matted with hair, remove the clog and test the drain again. If it still drains

sluggishly, use an auger to clear the drain line all the way back to the vertical stack (3 to 6 feet away).

If the drain flows well with the tripwaste removed but slows when it's back in place, you probably have an adjustment problem. Years of use can stretch the lift wire, leaving the mechanism riding too low in the drain. You'll have to pull the tripwaste out and shorten the wire. The lift wire will be attached to a notched clip or threaded. With a clip, loosen the setscrew and raise the wire one notch. **2.** If the wire is threaded, loosen the locknut. Then turn the wire clockwise until it moves up roughly ¼ inch, and tighten the locknut.

1 *To remove the linkage of a bathtub pop-up drain that's not working properly, grip the plug and pull the linkage out of the drain hole.*

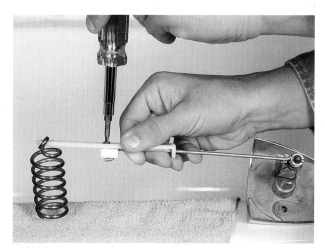

2 *Some tripwastes have a plastic adjustment mechanism. Set it to the slot you want, and tighten the locknut with a screwdriver.*

9 Clearing Drainpipes

Clearing Other Traps

Clearing Bathroom Drum Traps

Bathrooms plumbed in the early half of this century did not have dedicated fixture traps. Instead, the tub and sink drained directly into a drumlike canister called a drum trap in the bathroom floor. From there, a third pipe carried the water into the toilet drain piping. (See the drawing on page 50.)

If you have a house built prior to the 1950s, look for a cleanout plug in the bathroom floor to determine whether you have a drum trap. If you don't see a cleanout plug in the floor, there are other ways to tell whether you have a drum trap. If the bathroom sink backs up into the tub or you have a freestanding vintage tub with legs, a drum trap is likely. Another indicator is when the sink sits between the toilet and the tub. Modern methods favor the toilet in the center. To make sure, run a cable through the tub's overflow.

The only sure way to clear a drum trap is to open it up and clean it out. If a floor covering conceals the cleanout plug, look for a depression in the floor between the toilet and sink or tap the floor lightly with a hammer. The area above the drum trap will sound hollow.

Use a wrench to remove the threaded cleanout plug. If this doesn't work, tap the plug counterclockwise with a sharp cold chisel and hammer. With the trap open, auger each of the three pipes. Clean out any debris in the bottom of the trap. Then apply pipe joint compound to the threads, and replace the cleanout plug.

Clearing Shower Drains

Shower drains often clog because hair catches on the drain screen or a ragged pipe or fitting edge. These are simple, easy-to-clear clogs. Start by removing the screen that covers the drain opening. If the screen is held in

Clearing a Drum Trap

Cleanout Plug
Auger
1¼" Inlet from Tub
1¼" Inlet from Sink
1½" Drain Line to Toilet
Drum Trap

place by two screws, remove them. If not, it will have friction tabs. Pry up the screen with a knife or flat-blade screwdriver, and shine a flashlight into the drainpipe. If you see a clog, pull it out and look for the sharp edge that caused it. If possible, file down the edges before replacing the screen. If you don't see the clog, insert an auger cable and clear the entire line, back to the stack.

Clearing Floor Drains

Look for a 1¼-inch cleanout plug, usually made of brass, threaded into the side of the drain bowl. Remove the plug, and insert the auger cable directly into the line. When you've finished, replace the brass plug with a plastic plug or rubber expansion plug. If you seldom use the floor drain, you may experience a sewer-gas problem. Gas will flow into your living space when the trap water evaporates. To solve the problem, add water once a week or install a float-ball kit. A kit consists of a ball and matching seat. Drop the ball into the drain, thread the seat in place, and add water. The ball allows water but not gas to flow through.

Clearing Shower Drains

Pry up the drain screen with a knife or flat-blade screwdriver if it is not held in place by screws.

Insert an auger cable directly into the trap, and turn the handle clockwise as you feed the cable.

Clearing Floor Drains

To gain access to a floor drain, remove the cleanout plug.

Insert the auger cable directly into the cleanout opening.

Install a float ball in a seldom-used drain to prevent gas leakage.

Clearing Toilet Drains

A toilet's trap is smaller at its top (weir) than it is in the bowl. The reason is that toilets function in part by siphoning. Once water fills the top of the trap, water from the bowl is siphoned over the trap. The reduced trap weir makes a more efficient flush, but it can also cause clogs.

If you see that your toilet is about to overflow, quickly remove the tank lid and lift the float. If the water is already up to the rim, reach into the tank, close the flapper, and lift the float. In a few seconds, the water in the bowl will usually recede enough for you to lower the float. Turning off the shutoff valve is another alternative, but it usually takes longer.

Plunger. First, use a plunger. Fold the extension cup out, and press the plunger into the outlet. Pump the plunger vigorously until the water level drops. While remaining ready to lift the float if necessary, flush the toilet to see whether the obstruction has been forced over the trap. If everything seems normal, flush several more times to make certain the drain is clear. If the toilet flushes sluggishly, with large bubbles rising late in the flush cycle, the drain is still partially blocked. Use the plunger again, and test the flush.

Auger. If a plunger won't clear the blockage completely, then it's time to use a closet auger. Pull the handle and cable back, and insert the bend of the tube into the outlet. Slowly push the cable forward while cranking in a clockwise direction. When the crank handle bottoms out, retrieve the cable and repeat the process. Run the cable through at least three times, forcing it left, right, and center.

If this method doesn't work, empty the bowl with a paper cup and hold a pocket mirror in the outlet. Shine a flashlight into the mirror so that it illuminates the top of the trap. This should reveal what's causing the problem. Bend a length of wire into a hook, and pull the blockage back into the bowl. If you can't see the blockage, you'll have to take up the toilet and work from below. (See "Taking Up and Resetting a Toilet," page 121.)

Clearing Toilet Drains

To clear a toilet clog, first use a plunger that has a fold-out cup.

Use a closet auger if you can't clear a clogged toilet using a plunger.

CHAPTER 10

CAUTION

WHEN SOLDERING, DO NOT HEAT ANY VALVE ANY HIGHER
WHAT IS NECESSARY TO FLOW THE SOLDER. OVERHEAT
MAY DAMAGE THE CARTRIDGE. FOLLOWING THIS
WILL ALLOW YOU TO SOLDER WITHOUT REMOVIN
CARTRIDGE

Repairing & Installing Tubs & Showers

ubs and showers have the look of permanence, enough so that when they wear out, many homeowners are reluctant to replace them.

But they're *not* permanent, and they're not that difficult to repair or replace. Acrylic and fiberglass prefabricated units make the installation of a shower-tub fairly straightforward. Newer tubs are lighter than their cast-iron ancestors are. And there's no real mystery behind faucets and drains.

The hardest part of the job may be the wall and ceiling finishing you will have to do (or have done by a drywall contractor) when you've replaced or fixed the units.

Waste & Overflow Repair & Replacement

Bathtubs have two outlets: drain and overflow. Most also contain a tripwaste mechanism, an internal linkage that controls a drain stopper. Traditional tripwastes take

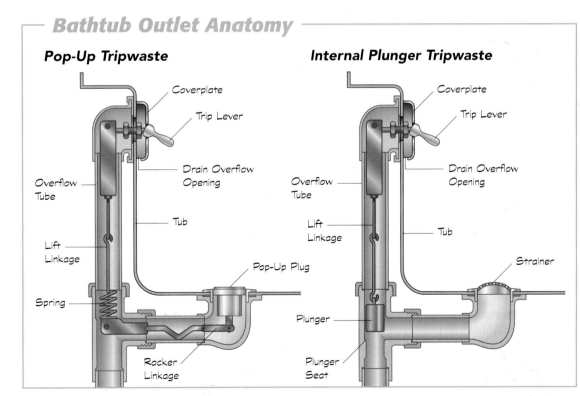

Bathtub Outlet Anatomy

Pop-Up Tripwaste

- Coverplate
- Trip Lever
- Drain Overflow Opening
- Overflow Tube
- Tub
- Lift Linkage
- Spring
- Pop-Up Plug
- Rocker Linkage

Internal Plunger Tripwaste

- Coverplate
- Trip Lever
- Drain Overflow Opening
- Overflow Tube
- Lift Linkage
- Tub
- Strainer
- Plunger
- Plunger Seat

two forms. One has a pop-up drain stopper, visible in the drain, while the other has an internal brass plunger. (Plastic versions of traditional drains are also available.) If your tub drain has a screen over it, expect an internal plunger. If it has nothing in it, you either have a very old drain or the handiwork of a frustrated homeowner. Many a homeowner has pitched the mechanism in favor of a rubber plug. Tripwastes require periodic tinkering, and if ignored grow less and less functional.

A third type—a European design—has an external cable. External linkage is less likely to clog with hair. These sturdy plastic drains are also available in longer lengths, making them ideal for jetted tubs, which are often taller than conventional tubs.

A foot-operated drain plug just threads into its drain fitting. Press it down, and it seals the drains. Press it again, and it pops up to open the drain.

Hair Clogs and Minor Adjustments. When a tripwaste malfunctions, it's usually because hair has accumulated around the stop mechanism or the internal lift wire has gone out of adjustment. (See "Clearing a Stopper Mechanism," page 214, and "Clearing a Pop-Up Mechanism," page 215.)

If your tub is old enough to have a rubber stopper or if you're just tired of dealing with tripwaste linkages, then I suggest an aftermarket drain insert. These toe-operated devices are made slightly larger than standard drain openings, for a friction fit. You just press the insert into the drain. Some new drains now come with toe-operated pop-ups.

Replacing a Tub Drain Assembly

At some point, every drain assembly needs to be replaced. Perhaps its finish has deteriorated, or the linkage is broken, or you'd like to switch from chrome to polished brass.

Start by removing the overflow plate and pulling the tripwaste linkage from the overflow tube. **1** (inset). If your drain has a pop-up stopper in place, remove it as well. Then insert the handles of an old standard set of pliers into the drain opening, and engage the crosspiece in the bottom of the drain fitting. **1.** With a pop-up style drain, engage two brass tabs protruding from the inner rim of the fitting. (Special drain-spud wrenches are also made for this task.) Grip the jaws of the pliers with an adjustable wrench, and turn the pliers counterclockwise. You should be able to unscrew the fitting from the threaded drain shoe.

Disconnect the Drain. If the fitting won't budge, move to the underside of the drain. Between the drain shoe and the bottom of the tub, you'll see a rubber gasket. Place a hacksaw against the gasket,

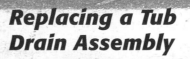

Replacing a Tub Drain Assembly

Tools and Materials

- Screwdriver
- Groove-joint pliers
- Hacksaw
- Pipe joint compound

Time Needed: 1–2 Hrs.

- New drain kit
- Plumber's putty

PLUMBING TIP: *If you have trouble getting the overflow gasket to seal, loosen the drain's friction nuts a little, tighten the overflow screws, and then retighten the nuts.*

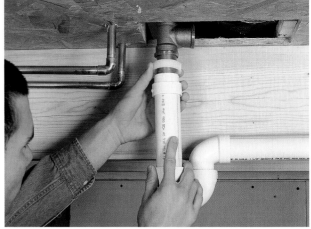

3 Loosen the trap connection to free the overflow tube. Expect to find a friction washer or compression washer.

and saw straight through it and the drain spud. **2.** (You can also use a reciprocating saw.)

With the drain connection severed, the P-trap will hold the entire assembly in place. If you have room to maneuver, loosen the trap's friction nut and lift the entire assembly out in one piece. If not, loosen the friction nuts that hold the waste and overflow components together and take out the assembly in pieces. In most cases, the trap will be attached to the waste assembly by means of a friction nut and flat washer. If the trap is made of plastic, the joint usually comprises a ground-joint adapter and compression-style nylon washer. **3.**

Install the New Tub Drain. With a conventional brass waste-and-overflow assembly, begin by pressing plumb-

er's putty around the underside of the drain flange, rolling the putty as you would for a sink drain. **4** (inset). Then have a helper place the rubber gasket on the drain shoe, and hold the shoe up to the tub's drain outlet from below. Feed the drain fitting through the tub opening, and thread it into the shoe. **4.** Insert pliers handles into the drain opening so that the handles engage the side tabs or crosspiece. Grip the pliers with an adjustable wrench, and tighten the fitting until most of the putty squeezes from beneath the flange. Trim the excess putty, and continue to tighten the fitting until it feels snug.

Next, slide a nut and washer onto the overflow tube, and tighten the tube into the waste T-fitting. Press the large rubber gasket onto the overflow flange, and lift the tube into place. **5.** Place a second nut and washer over

1 Begin by unscrewing the tripwaste cover plate and pulling the tripwaste linkage from the overflow (inset). Then unscrew the drain fitting.

2 If you can't free the old drain spud nut, cut through it using a hacksaw blade or a reciprocating saw with a metal-cutting blade.

4 Stick plumber's putty to the drain flange (inset), and screw the spud into the drain shoe and gasket while a helper holds them in place.

5 Install the rubber gasket on the bathtub overflow tube, and slide the tube upward into the wall cavity from below.

Sequence continues on next page

10 Repairing & Installing Tubs & Showers

Continued from previous page

6 *Join the drain and overflow pipes in the drain T-fitting, and tighten all the nuts using large groove-joint pliers.*

7 *Pull the plastic trap down far enough to allow you to screw the tailpiece into the drain T-fitting. Coat the threads with pipe joint compound.*

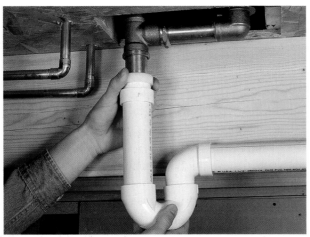

8 *Slip the compression nut and washer onto the tailpiece, and tighten the nut to secure the tail-piece in the trap riser.*

9 *From inside the tub, slip the tripwaste linkage into the overflow tube until the cover plate sits against the tube's gasket, and secure the plate.*

the drain shoe, and connect it to the waste T-fitting using groove-joint pliers. **6.** Apply a light coating of pipe joint compound to the fine threads of the brass tailpiece, and turn the tailpiece into the bottom of the waste T-fitting. **7.** Slide a third nut-and-washer set onto the tailpiece; insert the tailpiece into the trap riser (or ground joint adapter); and tighten the compression nut. **8.** If the trap riser is fitted with a ground joint adapter, you'll be able to reuse the original nylon compression washer. If the riser is made of metal pipe, buy a rubber friction washer to make the seal.

Connect the Tripwaste. With the tubing components assembled and connected, feed the tripwaste linkage into the overflow tube until the cover plate meets the tub. Thread the two bolts through the cover plate and into the overflow flange. Tighten these bolts until they feel snug. **9.**

If your tripwaste has a pop-up plug and lever, feed them into the drain shoe with the trip lever in the open position. If your tripwaste has an internal plunger, install the hair screen over the drain fitting. If your screen needs to be fastened with a screw, be careful not to overtighten the screw, or you'll bend the screen.

The only way to know whether your tripwaste was adjusted correctly at the factory—they're usually close—is to test it. If it leaks or drains too slowly, make the adjustments, as described on pages 214 and 215. When it seems to be working well, test the overflow seal by filling the tub to overflowing. Look for water around the rubber gasket on the back side of the connection. If it leaks, remove the cover-plate screws and look for an

SMART TIP

Tub and Shower Drain Access

If you want to replace an inaccessible drain (that is, when the tub is installed on a concrete slab or above a finished ceiling below), you'll need to do the work through the back of the plumbing wall. If your tub has an access panel already in place behind the tub, you're in luck. If not, you'll need to create one. To gain access, cut out the drywall between the two studs that straddle the center of the tub. When you've finished the installation, you can either patch the drywall or install a permanent access cover. You can make the cover out of plywood and door casing or purchase a ready-made plastic panel. When the opening is in plain sight, repair the wall. When it's in a closet or concealed by furniture, install a permanently accessible panel.

Oversized trim plates *often come with retrofit faucet kits.*

obvious problem. Some gaskets come with a front flange designed to fit through the bottom half of the tub opening. Also, check to see that the overflow flange is centered in the tub opening. If it's not, loosen the nut securing the tube to the waste T-fitting, and adjust the flange up or down as needed. If a minor leak persists, caulk the gasket with silicone.

Tub & Shower Faucets

To replace a tub/shower faucet that's behind tile or a plastic wall surround, cut out a section of the back side of the plumbing wall and make the repair from the rear. In this way, you can leave the tile or plastic surround undisturbed. Of course, your new faucet will need to match the wall openings left by the old faucet. A two-handle faucet, for example, would need a two-handle replacement. Most tub faucets have 8-inch spreads.

When the tub doesn't have a shower, consider removing the few rows of tile above the tub and make new tiles part of a general upgrade. With back-to-back tubs, which prohibit rear access, you'll need to remove at least several tiles surrounding the faucet. Cut through the wallboard exposed by the removed tile, and replace the faucet through this opening. When you're finished, repair the wall, cement the old tiles back in place, and grout the joints. While this method usually works, it's not easy, and there's always a chance that you'll break some tiles.

And finally, most manufacturers offer retrofit faucet kits for tubs and showers. The kit includes a standard faucet and an oversized trim plate. With care, you can cut out just enough tile or plastic surround to make the switch and then cover the opening with the trim plate.

SMART TIP

Matching Faucet Types

When you replace a tub/shower faucet, the easiest option is to install a brass faucet that matches your old faucet's spread (it's openings in the tile), especially if your piping is galvanized steel. In this case, you can use the new faucet's unions to connect the supply pipes. This approach is especially easy if the faucet has a union connecting the shower riser pipe. Of course, you may not want the same type of faucet. If not, you'll need to buy new tiles to patch the old openings, and you may need to make more complicated piping connections. When switching faucet types, it's usually better to convert to copper pipe.

A replacement faucet *with the same center spread as the original is the easiest to install.*

These kits can be real wall savers, but they have limits. First, maneuvering wrenches and soldering torches in such tight spaces is challenging, especially if a backing board is in the way. Secondly, bath tiles usually don't come off as neatly as these systems require. The tiles are square, but the trim plates are tapered. The trim never seems to cover all the removal, so these kits really work better on plastic surrounds. And finally, the large trim plates are big enough to be conspicuous.

Replacing a Tub-Shower Faucet

Begin by turning off the water at the shut-off valve. Pry the index caps from the handles, and remove the handle screws. Pull the handles off, and remove the stem escutcheons or trim plate. Escutcheons are threaded and screw on and off; trim plates are secured by two screws. Your faucet will have one type or the other.

Remove the Faucet. The tub spout will also be mounted in one of two ways; either threaded onto a ½-inch-diameter nipple or clamped onto a copper stub-out with a setscrew. Reach under the spout, and feel for an Allen screw recess. If you find a screw, loosen it and pull the spout off. If you don't find a screw, the spout is threaded. Grip the spout with a strap wrench (or padded pipe wrench or large pliers), and back it out. **1.** (You can also insert pliers handles or a large screwdriver into the spout opening and twist.)

For removing tile, it's best to buy an inexpensive grout-removal tool. Plan on removing an area of wall around the faucet measuring about 12 × 16 inches. Try to confine the opening to the space between studs. Draw the grout-removal tool along each seam repeatedly until you've gouged most of the grout from the joints. **2.** Then, using a sturdy putty knife, pry under one of the ceramic tiles until it pops loose. Pry at several points and

---

SMART TIP

Faucet and Piping Variations

The installation in "Replacing a Tub-Shower Faucet" (at right) is generally consistent with what you can expect to find inside tub walls. In the interest of completeness, it shows a change in piping materials, the most difficult kind of installation, from steel to copper, a more user-friendly material (even with the requisite soldering skills). If your piping system is already made of copper, everything gets easier. Just cut the existing copper risers, and solder new copper in place, using sweat couplings and 90-degree elbows.

If the faucet you've purchased has threaded ports instead of sweat fittings, use copper male adapters to make the conversion to copper piping. Use pipe-thread sealing tape instead of pipe joint compound, but don't overdo it. Two or three rounds, stretched slightly over the threads and applied in a clockwise rotation, is ideal. Make sure the final wrap of tape covers the end threads of the fitting.

And finally, if you live where plastic is allowed for water piping, using CPVC, with its cemented joints, is even easier.

Replacing a Tub-Shower Faucet

Tools and Materials

- Strap wrench
- Screwdriver
- Grout removal tool
- Pipe wrenches

TIME NEEDED: 2 HRS., PLUS TILE

- New faucet
- Solder, flux, torch

PLUMBING TIP: Tiles are sometimes hard to remove without breaking a few. It's a good idea to make sure you have matching replacements in advance of your work.

3 Start near the spout or faucet stems, and carefully pry each tile away from the wall. Set the tiles aside for reuse.

in several directions. If the tile won't budge, try one of the tiles next to the faucet opening. Grip the edge of one of these tiles and pull. Remove the remaining tiles, working from the center outward. **3.** When you've pried all tiles from the removal area, cut the wallboard just inside the remaining tiles and pull this section out.

How you remove the old faucet will depend on the piping material in place. If you find galvanized steel or brass, slip a 10-inch pipe wrench into the opening and loosen the two union nuts at the bottom of the faucet. **4.** If the shower riser pipe is joined to the faucet with a union, loosen it as well. If the riser is threaded into the faucet, use a hacksaw or reciprocating saw to cut it just above the faucet. Finally, push the faucet back until the spout nipple clears the wall. If you find copper pipe and soldered joints,

the easiest approach is to cut all pipes near their faucet connections and pull the faucet straight out.

Install the New Faucet. The faucet connection methods will be dictated by the kind of unit you buy: whether it's a single- or dual-control model; whether it has union fittings, threaded ports, or soldered joints; and so on. If your piping is made of galvanized steel, you'll also need to consider the problem of electrolytic corrosion, which results when you join copper and steel piping directly. (See "Electrolysis," page 84.)

If direct copper-to-steel connections are not a problem in your area, begin by threading galvanized-steel couplings onto each riser, using pipe-thread sealing tape. (It's a good idea to use couplings, with their female

1 *If you'd like to save the old spout, use a strap wrench to unscrew it from the faucet and avoid damaging the finish.*

2 *With the spout and escutcheons removed, use a grout saw to strip the grout from the tiles in the removal area.*

4 *Loosen the faucet unions with a pipe wrench, and lift out and discard the old faucet. Remove and discard the unions.*

5 *Apply pipe-thread sealing tape, and then thread ½-in. galvanized couplings to the old faucet supply tubes.*

10 Repairing & Installing Tubs & Showers

Sequence continues on next page

Continued from previous page

6 *Using pipe-thread sealing tape (not pipe joint compound), screw ½-in. copper male adapters into the couplings.*

7 *When adding piping for the showerhead, cut an opening in the wall to secure the drop-eared elbow to blocking.*

ports, because copper stretches when threaded over steel, often enough to cause a leak.) As always, be sure to use a second wrench to backhold the supply pipes when tightening the new fittings. **5.** With the steel couplings in place, wrap three rounds of pipe-sealing tape counterclockwise over the threads of two copper male adapters, and tighten the adapters into the couplings. **6.**

If you had to cut the old steel shower riser to remove the faucet, you'll have to install a new one. There are several options. You can remove the old riser and fish Type L soft copper in its place through the faucet opening, uncoiling the pipe as you go. This requires cutting a second opening at showerhead level. If the basement ceiling beneath the tub is open, you can usually install rigid piping from below. In any case, solder a drop-eared elbow to the top of the pipe, and feed it into the wall. Screw the elbow to a backing board. **7.**

With a new shower riser ready, solder copper inlet stubs into the side ports of the valve. The easiest approach is to make them a little long, then hold the faucet in place and measure between the stubs and the copper adapters on the supply tubes. Cut these lengths, and test-fit the riser-to-faucet connections.

With the faucet temporarily connected to the supply tubes and shower riser, cut stubs for the tub spout. If your new spout is threaded, solder a ½-inch-diameter male adapter to the end of the horizontal pipe so that the threads of the adapter protrude through the finished tub wall about ½ inch. If the spout clamps onto the pipe with an Allen screw, bring the copper pipe through the wall about 3 inches. **8.**

When you have all of the pieces fitted, pull the assembly apart and flux the ends of the stubs. Before soldering, remove the faucet cartridge or stem to keep from warping the plastic components.

Solder as much of the assembly as possible outside the wall. Insert the stubs into the faucet ports; lay the faucet on the floor; and solder each joint carefully. After the valve cools, flux the remaining joints; connect the faucet to the in-wall piping; and solder these joints. **9.** Be careful when soldering next to combustible surfaces inside the wall. Use a flame-shield and wet the wood near the faucet. When the faucet cools, reassemble it and turn the water on to test your work. When you're sure you have no leaks, repair the wall and install the spout, showerhead, and faucet trim.

Bathtubs

As you shop for bathtubs, you'll see five basic types: traditional enameled cast iron and porcelain-coated steel tubs and the newer plastic-coated porcelain steel, fiberglass, and acrylic-plastic tubs.

Of the two traditional types, cast iron is the more durable. It retains heat better than steel and is much quieter when it's being filled. Expect cast-iron tubs to cost $300 to $400, compared with $100 to $175 for steel tubs. Steel tubs have always earned their keep in starter homes and, with care, hold up reasonably well.

The third type, a steel tub with a flexible-plastic coating separating the porcelain from the steel, is priced midway between traditional steel and cast iron and combines their best features: it is warmer, quieter, and

8 Complete the new faucet piping in copper. Install the spout pipe so that the spout will be 6 in. below the faucet body when installed.

9 Remove the nylon faucet cartridge from the faucet body, and sweat all copper fittings using lead-free solder.

more durable than traditional steel but without the weight of cast iron.

Fiberglass and acrylic-plastic tubs often come with matching wall surrounds. These tubs have better insulating properties than cast-iron but are generally less substantial. They're easier to install, however. Of these, acrylic is the most attractive, colorful, durable, and costly. Fiberglass is more affordable, and it can be repaired seamlessly and cheaply. The advantage of plastic, generally, is that it's easy to mold into attractive shapes and textures. Acrylic plastic is also available in a wide variety of colors, and unlike cast iron and steel, darker colors don't cost substantially more.

Fiberglass and plastic are also used to make one-piece tub-shower stalls. These units are generally too big for retrofits because they won't fit through doors or down hallways. Their chief advantages are durability, affordability, and ease of maintenance. When properly installed, they're virtually leak-proof. However, a frequent complaint with these tubs, especially fiberglass models, is that they're uncomfortable for bathing.

Tubs are available with right-

hand and left-hand drains, as determined when you face the tub. A tub drain and faucet should be installed in the same wall, so order your tub accordingly. Standard tubs are 60 inches long, but special-order tubs are available in lengths ranging from 48 inches to 72 inches, graduated in 6-inch increments. Special-order lengths are naturally more expensive.

Bathtub Installation Anatomy

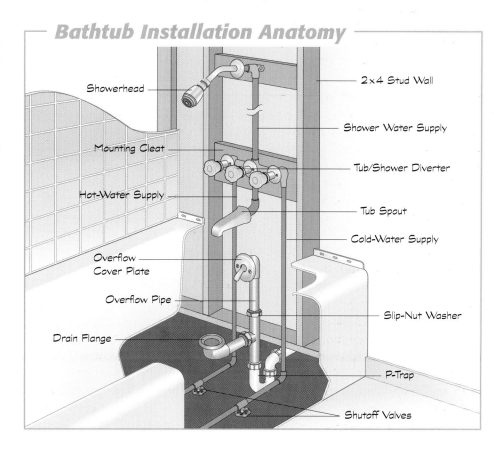

Showerhead

Mounting Cleat

Hot-Water Supply

Overflow Cover Plate

Overflow Pipe

Drain Flange

2×4 Stud Wall

Shower Water Supply

Tub/Shower Diverter

Tub Spout

Cold-Water Supply

Slip-Nut Washer

P-Trap

Shutoff Valves

Whirlpool Tubs

There are two styles of whirlpool, or more properly jetted, tubs sold today: apron-style tubs and drop-ins. Those with conventional aprons are typically smaller, and most are designed to fit a standard 32 × 60-inch tub opening. Drop-ins can be quite large, up to 48 × 84 inches. The term drop-in is a misnomer, because these tubs are really freestanding. Drop-ins require a surrounding deck, however, so the impression is that of a tub suspended, like a sink. The tub and pump motor rest on a sturdy base, and the circulation piping wraps around the tub. The usual approach is to build a treated-lumber framework, cover it with backer board, and finish it with solid-surface resin, marble, granite, or ceramic tile. All support equipment, including the motor, pump and piping, is concealed by the apron or decking. Apron models usually have a removable panel, while drop-ins require you to build an access panel into the deck. Make sure this service opening is large enough to allow you to replace a pump and motor.

Features. Most jetted tubs sold today are made of acrylic or a similar composite plastic. They range widely in price and are now sold just about everywhere. There are three types of motors in use today: brush-style motors and single and multi-speed induction motors. Brush-style motors are used almost exclusively in builder's grade tubs. Brush style-motors are noisier and have a shorter expected service life. For a little more

Jetted tubs *not meant to be deck-mounted come with aprons, which often provide pump access.*

money, you can have a quiet, long-lasting induction motor, and for $300 to $400 more, a two or three-speed motor. Pumps are sized between 1 and 3 horsepower. At the high end, manufacturers also vary jet speed with flow control devices. In any case, more speeds offer greater control and comfort. The high-volume jetting that feels so good when you first climb in can feel like a beating 10 minutes later, so variable speeds are a real benefit.

You'll hear a lot about jet technology, which is where most manufacturers try to differentiate themselves. If relaxation is what you're after, the most basic jets will do, but for massage therapy to specific areas of the body, specialty jets can make a difference. The better tubs also have built-in heaters. Injecting room-temperature air into churning water cools the water quickly, so booster heaters really improve comfort.

Hot Water Concerns. Jetted tubs take a lot of hot water from the start, enough that your current water heater may not be up to the task. With the heater set properly, household faucets should deliver comfortably hot water at a ratio of two-thirds hot water to one-third cold water. At that rate, a 40-gallon gas water heater will deliver a maximum 60 gallons of hot water. For a larger tub, you'll either need a larger water heater

Whirlpool Tub Anatomy

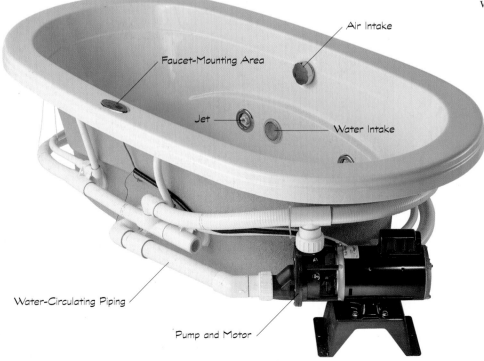

Air Intake

Faucet-Mounting Area

Jet

Water Intake

Water-Circulating Piping

Pump and Motor

SMART TIP

Resurfacing Bathtubs

If you have an old bathtub, you can hire a company to resurface it for about $300. This might be worth the cost to you when you consider the combined costs of replacement, including wall repair and a new tub, faucet, drain, and shower surround. The resurfacing process usually consists of removing the drain fittings, masking off the tub area and applying an etching solution or some other chemical-bonding agent. The installer then sprays on several coats of a plastic top coat, removes the masking tape, and installs the drain fittings. These thick finishes are available in many colors.

The materials used in these preparations have been improved, but the key factors in durability still have more to do with the diligence of the installer and the cleaning habits of the owner. If you use the tub only occasionally or are good about wiping it clean with each use, a new synthetic finish should last 10 years or more.

Refinishing a tub *includes several applications of a plasticized finish.*

Finishing touches *include buffing out any imperfections in the final surface.*

or two standard heaters, plumbed in series. In this case, the first heater feeds the second and the second feeds the house. Luckily, the water supply and drain hookups for these tubs are very similar to those of standard bathtubs.

Caution: *large tubs of water are heavy. If you plan to install a large tub on an older wooden floor, check with an engineer. Building and safety officials may also be able to help. You may need to add floor joists to handle the extra weight.*

Installing a Cast-Iron Bathtub

Whether working with new construction (in a new home or addition) or replacing an old tub, the process is similar. A new installation requires a few more steps, so this procedure assumes a new tub in a new bathroom. The time to install the tub is when the piping is roughed-in and before the drywall goes up.

Removing a Built-In Bathtub

When replacing a built-in tub, expect the old bathtub to be locked in place by the plaster or wallboard above and in front of it. It may also be held in place by a layer of flooring. With a standard tub, you'll need to remove about 3 feet of drywall above the tub and 1 foot in front of it. In the case of a plaster wall, remove both plaster and lath. Use a reciprocating saw to cut away drywall or plaster. Cut out the old faucet and drain, as well.

With steel or cast-iron tubs, pry between the tub apron and the floor, using a flat bar. Pry from one end only, and when it pops loose, slide a shim under the apron and pry again. With a steel tub, you can then just lift that end and stand it up. In the case of a cast-iron tub, weighing over 300 pounds, continue to shim until you can get a 2x4 under the apron. Pry with the 2x4, and block the tub until you have the apron about 2 feet off the floor on one end. Then, with the aid of a helper or two, lift it upright. If you'll be gutting the entire room, an easier method is to lift the tub with a cable ratchet. Loop one end over a ceiling joist and the other through the overflow hole; then winch the tub upright.

In the case of a fiberglass or plastic tub-shower, cut it into pieces with a reciprocating saw and carry out the pieces. These units are usually too big to fit through doors and down hallways.

First, you need to cut a drain opening in the floor. This should be an oversize rectangular hole, because the drain shoe will extend below the tub about 10 inches back from the wall. **1.** The hole will need to be centered in the tub space, which is typically 30 inches, so mark a cutout that is centered 15 inches from the long wall. The actual size of the hole should be 8 × 12 inches, with the longer dimension extending away from the plumbing wall. Use a circular saw or reciprocating saw to make the cut.

Set the Tub. A cast-iron tub weighs more than 300 pounds, but if you're careful you can set one with little or no help. Uncrate the tub, and stand it up. **2.** The easiest way to move an upright tub is to "walk" it. Grip the upper end, tilt it toward you slightly, and then rock the apron from corner to corner. Each time a corner leaves the floor, pull the tub toward you a little. Walk it, corner to corner, into the bath until you have it standing upright in the tub area. Maneuver it into one corner, and carefully lay it over until the high end comes to rest against the opposite wall. In new construction, where the walls are open, use a 2×4 stud to pry under the low end of the tub, through the wall. Each time you lift, the high end will settle closer to the floor and the low end will slide closer toward you. When the tub drops to the floor, push it against the long wall.

Cast-iron tubs are not meant to be secured. They stay put because they are so heavy and are locked in place by underlayment and drywall. You should support the tub along the long wall, however. Begin by stepping into the tub and walking around. If the tub rocks corner to corner even a little, make an effort to find out why. The problem can be an out-of-level floor or a slightly warped tub. With the tub pushed firmly against the back wall, lay a spirit level across the ends of the tub. If you see a discrepancy, slide a wooden shim under one corner of the tub. If this corrects the level and the rocking, mark the exact position of the shim and remove it. Apply a dab of construction adhesive to the bottom of the shim and slide it back in place. Then measure between the bottom of the tub deck, along the wall, and the top of the wall's soleplate. Cut two pieces of 2×4 to this length, and wedge them between the tub and soleplate. **3.** Nail them to nearby studs. These supports help spread the weight.

Install the Faucet Plumbing. When assembling the faucet piping for a tub or tub-shower, it's important to keep all the piping square and straight. Most plumbers assemble and solder the piping to the faucet on a flat surface, like a floor, and install the resulting "shower tree" in one piece.

Begin by laying three 16-to-24-inch pieces of 2×4 lumber on the floor. One piece should be near the showerhead, one just below the valve and one near the bottom of the supply tubes. For a tub, cut two lengths of type M rigid copper 36 inches long, to be used for the supply tubes. Cut a second length for the shower riser, 44 to 48 inches long. Finally, cut two short stubs for the horizontal connections to the faucet inlets, and two 5-inch stubs for the spout piping. Clean and flux the pipe ends, and install a drop-eared elbow on the top of the shower riser. Insert the shower riser and pipe stubs into the remaining ports of the valve. Finish by joining the supply risers to the inlet stubs, using 90-degree elbows.

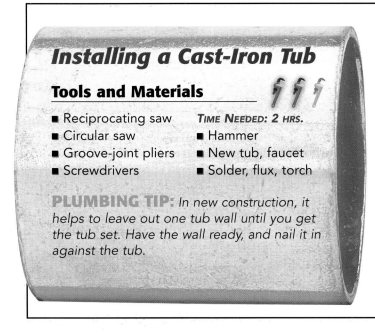

Installing a Cast-Iron Tub

Tools and Materials

- Reciprocating saw
- Circular saw
- Groove-joint pliers
- Screwdrivers

TIME NEEDED: 2 HRS.
- Hammer
- New tub, faucet
- Solder, flux, torch

PLUMBING TIP: *In new construction, it helps to leave out one tub wall until you get the tub set. Have the wall ready, and nail it in against the tub.*

1 Cut the tub's drain opening (8 x 12 in.) with a reciprocating saw. Center the cutout 15 in. from the long wall.

Setting Steel and Plastic Tubs

Unlike a cast-iron unit, a steel tub should be light enough to muscle into position. There are two significant design differences between steel and cast-iron tubs. First, cast-iron tubs have support legs; steel tubs do not. Instead, a flat slab of polystyrene foam is glued to the bottom of the tub. On a level floor, this foam slab supports the tub. Secondly, a steel tub has a top lip, or flange, on three sides. On some models, the flange has a series of screw holes, allowing you to screw the tub to the wall. Don't drywall over this flange, however. Hold the wallboard about ⅛ inch above it.

Step into the tub and walk around a bit. If you feel the tub rock, even slightly, investigate to determine why. If the floor is out of level—a common situation with concrete—then you can't rely on the polystyrene foam slab for full support. Place a level on the tub, along each wall, and make whatever adjustments are necessary. When you have it right, reach under the tub, mark each stud along the back wall where the tub meets the stud, and then pull out the tub. Cut a straight 60-inch 2x4, and nail it to the wall so that its top meets the marks on the wall studs. Push the tub back against the wall so that its deck rests on the 2x4. If the tub has flange holes, you can attach the flange to the back wall using 1½-inch-long

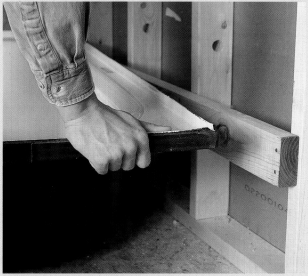

With a steel tub, *install the 2x4 support horizontally. (See step 3 below.) Check it with a 4-foot level.*

drywall screws, though this is usually unnecessary.

When setting a fiberglass or plastic (acrylic) tub-shower unit, use a spirit level to level and plumb the tub in all directions. Because the contours of the tub will yield a false reading, lay the level against the drywall flange on both the vertical and horizontal surfaces. When you get it right, use galvanized roofing nails or screws to secure the flange to the studs. Lay a piece of sheet metal or hardboard against the finished edge to avoid hitting it when nailing.

2 *An easy way to move a heavy cast-iron tub is to walk it, corner-to-corner, across the floor.*

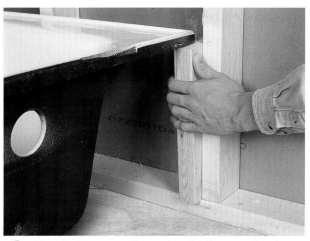

3 *Use 2x4s, vertically, under the long-wall-side corners of the tub. Nail the blocking to the wall's corner studs.*

Sequence continues on next page

Continued from previous page

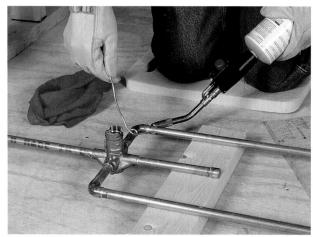

4. Assemble the shower-tree assembly on blocking laid on the floor, and when everything's straight, solder the copper tubing together.

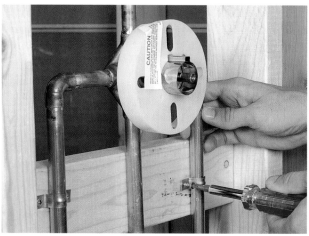

5. Install backing boards behind the faucet and showerhead fittings for support, and secure the piping with straps.

Lay this assembly on the three 2×4s, and check for straightness. When it all looks right, solder and wipe all joints and let the assembly cool. **4.** Then set the tree in place so that the front of the faucet's rough-in plate matches the approximate plane of the finished wall. Mark the wall's sole plate for the supply tube holes, and drill ¾-inch holes at each mark. Insert the supply tubes through the floor holes until the center of the valve is 28 inches off the floor. With a plastic tub/shower unit, insert the tubes through the tub's drain hole.

Let the tree stand by itself while you cut two 2×4 braces to fit between the studs. Nail these braces in place, positioned so that the valve's rough-in plate will be on the same plane as the finished wall, and that the showerhead's drop-eared elbow is held behind the face of the studs. Screw the ears of the elbow to the upper brace so that it is centered above the tub drain, and then center the valve above the tub drain and secure the supply risers to the lower brace, using two-hole copper straps. **5.** Loosely thread a ½ × 4-inch nipple into the drop-eared elbow. **6.** Connect the supply risers to the system water piping, and test your work. Install the tub's drain assembly as described in "Replacing a Tub Drain Assembly," page 218, or "Connecting to a Drain beneath Concrete," at right.

Showers

In a typical shower-stall installation, the in-wall faucet should be plumbed so that its spray hits a side wall and not the door or curtain. The showerhead should be roughed-in at around 76 inches off the floor, while the

faucet should be positioned 48 inches off the floor. The faucet and shower head do not need to be on the same wall, though it's easier to plumb that way. The shower tree should be preassembled and soldered as described in "Installing a Cast-Iron Bathtub," page 227. As with a tub-shower tree, both the valve piping and showerhead should be firmly anchored.

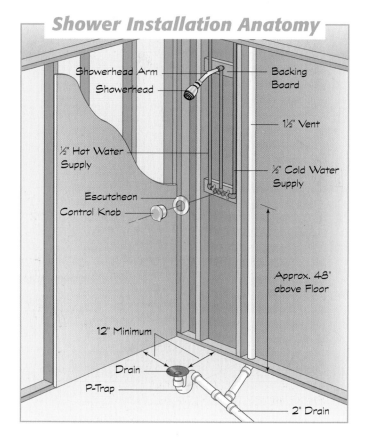

Shower Installation Anatomy

- Showerhead Arm
- Showerhead
- Backing Board
- 1½" Vent
- ½" Hot Water Supply
- ½" Cold Water Supply
- Escutcheon
- Control Knob
- Approx. 48" above Floor
- 12" Minimum
- Drain
- P-Trap
- 2" Drain

6 Screw the showerhead's drop-eared elbow to the backing board, and install a temporary nipple in the fitting.

SMART TIP

Installing a Tub on an Exterior Wall

If you plan to install a tub against an exterior wall, make sure that the wall is well insulated and that a plastic vapor barrier covers it. After you set the tub, and before installing drywall, stuff more fiberglass-batt insulation into the cavity between the wall and the tub. This simple step can greatly reduce heat loss. If the tub is made of porcelain steel, the insulation will also muffle the noise associated with steel tubs when they are filled. It also helps to stuff insulation between the tub and the apron. Don't use expandable foam under tubs, however.

Connecting to a Drain beneath Concrete

When a tub will be set on concrete, a 2-inch drain line is usually brought to a boxed out area and taped off. The box, usually made of framing lumber, is then partially filled with gravel. If a tub will not be installed immediately, concrete is poured over the top of the gravel and finished. This keeps insects, radon, and moisture from entering the living space but leaves a weak spot for easy access. If the tub will be installed as part of the primary construction, the box is usually left open.

Only after the tub and drain assemblies are installed is this pipe connected, using a PVC P-trap. If the waste pipe is made of cast iron and ends in a hub, press a rubber gasket into the hub. Then dull the end of a short length of 2-inch PVC pipe, lubricate both the pipe and gasket, and push the pipe into the hub. Immediately out of the hub, install a 2-inch plastic coupling with a 2 x 1½-inch reducing bushing. Pipe a 1½-inch P-trap into this bushing. All other aspects of the drain connection are the same as those of an upper-story connection.

If a cast-iron line is without a final hub, join the plastic to the iron with a banded coupling. If the drain line is also plastic, make the connection with solvent-cemented fittings. When you've completed the connection and tested it with water, mix a small batch of concrete and seal the opening around the trap.

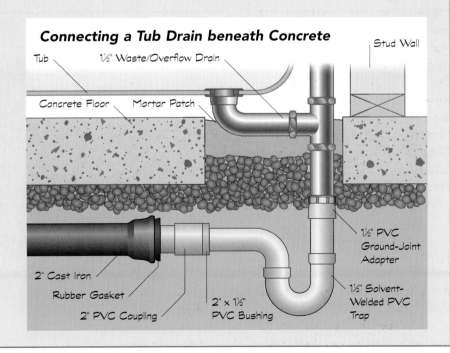

Connecting a Tub Drain beneath Concrete

Tub
1½" Waste/Overflow Drain
Stud Wall
Concrete Floor
Mortar Patch
1½" PVC Ground-Joint Adapter
2" Cast Iron
Rubber Gasket
2" PVC Coupling
2" x 1½" PVC Bushing
1½" Solvent-Welded PVC Trap

Component showers can be made of several materials, but they usually start with a premolded plastic or fiberglass pan. These floor pans come in sizes ranging from 32 × 32 inches to 40 × 60 inches. You'll need to frame the opening to fit the pan dimensions. Side walls should extend beyond the front of the pan at least 2 inches so that drywall can be wrapped around the edge. As with a tub, you should install a shower pan before the drywall (and cement backer board if necessary) goes up on the walls. The drywall (or cement board), when installed, should be held just above the pan flange. You can buy pans alone or with surround walls. Most shower combinations are made for rectangular, three-wall stalls, with a glass door or shower curtain shielding the open end.

Installing a Shower Stall

After framing the stall, you need to install the shower pan. Some shower pans come with the drain fitting packaged separately. The pan or stall is easier to ship that way. This means that you'll need to install the drain in the pan before you install the pan in the framed opening.

Set the Shower Pan. Before installing the shower pan in its opening, measure off the back wall and cut a 6-inch circular opening in the floor. A good way to make sure you spot the drain in the right location is to set the pan in place and mark the floor though the pan opening. **1.**

Insert the rubber-gasketed drain spud through the opening in the pan. **2** (inset). Then slide a rubber washer and paper washer over the spud from below. Thread the large plastic spud nut onto the drain, and tighten it. **2.** As with other spud-type drain fittings, tighten the nut until it feels snug. Don't overtighten it.

You'll need to plumb a 2-inch vented P-trap below the drain opening with a riser long enough to reach the pan drain. To determine the exact riser height, either set the pan in place or measure down from the floor. It helps to lay a straightedge across the opening. **3.** There are two possible connections. Some drains require that the trap riser be brought through the spud, stopping just below the drain screen. (These drains may be plastic or metal.) The seal is made with a rubber gasket, which you tamp into the gap between the pipe and spud with a hammer and packing iron or flattened piece of ½-inch copper pipe. Don't lubricate this gasket. Just set it in place and tamp it down. **4.** Other drain fittings require that you cement the riser pipe right into the hub. (These drains are always plastic.)

After you set the pan, install the water piping. (See "Shower Installation Anatomy," page 230.) Finish the enclosure with moisture-resistant drywall, or if you'll tile the walls, with a combination of moisture-resistant

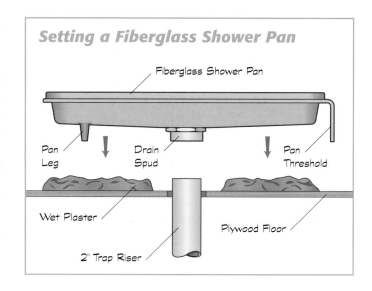

Setting a Fiberglass Shower Pan

Fiberglass Shower Pan

Pan Leg

Drain Spud

Pan Threshold

Wet Plaster

Plywood Floor

2" Trap Riser

Installing a Shower Stall

Tools and Materials

- New shower stall
- Measuring tape, pencil
- Saber saw
- Groove-joint pliers
- Cement backer board
- Hammer, packing tool

TIME NEEDED: 1–2 HRS.

- Level
- Drill, hole saw
- Adhesive
- Tub-and-tile caulk

PLUMBING TIP: *The best way to hold the shower pan in place is to install underlayment flooring along its front.*

3 *Install a PVC drainpipe riser to meet the drain fitting. Use a straightedge to check the riser's length.*

drywall and cement backer board. Cover the lower 24 to 30 inches of the walls with backer board, and drywall the rest. Attach the tile backer with construction adhesive and deck screws or galvanized roofing nails. **5.**

Install the Surround-Panel Kit. Next, you'll need to make the shower enclosure watertight. You can line the walls with ceramic tiles, but installing a plastic shower-surround kit made of PVC or ABS plastic or fiberglass is quicker and less skill intensive, and the installation is likely to be longer lasting.

Some surround kits come with three panels, others with five. A five-panel kit has separate corner panels, while a three-panel kit has the corners built into the end panels. If your walls are reasonably square and plumb, a three-panel kit is your best choice. (Use a 4-foot level to check the walls.) If not, a five-panel kit is more accommodating.

Surround panels are held in place by two-sided foam-rubber tape and panel adhesive. You should seal the wall behind the panel with satin or semigloss latex or oil-based paint. If you use semigloss, scuff it with sandpaper before installing the panels.

Begin by laying the panel that will cover the plumbing wall on a set of sawhorses. Then measure carefully to determine the exact locations of the plumbing holes to be cut into the panel. Use the back wall and the shower pan as reference points, and take the measurements from the exact center of each plumbing feature, such as a faucet cartridge or stem.

Use a hole saw and electric drill to cut the openings

1 *Set the pan in place, and mark the floor through the drain. Remove the pan, and cut a 6-in. floor opening with a saber saw or reciprocating saw.*

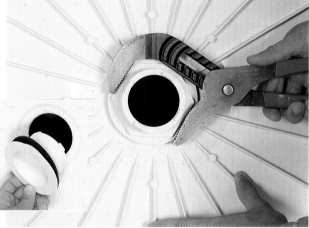

2 *Insert the drain spud through the pan and thread the spud nut over it. Tighten with pliers or a spud wrench.*

4 *With drain installed over the riser, press the rubber gasket around the riser. Tamp it in using a hammer and packing tool.*

5 *Nail concrete backer board along the bottom 24 in. of the shower wall, and then continue with moisture-resistant wallboard.*

10 Repairing & Installing Tubs & Showers

Sequence continues on next page

Continued from previous page

6. *Drill a faucet hole in the plumbing-wall panel using a drill and 3-inch hole saw. Measure carefully before cutting the hole.*

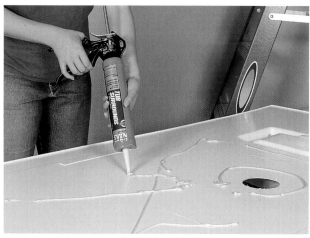

7. *Peel the paper from the foam tape around the panel edges and wherever else it appears; then apply panel adhesive with a caulking gun.*

for the faucet, and in some cases, the showerhead. **6.** Lacking a hole saw, drill pilot holes with a smaller bit and cut the openings with a saber saw. If you use a saber saw, however, tape the bottom of the saw's baseplate to keep from marring the finish. With the holes drilled, test-fit the panel to make sure there are no last-minute surprises. At this point, the rough-in plate should also be removed from the faucet.

When you're confident this first panel will fit, tape cardboard spacers around the perimeter of the shower pan deck. These spacers will keep the panels from making direct contact with the pan. Then, peel the paper from the two-sided foam tape and apply several heavy beads of panel adhesive to the back side of the panel. **7.** Apply one bead around the entire perimeter, about 2 inches inside the tape, another around the faucet holes, plus an X pattern across the panel.

Pull the paper from the two-sided tape, carry the panel into the shower stall, and carefully set it on the cardboard spacers. Make any last-minute adjustments. Then press the bottom of the panel against the wall while holding the upper portion of the panel away from it. This progression is critically important. Make sure that the bottom of the panel sticks to the wall first. While continuing to hold the top away from the wall slightly, press more of the panel in place, working gradually upward. Finally, press the top in place. To make sure that the adhesive makes full contact, rub the entire panel with a towel, pressing firmly. Prepare the opposite side panel and install it in identical fashion. **8.** Finally, press the center panel in place, and wait two days for the adhesive to cure. **9.**

Seal the Wall Panels. After a couple of days' wait, caulk all the seams. **10.** (At the very least, the top of the panel should remain open temporarily to release the curing gases.) Silicone caulk is by far the best material here. However, it has a working time of only about 30 seconds. After that, it balls up under your finger when you try to smooth it. To make the job easier, don't apply more caulk than is absolutely necessary (just enough to fill the gap), and don't apply more than 2 or 3 feet of caulk at a time. Lay a 2-foot bead, wipe it smooth with your finger, and then lay on another few feet. If your finger starts to drag, dip it in rubbing alcohol.

If, when you smooth the bead, caulk squeezes out on both sides of your finger, you've made the bead too large. The thin layer at the sides will eventually peel back, exposing the rest of the joint to water. If you see that you've put on too much, wipe it off with a paper towel. If the caulk starts to set before you get it smoothed out, dip your finger in rubbing alcohol and try again. If you've applied too little caulk in a few spots, smooth the bead and leave it. Add more when the caulk cures.

Caulk the faucet trim as well. Apply a very thin bead around the top half of the trim plate, with the tube's applicator tip trimmed to its smallest opening. Then immediately wipe almost all of it off. Use the tip of your finger, and keep a paper towel handy. **11.** Press hard, leaving only a thin bead in the joint, roughly $\frac{1}{16}$ inch wide. It should be all but invisible.

Finally, caulk the seams between the panels and the wall, this time with latex tub-and-tile caulk. Don't forget the seam at the top of the panels, because shower water bounces up, as well as out.

8 Tape strips of cardboard to the shower pan; set the first panel on the strips; and press it against the wall from the bottom up.

9 Install the other side panel, then the back panel. Wipe all panels with a towel, pressing hard to spread the glue.

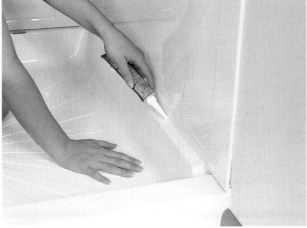

10 Use silicone caulk in the joint between the shower pan and panels. Caulk the vertical seams, too.

11 Caulk the shower faucet trim with a thin bead of silicone, and then wipe away all but an inconspicuous line.

CHAPTER 11

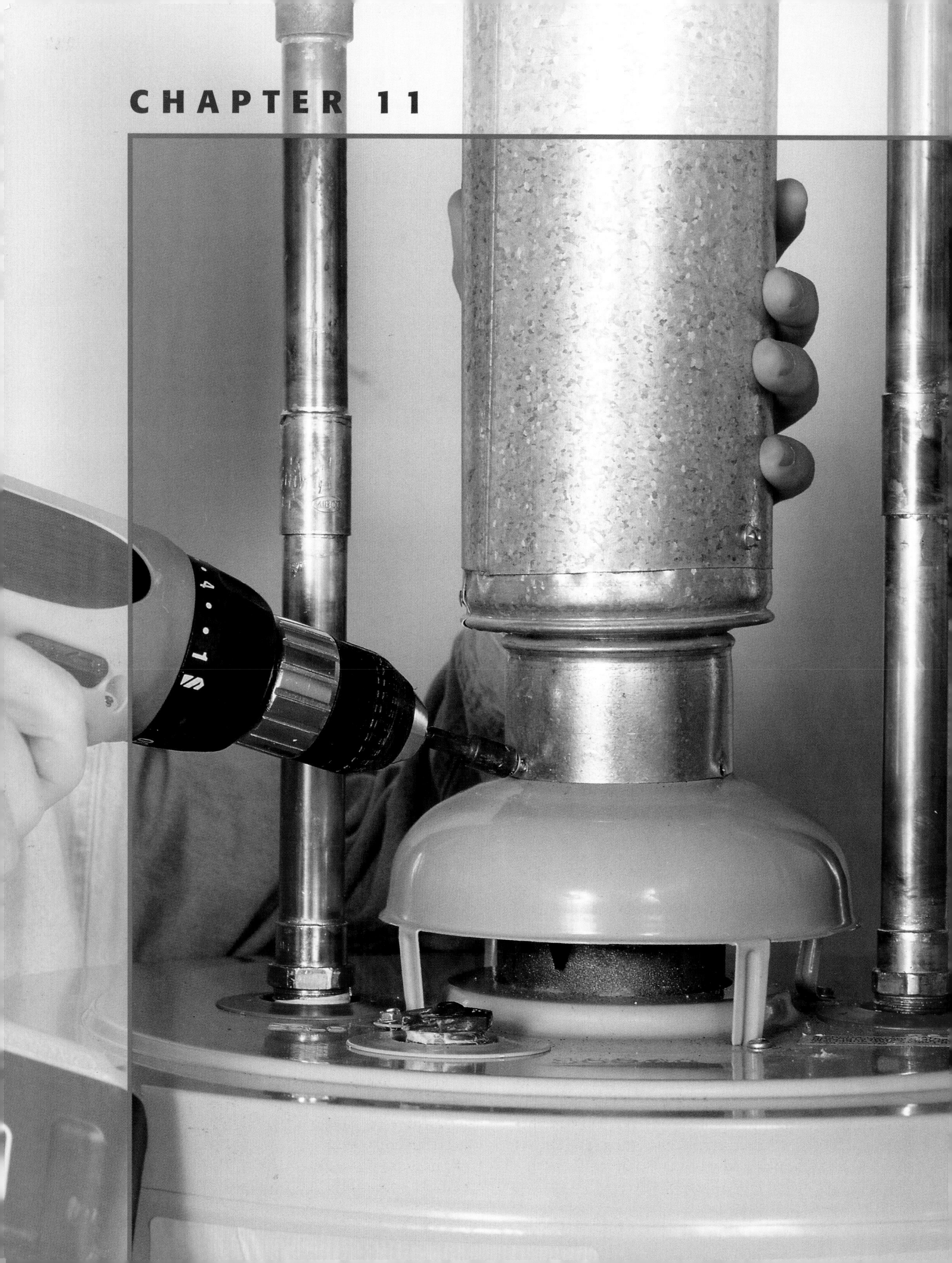

Maintaining & Installing Water Heaters

hile the range of water-heater options has grown in recent years, most of the units in current use are similar to those of generations past. The reason is that conventional electric and gas-fired water heaters are affordable and fairly inexpensive to operate, and they require little maintenance. High-tech, high-efficiency models use less fuel, but they are more expensive to buy and maintain.

Electric & Gas Water Heaters

Conventional tank heaters are basic-technology appliances, though these days they are more efficient than they used to be. Because of their no-frills mechanics, they are the most affordable and most popular heaters sold today.

Electric Water Heaters

An electric water heater consists of a welded steel inner tank covered by insulation and a metal outer cabinet. The inner surface of the steel tank is coated with a furnace-fired porcelain lining, often described as a glass lining. The bottom of the tank is slightly convex, which helps to control sediment, and a drain valve sits just above the bottom of the tank. The top of the tank has two water fittings and sometimes a separate anode fitting. The top (or upper side) of the heater also contains a fitting for a temperature-and-pressure (T&P) relief valve.

Two resistance-heat electrodes, called elements, heat the water in the tank. Each element is controlled by its own thermostat. The thermostats are joined electrically so that the elements can be energized in sequence: the bottom element comes on only when the top one shuts off. The elements are threaded or bolted into the unit, and the thermostats are surface-mounted next to the elements, covered by access panels and insulation. To help keep the tank from rusting, a magnesium anode rod is installed through the top of the heater. And finally, a dip tube usually hangs from the inlet fitting and delivers incoming water to the bottom of the tank.

Plastic Tanks. Electric water heaters with plastic tanks carry a lifetime warranty and cost about double the price of standard water heaters. Plastic makes an ideal tank because it can't corrode. In hard-water situations, steel-tank heaters tend to accumulate precipita-

Plastic Tank

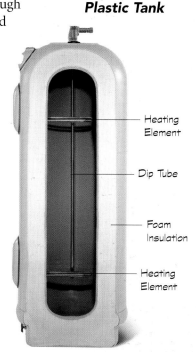

Heating Element

Dip Tube

Foam Insulation

Heating Element

Water Heater Anatomy

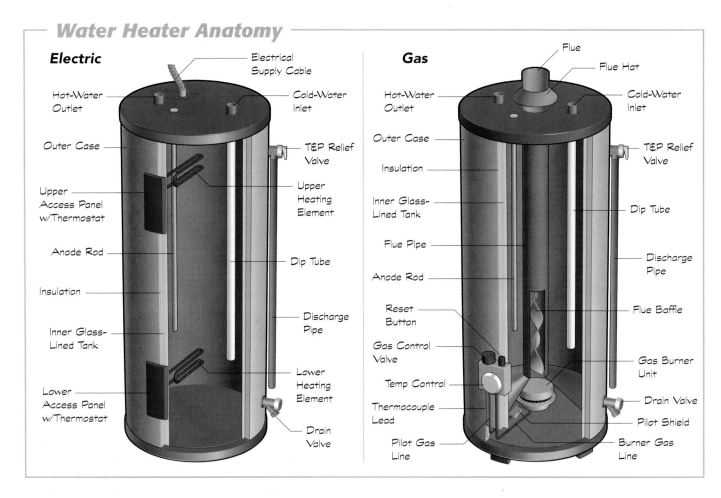

Electric

- Electrical Supply Cable
- Hot-Water Outlet
- Cold-Water Inlet
- Outer Case
- T&P Relief Valve
- Upper Access Panel w/Thermostat
- Upper Heating Element
- Anode Rod
- Dip Tube
- Insulation
- Inner Glass-Lined Tank
- Discharge Pipe
- Lower Heating Element
- Lower Access Panel w/Thermostat
- Drain Valve

Gas

- Flue
- Flue Hat
- Hot-Water Outlet
- Cold-Water Inlet
- Outer Case
- T&P Relief Valve
- Insulation
- Inner Glass-Lined Tank
- Dip Tube
- Flue Pipe
- Anode Rod
- Discharge Pipe
- Reset Button
- Flue Baffle
- Gas Control Valve
- Gas Burner Unit
- Temp Control
- Thermocouple Lead
- Drain Valve
- Pilot Shield
- Pilot Gas Line
- Burner Gas Line

ted minerals, shortening service life. Sediment can be a problem in plastic heaters, but it's more manageable: they have rounded bottoms with large, centered drain plugs for easy draining. Plastic tanks are also highly insulated with non-ozone-depleting foam insulation. Along with better insulation comes lower fuel costs. You can earn back the price difference of these units in five to ten years.

Gas-Fired Water Heaters

A gas-fired water heater is like an electric unit in many respects (glazed tank, anode rod, dip tube, relief valve), but its open-flame heating components require design differences. A flue tube runs through the center of the tank, from bottom to top. Viewed from above, the tank looks like a donut. To capture latent exhaust-gas heat, a wavy steel damper is suspended in the flue like a ribbon. The bottom of the tank is convex, which helps send sediment to the outer edges and away from the area just above the burner. At the bottom of the heater is the circular burner, and at the top, the exhaust-gas flue hat.

Gas goes to the burner through a thermostatically triggered control valve mounted on the lower front of the heater. The burner is joined to the control valve by three tubes. The largest of the tubes is the main gas feed. The mid-size tube is the pilot-gas feed, and the smallest is the

thermocouple lead. A thermocouple is little more than a copper wire with an expansion plug controlling the gas valve at one end and a heat sensor at the other. The heat from the flame sends a millivolt of electricity to the expansion plug, which holds the gas control valve open.

Power-Venting. A power-vented, or direct vent, heater has a sealed burner. A fan expels its gases, so the vent pipe does not need to be vertical (photo below). You can run the vent pipe horizontally down a long joist space and have it exit at a rim joist, for example. Power-vented units have a price tag two to three times that of a conventional gas-fired water heater and higher repair costs. They are a little more efficient, but not enough to earn back the price difference over a unit's useful life.

Power-Vented Water Heater

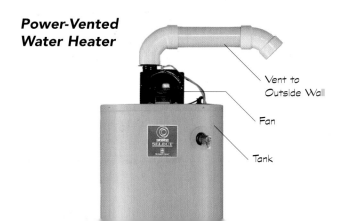

- Vent to Outside Wall
- Fan
- Tank

Common Water-Heater Problems

You will generally come across just a few main problems with a water heater: a faulty T&P relief valve, accumulation of sediment in the bottom of the tank, and a corroded anode rod. You'll learn how to deal with other more-specific problems on pages 242 to 245.

Faulty T&P Relief Valves

A temperature-and-pressure (T&P) relief valve is a water heater's primary safety device. Should a thermostat stick and the heater not shut off, the resulting increase in heat and pressure would be relieved through the T&P valve. Otherwise, the heater could explode.

The problem with T&P valves is that you can't always tell when they are no longer working. A leaky valve may signal a defect, but just as often, it indicates that the valve is working just as it should. A temporary pressure surge elsewhere in the system may have been relieved through the T&P valve.

The best way to know for sure is to keep track of when the water appears. If it only happens when you do laundry, for example, your washer solenoid, which can produce substantial back-shock in the water system when it abruptly shuts off the water flow to the machine, is the likely culprit. (See "Water-Hammer Arrestors," on page 240.)

Replacing a T&P Relief Valve. It's good practice to test your water heater's T&P valve every six months or so. Just lift the test lever and let it snap back (inset photo below, left). This should produce a momentary blast of hot water through the valve's overflow tube. If no water appears or if the lever won't budge, replace the valve immediately. If water does appear but you notice that the

SMART TIP

Top-Mounted and Replacement T&P Valves

If your water heater's T&P relief valve is threaded into the top of the unit, you may need to cut the overflow pipe to remove it. After you've installed the new valve, reconnect the old overflow pipe, using a soldered coupling or compression coupling to repair the cut. If your old valve was without an overflow pipe, install one. Run it to within 6 inches of the floor.

When buying a replacement T&P valve, be sure that it has a pressure rating lower than that of the water heater. If your heater is rated at 175 psi, as noted on its service tag, buy a valve that is rated at 150 psi. Local codes may specify a pressure rating.

valve now drips steadily, your test probably deposited flakes of scale in the valve seat. This scale will often clear itself if you open and close the valve several times. If it doesn't, tap lightly on the lever pin with a hammer and then retest. If it still leaks, replace the valve.

To replace a T&P relief valve, shut off the water and power and let the water cool for at least a few hours. Open an upstairs faucet and the tank's drain valve. You won't need to empty the entire tank, just drain it to a point below the valve fitting. The T&P valve may be mounted on the top or in the side of your heater. In either case, remove the overflow pipe from its outlet. Then use a pipe wrench to unscrew the old valve from the tank (photo below, left). Coat the new valve's threads with pipe-thread sealing tape or pipe joint compound, and tighten it into the heater (photo below, right). Stop when

Replacing a T&P Relief Valve

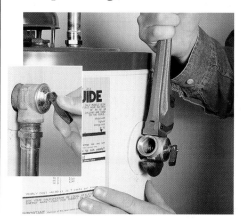

Test the T&P valve periodically (inset), and remove it if it seizes up or doesn't seem to work properly.

Wrap pipe-thread sealing tape around the threads of the new valve, and tighten it into the opening in the water heater.

Water-Hammer Arrestors

If you hear a pounding noise in your water system and see an occasional spill of water near your water heater, you have a water-hammer problem. (See page 90.) Water-hammer arrestors have internal rubber bladders that act as shock absorbers for high-pressure back-shocks. You typically install them between the water piping and fixture. For a clothes washer, screw the arrestors onto the stop valves and the hoses onto the arrestors.

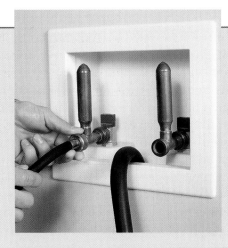

To stop T&P valve leaks, *install water-hammer arrestors on the washing machine shutoffs.*

the valve's outlet points straight down. Screw the overflow pipe into the valve's outlet, and turn the water back on. Bleed all air from the tank through an upstairs faucet, and turn the power back on.

If the new valve also spills water, the water heater's thermostat is sticking. Either replace the unit or call a professional plumber to replace the control valve.

Sediment Accumulation

If you know you have a problem with sand, rust, or scale in your water system, your water heater is likely to experience a buildup of sediment over time. If you have a gas-fired water heater and it makes a steady, rumbling noise each time it cycles on but otherwise seems to work fine, then you'll know that it has accumulated several inches of sediment. The rumbling occurs when heat from the bottom of the tank percolates through the sediment.

Remedy this problem by flushing as much sediment from the tank as possible. Start by turning the gas control to "Pilot" or turning off the electricity at the electrical panel. Then shut off the water above the heater and connect a hose to the drain valve. Lay the other end on the

floor, near a floor drain or in a bucket. Open the valve, and drain all water from the tank. A good deal of sediment should flow out with the water. With the drain still open, turn the water back on for a moment. This should flush more sediment from the tank. Repeat the procedure several times. Finally, close the drain and fill the tank half full; then drain it through the hose once more.

Scale is produced at a faster rate when the water temperature is above 140 degrees F. To limit further accumulations of scale, turn the heater down to 130 degrees. If the sediment is mostly sand, install a sediment filter early in the cold-water trunk line.

Replacing a Sediment-Clogged Drain Valve. If you find that the drain fitting drips, especially after clearing out the water heater, sediment is probably blocking the stop mechanism. You may be able to get rid of the sediment by operating the valve under pressure. If not, replace the drain valve. Start by turning the gas control to "Pilot" or turning off the electricity at the electrical panel and letting the water cool until it's comfortable. (There's no need to drain the tank if all of the faucets

Replacing a Sediment-Clogged Drain Valve

Remove *the leaky old drain valve using large groove-joint pliers.*

Install a new valve, *turning it clockwise. Use pipe-thread sealing tape or pipe joint compound on the threads.*

remain closed.) If the drain valve is a standard hose bibcock, just back it from the tank with a wrench (photo opposite, bottom left). If it's a round plastic fitting, removal can be tricky. Start by rotating the valve counterclockwise while pulling back. After five or six turns, you'll cease to make progress. At this point, rotate the valve clockwise while pulling back.

With the drain valve removed, you may want to flush the tank one more time. Sometimes, getting the drain out of the way makes a difference. When you've finished, install a brass hose bibcock in the opening, using pipe joint compound or pipe-thread sealing tape (photo opposite, bottom right).

Anode Rods

Even though steel water-heater tanks are lined with a vitrified porcelain finish, the coating process is far from perfect. In fact, every glass lining has dozens of tiny pinholes where rust can start. The tank could rust through were it not for its sacrificial anode rod.

An anode rod works by sacrificing itself to corrosion, thereby preventing the tank from corroding. Most metals corrode, but at different rates. Water-heater anode rods are typically made of magnesium because it corrodes at a faster rate than does iron. As the magnesium corrodes, it sheds electrons, which migrate to the pinholes in the lining. This electron-rich environment keeps the tank from rusting. Under normal conditions, it takes 4 to 5 years for an anode to fail; thus, the five-year tank warranty. Ten-year heaters have larger anodes or two anodes. It's a good idea to replace the anode rod at the end of the warranty period.

The anode rod in some water heaters is attached to the hot-water outlet fitting.

Changing an Anode Rod. Anode rods are installed in heaters in one of two locations. The easiest to reach are those screwed into a female fitting in the top of the heater with a 1 1/16-inch nut. These are usually visible through a hole in the top of the cabinet but are sometimes hidden under the top. In that case, you'll need to lift the sheet-metal top to reach the anode. The other type is threaded into the hot-water outlet. Called in-line anode rods, they are fused to a plastic-lined steel nipple (photo above).

To remove a top-nut anode, turn the water off and use a socket and breaker-bar wrench to remove the nut. **1.** If the nut won't budge, drain some water, peel the insulation away from the nut, and heat the tank fitting with a torch. This will expand the threads enough to allow you to wrench the nut free. Then lift out the old anode. **2.** To install the new anode, coat its threads lightly with pipe joint compound, and tighten it into the water heater. In order for the anode to work, it has to be in direct contact with the tank's iron fitting, so don't use tape and don't use much pipe joint compound. **3.**

Changing an Anode Rod

Tools and Materials

- New anode rod   TIME NEEDED: 1 HR.
- Breaker bar with 1 1/16-in. socket
- Torch (as necessary)
- Pipe joint compound

PLUMBING TIP: *If the old anode is really stuck, have one helper grip the tank piping to hold the tank in place, while another helps with the wrench.*

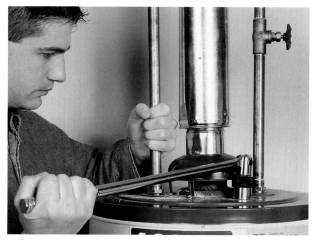

1 Use a breaker bar and 1 1/16-in. socket wrench to break the top nut of the anode rod free. Unscrew it, and lift the rod out.

Sequence continues on next page ▶

11 Maintaining & Installing Water Heaters

Continued from previous page

2 This 5-year anode rod has exceeded its service life. It looks like a corrosion sculpture.

3 Use just a little pipe joint compound on the threads of the top nut, and tighten the new anode rod in place.

Servicing Gas-Fired Water Heaters

Gas-fired water heaters have service needs that are different from those for electric units. You may experience problems with the combustion process, the vent pipe, the burner itself, or the thermocouple and pilot.

Combustion-Air Problems

If your gas-fired water heater makes a puffing sound at the burner, it's not getting enough air. Air shortages are especially common in utility rooms, where a water heater, furnace, and clothes dryer all compete for air. Allow the water heater to run for a few minutes with the utility-room door closed. When it starts puffing, open the door and a nearby window. If the flame settles into smooth operation, inadequate combustion air was the culprit. Either cut a large vent through the utility-room wall or replace the solid door with a louvered door.

Vent-Pipe Problems

When a gas-fired water heater runs, it creates a thermal draft, in which air from the room is also drawn up the flue. If there is insufficient secondary air or if the flue is partially clogged, deadly carbon monoxide gas may spill into your living space. Because carbon monoxide is odorless and invisible, it pays to test the efficiency of the flue from time to time. You can call your gas company for a sophisticated test, but the following method works. If the utility room has a door, close it. Wait a few minutes for the heater to develop a good draft, and then hold a smoking match, incense stick, or candle about 1 inch from the flue hat at the top of the heater (photo above, right). If the flue

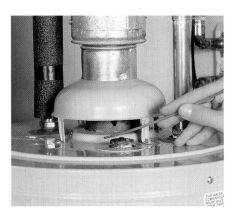

Use the smoke from a match, incense stick, or cigarette to test the flue.

draws in the smoke, all is well. If the smoke is not drawn in or is pushed away from the flue, there's a problem. To determine whether the problem is an air-starved room or a clogged flue, repeat the procedure with a door and window open. If the smoke is now drawn into the flue, make the corrections noted in "Combustion-Air Problems," at left. If not, call in a professional to inspect the flue.

Maintaining the Thermocouple and Burner

The job of the thermocouple is to hold the gas valve open so that gas can flow to the burner and pilot. If the pilot on your gas-fired water heater goes out and the heater goes out again after you re-light the pilot, the thermocouple is probably misaligned or defective.

Before buying a new thermocouple, check to see whether the existing thermocouple's sensor is positioned directly in the path of the pilot flame. If not, bend the fastener clip so that the pilot flame surrounds the sensor. Then light the pilot to see whether it keeps burning. If not, a new thermocouple is in order.

Clean the Burner. As combustion gases degrade the inner surface of the water heater, flakes of rusty metal may fall onto the burner. The rust can cover gas jets around the burner's perimeter. With some jets blocked, the rest will flame orange and high, signaling a loss in efficiency.

Check the burner for rust as part of your routine maintenance. With the heater turned to pilot, remove the outer and inner access panels at the base of the heater. Shine a flashlight onto the burner. If you see rust on top of the burner, vacuum it off. Then turn on the water heater. If some of the gas openings still appear clogged, you'll have to remove the burner to clear them out. To do so, turn off the gas and loosen the nuts securing the three burner tubes to the gas control valve. **1.** Slide out the burner, and poke through the openings with a piece of wire. **2.**

Replace the Thermocouple. If you need to replace the thermocouple, pull the sensor from its clip. (Some are held in place by a screw.) Take the old thermocouple to a hardware store, and buy a matching one. Connect the new thermocouple, making sure that the sensor will catch the pilot flame. **3.** Reinstall the burner, and reconnect the burner tubes to the control valve. **3** (inset).

To re-light the water heater, press down on the pilot button and hold it down for 30 seconds before lighting a match held with needle-nose pliers. Feed the flame into the heater. If the pilot goes out when you let up on the button, repeat the procedure. You may need to do this several times for the gas to push all the air from the pilot feed line. When the pilot stays on, replace the access panels and turn the control knob to "On."

Maintaining the Burner and Thermocouple

Tools and Materials

- Adjustable wrench   TIME NEEDED: 30 MIN.
- Wire
- Vacuum cleaner

PLUMBING TIP: *Thermocouples tend to fail after a period of disuse, so if you own a weekend cabin, it usually pays to leave the pilot light burning.*

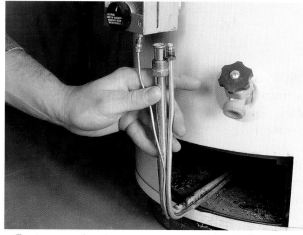

1 Loosen the three connecting nuts, and remove the burner assembly. Tip the assembly down and out.

2 While you have the burner out, ream its jets with a piece of wire. Also, vacuum any rust from the floor of the water heater.

3 Snap the new thermocouple into the burner, and secure the clip. If the thermocouple wire is too long, coil it a bit.

11 Maintaining & Installing Water Heaters

Servicing Electric Water Heaters

Electric water heaters are simple appliances. Diagnosis is easy using a volt-ohmmeter, which most plumbers carry. However, few homeowners own testing equipment, so a symptomatic is best.

Troubleshooting the Wiring and Thermostat

If the water heater stops working, the trouble may be as simple as a tripped circuit breaker, blown fuse, or loose wire. Or it could be the thermostat. Do the easy things first. Check the electrical service panel and the thermostat reset button.

Wiring. While tripped breakers often signal a defective heater component or a loose wire, the problem may be as simple as a momentary voltage spike. Reset the breaker or install a new fuse. If the breaker trips immediately or in a day or two, look for a loose wire.

Turn off the power, and remove the upper and lower access panels. **1.** Peel the insulation back, and look closely at all wire connections. If you see a wire that looks charred, loosen the binding screw holding it in place and trim the wire beyond the char mark. **1** (inset). Strip about ⅝ inch of insulation from the end of the wire. Slide the wire under the terminal, and tighten the binding screw. **2.** Follow by tightening all other binding screws you can see. Expansion and contraction from heating and cooling loosens terminal screws.

Troubleshooting the Wiring and Thermostat

Tools and Materials

- Insulated screwdriver **TIME NEEDED: 30 MIN.**
- Electrician's pliers

PLUMBING TIP: Don't assume that you need a new thermostat if the water heater stops working. The problem may be as simple as a loose wire. Turn off the power at the main service panel before checking, though.

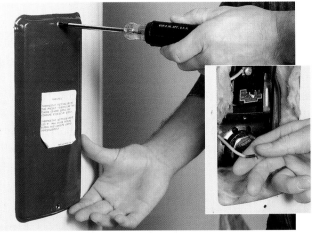

1 With the power shut off at the electrical service panel, remove the water-heater access panel and insulation. Check for charred wires (inset).

2 Trim any charred wires, and strip the insulation back ⅝ in. Insert the wire back into its slot, and tighten the terminal screw.

3 With the power still turned off, loosen the wiring connections and replace the thermostat. Snap it into its clip (inset), and tighten the screws.

Thermostat. If a thermostat should stick in the "On" position, the high-limit switch (usually with the upper thermostat) will sense the added heat and open the circuit, putting the heater out of commission instantly. Press the reset button, and let the heater cycle. If it trips again, investigate.

High-limit switches don't often fail, so suspect a faulty thermostat. But is it the upper or lower thermostat? Because the lower element won't come on until the upper element kicks off, this sequence offers a clue as to which thermostat has failed. With the power on, start by pressing all the reset buttons. Cover both thermostats with insulation. Then, listen for the expansion noises in the tank that signal a heat cycle. When the high-limit switch snaps off, you should be able to hear it. If it trips early in the 40 minute heating cycle, expect a faulty upper thermostat. If it trips much later, expect a defective lower thermostat.

Replace the Thermostat. If you find a defective thermostat, you can buy an inexpensive, universal replacement at most hardware stores. Just make sure that it has the same voltage and wattage rating as the old one. *With the power off,* undo the wiring connections and push the wires aside. Note which wire goes to each terminal, however. Snap the thermostat into the clip on the face of the heater, and reconnect the wires. **3** (inset). Press the reset button. Then, using a screwdriver, adjust the temperature setting to 130 degrees F. **3.**

The thermostat doesn't have an in-tank sensing probe and instead senses the heat of the tank. Therefore, it's critically important that you replace the insulation and cover the thermostat completely.

Replacing a Heating Element

Faulty thermostats and heating elements can display some of the same symptoms (only testing will tell for sure), but elements are subject to more stress and generally fail more often than do thermostats. But short of testing, how will you know which element has failed? If the heater produces plenty of warm water, but no hot water, the upper element has probably failed. If you get a few gallons of hot water, followed almost immediately by cold water, it's most likely the lower element. Most residential heaters use 4,500-watt elements. Check the old one to make sure.

To remove a defective element, *shut off the power* and drain the tank. If you need to replace an upper element, just drain the tank to that level. Remove the access panel, and loosen the two terminal screws securing the wires to the element. If your heater has a bolted flange, remove all four bolts and pull the element out. If it's threaded-in, grip the wrenching surface with a pipe wrench and back it out. If the sheet-metal cabinet keeps a pipe wrench from reaching the element, as it often does, use an element wrench (photo below, left). They're not expensive.

To install the new element, slide the rubber gasket in place and coat both sides with pipe joint compound (photo below, right). Then thread or bolt the element into the tank. Trim the stressed ends of each wire, and strip the insulation back about ⅜ inch. Insert the wires under the binding clips or around the screws. Tighten both screws, making sure the wires don't drift outward (inset photo). Press the reset buttons, and replace the insulation and access panel. Before turning the power back on, fill the tank and bleed all air through an upstairs faucet. Expect the heater to take 45 minutes to recover.

Replacing a Heating Element

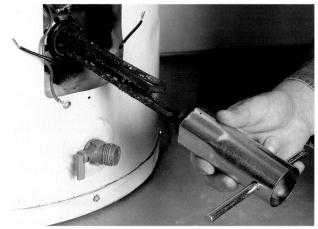

Use an element wrench to remove the old element from the heater. Some are held in place by four bolts.

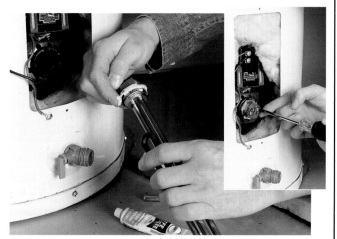

Coat the element's threads and rubber washer with pipe joint compound, and screw the element in place.

Replacing a Gas-Fired Water Heater

Remove the Old Water Heater. Shut off the water; attach a hose to the heater's drain valve; and open the drain. **1.** Open some faucets to relieve air lock. Shut off the gas, and disconnect the gas line. If the gas piping is made of black iron, break the line apart at the union. **2.** Grip the union collar with one pipe wrench and backhold the upper nut. Disassemble the nipples and fittings between the union and water-heater connection. If the gas line is soft copper with flare fittings, loosen and remove all fittings below the shutoff valve. If a flexible connector is present, loosen the end nuts and remove the connector.

Remove the sheet-metal screws that join the vent pipe to the hat, and lift the vent pipe. **3.** If need be, wire the vent to the overhead pipes to keep it from falling. If the vent pipe enters a brick chimney, don't disturb that joint. If the vent pipe or its connection to the house is rusted, contact a professional to replace defective components.

With much of the water drained from the tank, disconnect the hot- and cold-water piping. If yours is an older home, with galvanized-steel or brass piping, loosen the union fittings just above the heater. Save the unions and nipples for now. The same approach applies to copper piping that joins the heater with dielectric unions. If you find a direct connection, with soldered copper or threaded female fittings, cut the copper 6 to 12 inches above the heater or at least 2 inches below the cold-water shut off. **4.** Walk the unit out from under the pipes.

Replacing a Gas-Fired Water Heater

Tools and Materials

- New heater, T&P valve TIME NEEDED: 1–2 HRS.
- Garden hose
- Pipe wrenches
- Nut driver
- Tubing and cutter
- Self-tapping screws
- Power drill-driver
- Pipe joint compound
- Solder, flux, torch

PLUMBING TIP: *Gasoline vapors settle near the floor, so in a garage or work room, install a gas heater on a platform at least 18 inches high.*

1 To begin, turn down the thermostat on the water heater and shut off water supply. Drain the unit through a garden hose.

4 Grip the water heater by the supply pipes, and walk it out of position. Cart it away using a two-wheel dolly.

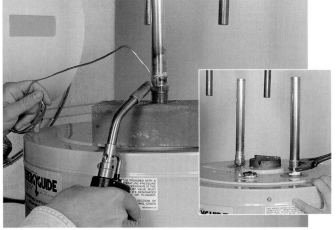

5 Pre-solder stubs into male adapters, and then tighten the adapters into the new water heater (inset). Use pipe-thread tape on the threads.

Connect the New Unit. Walk the new unit under the water pipes. The water-piping alignment is the most critical, so make these connections first. Sometimes you can make the connection with existing unions and nipples. In most cases you'll need to adapt the piping. If your piping is threaded galvanized or brass, you'll be able to buy threaded nipples to extend the pipes. If the pipes are too long, you'll need to dismantle the pipes back to the first joint. If the local hardware store has a selection of longer nipples, in the 18-to-24-inch range, you can build back with those. If not, you'll have to cut and re-thread the existing pipes. Coat all the connections with pipe joint compound, and make the final connection with unions. (You might also convert, codes allowing, to plastic, flexible copper, or stainless-steel connectors.)

If the piping is made of copper and electrolysis is not a problem, adapt the lines with sweat couplings and male or female adapters. The heater connection is usually a threaded female fitting, so pre-solder ¾-inch copper pipe stubs into male adapters. **5.** Then thread the adapters into the heater fittings using pipe-thread sealing tape. **5** (inset). Trim the stubs to length, and prepare them for soldering. **6** (inset). Slide the unit into place, and check it for level. If the floor slopes toward a floor drain, shim the water heater's legs. Join the stubs to the existing pipes with repair couplings, and solder the couplings using lead-free solder. **6.** Coat the threads of the T&P relief valve with pipe joint compound, and tighten the valve into the tank fitting. **7.** With the valve in place, solder a copper male adapter to ¾-inch copper pipe that's long

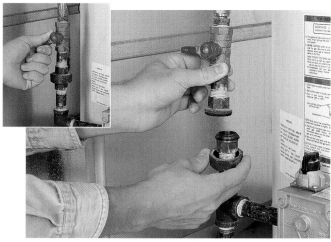

2 Shut off the gas going to the water heater (inset), and break the gas line apart at the union fitting.

3 Use a nut driver to remove the screws from the flue hat, and then cut the water lines with a tubing cutter (inset).

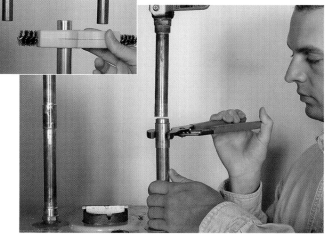

6 Cut and clean the pipe ends (inset). Install slip couplings with flux; slide the couplings up to meet the water piping; and solder the joints.

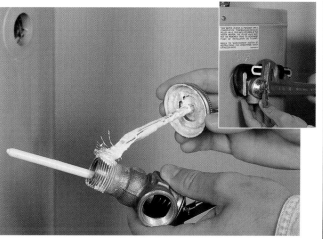

7 Lightly coat the threads of a new T&P valve with pipe joint compound, and tighten the valve into the water heater using a pipe wrench (inset).

11 Maintaining & Installing Water Heaters

Sequence continues on next page

Continued from previous page

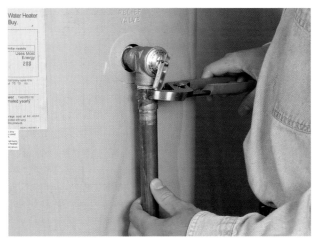

8 Thread a copper or plastic discharge pipe into the T&P valve. Extend the pipe to within 6 in. of the floor.

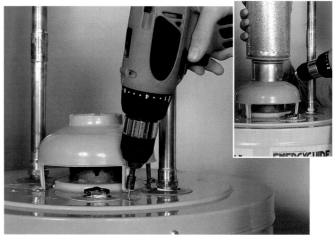

9 Use self-tapping hex-head screws to fasten the flue hat to the heater, and then screw the flue to the hat (inset).

enough to extend from the valve to within 3 inches of the floor. Thread the pipe into the valve port to serve as an overflow tube. **8.** In earthquake zones, secure the water heater to the wall with straps.

Connect the Vent Pipe. In most cases, you'll be able to adapt the existing vent pipe to the new heater. If the heater comes with a 3-inch flue hat and the vent pipe is 4 inches in diameter, you'll need to screw a 3 × 4-inch sheet-metal

increaser to the flue hat. Most codes require a 4-inch vent pipe. All joints, including the hat-to-heater and the hat-to-vent-pipe connections, should be screwed together. Use self-tapping, hex-head screws. **9.**

How you approach the gas-line hookup will depend on the existing material. Many codes now require soft copper or CSST (pages 13 and 80) in new construction. Existing black-steel piping need not be replaced, however, so continue the line to the heater with the same material. Install a drip-leg near the gas-control valve to keep dirt and condensation away from the valve. A drip leg is made with black steel or brass fittings and nipples. **10.** (inset).

If your codes allow flexible copper or require CSST connectors, the gas hookup is quick and easy. Even with a CSST connector, however, a shutoff valve needs to be installed within 36 inches of the gas-control valve. Make all connections with pipe joint compound, but use it sparingly. **10.** A light coating on the male threads will do. When you're finished, light the burner and replace the access panel. **11.**

Installing an Electric Water Heater

An electric water heater is easier to install than a gas-fired one. There are no flue or gas connections to make, and electric heaters usually come without legs, so any minor unevenness in the floor can be ignored. (A significant slope will still require shims, however.) The water and T&P relief valve connections are the same as those for a gas-fired heater.

SMART TIP

Saving Fuel Costs

Today's water heaters are better insulated than were those of even a few years ago. Still, you can boost efficiency by installing an aftermarket insulation blanket. The more hours you spend away from the house, the more benefit you'll get from this add-on. **Caution:** *Be careful not to cover the access cover, T&P relief valve, or control valve. You'll also need to hold the insulation away from the flue hat by several inches on gas-fired heaters.*

An even better investment is to insulate all hot-water pipes. These pipes shed a good deal of heat, and the more you can do to slow heat loss, the lower your energy bills. You'll find several kinds of pipe insulation on the market. The best is pre-slit foam rubber.

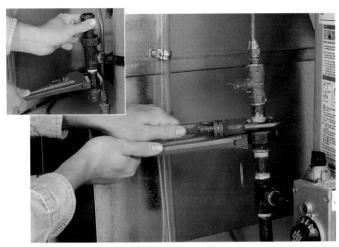

10 Reconnect the gas piping. Be sure to include drip-leg piping (inset), and use a union as the final fitting.

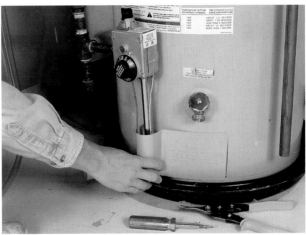

11 Light the pilot for the water heater. A gas-grill lighter works best. Then install the access panel and cover, and turn on the water.

The big difference, of course, is the electrical connection. The heater will come with its own built-in electrical box, but you'll need to connect electricity to the box using a box connector and conduit. The conduit needs to run from the water heater to a disconnect box on the wall or into a joist space overhead. (Check with your building department.) Once in the joist space, the cable usually doesn't need to be in conduit. If your old heater was installed without conduit, it's a good idea to install it now. Use rigid, thin-wall conduit from the ceiling or flex conduit from a disconnect box on the wall.

Begin by punching the knockout plug from the heater's box, and then install a conduit-to-box connector (photo below, left). Bring the existing 240-volt cable through conduit and through the box connector. (If running new cable, make it a 3-wire with ground sized to meet the heater and breaker requirements, usually 10-gauge wire with a 30-amp breaker.) Tighten the conduit in the connector. Then, using approved twist connectors, join the black and red circuit wires to the black and red (or black and black) lead wires in the water-heater box (photo below, right). Join the ground wire to the ground screw near the box. If you used rigid conduit, secure its upper end to the joists or a brace nailed between joists. Before turning on the power at the service panel, fill the tank with water and bleed all air from the tank through the faucets.

Installing an Electric Water Heater

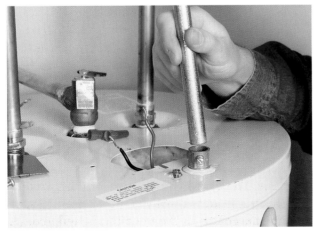

Thread a conduit connector into the water heater, and run the wires in ½-in. EMT conduit.

Bind the grounding wire under the grounding screw, and join the like-colored wires in connectors.

11 Maintaining & Installing Water Heaters

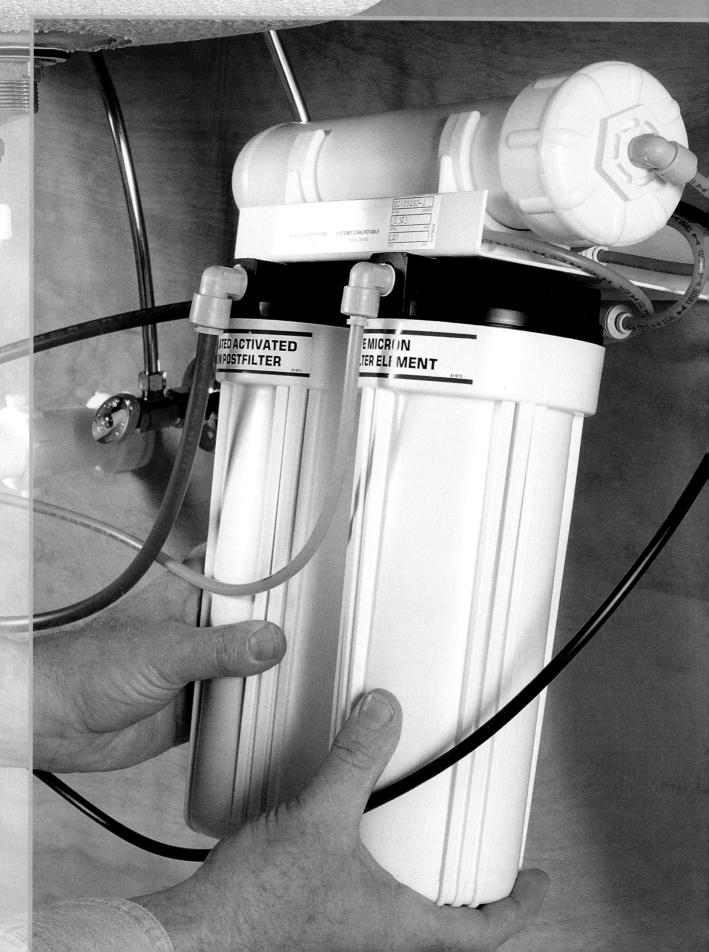

CHAPTER 12

Sump Pumps, Filters & Softeners

Many plumbing systems function well with basic equipment, but problem situations may call for additional equipment. Sump pumps, filters, and water softeners are the most common residential problem solvers. Sump pumps remove unwanted ground water, gray water, or sewage. Filters strain contaminants from drinking water, and water softeners protect plumbing equipment by altering the chemical/electrical composition of water.

Sump Pumps

There are three types of sump installations:

• **Conventional sumps** pump seasonally high groundwater from under a basement floor and require a below-floor drain tile system and sump pit. You'll find several types of pit liners, or plastic sump containers. Some have perforations around the top half, while others are solid. The perforated models are for groundwater installations. A typical groundwater setup includes a 12-to-14-inch-deep trench, which contains perforated plastic drain tile and coarse gravel, around the basement perimeter. Water drains into the pit liner and is pumped onto the lawn.

• **Gray-water installations** are similar, but the water comes from plumbing fixtures and must be pumped into a plumbing stack.

• **Ejector pumps** grind solid sewage, so they can drain a bathroom or an entire house.

Groundwater/gray water pumps come in two forms. Some are submersible, motor and all; others have the motor elevated above the pump on a pedestal. Pedestal models are less expensive, but they're a bit noisy. For this reason, submersibles are more popular.

Sump Pumps for Groundwater and Runoff

Many homes have groundwater and runoff problems. In the worst cases, a system made up of a sump pump and drainage tile (or nowadays, more likely perforated plastic pipe) can mean the difference between a dry, usable basement and a damp, crumbling foundation. If you plan to build a home and seasonally high groundwater is even a remote possibility, install a drainage system and a sump pit. You may never need to buy and install the actual sump pump, but doing this preparation work in the open stages of construction

Submersible Sump

Solid Pit Cover

Perforations

Check Valve

Sump Pump

Float

Gravel

Undisturbed Soil

is a fraction of the cost of a retrofit. Each site is different, of course, but if a new-construction drainage system costs $350 (without a pump), you could easily pay $3,500 for a retrofit installation.

Installing a Submersible Sump Pump

Once you've worked out a perimeter drainage strategy to direct water to the sump pump (either installing a perimeter drain in new construction or using a rented concrete saw and jackhammer to cut out 18 inches of concrete along the basement walls and dig in a trench, gravel, and tile in an existing house with drainage problems), you need to install the pump and attach the discharge piping.

Install the Pit Liner. You'll find two types of sump-pit liners on the market. One has perforations around its upper half; the other doesn't. Use the perforated liner for groundwater sumps and the non-perforated type for gray-water pits. (See "Gray-Water and Ejector Sumps," page 254.) Dig a hole for the pit liner so that its top rim is flush with the top of the concrete floor.

If your drainage piping installation was made on the outside of the footing, use a tile spade to tunnel under the footing. Slide a length of pipe through the tunnel, and join it to the perimeter perforated pipe with a T-fitting. Then cut an opening in the pit liner (usually at its midpoint), and run the pipe through this hole several inches. **1.** Backfill the pit below the pipe connection with soil, tamping it in 4-inch lifts. Fill the upper half of the excavation with coarse gravel, packing as much as possible into the footing tunnel. Finally, backfill the exterior, and pour concrete for the basement floor.

Set and Pipe the Sump Pump. To install a submersible pump, begin by threading a 1½-inch plastic male adapter into the outlet fitting. **2.** Glue a 2- to 3-foot length of PVC pipe into the adapter to bring the riser up to check-valve level, preferably just above the liner lid. (For more about check valves, see "Checking a Sump Pump," page 94.) Lift the pump into the pit. **3.** If your check valve has threaded ports, make the connection with male adapters. If it has banded rubber connectors, tighten its lower end over the riser. **4** (inset). Make sure the arrow on the side of the valve points up.

Before extending the riser, determine where you'll take it through the wall. The easiest spot is through the rim joist overhead. You may need to run to the right or left along the joist a bit to reach the best exit point outdoors.

Installing a Submersible Sump Pump

Tools and Materials

- Sump pump kit
- Drill, saber saw
- Pliers, nut driver
- Hacksaw

TIME NEEDED: 2 HRS.
- PVC pipe, fittings
- Primer, cement
- Pipe hangers

PLUMBING TIP: *Dry sump pits can be used to remove radon gas. If tests reveal radon, seal the top of the liner with plastic glazing and caulk. Drill a 1½-inch hole in the glazing, and vent the pit outdoors with 1½-inch PVC pipe.*

3 *Cement a length of PVC pipe into the adapter, and lower the sump pump and pipe into the pit liner.*

SMART TIP

Runoff Drainage Solutions

Most wet basements can be fixed above-ground, without a sump pump, by improving the gutter system and sloping the ground away from the house. If your gutters overflow, clean them. If they leak, replace them. If downspouts empty near the foundation, install downspout extensions or splash blocks. If a raised flower terrace next to the house can't be properly drained, remove it. If a concrete patio slopes toward the house, replace it. And if the soil around the foundation does not slope away from the house for a distance of at least 4 feet (past the permanently absorbent backfill), haul in new soil and make sure that it does.

Offset the riser, and extend it to joist level. **4.** Install a 90-degree elbow, and travel under the joists until you reach the target joist space. Use two more elbows to enter the joist space, and run the pipe to within a few feet of the rim joist. Make sure this length of pipe has adequate slope.

Connect the Discharge Pipe. To keep from damaging the siding at the discharge spot outside the house, drill from the outside. Measure up the basement wall to determine the best exit point, and mark the rim joist several inches above the sill. Drill a ⅛-inch hole at the centerpoint to transfer the mark to the outside of the house. Drill a 1⅞-inch hole through the siding and rim joist from outside, and slide a short length of 1½-inch pipe through the hole.

Join this pipe to the drain line with a coupling. **5.**

Replace any insulation you've removed to expose the rim joist, and secure the piping with hangers. The pump can cause the drain line to surge at start up, so you'll need good support to keep it from moving and making noise. Pipe movement can also break the exterior caulk seal.

On the outside of the house, trim the horizontal pipe stub ½ inch away from the siding, and cement a 90-degree elbow to this stub, with the open end pointing down. Extend the line down to ground level, and use another 90-degree elbow to direct the flow onto a splash block. To make the through-wall piping insect- and water-tight, caulk the joint with siliconized exterior latex caulk.

To test the pump, pour water into the pit. The float should activate the pump when water exceeds 8 to 10 inches and deactivate at about 3 inches.

1 Cut a 3-in. hole in each side of the pit liner corresponding with drainage pipes, bury the liner, and connect the plastic perforated pipe.

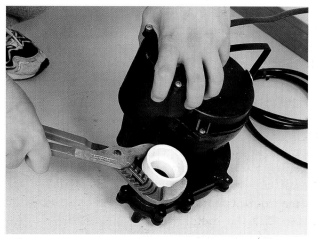

2 Thread a 1½-in. PVC male adapter into the sump pump using pipe-thread sealing tape on the threads. Tighten the fitting until it's snug.

4 Install a check valve above the lid, and secure it with a nut driver (inset). Offset the riser pipe against the wall using 45-deg. elbows.

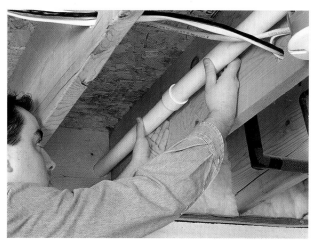

5 Run the discharge pipe outdoors through the rim joist, using couplings for connections. Cover the open exterior end with plastic screen.

Gray-Water and Ejector Sumps

If your house drain exits a basement above floor level, the only way you can have a sink or laundry in the basement is to install a gray-water sump. The only way to have a full bath in the basement is to drain it through an ejector sump.

The difference between a groundwater and gray-water sump installation is in where the water must go. Groundwater is pumped outdoors, while gray water must be pumped into the plumbing system. Gray-water installations are usually low volume. The fixture drainpipe can enter the pit through the lid (below) or through the side of the liner, below the floor. A below-floor installation looks neater and tends to be less noisy than the alternative.

An ejector sump differs in that it handles—

grinds and pumps—solid sewage. (It cannot handle other solids, like cigarette filters or tampons.) The inlet drainpipe always enters the pit liner under the floor through a watertight fitting. Because raw sewage is involved, the pit must be airtight and vented. Both the pit-liner lid and the soil-pipe connection have gaskets and are bolted in place.

Ejector pumps are expensive, but they are quite reliable. Like all mechanical things, however, they will eventually fail. When this happens, it can make quite a mess. For this reason, some manufacturers use two pumps that kick on alternately. When one of the pumps fails, it triggers an alarm.

A sump-box kit, left, or ejector pump, right, won't handle a lot of volume. The former works with a sink; the latter with sink and toilet.

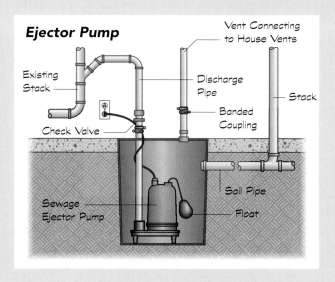

Ejector Pump

- Vent Connecting to House Vents
- Existing Stack
- Discharge Pipe
- Stack
- Banded Coupling
- Check Valve
- Sewage Ejector Pump
- Soil Pipe
- Float

Filters

The quality of groundwater across the country varies a great deal. There are two basic problem water categories: the unhealthy and the unpleasant. Unhealthy water might contain nitrates, heavy metals (like lead and mercury), disease-causing bacteria, organic and inorganic compounds (arsenic, atrazine, benzene, and the like), and dissolved gases such as radon. Unpleasant water might be high in iron, sulfur, manganese, sediments, non-hazardous bacteria, and so on. Municipal water is rarely unhealthy, but it may be unpleasant; private well water may be unhealthy, unpleasant, or both.

Common Water Problems. Private well water may be high in mineral salts, sediments, and chemicals. It may contain soluble iron, which leaves fixtures black or rusty. A harmless but nasty-looking bacteria, called bacterial iron, can feed on iron particles in well water and coat pipes and fixtures with an orange slime. (If so, you should

have the well chlorinated.) Water may have a high sulfur content, making it taste and smell awful. It may contain Giardia, a common microorganism that causes flu-like symptoms. And finally, it can contain nitrates, disease-carrying bacteria, lead, cadmium, and the like. Most public water is monitored and treated, but treatment facilities can't do everything. They can't soften water, for example. And they can't prevent aging city piping systems from adding minute traces of lead, rust, copper, or asbestos.

Filter Types
The first line of defense is usually a filter or series of filters. If you think you need a series of filters (to treat a variety of problems) you should get professional help in deciding which filters to use and in which order. A private testing lab, your local health department, or a state university are good sources.

Sediment Filters. If your only problem is sediment, a single sediment filter will do. These in-line filters consist of a filter body, a reservoir, and a filter medium. In most models, the filter must be replaced regularly, but expensive models have a filtering screen and reservoir. These have no filter cartridge to replace. Instead, a drain valve allows you to backflush the sediment from the filter.

Carbon Filters. If tests reveal high levels of organic or inorganic contaminants, granular carbon filters may work. (The porous surface of activated carbon traps particles.) High-volume carbon filters are installed in supply lines; low-volume carbon filters serve a single fixture.

Carbon and other media filters have a serious drawback. There's no foolproof way of knowing when the media is saturated with contaminates. (Some filter systems have flow meters or built-in timers to remind you to change them.) If you don't change the filter in time, it can dump contaminants (nitrates, chemical compounds, and so on) into the water in high amounts.

If you can stay on top of the maintenance, activated carbon filters will do a reasonably good job on contaminants in gas, liquid, and particle form. They also cost a good deal less than the other options.

Reverse-Osmosis Units. Reverse-osmosis (RO) units are reliable in dealing with nitrates and chemical contaminants. They should not be used with water high in dissolved minerals (hard water), and they can't remove biological contaminants. In an RO unit, water is forced through a permeable membrane. Though the water makes it through, the contaminants do not. The membrane is dense, so RO units have an extremely low output, and they can't purify an entire plumbing system. They use a 2-to-3-gallon storage tank. Most are installed under kitchen sinks in series with sediment and carbon filters.

Reverse-Osmosis Filter System

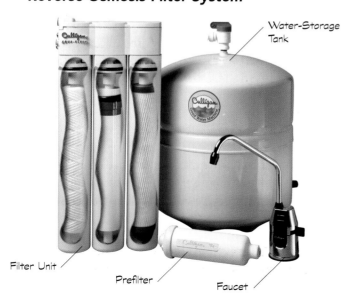

Water-Storage Tank

Filter Unit

Prefilter

Faucet

The Question of Water Quality

Should you be concerned about the quality of your drinking water? It depends largely upon where the water originates. If you live in a city or even a small town, rigorous testing is federally mandated and any problem is corrected at the distribution center. If it can't be corrected immediately, a public notice must be given, warning you to drink bottled water or take other precautions until further notice.

Public water systems serving fewer than 100 people and private wells are exempt from federal requirements, although they are within the purview of state and county health departments when new and when put back into service after a period of disuse. In these cases, it's not a bad idea to test your water every five years or so. Basic testing is quite affordable ($20 to $50), but the more substances you identify for screening, the more it will cost.

Disinfection Units. When water contains only biological contaminants, sending that water through a disinfection chamber is a good choice. The chamber can be treated with chlorine, bromine, or iodine, but it might also be bombarded with ultraviolet light or saturated with ozone. These units should be professionally installed.

Distillers. One of the most effective ways to purify water is through distillation. In a distiller, water is heated until it steams, or vaporizes. The vapor rises into a cooling chamber, where it condenses back into liquid. Heavy metals, trace chemicals and minerals are left behind in the heating chamber. Biological contaminants are killed in the heating process. (see the illustration on page 256.)

Distillers do an excellent job on a variety of contaminants, including nitrates, lead, mercury, radium, iron, calcium, magnesium, copper oxide, copper sulfide, coliform bacteria, Giardia and more. In fact, no other system does as much, as simply. However, distillers have limited capacity; they use quite a bit of electricity; the larger units are fairly expensive; and the heating chambers must be cleaned of minerals and contaminants frequently. Because the heating source is usually an electric resistance-heat element, you'll have to replace an element occasionally.

While large freestanding distillers are available, most residential distillers are counter-top models. Larger units are usually piped directly, while smaller models are either piped through a saddle-tap valve (like an ice maker) or have no connection at all: you pour tap water into the unit's reservoir.

Installing In-Line Filters

In-line filters must be installed so that the body is vertical. They usually require a shutoff valve on both sides, so cartridge changes can be made without draining the entire system. Some models come with a shutoff mechanism built-in, making valves in the piping unnecessary.

Filter bodies normally come with threaded connections. When joining copper or plastic male adapters to threaded ports, solder or solvent-cement the adapters to pipe stubs first. Then thread the adapters into the filter.

In a horizontal installation, the piping connection is a simple splice in the water pipe (below). In the case of a vertical pipe, you'll need to create a horizontal offset so that you can install the filter with its reservoir vertical.

Assuming a horizontal installation in copper, begin by cutting out a section of pipe about 14 inches long, or long enough to accommodate the top of the filter body, the soldered stubs, and the male adapters. Then install two full-flow shutoff valves. Valves with compression nuts eliminate the need for soldering. Finally, if your copper or galvanized-steel piping system serves as a partial ground for the electrical system, install a jumper wire. Bolt an approved grounding clamp onto the pipe on each side of the filter, and join them with 6-gauge copper wire.

Installing Reverse-Osmosis Units

Identify and label all the color-coded tubes attached to the filter unit. Then hang the unit on the side or back wall of the cabinet, using the screws provided. **1.** Set the storage tank in another corner of the cabinet. Most codes require a backflow-preventing air gap for the drain tube, with the gap at countertop level. (Faucets with a built-in

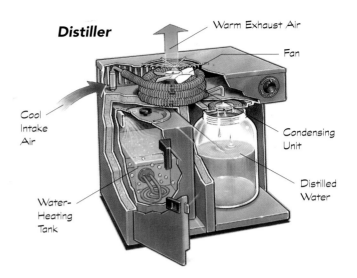

Distiller

Warm Exhaust Air
Fan
Cool Intake Air
Condensing Unit
Distilled Water
Water-Heating Tank

air-gap connection are typically sold with RO units.) The faucet will have two barbed fittings next to the faucet shank. Insert the faucet through the fourth sink hole, and tighten the jamb nut onto the shank. **1** (inset).

With the faucet, tank, and RO unit in place, tap into the cold-water line with a saddle valve, and attach the blue supply tube that goes to the unit. Then attach the faucet supply tube (blue tube that runs from the tank) and both drain tubes to the faucet fittings. **2** (inset). Run the remaining blue tube from the RO unit to the storage tank, and push it into the compression fitting. **2.** With the supply tubes and one drain tube (to the RO unit) connected, install the drain saddle. Bolt the saddle onto the sink's horizontal drainpipe, and drill the pipe with a ¼-inch bit. Finally, connect the drain tube looping down from the faucet. **3.** Turn on the water at the saddle valve to test your connections, and run several gallons of water through the system before using any of it for cooking or drinking. RO units come packed with a sanitizer that needs to be flushed out completely.

Installing an In-Line Filter

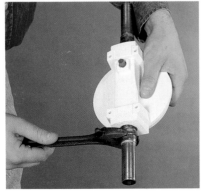

Thread male adapters, with attached stubs, into the filter head.

Splice the filter into the water supply line with shutoff valves.

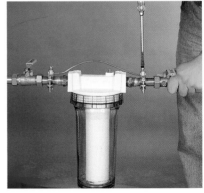

Install a jumper wire to restore the electrical path to ground.

Installing a Reverse-Osmosis Unit

Tools and Materials

- RO filter kit
- Drill and bit
- Adjustable wrench
- Screwdriver

TIME NEEDED: 1 HR.

PLUMBING TIP: *RO membranes need to be replaced periodically. They are cylinders that slide out one side, so position the unit with extra fitting room on that side.*

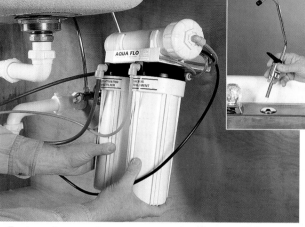

1 Install mounting screws on a cabinet wall, hang the unit, and tap into the water line with a saddle valve. Install the faucet in the sink deck (inset).

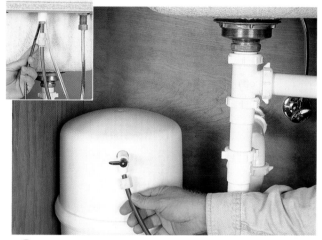

2 Connect the supply and drain tubes to the faucet (inset.) Set the storage tank in a corner of the cabinet, and attach the hose from the filter unit.

3 To make the drain connection, drill into the waste tube and install the saddle valve. Connect the waste tube, and turn on the water.

Ion-Exchange Equipment

The common water softener is designed to strip water-soluble minerals from "hard" water. (See "Do You Need a Water Softener?" at right.) It does so by substituting sodium (or potassium, depending on the kind of salt you use) for calcium and, to a lesser degree, magnesium and iron. The water passing through a softener is diverted through synthetic granulated resin that effects an ion exchange: calcium and/or magnesium ions for sodium or potassium ions. The resin becomes saturated with mineral ions every two to seven days, depending on the hardness and volume of the water being treated. To clear the minerals from the resin, the softener periodically backflushes the resin with salt water from a brine container. The brine-mineral wastewater is then sent into a drain or

Do You Need a Water Softener?

Hard water contains high levels of calcium and magnesium, which form a crusty scale on metallic surfaces. (On the plus side, this scale can seal off lead in old solder.) Also, detergents and soaps don't work well in hard water because they react with the dissolved metal ions. Most water has some hardness, measured in grains per gallon. The surest way to tell whether you have hard water is to have it tested. Generally, anything above about ten grains of hardness may pose a problem.

saved for disposal. You must replenish the salt in the system (to create the brine) on a regular basis.

Softeners use one of three approaches to managing purge cycles. The most efficient (and expensive) units have probes that detect the point of mineral saturation in the resin. Other models have flow meters that are programmed to purge when a given volume of water has been treated. The least efficient units have timers, and they purge at set times, regardless of how much water has passed through the system.

Installing Water Softeners

Shut off and drain the water at the main valve. When using copper male adapters, solder them to pipe stubs before threading them into the head of the softener. A softener piping loop needs a bypass just above the softener so that the water system can be kept in use when the softener is shut down for servicing. Factory-made bypasses are available, but you can also make your own using three ball valves.

Install the Bypass. If the softener comes with a built-in bypass, you won't need one in the piping loop. In this case, start by sliding the factory union nuts onto the provided copper stubs, and solder the stubs to ¾-inch copper risers. **1.** Follow by installing the plastic purge line on the unit's head, locking it in place with a hose clamp. **2.** Attach the same type of hose to the brine tank's overflow fitting.

The bypass valve comes with lubricated O-rings, so just push it into the head until it locks in place. **3.** Slide rubber washers onto the copper stubs, and connect the copper to the bypass. **3** (inset). Tighten the unions to secure the pipes. **4.** To preserve the piping system's electrical path to ground, install the copper clip that bonds the two pipes together. **4** (inset).

Plumb the Unit. Slide the softener against the wall. **5.** Cut into the cold water line. Use 90-degree elbows to route the hard water line toward the softener and install a second line for the return. **6** (inset). Cut a T-fitting into the supply line, and run a ¾-inch branch to serve any faucets and sillcocks that you want to get hard water. **6.** You can pipe one sillcock with soft water for washing the car, but try to pipe one with hard water for the lawn. If you can't isolate at least one, shut down the softener to water the lawn.

Secure the two lines to the wall, and make the softener connections. Solder all piping connections with lead-free solder. **7.** Finally, turn the water back on, purify the softener with bleach, rinse thoroughly, and add salt to the tank. **8.**

Installing a Water Softener

Tools and Materials

- Water softener kit
- Pipe cutter
- Copper pipe, fittings
- Flux, solder

TIME NEEDED: 2 HRS.
- Torch
- Groove-joint pliers
- Flame shield

PLUMBING TIP: *Softeners can be shoe-horned into tight spaces, but they need front access. Also, avoid blocking access to the furnace and water heater.*

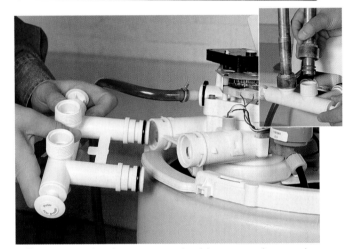

3 *Mount the factory-supplied bypass valve on the softener head, and then attach the copper risers (inset).*

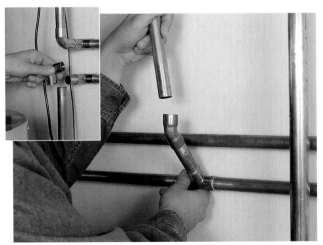

6 *Splice into the cold-water supply line to feed the softener. Use a T-fitting to maintain one line (usually for an exterior hose bibcock) as hard water.*

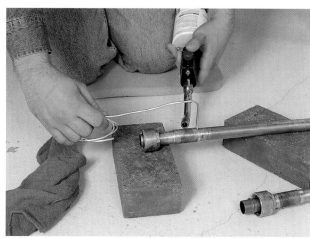

1 Slide the factory-supplied union nuts onto the pre-fitted stubs (also supplied), and solder the stubs to the copper riser pipes.

2 A softener needs a purge line and overflow tube. Slide and clamp these plastic tubes onto their barbed fittings.

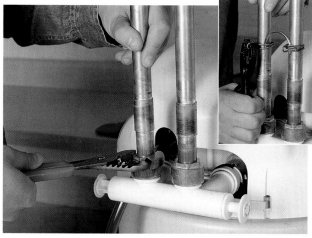

4 Use large groove-joint pliers to tighten the union nuts over the riser pipes. Connect the copper electrical-ground bonding wire (inset).

5 Slide the softener in place, and route the purge and overflow tubes to a nearby drain.

7 Solder all water-pipe connections with lead-free solder, and protect combustible surfaces with a flame shield.

8 After disinfecting the unit, pour several bags of special water-softener salt into the reservoir. The salt is available as sodium chloride or potassium chloride.

CHAPTER 13

Private Septic Systems & Wells

Those who live beyond the reaches of public water and sewer systems rely on private water wells for fresh water and septic systems for sewage and wastewater disposal. Keeping these systems up and running is not difficult or complicated, but they require some maintenance. And knowing how these systems work is important because you'll be less likely to push them beyond their limits.

There are three types of code-approved waste-disposal systems in use today:

• *Anaerobic (Septic) System.* The septic system is the most common private waste system, consisting of a buried septic tank, a distribution box, and a gravel-lined leach, or drainage, field.

• *Aerobic Lagoon System.* The lagoon system, the second most popular waste-disposal design, is a precisely constructed open-air sewage pond. Lagoons are also known as stabilization ponds.

• *Hybrid Aerobic/Anaerobic System.* The least popular (and little used) system is a mechanical version of the buried tank and leach field. In this system, electrically powered equipment in the tank stirs and aerates the sewage, thereby speeding the digestion process. While the tank is aerobic, the leach field is anaerobic.

All three processes use naturally occurring bacteria to break down and consume solids. In an aerobic, or aseptic, system, a form of bacteria that thrives on the oxygen present in air does the work. Anaerobic systems use bacteria that cannot tolerate significant quantities of air.

Septic Systems

In a septic system, sewage flows from the house by force of gravity through a 4-inch soil pipe that spills into the inlet baffle of the tank. The tank and distribution box may be made of steel, concrete, ABS plastic, or fiberglass. Once in the tank, the sewage solids are digested by naturally occurring anaerobic bacteria in human waste. The bacteria also produce heat, which keeps the tank and leach field from freezing. The digestion process yields two tank-bound by-products. Insoluble particles settle to the bottom of the tank to form sludge, while grease and soap float to the top to form a surface scum. The sludge and scum must be pumped out periodically to keep the system functioning properly.

Distribution. Every time wastewater enters the tank, an equal volume exits through the outlet baffle. This water, called effluent, flows into the distribution box and then into the leach field. Ideally, effluent contains no solids but is rich in urea and organic nitrogen compounds. Once it's in the leach field, another digestion process begins. Naturally-occurring microbes that inhabit the top 2 feet of soil convert the waste in the water to compounds that can be used by plants. The water is either evaporated (60 percent by volume) or absorbed by soil and plants.

Avoiding Permanent Failures. If scum is allowed to accumulate for long, it will eventually become so deep

Septic System Anatomy

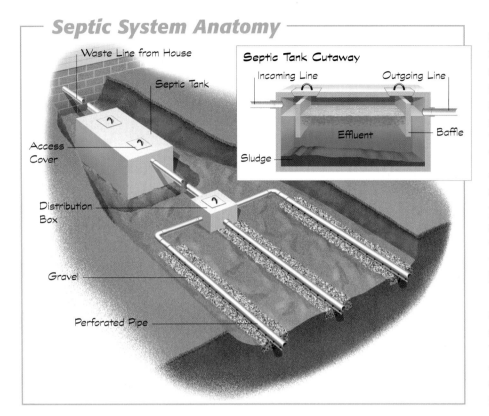

Waste Line from House
Septic Tank
Access Cover
Distribution Box
Gravel
Perforated Pipe

Septic Tank Cutaway
Incoming Line
Outgoing Line
Effluent
Baffle
Sludge

ration. Spring snow melt and heavy rains can saturate the soil above and around the leach field. Saturated soil not only fails to absorb water but also stops—even reverses—the nitrification process. The very term "septic" implies a lack of oxygen. When oxygen-rich surface water enters a field, the soil shifts from a septic to an oxygenated state. At this point, the leach field is merely a storage chamber. It does almost no work. As you add more sewage to the system, it's almost certain to back up.

In a well-designed, properly sized system, these temporary setbacks are accommodated, but in marginal systems, sewage backups are an annual occurrence. To help a seasonally stressed septic system, try to keep the field as dry as possible.

that it extends below the outlet baffle, flows into the leach field, and plugs up the trench. (Sludge contributes to the problem by reducing, from the bottom, the volume of water the tank can hold.) This reduces storage capacity and halts most of the absorption and nitrification. At this point, the leach field is ruined. The tank and distribution box still work, but the leach field must be replaced. *For this reason, it's important that you have the septic tank pumped every three to four years.* You'll find septic-pumping companies in the Yellow Pages.

Minimizing Temporary Failures. Temporary failures, which often occur in the spring, may be due to soil satu-

• Change the roof-gutter downspout locations or extend them with underground diversion pipes if they send water in the direction of the field.

• Move some soil to divert runoff, if necessary.

• Use less water during the wettest weeks of the year. You might take your clothes to a coin-operated laundry, shorten the length of your showers or the depth of your bath water, wash the dishes by hand, and flush your toilets less often.

Other Septic-System Considerations. A well designed septic system will handle a range of household materials, from toilet paper to food waste. (White toilet paper is best.) However, septic systems can't tolerate large amounts of cleaning solvents or furniture strippers, strong acids, paint thinners, petroleum-based lubricants, antifreeze, and some chemicals used in photography.

Septic-System Additives. According to health department officials and other experts, "enzyme" additives available in supermarkets and from other sources won't hurt your system and may even help a bit, but they're not needed. While it takes several months for a new system to develop a full-strength colony of bacteria, the official consensus seems to be that additives don't do much to speed up the process. And of course, once the system is up and running, it will regulate itself.

SMART TIP

Cleaning the Septic Tank

Having the septic tank pumped out periodically is vitally important for long-term, trouble-free operation of a septic system. Some homeowners find it helpful to use a well-recognized recurring event as a reminder to have the job done. For example, you might want to time your pumping ritual with the presidential election. That way, when election time comes, you know it's time to pump out the septic tank.

Aerobic Lagoon Systems

When soil drainage is extremely poor, lagoon systems are an alternative. Lagoons, or stabilization ponds, are conically shaped earthen enclosures designed for sewage disposal. The wastewater is always exposed to air, so treatment is accomplished with aerobic bacteria, algae, and surface evaporation. Lagoons must be built to exacting specifications if they are to last. When properly constructed, they work efficiently and odorlessly for decades with little maintenance.

The perimeter of the lagoon must be fenced with wire mesh, and because surface breezes must sweep a lagoon for it to work properly, no tall vegetation should be allowed to grow near it.

As for the digestion process, heavy solids settle to the bottom and are consumed by bacteria. Suspended bacteria break down lighter particles, giving off carbon dioxide. In the presence of nitrogen, phosphate, carbon dioxide, and light, algae flourish. The algae produce oxygen, which in turn feeds the bacteria. As in a septic system, the digestion process keeps the water from freezing. Unlike a septic system, however, a lagoon and its digestive process are all but odorless.

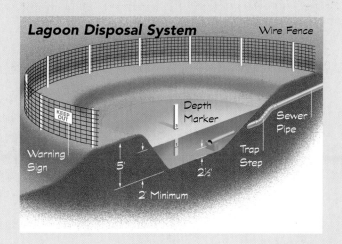

Lagoon Disposal System

Private Water Wells

Well types range from the tireless windmill wells of generations past to shallow-well jet pumps to deep-well submersible pumps (most common). Most deliver water to a pressure tank located in a well pit or basement. Most wells these days are drilled by professionals and can be a couple of hundred feet deep. Well casings are 5 to 6 inches in diameter—large enough to fit a submersible pump.

The Pressure Tank. Pressure tanks maintain a steady line pressure and keep the pump from kicking on with every small draw of water. A pressure switch installed in the tank piping controls the electric well pump. The switch turns the pump on at a given low pressure and off it at a given high pressure. Different switches are used for different pressure combinations, but some adjustment is possible. Common "On-and-Off" settings are 20 and 40 psi for smaller tanks and 30 and 50 psi for larger tanks.

The most common pressure-tank problems are waterlogged tanks and pressure switches that have drifted off their settings or have simply worn out. Some pressure tanks (especially older ones) are simply hollow, galvanized containers that have a top-mounted snifter, or air, valve. The snifter, sometimes called a Schrader valve, looks and acts like a valve stem in a car tire. In these tanks, a quantity of air is held in the top of the tank as a pressure buffer and is in direct contact with the water in the tank. It's not uncommon for them to have waterlogging problems. Most modern tanks have an air-filled rubber bladder inside, at the top. It has a snifter valve as well, but it's charged at the factory and usually needs no on-site adjustment. With the air contained in the bladder, the water can't absorb it, so these tanks are nearly maintenance free.

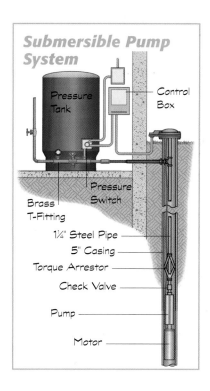

Submersible Pump System

Minor Well Problems and Solutions. If your well stops working abruptly, look first for tripped breakers and blown fuses, either in the main service panel or at a fused disconnect switch. Pump motors require roughly ten times the power to start than to keep running. Breakers and time-delay fuses usually accommodate this momentary overcurrent, but occasionally they will trip.

Reset the breakers, and install new time-delay fuses. Don't use standard fuses.

The tank pressure must be drawn down for the pump to kick in when you turn the system back on, so open a few faucets to test your work. If the breaker trips or the fuse blows when the pump comes on, call a professional.

If the pump runs for an extended length of time before tripping the breaker or shuts off normally but seems to run much longer than it used to, you may have a pressure-switch problem.

Fixing a Pressure Switch. To gain access to the pressure switch, shut off the power, loosen the captive nut on the top of the switch cover, and remove the cover. You'll see several wire connections and two spring-loaded pressure sensors: one long and one short. The short spring will control the cut-out pressure (the range), which is usually the culprit, while the larger spring will control the cut-in (low) pressure while maintaining the cut-in/cut-out pressure differential. Both springs can be adjusted with the range nuts on top of the springs. Adjust the larger spring nut first. For a higher cut-in pressure, rotate the nut downward. For a lower cut-in pressure, rotate the nut upward. Follow with similar adjustments for the smaller cut-out spring. If the contacts are fouled, clean them according to the manufacturer's instructions. Then restore power, and test your work. If these corrections don't help, or if the pump cycles erratically, have the pressure switch replaced.

If your pump seems to kick on every time you use a little water, expect a tank with too little air. While this problem is mostly limited to bladderless tanks, it is possible for a bladder style tank to leak as well, usually through the snifter valve. To make sure, test the tank pressure with a tire tester. If the high pressure is not as high as the tank specifications require (usually about 28 pounds), add some air.

If these simple procedures don't put your well equipment back in working order, call a professional.

Fixing a Pressure Switch

To set the cut-in pressure while maintaining the pressure differential, adjust the nut on the long spring.

To set the cut-out pressure only, adjust the nut on the short spring.

How to Replace a Leaking Pressure Tank

Tools and Materials

- Pipe wrenches
- Adjustable wrench
- Screwdriver
- Wire-cutting tool

TIME NEEDED: 1–2 HRS.
- Thread-sealing tape
- Pressure-relief valve
- Pressure switch

PLUMBING TIP: *Pressure switch contacts foul over time, so your first troubleshooting step should be to sand the contact points. But first make sure that the power is turned off.*

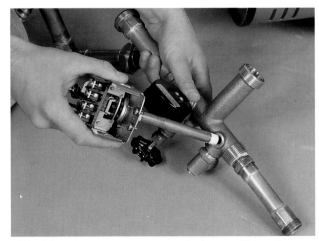

3 Mount a new pressure switch on a ⅜-in.-dia. threaded nipple, and thread the nipple into the tank T-fitting.

How to Replace a Leaking Pressure Tank

Begin by shutting off the power and water and draining the system through the boiler drain next to the shutoff valve. Disconnect the power supply at the pressure switch. **1** (inset). Then undo the feed line from the well and the union on the house side of the tank T-fitting. **1.** Slide the old tank out, and remove the tank fitting.

Fit the T-fitting with new components. Be sure to install a pressure-relief valve in one of the openings. **2.** Follow with a new pressure switch on a ⅜-inch brass nipple. Thread the nipple into the tank T-fitting with pipe-thread sealing tape. **3.** With the T-fitting's components in place, tighten the fitting into the new tank's fitting. **4.** Reconnect the unions on the inlet and outlet piping, and snug them with a pipe wrench. **5.** Finally, make the new wiring connections according to the manufacturer's directions, and recharge the system. **5** (inset).

Adjust the Pressure Switch. Have a helper open a faucet until the pump kicks in. With a 20-40 switch, check that the pump comes on when the gauge nears 20 pounds and shuts off near 40. If it shuts off before 40 pounds, adjust the switch's high-pressure spring. Next, wait for the pump to shut off and then have a helper open a faucet. The pressure should drop slowly; the pump should not come on until the gauge reads 20 pounds. If the pressure drops immediately, bleed the system of all water and take an air pressure reading. The tanks's air pressure should be within two pounds of the cut-in pressure. Add air through the snifter valve if needed.

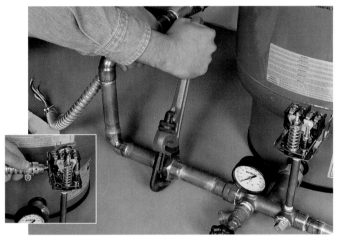

1 With the power and water turned off, disconnect the wires and undo the box connector (inset). Then loosen the water-pipe unions.

2 Tighten a new pressure-relief valve into one of the openings in the tank T-fitting. Use pipe-thread sealing tape on the valve's threads.

4 With the T-fitting assembled, install it on the pressure tank. Use the half union mounted on the tank for attachment.

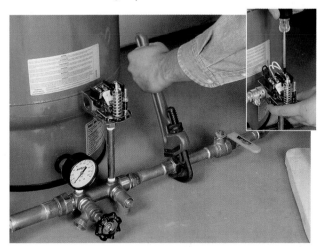

5 Attach the tank to the piping using unions with thread-sealing tape on the mating surfaces. Then reconnect the wiring (inset), and recharge.

Glossary

Clamp-type flaring tool For flaring soft copper tubing. It consists of a base clamp, which bites onto the pipe, and a flaring vise with a threaded stem and cone-shaped flare head, which slides over the clamp. As you screw downward, you force the head into the end of the pipe.

Close-quarters tubing cutter A much smaller version of a tubing cutter, it is handy when working in confined spaces.

Closet flange The rim on a closet bend by which that pipe attaches to the floor. See *Toilet flange.*

Compression fittings Replaced most cone and friction washers in the 1960s. These fittings tighten, or compress, over the tapered seats with pressure to lock into place.

Cone washers Also known as friction washers, these transition fittings were used to join permanent pipes to fixture-supply tubes prior to the 1950s.

Corpcock (or corporation stop) The first shutoff in the water line that is tapped directly into an iron or plastic water main and can be reached only by excavating the soil above it.

Coupling A transitional fitting that joins pipes end to end.

CPVC (chlorinated polyvinyl chloride) pipe Plastic water piping.

Curb stop (or stop box) The second shutoff in a water line. It is usually found underground in a public area such as between the street and the sidewalk.

Deglaze (plastic pipe) The process of priming pipe ends and fittings to roughen the surfaces and make it easier for the solvent to achieve a good bond. You can also use an abrasive pad to achieve this.

Dielectric union A special coupling used when connecting piping made of dissimilar metals. It prevents the transfer of electrons, which results in electrolytic corrosion.

Drainpipe Pipe that directs wastewater away from the fixtures and house to the sewer or septic tank.

Drum trap An outdated waste trap that has a juglike shape, with two inlets and one outlet. It was used almost exclusively in bathrooms and can be found in the floor of older houses, near the toilet. It cannot be vented and is no longer allowed by code.

Dual stop A valve with two outlets that splits one water line (usually hot) into two—for example, joining a kitchen's hot-water supply line to the kitchen faucet and a dishwasher.

Elbow A fitting used for making directional changes in pipelines.

Escutcheon A decorative plate that covers the hole in a wall through which a pipe or faucet body passes.

Extension tube A copper tube with compression fittings at one end. The tube bridges the gap between the supply risers and faucet stubs.

Faucet stem (compression) The main vertical component of a compression faucet. It has a handle at one end and a seat washer at the other. It is threaded and moves up and down to control water flow.

Female thread The end of a pipe or fitting with internal threads.

Ferrule On a compression fitting, the beveled compression ring that is driven into the tapered seats to lock the fitting in place.

Fill valve The device in a toilet that allows water to refill the tank after each flush.

Fixture Any of a number of water-using devices hooked up to the main water supply network: sinks, showers, bathtubs, and toilets.

Fixture riser Any length of vertical pipe that supplies or drains water to or from a fixture. See *Riser.*

Flapper A rubber seal that controls the flow of water from a toilet tank.

Flush bag (also called blow bag) A special bag that attaches to a garden hose and is inserted into a large drainpipe. It uses water pressure in order to clear clogs.

Flush valve A device at the bottom of a toilet tank for flushing. See *Flapper.*

Freeze-proof sillcock A sillcock with an extended stem that allows water to be shut off inside rather than outside the house. It prevents the water line from freezing in the cold winter months.

Freeze-proof yard hydrant The equivalent of a freeze-proof sillcock, but installed in the yard. These faucets supply water to gardens and livestock tanks and drain underground rather than through the spout.

Friction washer A flat, rubber washer used to make a water seal in chrome P-traps.

Frost-proof flashing Flashing that has double sheet-metal walls with an air space in between them. This air space acts as an insulator to prevent freezing in colder climates.

Gallons per flush (gpf) The amount, in gallons of water, used for each flush of a toilet.

Galvanized-steel pipe Once used for in-house water systems, steel pipe is now used mostly in repair situations only.

Gate valve A valve that allows an unrestricted flow of water via an internal gate. Gate valves are predominately used at or near the beginning of water supply systems.

Gravity-flow toilet A toilet designed to use the force of gravity to flush wastewater away, through the drainage system.

Gray water Wastewater from sinks, baths, and kitchen appliances.

Hammer-type flaring tool A cone-shaped stud that's hit by a hammer to create a flare in the end of copper tubing for a flared fitting.

Hole strapping Plastic or copper strapping used to support pipe against studs and joists.

Hootie wench A special sink-clip wrench used to remove the rim clips that hold a sink in place on the counter.

Hose bibcock An external-threaded faucet onto which a hose is attached.

Integral trap A trap molded into a fixture. It sweeps up before it sweeps down, keeping standing water in place.

Laundry box A recessed connection box for water and drain lines. It is mounted on top of the standpipe.

Lavatory basin A sink, or wash basin, that is located in a bathroom or powder room.

Line friction Water pressure loss due to friction caused by pipe walls and fittings.

Low-flow toilet A water-saving toilet now mandatory in residential homes since the passing of the Clean Water Act in 1994. These toilets use only 1.6 gallons per flush (gpf).

Male thread The external threads located at the end of a fitting, pipe, or fixture connection.

Meter pit Underground container—usually near the street, on either side of the sidewalk—that houses below grade water meters.

Oakum An oily ropelike material that was commonly used years ago in combination with lead to make watertight seals on joints.

O-ring packing Modern alternative to traditional packing. It consists of a lubricated o-ring that fits over the stem.

PEX Acronym for cross-linked polyethylene plastic pipe. PEX is a strong, flexible water pipe used for radiant floor heating and water pipe.

P-trap A U-shaped bend and a trap arm, this is the most common type of trap. It may be made of plastic or chrome-plated brass and is commonly used to drain sinks, tubs, and showers.

PVC (polyvinyl chloride) plastic pipe Piping used for drainage and venting systems; it is corrosion-resistant and easy to install.

Packing (compression valve/faucet) Material, often graphite, used to create a seal around the stem in a compression faucet.

Pipe chase A boxed-out cavity, vertical or horizontal, through which pipes may travel from floor to floor or room to room.

Pipe joint compound A pastelike filler material applied to threaded connections to help prevent leaks.

Plumber's grease Heatproof nontoxic grease applied to washers and other moving parts as a lubricant.

Plumber's code The rules and regulations determined and enforced by a state, local, or municipal authority governing all plumbing work done in that jurisdiction.

Pounds per square inch (psi) The measure of water pressure in a system, expressed in pounds of pressure per square inch of surface. Too much pressure causes water-heater relief valves to leak, toilets to keep running, and faucets to pulse and pound when turned off and on.

Potable Water that is free from impurities in amounts sufficient to cause disease or harmful physiological effects.

Pressure-assisted toilet A toilet designed to push water through the system more forcefully with the help of compressed air.

Pressure-reduction valve A valve that reduces excessively high, damaging water pressure and conserves water.

Public parking The area outside a house that lies between the sidewalk and the street.

Reducer A fitting used to join two pipes of different diameters.

Re-vent A pipe installed to vent a fixture trap that connects to a main vent.

Rim holes (toilet) Holes around the underside perimeter of the toilet rim through which water flows into the bowl from the tank.

Riser A water supply or drainage pipe that carries or drains water vertically.

S-trap A sink trap that connects to drainpipes at floor level. These traps are impossible to vent and are no longer allowed by code.

Seat The stationary base in a compression valve onto which the stem closes to shut off water supply. The stem holds a washer that fits into the seat.

Seat-dressing tool A threaded stem with a T-handle and several grinding blades that cut into a pitted seat to make it smooth.

Seat washer The rubber or neoprene washer that covers the lower end of the faucet stem and fits into the seat of the faucet body to form a seal.

Septic system The intricate network of pipes and tanks that collect and dispose of wastewater from the house.

Sewer A public drainline, usually underground, that carries away waste or rainwater.

Shutoff valve A device set into a water line to allow for interruption of the flow of water to a fixture or appliance.

Sillcock An outdoor water faucet; also called a hose bibcock.

Siphon jet A hole at the bottom of a toilet's water bowl through which water from the tank flows to aid in creating a flushing siphon.

Siphoned trap A situation in which the flow of water from a sink fills an improperly vented trap and thereafter pulls excess water through the pipe, leaving too little water behind to seal the trap.

Soil pipe A drainpipe that carries wastes to the sewer drain; also, the main drainpipe that receives all the wastewater from a group of plumbing fixtures, including a toilet, or from all the plumbing fixtures in a given installation.

Spigot (cast-iron fitting) The male end of a cast-iron waste pipe that requires a neoprene gasket or packing material to fit into the female end, or bell, of another pipe to make a seal.

Spud gasket (flush valve) Rubber gasket that fits over the flush-valve's shank threads that will connect to the spud nut and washer joining the two sections of toilet.

Spud washer (flush valve) A large rubber seal that fits over the spud nut connecting the toilet tank to the base and bowl of the toilet.

Stem The component in a faucet that rises up and down via its threads, when the faucet handle is turned, to control the flow of water.

Stem nut The nut that connects to and tightens on the faucet stem. It may also serve as the packing nut in some faucet designs.

Step-up An abrupt vertical offset in a horizontal piping run.

Stop valve A valve, mandatory under toilets and often under sinks as well, that allows you to shut off a water line completely. There are two basic types: compression stops and ball-valve stops.

Stop-and-waste valve Usually globe valves with a drain screw on the downstream side of the shutoff. These valves are widely used in the winter months to shut down water running through dedicated outdoor lines.

Stop box The vertical extension of a curb stop that extends from the water service line up to grade level.

Stub-out The termination of water-delivery or drainage-network pipe extended into a room through a wall or floor to which a fixture or appliance is to be connected.

Supply tube The flexible tubing that carries water from the shut-off valves to the fixture above.

Sweat fittings Copper or brass fittings that are made to be soldered.

Sweep bend A fitting used for vent and waste piping that has a gradual 90-degree bend. It may have either a short or long vertical bend.

T-fitting A T-shaped pipe fitting with three points of connection.

Takeoff fitting A fitting that branches off a drainpipe or vent pipe. The location of a vent takeoff fitting is crucial to proper venting.

Tank ball (toilet) A hollow ball attached to a lift wire that opens and closes the tank water outlet with each flush.

Temperature-and-pressure (T & P) relief valve The device installed in a water heater that prevents temperature and pressure from building up inside the tank and causing it to explode.

Thumb cutter See *Close-quarters tubing cutter.*

Toilet flange A slotted ring connected to a vertical collar that rests on the floor. Toilets are bolted directly to this fitting.

Trap The water-filled curved pipe that prevents sewer gas from entering the house through the drainage network.

Trap-preserving vent A vent added to a drainage line to ensure that a trap receives enough makeup air and functions properly.

Trunk lines The hot- and cold-water supply lines that usually run side by side along the center beam of the house, branching to serve isolated fixtures or fixture groups along the way.

Tube trap A conventional P-trap for a sink or other fixture that usually comes as a kit, with all components needed for complete installation.

Union fittings Threaded fittings that join two lengths of pipe together, allowing you to connect or disconnect pipes repeatedly anywhere they are installed.

Vacuum breaker A device that prevents back-siphoning of water into a water supply line, usually mounted on the faucet.

Vents Pipes that pull system makeup air from above the roof. Vents control the water seals for traps. Some may also carry water. See *Wet vent.*

Vent stack A vertical vent installed for the sole purpose of providing relief air. It does not carry water.

Water hammer A back shock in water pipes caused by a sudden change in pressure after a faucet or water valve shuts off.

Water spot (toilet) The amount of water held in the bowl of a toilet. The larger the water spot, the more likely the bowl will remain clean.

Weir The highest point in any fixture trap or built-in trap of a toilet. It regulates the amount of water held in the trap. In toilets, it determines how much water remains in the bowl.

Wet vent An extension of a waste pipe that also acts as a vent. It is not permitted to receive waste coming from a toilet or kitchen sink.

Wiped-lead joints A hand-formed splice between lead and galvanized-steel pipe. Outdated and no longer used.

Index

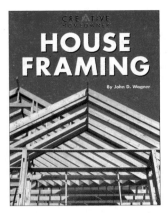
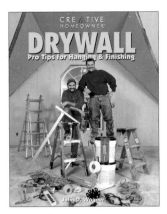
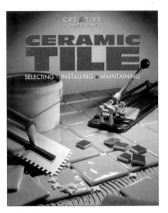
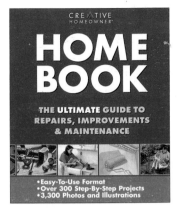
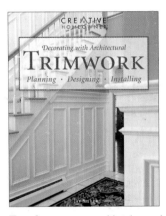
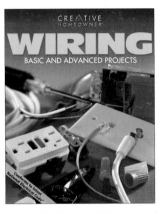